THE MEMOIRS OF
WILLIAM JENNINGS BRYAN

WILLIAM JENNINGS BRYAN
From the painting by Irving R. Wiles in the State Department at Washington.

THE MEMOIRS OF
WILLIAM JENNINGS BRYAN

BY HIMSELF AND HIS WIFE
MARY BAIRD BRYAN

Illustrated

THE JOHN C. WINSTON COMPANY

CHICAGO   PHILADELPHIA   TORONTO

Printed in the United States of America

INTRODUCTION

By Mary Baird Bryan

IT has fallen to me to take up the pen which Mr. Bryan laid down.

In justice to him, it should be borne in mind that his chapters are in the first draft; he had no opportunity to revise or polish them.

While I am willing to carry out his ideas, the fact remains that it is impossible for me, or for anyone else, to do this work as he had planned it. The intimate knowledge of people and of small happenings has passed with him.

However, from his private correspondence, from his documents, and from my diary, I hope to bring to light the truth on several controversial questions.

I wish, too, to give a careful and just analysis of his character. His dominant traits will explain his course of action in several crises.

In this work I have been assisted in research and collation by our children, by other members of the family, by faithful friends, and by the competent staff which was furnished me by the Publishers.

Mary B. Bryan

CONTENTS

5

CONTENTS

PART I

PREFACE

By William J. Bryan

IN giving the public the story of my life I trust I may be credited with something more than a desire to acquaint the public with myself. The time has passed when I could have any ulterior motive in a heart-to-heart talk with the American people. Whatever ambition I have had has been more than gratified; I feel that I have received more than I have deserved and been abundantly repaid for the efforts I have made in behalf of the American people.

It is my purpose to show that in my own case good fortune has had more to do with such success as I may have achieved than any efforts of my own. Success in politics—and, to a large extent in other lines of activity—is the conjunction of opportunity and the preparedness to meet it. Opportunity comes independently of one's own efforts; and his preparedness to meet opportunity is due, as I shall show, largely to others. The facts as I present them will prove that I have been wonderfully fortunate in the opportunities that have come to me and that I am indebted to a multitude of individuals known and unknown for such preparation as I have had to improve the opportunities as they came.

My second purpose is to show the goodness of the American people, their patriotism, their moral courage, their high ideals, their willingness to sacrifice for their convictions— the virtues that not only make popular government possible but insure its success. No man in public life has ever been in a better position to record these virtues of the people or under deeper obligation to give them the credit they deserve.

I trust that with the two purposes in view I may be able so to shift the accent from "I" to "they" as to purge my Memoirs of every trace of egotism or self-assertion. I shall

9

relate my own connection with individuals, measures, and events, but I shall endeavor so to interweave the actions of others with my own acts as to make the results appear as the result of a joint effort in which I have played but a part, and often but an inconsequential part.

In politics as in the army, the generals receive the glory while the enlisted men die in the trenches. The names that are prominent become household words, while the multitude who bear the burden are nameless in history.

That which was called Bryanism in derision by many, represented a group of substantial reforms; it was not an individual thing but rather the result of united effort of some six and a half millions of American voters. I was but one of the millions, but because I was in a position of leadership I received the glory and the censure, while others equally earnest and often with more sacrifice labored and died unknown to fame.

To begin the story of my good fortune. I was born in the greatest of all ages. No golden ages of the past offered any such opportunity for large service and, therefore, for the enjoyment that comes from consciousness that one has been helpful.

I was born a member of the greatest of all the races—the Caucasian Race, and had mingled in my veins the blood of English, Irish, and Scotch. One has only to consider the limitations upon one's opportunities imposed by race to understand the incalculable benefit of having the way opened between the child and the stars.

I was born a citizen of the greatest of all lands. So far as my power to prevent was concerned, I might have been born in the darkest of the continents and among the most backward of earth's peoples. It was a gift of priceless value to see the light in beloved America, and to live under the greatest of the republics of history.

And I was equally fortunate, as I shall show, in my family environment. I cannot trace my ancestry beyond

10

the fourth generation and there is not among them, so far as I know, one of great wealth or great political or social prominence, but so far as I have been able to learn, they were honest, industrious, Christian, moral, religious people—not a black sheep in the flock, not a drunkard, not one for whose life I would have to utter an apology. The environment in which my youth was spent was as ideal as any that I know.

At the age of fourteen I became a member of the Church, as the result of a spiritual awakening that took place in the little town in which I was born. I shall elaborate upon it in the proper place in my story; I mention it now because it has had more influence in my life for good than any other experience, and I have been increasingly grateful for the circumstances that led me to take a stand on religion before I left home for college. It was of incalculable value to me during the period of questioning that seems unavoidable in the life of students. The influences of the Church, the Sunday school, the prayer meeting and the Y. M. C. A. were about me and sustained me until my feet were upon the Solid Rock and my faith built upon an enduring foundation.

I have often been reminded of one of the concluding verses of the Twenty-third Psalm: "Thou preparest a table before me in the presence of mine enemies." And still more frequently do I recall that wonderfully expressive description of superlative blessings: "My cup runneth over." If judging the future by the past can be made the basis of a firm hope, I can say, "Surely goodness and mercy shall follow me all the days of my life."

No one has been the recipient of as large a measure of unselfish devotion; no one is in better position to record with grateful appreciation the kindnesses received. I have never been in a position to repay friends in a political way. During my first term in Congress, the Republicans were in control of the national administration, so that I had no patronage at my command. During my second term in Congress, I was not in harmony with President Cleveland on the money question and soon ceased to be influential in the securing of appointments. Thus, during the four years in office in the earlier part of my life, I was unable to pay my debts with lucrative positions or to secure support by the hope of appointments. Even when I was Secretary of State, as I shall later relate, I was not able to reward any considerable number of political friends. My debts were larger and, in an appointive way, my assets smaller than those of any other cabinet member. All of the clerical force of the State Department is under the Civil Service, as are also the Consular offices. There are but a handful of assistants in the whole office who hold appointing power. Our ambassadors and ministers are largely chosen upon recommendation of the United States Senators.

And yet, while during the six years and three months of my official life I was practically powerless to reward those who had contributed to my success, I am sure that no one in this country—probably no one who ever lived—has had more friends, kept them for a longer period or received from them greater loyalty or more constant support. I have reason to know that the masses are patriotic and incorruptible. They cannot be purchased and they cannot be terrified. No matter how they may err or be led astray, the American people are sound at heart. They have solved successfully all problems that confronted them during the momentous years of our nation's history and there is not the slightest reason to doubt that they will meet every emergency, rise to every responsibility and prove that their capacity for self-government is as undeniable as their right to self-government.

The story of my life is but an account of opportunities improved and of circumstances of which I have taken advantage, but for the wisdom to see opportunities and the ability to take advantage of circumstances, I am indebted to others more largely than to myself. In tracing my life from the beginning up to the time of the completion of this volume, I am simply showing what anyone, equally fortunate and with equal opportunities, can accomplish in this favored land of ours in this golden age.

If to. the encouragement that my words may bring to the young men of our land I can add a moral, it is this: Truth, being of God, is omnipotent. It has within itself the power to propagate itself. Man may delay, but cannot prevent its triumph. Man borrows more strength from a great truth than he gives to it. It is of little importance to truth whether any individual espouses it, but to the individual it is of vital importance that he shall know the truth and, knowing it, adhere to it.

Jefferson said that he had learned that firm adherence to principle was the best handmaiden, even unto ambition.

If my Memoirs prove of benefit to others they will pay in part the debt I owe to those who in the past have contributed to the spread of the Christian religion, the safeguarding of society, and the establishing of popular government—the causes to which the mature years of my life have been dedicated.

13

"HE BELONGS TO THE AGES"

"The message of Mr. Bryan was not alone to the men of his day, but to the men of the ages."

CHAPTER I

IN THE BEGINNING

I WAS born on the nineteenth day of March, 1860, at Salem, Illinois. A picture of my birthplace to be found among the illustrations shows the house in which I first saw the light. The house stood on Broadway about halfway between the public square and the Baltimore and Ohio Railroad—prior to 1872 called the Ohio and Mississippi. It had never been materially changed from the time when it was built in 1852. My father, then a young lawyer just starting in at the practice, helped to hew the timbers to build the house. Being thus doubly attached to the homestead, I purchased it and gave it to the city of Salem, moving it a few feet to the west in order to give room for the erection of the Bryan Bennett Library, to which reference will be made in another chapter.

I do not know the hour of my birth, because the hour never became material until after the death of my parents. As soon as I was nominated for the Presidency, astrologists made their appearance and offered to consult my horoscope with a view to ascertaining whether I would be elected. I never had any faith in their calculations but, complying with my general rule, gave the specialists along various lines such information as I could furnish. I remember that one astrologer wrote a letter which my wife answered in my absence. He asked for the hour of the birth both of Mrs. Bryan and myself. She responded giving the day of my birth and the day and hour of her birth. Her parents were then residing with us and she was able to secure the information desired. The astrologer cast my horoscope, based upon such facts as he had, and declared that it indicated my election. He was very much mortified at my defeat— seemingly more than I was myself—and hastened to explain

15

to Mrs. Bryan that his failure was due wholly to the fact that she did not give the exact hour of my birth. Having the hour of her birth, he had, since the election, cast her horoscope and felt sure that I would be yet elected for the Presidency. My wife enjoyed the humor of it and informed me that if I would stick to her she would land me in the White House yet. I responded, expressing my appreciation but admitting it was a little mortifying for a Presidential candidate to keep his horoscope in his wife's name.

I did not, until after the Chicago convention, hear much about the incidents of my childhood. I only know that I was blessed with as happy an environment as a child could hope for or ask. The two older children, John and Virginia, had died before the third child was born. As she was a daughter, I became the oldest son and had all the care that a mother could bestow upon a child and all the interest that a father could feel. A letter written just after my birth conveyed to the distant relative at whose home I lived while in college the fact of my birth. My father, who was suffering from a serious attack of diabetes, wrote to this relative that the birth of a son had increased his desire to live.

After my nomination, I met a Salem friend who told me that he had visited our home when I was just beginning to walk. It was evening and they were getting me ready for bed. According to this friend, my father stood me up before the visitor, and boastingly remarked, "He will be President some day." As my father never divulged to me any such expectations, I will be pardoned for considering the remark apocryphal.

The first thing that I can recollect is the younger child, Harry, crawling upon the floor. As he died when less than a year old, I could not have been more than three. My next recollection is of looking at the corpse of a neighbor who was a minister. They lifted me up so that I could see his face.

IN THE BEGINNING

According to family tradition, I was not a perfect child by any means, unless the word "perfect" is used to describe a boy with all the natural inclinations to mischief. Tradition has it that I used to disobey the injunctions of my mother and slip away from home to play with other children. Our yard was enclosed with the old-fashioned paling fence with a baseboard about a foot deep. By crawling close to the ground, I could conceal myself behind this broad board and thus get to the side of the fence without being noticed. More than once I was brought back and chastised and tied to the bed-post as a punishment.

My Ambitions Before Six

Three ambitions entered into my life before I was six years old—I fix the age at six because one of the first things to stay in my memory is the removal to our farm home which occurred in the summer of 1866. The incidents of my boyhood are roughly classified as having occurred while we lived in town or after we moved to the country. That is the way I know of these three early ambitions. The first was to be a Baptist preacher—due doubtless to the fact that my father was a member of that church. Of course, I was too young to have any distinct recollection of either this ambition or its abandonment, but the record as given by my parents is that my father took me to an immersion one night during a protracted meeting held in a Christian Church. I saw the convert going down into the pool of water to be baptized. I evidently watched the ceremony with great interest and was deeply impressed by it. On my return home, I asked my father whether it would be necessary for me to go down into the pool of water in order to be a Baptist preacher. He answered in the affirmative, and after that they never could get me to say that I was "going to be a Baptist preacher." I do not know that any conclusion can be drawn from this incident unless it be that at this early age my parents had impressed upon me the virtue of truthfulness and that therefore I was not willing to avow an ambition from which I had been turned by fear of water.

My second ambition was to be a farmer and raise pumpkins. This did not last long, but long enough to be a matter of remark in the family. It may have been due to the plans we were making to remove to the country. I remember that a young lady by the name of Hester, daughter of Brother Williams, the much beloved pastor of the Christian Church, came into my life about that time and promised to wait for me. She was a very handsome girl, nearly grown, and encouraged me in my taste for agricultural pursuits. When I shortly afterwards decided to be a lawyer, she gave my change of plans as an excuse for refusing to look forward to a life partnership, and married a farmer cousin of mine.

My third ambition was probably due to the fact that my father was a lawyer, and at that time a circuit judge. I used to go down to the courthouse and sit upon the steps leading up to the bench and listen to the trial of cases. This ambition was more permanent than the ones which it succeeded. It remained with me during my school days and my college days, as the reader will see if he follows this narrative.

My Ancestry

Ancestry counts. We inherit more than we ourselves can add. It means much to be borne of a race with centuries of civilization back of it. Blood, if it be good, inspires one to great effort—if it be bad it may paralyze ambition and fix the boundary to one's possibilities. I am speaking of the rule, not of the rare exceptions; many have become degenerate in spite of inheriting the stimulus to better things, and a few have, to a degree, overcome handicaps of their life and early environment.

If one is tempted to boast that he is self-made, a few reflections will puncture his pride. Let him analyze himself, separate all that has come to him into three factors: one representing that which has come to him by inheritance; another representing that which has entered his life through environment; and the third representing what he can fairly credit to himself—that which is not based upon either inheritance or environment—and the third factor will not be large enough to flatter his vanity.

The child comes into the world without its own volition, containing within himself capacities and weaknesses for which he is in no way responsible; he finds himself in an environment which he did not choose and cannot control. His first impressions come to him with breath and his life is largely moulded for him before he has intelligence to choose or standards by which to measure effort.

It is a consciousness of the helplessness of the new-born babe and of his dependence upon an unknown past and upon surroundings that he cannot comprehend that makes me increasingly grateful for the parentage with which the Heavenly Father blessed me and for the home in which my life began.

My father, Silas Lillard Bryan, was of Irish extraction. I do not know from what part of Ireland his ancestors came, nor when they crossed the ocean. I learned this since his death from a biographical sketch which I have reason to believe was written by him or submitted to him for his approval. William Bryan is the most remote forefather of whom I have knowledge. He lived in what was then a part of Culpeper (now Rappahannock) County and near the town of Sperryville, Virginia. He owned a tract of timber land in the Blue Ridge Mountains of which we learned when I was a young man because of a ninety-nine-year lease which expired about that time. We knew nothing of William Bryan's parents, brothers, or sisters. He belonged to the Baptist Church in that neighborhood, which was known as the Bryan Meeting House.

I digress at this point long enough to relate the experience which I have had with my name. I had scarcely entered upon the practice of law when my business brought me into acquaintance with a number of people of Irish birth who frequently addressed me as "Mr. O'Brien." I was at first in doubt as to whether I should correct the mistake or allow it to pass unnoticed, but, deciding that honesty was the best policy, I said to a very typical son of the Emerald Isle, "My name is not O'Brien, but Bryan."

"It's all the same," he replied. "When Bryan Boru became king his descendants put on the 'O.' The Bryans are the same stock, but just common people."

I have had frequent occasion to use this explanation. The most notable opportunity was a dinner in Ireland tendered me by the Mayor of Dublin in 1903. One of the speakers jestingly called upon me to tell when I had dropped the "O." I replied by asking whether any of them ever knew of an O'Brien prior to the line of King Bryan Boru. When no one could name an earlier O'Brien, I explained to them that Bryan was the original name and that the "O" had been *added* by them, not eliminated by my ancestors.

After the campaign of 1896 I received a letter from a man in California named Bryan. He sent me an interview which he had given to the newspapers.

It seems that some one had claimed to have seen my name printed as "O'Brien" when I began the practice of law at Jacksonville, Illinois. My correspondent had given out an interview denying that there had been any change in my name and saying that he was a relative of mine. He explained to me that he was not a relative, but added that it was a poor friend that could not lie for another.

We know nothing of the parents, brothers, or sisters of William Bryan, my great-grandfather, and therefore have been unable to answer a multitude of questions which have been asked from time to time, the most persistent being whether our ancestor was related to the wife of Daniel

JUDGE SILAS L. BRYAN   MARIAH ELIZABETH BRYAN

Father and Mother of William Jennings Bryan.

Boone, whose maiden name was Bryan. William Bryan had three sons, Aquilla, James, and John. Aquilla Bryan, the oldest of the three sons, left Sperryville before or soon after my father's birth, to try his fortune in the Great West which was then inviting adventurers. When he reached the Ohio River the water was so high that instead of descending the river as he had intended, he crossed into Ohio and then waited for the waters to subside. That is the last knowledge we have of him that is authentic. We have met persons who with varying degrees of uncertainty thought they traced their ancestry back to this Aquilla Bryan, but no connection has been established with certainty.

James, the second son, went to Kentucky and located at Glasgow, where some of the family still reside.

John Bryan, my father's father, moved from his birthplace to Point Pleasant in what is now West Virginia. There my father spent part of his boyhood, but his mother died when he was twelve and his father when he was fourteen years old and Silas was entrusted to the care of different members of the family. His oldest brother, William Bryan, to whom I am indebted for the first part of my name, located on a farm near Troy, Missouri, where some of his descendants still live. Russell Bryan, his younger brother, located at Salem, where he raised a numerous family. His children were among my earliest playmates and most beloved companions.

John Bryan, my grandfather, was married to Nancy Lillard, a member of an English family. They lived in Culpeper County. This family was quite large and made up of men and women of character and virtue. My father was named after Silas Lillard, his mother's brother. When I went to Washington as a Member of Congress, I visited Virginia and became acquainted with a number of members of the Lillard family between whom and myself there grew up and has continued a warm friendship.

21

WILLIAM JENNINGS BRYAN

My Father

As none of the brothers or sisters of my father were rich, he had the advantage of having to work. I do not know that this spur of necessity was absolutely necessary, but it is no disadvantage and it is possibly the best insurance against the influences that sap the energies and industry of young men. He had caught from some one the ambition to learn and though he had to work his way through school, he went further than any of his brothers or sisters in the pursuit of learning. When he was far enough advanced to teach he earned, by teaching, the money necessary to complete his college course, which was taken at McKendree College, Lebanon, Illinois. He had intended to attend a Baptist college, but for some reason changed his plans and entered the Methodist college above named. He took the classical course, graduating in 1849, and was always an enthusiastic believer in classical education for the young. He was a good student and interested also in the literary societies.

As father did not graduate until he was twenty-seven, he was one of the older students, although the age of graduation was probably older then than now. I have had the good fortune to meet several persons who were schoolmates of my father at Lebanon. From these I have learned something of my father as a student.

One incident seems to have made an impression at the time. Father used tobacco—I do not know in just what form at this time, later in life before he quit it entirely he indulged in chewing, smoking, and the use of snuff. He was in the habit of chewing tobacco while he was a student, as I learned from the following incident. Some teacher from another college made a speech to the boys. In the course of the address, the speaker commented upon the use of tobacco, criticizing it quite strongly, paying special attention to chewing. My father thought from what the speaker said he was making personal reference to him—whether true or

not I do not know—but at the conclusion of the address
father arose and made a speech in defense of the use of the
weed.   Later in life he became convinced that the use of
tobacco was harmful, and just before the date of my birth
he quit its use in every form.   We thought it responsible
for the dyspepsia which manifested itself about 1859 and
continued to afflict him sorely until his death twenty-one
years later.

Father was a very devout Christian.   Just when he
joined the Church I do not know, but it was probably at
an early age.   There came a day, however, when he was a
young man, when religion took a very strong hold upon him
and held him and became a controlling influence in his life.
As a young man he was fond of fun and took delight in the
frivolities of his day.   One night as he went to a party he
took cold and the cold developed into pneumonia.   His
condition finally became so critical that the attending
physician thought it wise to inform him that, while his life
was not despaired of, it would be the part of wisdom for
him to make such provision for the future as he might
think best.   When the physician retired, father prayed as
he had never prayed before and promised the Heavenly
Father that if restored to health he would pray three times
a day as long as he lived.   He was restored to health and
kept the promise.

I knew there was some such incident in his life, but did
not learn the details until many years after his death and a
few years after my mother's death.   The facts were related
to me by a caller who lived at one of the county seats which
father visited when he was on the Circuit bench.   My
informant was then a boy and noticing that Judge Bryan
bowed his head upon the desk when the noon whistle blew,
asked his father why he did so.   His father replied, "Judge
Bryan is going to eat with us today and you had better
ask him for an explanation."   When the guest was at the
table and the boy hesitated about asking the question, the

father came to the boy's rescue and explained to Judge Bryan what the boy had noticed and asked the question the boy had intended to ask. Father moved his chair back from the table and said, "I am glad to answer the question," and then related the incident as it was told to me by the man, then the boy in the story.

This thrice-a-day prayer is the basis upon which numerous elaborations have been built. After my nomination for the Presidency a great many stories were told, differing in detail but all emphasizing the devotional side of my father's life. One story was that he opened court with prayer. Another, that he always prayed for guidance before rendering a decision. The first was not true, but knowing as I do his dependence upon God for guidance, I have no doubt that he invoked aid when entering upon anything important. I may add that my father's attitude on spiritual matters made a very deep impression upon me. There was a family altar in our house and the children were brought up according to the strictest views in religious matters, and my gratitude for such a home environment increased with the years. I shall be happy if my children feel toward me in mature life as I feel toward my father; if they revere my name as I revere my father's name and feel as deeply indebted to me for whatever there is in me of good.

After graduation at the age of twenty-seven, my father moved to Salem, the county seat of Marion County, Illinois, in which two of his sisters lived. At the age of twenty-nine he was admitted to the bar and about the same time or possibly a little earlier was elected superintendent of schools of that county. He began the practice of law in 1851 and in 1852 was elected to the Senate of the State of Illinois, where he served for eight years. He soon became prominent at the bar and prominent also as a public speaker. In 1860, at the age of thirty-eight, he was elected a judge of the Circuit that included about half a dozen counties and was re-elected in 1866, serving until 1872.

IN THE BEGINNING

In 1869 he was elected a member of the Constitutional Convention of Illinois and assisted in the drafting of that constitution. After his death I found in his library two volumes containing a record of the proceedings of the Constitutional Convention. On the fly leaf of the first volume I found a dedication of the books to myself. I immediately examined it, desiring to see what part he took, and was interested to find that at the very beginning of the session he introduced a resolution which reads as follows:

"*Resolved*, By the Convention: First—That all officers to be provided for in the new Constitution in the executive, legislative, and judicial departments, shall be elected by the people. Second—That the compensation to be allowed for official service in the several departments of the government shall be fixed in the Constitution, and shall not be increased or lessened by the legislative department."

It interested me to know that he shared Jefferson's confidence in the capacity of the people for self-government as well as in their right to self-government. He believed in entrusting them with their own affairs, as this resolution indicated. I have credited him with a definite influence in the shaping of my religious views; I am also indebted to him for the trend of my views on some fundamental questions of government, and have seen no reason to depart from the line he marked out.

My father was married at the age of thirty to Mariah Elizabeth Jennings, who had been one of his pupils when he taught school at Walnut Hill, Illinois. Mother was twelve years younger than father and had been his pupil when as a college student he was teaching in the Walnut Hill District, Walnut Hill being in the southeast corner of Marion County, twelve miles from Salem and about four from Centralia. Mother did not have the educational advantages father had secured, but she was as enthusiastic as he in her appreciation of education and in her devotion to it. Her studies after marriage and her companionship with him enabled her to make up somewhat for the shortness of her school days.

MY MOTHER

But before speaking further of my mother, let me add a word here in regard to her lineage. As her maiden name indicated, she was of English ancestry, although, like my father's people, her family had been in the country so long, they were not able to trace any of them to the water's edge. The first of the Jennings of whom we have definite knowledge was Israel, my mother's grandfather. He moved to Illinois from Maysville, Kentucky, early in the eighteenth century and lived to a ripe old age, I think about a hundred years. Family tradition has it that he went from Maryland to Kentucky. His wife, Mary Waters, was a native of Maryland, but we have not been able to locate definitely any of her antecedents and but few of her collateral relatives. Israel Jennings had a large family, most of whom grew up in the neighborhood of Walnut Hill and Centralia.

My mother's mother was a Davidson and this family, too, had been in the United States long enough to lose its old-world connections. The Davidsons were of Scotch descent. Some of the family had been looking up the record recently and they found that there was a certain plaid that was worn by the Davidsons who, though not constituting a clan, were members of a clan. The earliest Davidson of whom we have a record lived in Virginia and went from there to Kentucky. From Kentucky the Davidsons, like the Jennings, moved to southern Illinois, evidently about the same time. I do not know whether it was because of the superiority in the attractiveness of the members of the two families or because of the scarcity of the population, but

26

it is a rather remarkable fact that four Jennings married four Davidsons.

Mother was born on May the 24th, 1834, at Walnut Hill, a rural community near Centralia, Marion County, Illinois. She was reared in the country and attended the public school in the neighborhood. She was married at the age of eighteen (1852) and began housekeeping in the home on Broadway, about halfway between the public square and the railroad. Father helped to hew out the timbers and build their house. The style of it was that which was customary in that day. It had a room on each side of a short central hall, with two rooms upstairs over these lower rooms and a dining room and kitchen in the rear. In this house, the first six children were born. The two older children, Virginia and John, died of whooping cough before the third child was born. Frances, the next child, was born on March 18, 1858. My birthday came on the 19th of March, 1860, two years and one day later. The fifth child, Hiram, called Harry, died in infancy, and the sixth one, Russell, died at the age of seventeen. In 1866, the summer after I reached the age of six, we moved to the farm, about a mile northwest of the center of Salem, where the three younger children, Charles Wayland, Nancy Lillard, and Mary Elizabeth, were born.

Mother was a very competent woman, of rare native ability, of lofty ideals, and as devout as my father. While during the first twenty years of their married life they were members of different churches, there was never the slightest religious discord in the family and I never heard a word said in regard to the differences between denominations. Both of them were firmly wedded to the fundamentals of Christianity, but charitable on all nonessentials. This liberality in the matter of denominations was early impressed upon my mind by the family gatherings. It was in the old days of simple social customs when family dinners emphasized companionship and friendly intercourse rather than elaborate bill of fare. We were in the habit of having all the ministers at our home once a year and I knew all the ministers as "Brother."

While religious subjects occupied a prominent place in the conversation, the meals were not without a sprinkling of humor. I remember on one occasion that the meat for the dinner consisted of a roasted kid. As the plates were being served the conversation turned on the various kinds of meat and the Methodist preacher, Brother Mosser, expressed himself quite strongly as liking all kinds of meat excepting goat meat. Father had spoken of the meat as a roast, without designating the kind of animal that furnished it. After Mr. Mosser's statement he purposely avoided the subject until Brother Mosser was well through with a second helping, when the company enjoyed the joke.

My attitude on the subject of religious tolerance has been inherited, so to speak, from my parents. In memory of these religious social gatherings my good wife has been led to set aside certain days for the bringing together of the representatives of the various denominations in a social way.

I also received from my parents the impressions that have controlled my views on the husband's relation to the mother-in-law. When my father built the commodious brick house in which he lived upon the farm, one room was known as Grandma's room. At that time, my mother's mother was in good health with the prospect of living to a ripe old age. But although my mother's family was one of the largest among the children, it was always understood that Grandma was to have a home in our family if she reached an age when it was not desirable for her to continue to occupy the old homestead at Walnut Hill. The children expected some day to have my mother's mother as a member of the family, and the time came when she was too old to keep house any longer and came to spend her declining years with us. She lived to be more than eighty and

THE BRYAN SISTERS AND BROTHERS

Left to right: Ex-Governor Charles W. Bryan, Mrs. T. S. Allen, Mrs. J. W. Baird, and William Jennings Bryan.

Photo. Kadel & Herbert, N. Y.

it was a pleasure to minister to her during her years of feebleness.

When my wife's parents came to live with us, I recalled this early experience and the respect shown by my father to the mother of his wife. My wife's mother lived with us from 1884 to the spring of 1896 and my wife's father till 1905, and they were welcome members of our family.

My mother had not carried the study of music to the point where she practiced regularly, but she was proficient enough to play many instrumental selections and to play the accompaniment when she sang. Some of the tunes still run through my mind and the words of the songs are still recalled. "When you and I were young, Maggie," was popular at that time, and the war song, "Farewell, Mother, you may never press me to your heart again." The words came back to me when I was for a little while a soldier and I found myself time and again humming the tune that I had heard her sing when I was a boy.

My father being absent at court a considerable portion of the time, the burden of directing the family affairs and taking full control of the children fell upon her. Every duty was faithfully discharged. As I look back upon those early days, I cannot recall a single word that she ever said or a single act of hers that to me seems worthy of criticism. I feel that she was as nearly a perfect wife and mother as one could be. When father died, her oldest child was twenty-two, I was twenty, and the youngest child was ten. She assumed with courage the double responsibility of being to the children both mother and father. She survived my father sixteen years and lived to see her children grown, settled, and successful in life, and was revered by all of them. As a mother, she had one advantage that can hardly be overestimated. Her husband set an example in word and conduct that she could always invoke in the training of the children. Not in a single matter was it necessary to warn the children against following their father's example. Thus the memory of the two is entwined as if of a single character, so much alike were they in all that contributed to character building.

In 1872 my mother took her letter from the Methodist Church to the Baptist Church and from that time until her death became more and more a defender of the creed of that church, though she never carried it to the point of criticizing the doctrines of any other denomination. She had a sense of humor that relieved the conversation in the home. As my father also turned occasionally to the lighter vein and indulged in stories that had a point, I am not sure to which one I am most indebted for my fondness of the stories which I have used in abundance in my speeches. As I proceed with the narrative of my own life, I shall have occasion to refer from time to time to things that my parents said. At this time, I venture to illustrate their sense of humor by two stories for which I am indebted to them.

Some years ago I met an old resident of Salem who had often heard my father speak. Having heard me use in a lecture a story in connection with prohibition, he said it reminded him of a story that my father told back in the sixties. A man who was stricken with lockjaw was taken to the hospital for treatment. The doctor advised, "Give him a little whiskey." In order to administer the liquor, it was necessary to bore a hole through a tooth and inject it through a funnel. It had a stimulating effect; the patient was aroused and making his voice heard through his closed teeth begged them to funnel him again.

I remember one day my mother told a story that was recalled by the charitable attitude of a visitor. It reminded her of another woman so kindly in her treatment of others that she never could bear to have anybody criticized in her presence. One day the children conspired together to see how far the mother could carry her charity. They assembled one by one in her room and began to criticize the devil just to see if their mother would take his part. They had not proceeded far when the mother interrupted them with the admonition, "Well, children, if we were all as industrious as the devil is, we would all accomplish more."

After the children were grown and the three older ones had established homes of their own, mother moved from the farm into Salem. I had then prospered sufficiently to be able to buy her a home near to the home of my oldest sister, and I never spent money that brought me more real pleasure.

In the fall of 1895, she was stricken down with an illness that resulted fatally the following June. I shall never forget her last Christmas with us. We took the children (Ruth was about ten, William six, and Grace four) with us to spend the holidays at Salem. Four of her five children were there and five grandchildren also. Mother sat up in bed and distributed the presents. I never saw her happier; her cheerfulness enlivened our Christmas reunion and is a cherished recollection.

She died ten days before my nomination for the presidency. I went from her funeral to the Chicago convention. Often I have thought of the joy it would have given her if she could have lived to see me nominated. And then I check the thought, for in her weakened condition the excitement might have been too much for her. The fact that she was not spared to share in the proud satisfaction that my nomination brought to the family made me glad that the mother of my successful rival lived to see her son in the White House. A mother's pride is so genuine and so excusable that we forget political differences as we are united in a common humanity.

Such were the parents to whom, and such was the home in which I was born.

My name was drawn from the two families that were united by the marriage of my parents. William was a family name with the Bryans; the name of my father's oldest brother and the name of their grandfather. Jennings was my mother's maiden name. A few years ago I met a man in Missouri who was a little more than a hundred years old. He had lived in Marion County at the time of my birth. In the conversation that I had with him, he claimed credit for having suggested my name. He said that my father wanted to name me William and that my mother desired me to bear the name Jennings. He made the quite natural suggestion that both names be given to me, and so it was. In my youth my name went through all the forms of which it was capable; like the boy of whom James Whitcomb Riley writes,

> "Father calls me William,
> And mother calls me Will;
> Sister calls me Billy,
> But the fellers call me Bill."

Possibly Willy was more frequently used by my mother and brothers and sisters during the early years, while Will became my settled name as I advanced from boyhood into young manhood.

In the spring of 1866 my father decided to move to the country, the reason being that he thought a farm a better place to raise a family. There were three of us at that time, Russell Jones, Frances Mariah, and myself. The site selected was about a mile northwest from the center of Salem—that is, a mile by the road, although not quite so far in a direct line. There were two ways of going out to the place. The Prairie Road way, as we used to call it, took us half a mile west of the square and then a mile north; or the Woods Road that turned to the north about a quarter of a mile from the square and passed through the strip of woods. The house stood in a level piece of land, approached from the east by an avenue a quarter mile long and leading up to what seemed to me quite an elevation. It was not more than twenty or twenty-five feet, and as I have revisited the place in later years I wondered how the hill could have seemed so high. Perhaps it is due to the magnifying power of time, for all the hills in the neighborhood have shrunk, and the streams that seemed deep appear shallow.

The house was of brick and faced to the east and had a porch set in on the front and back side of the main living room. It was of the style quite familiar in Virginia, with a hall running through the center.

A commodious yard about three hundred feet long and two hundred feet wide contained a row of cedars on each side of the walk and several rows of maples. I still measure distances by the distances that I learned to know in this country home. A hundred yards is still the distance between our front door and the gate, a quarter mile is the length of the avenue, and the half mile is the distance from our farm fence to the main street.

My father used to take me out to the farm while the house was being built and the workmen allowed me to help to the limit of my small ability. I would carry a brick on a shingle and in my boyish pride felt that I was having a part in the construction of the building that was to be my home for seventeen years.

A piano was the principal piece of furniture in the parlor and is often recalled. One of the pictures most clearly outlined in my memory is the picture of the family gathered in this room on Sunday afternoon, singing Sunday-school songs and church hymns. Mother played the accompaniment and led in the singing. The Bryan Choir, as father called it, joined with youthful enthusiasm. Father's favorite piece was "Kind Words" and we were wont to close the singing with his favorite song. To these Sunday afternoon exercises, as well as to the Sunday school, I am indebted for these tunes that have run through my mind ever since.

The spare bedroom was set apart for the special entertainment of politicians and divines. The bringing together of these two classes illustrated not only my father's views on the subjects but early taught me to regard the science of government as an entirely honorable one. My father was as much at home with ministers as he was with politicians and statesmen. He saw no necessary conflict—and I have never been able to see any—between the principles of our government and the principles of Christian faith.

One of the pieces of furniture of that day which seems to have disappeared in modern times was the trundle bed. It enabled the younger children to sleep in the same room with their parents and at the same time space in the room to be utilized in the daytime.

Our farm contained five hundred twenty acres in one block, nearly all of it prairie, with a small woods pasture near and an eighty-acre piece of timber about three miles away. We had a park of fourteen acres adjoining the farm where my father indulged his fancy for deer, the number running up at times as high as twenty. We had the usual farm animals, horses, cattle, hogs, sheep, and, of course, the usual supply of poultry which included turkeys, guineas, and ducks as well as chickens. As I look back upon those days, I feel a little disappointed that we did not have geese, fowls that I used to associate with the family visits which we made to our grandparents, who lived near Walnut Hill, Illinois, about twelve miles away. There was a creek in front of the house and the geese that frequented it, always on the lookout, gave their noisy warning at our approach.

My parents were not fanciers of pure-bred stock, although I remember several excellent males that were bought from time to time, as a bull to which we gave the name "White Cloud" which was sent to us from Jacksonville—he was a gift from Dr. Jones, whose name will become familiar to the readers of these memoirs. I remember that we were very proud of him until he became vicious, when we had to dispose of him. My first experience with pigs was with a Chester White boar. I took him to the fair one fall, and have a very distinct recollection of the amount of washing necessary to keep a white pig clean,

IN THE BEGINNING

As we rented the land out and cultivated only a few acres, our place might have better been called a suburban home than a farm, but we had enough farm life to give us experience as children. The boys had the wood to cut and the chores to do. I, being the oldest, used the laboring oar, so to speak, and learned to milk and care for the stock and to do the general chores. If I were required to select the days of my boyhood which were least enjoyed the lot would fall on the winter days of this period. My first business was to make the fire in the Franklin stove and then go to the barn and feed the horses, cows, and hogs. Then came the milking and then breakfast. Sometimes we had a farm hand and I played the part of assistant, but much of the time we did not have enough work to justify the employment of a man in the winter time and the burden fell on me.

More than fifty years have passed since those days and I can see myself engaged in this drudgery, my nose running, my fingers numb, and possessing feelings for which the Sunday-school songs I knew did not furnish fitting expression. And yet, I look back to those days as among the most valuable of my life and I would not for anything have them eliminated. They taught me industry and obedience and they gave me an exercise which no gymnasium can supply. My physical strength has been an invaluable asset and I feel that I am indebted to work upon the farm for the strength that has enabled me to endure fatigue and withstand disease. Our verdicts which we pronounce in youth are often reviewed and set aside in mature life. I am sure that the indictments which I would have framed about the time the chores were done are very unlike the judgments that I now render in retrospect.

RABBIT HUNTING

My favorite sport in those early days was hunting rabbits. My father had something of the spirit of the hunter. I presume it came down in his blood from a Virginia

35

ancestry. At any rate, he used to take me out squirrel hunting and I was all interest from the time we began to prepare for the hunt, moulding the bullets the night before for a muzzle-loading rifle, to the time when we came back with one or possibly two squirrels as a reward for an afternoon's tramp. But while I envied my father's skill as a marksman, I never attempted to rival him with the rifle. I began with a shotgun, first with a single barrel and then with a double barrel. These were given to me as soon as my parents thought it was entirely safe for me to use them, possibly a little earlier than it was entirely safe, for I remember three narrow escapes from death by gunshot.

One day I was cleaning the gun in the hallway and it went off, blowing a hole through the baseboard, but I was not in front of it at the time. It scared me and I was careful, but not, I fear, as careful as I should have been. A little later I was putting a double barreled shotgun through a rail fence and foolishly had the barrel pointed toward me. The hammer struck a rail and discharged the cap—but fortunately, the gun did not go off. I could not have escaped death if the fire of the cap had reached the powder. Why it did not, I do not know, for that was its only failure to fire during the hunt.

At another time Henry Webster, my nearest neighbor, went with me out to Tonti, the nearest station on the Illinois Central, to meet my father, who was returning from holding court in one of the courts of his circuit. We got out at a pond near the road to shoot some snipe. I suppose we must have forgotten to let down the hammer. At any rate, the gun that was between us went off and blew a hole through the back curtain. We were singing "O, you must be a lover of the Lord, or you can't go to heaven when you die." Our musical program was suspended by the discharge of the gun and we rode the rest of the way exchanging congratulations upon our escape and wondering how the gun could have discharged.

IN THE BEGINNING

Before I was old enough to use a gun I used to hunt rabbits with a stick, tracking them in the snow and killing them in the little sheltered spots so familiar to hunters of this familiar game.

I had two dogs, Carlo and Dixie, the latter a mixed breed with rat terrier predominating. Carlo was a dog of medium size. If any one pure strain could be multiplied by the many strains mixed in him, he would have been a very costly brute. But as prices are not determined in this way, he would have brought at auction as little as he cost me— nothing. The dogs hunted together, Dixie would go in under the brush piles and scare the rabbits out and Carlo jumped stiff legged around the pile and would take up the chase as soon as the frightened rabbit came out. I followed the dogs, scrambling over fences, helping to pick up the trail when there was snow on the ground, and returning as jubilant in defeat as in victory. Many times when I almost froze during the chores I would warm myself by a chase after a rabbit until all the hardships of work were forgotten. After I began going to school, a part of each Saturday was given over to some kind of sport, usually a rabbit hunt, and one rabbit seemed to be my normal luck, although sometimes I would come back with several.

At times I would get my first game soon after I started and carry it for several hours and sometimes I would trudge along without reward until nearly home and then unexpectedly catch a rabbit. We had a boardwalk which ran diagonally from the front porch to the garden gate and intersected the walk from the kitchen to the barn. As the boards were nailed crosswise on two by fours, the walk furnished a splendid hiding place for rabbits and it trapped many for me.

As I grew older I extended my hunting to quail, prairie chickens, and ducks. The quail, however, was never much endangered by my hunting. It seemed too small for my gun and I was frequently mortified by having a hunting

37

companion give me the first shot and then kill the bird after I had missed it.

With prairie chickens I had better success. Probably they furnished a larger target, but even here I was only a second-rate hunter. One time, I think it was in 1897, I went hunting in Idaho with the father of the famous Chicago lawyer, A. S. Trude. I think he was then about eighty. He had lost one eye, which to a hunter is quite a disadvantage. When we came in from the most successful chicken hunt I ever had we counted up thirty fowls and he was generous enough to insist that I had killed ten of them— half as many as he. I used to wonder what the relative success would have been if he had had two eyes.

Soon after the election of 1896 I became acquainted with William L. Moody, a prominent banker of Galveston. Governor Hogg, his attorney, made me acquainted with him and established him in my affections by telling me that he was the only prominent banker in Galveston who voted for me. When Governor Hogg was describing a hunt he gave a very vivid picture of the hunting at Lake Surprise. Three items of his description are recalled. The first was that you could hunt ducks there in a dress suit, and this I found to be true. We were entertained at a commodious house near the lake, where we had comfortable beds and the best of food. A spring wagon would take us to the lake, where we entered canoes and rowed to the blinds which were hidden in reedy islands in the lake. Here we would sit and shoot until our hunting hour was over. Then boatmen would gather up the ducks, carry us back to the landing place, from which the spring wagon would carry us back to the house. There was nothing to soil one's evening dress had he cared so to clothe himself. On one of my visits I took Mrs. Bryan with me and she sat in the blind and read to me while I waited for the waterfowl to appear. Another item in his description was that the ducks were so numerous that the noise made by their feet in the celery in the lake

sounded like the roar of a train and that the noise made by
their flying was like the rumbling of distant thunder. These
accounts seem quite extravagant, but they were true to the
letter. I have never found anywhere such hunting places
as Colonel Moody used to furnish at Lake Surprise and
never a more genial and hospitable host than Colonel
Moody, whose son J. L. or his younger son, Henry, or his
son-in-law, Northen, expert with the gun, went with us.

Our trips usually extended from the evening of the first
day through the morning and evening of the second day and
the morning of the third day. When I first went down there
I was inclined to joke about the game law, saying that a
law limiting each person to twenty-five ducks a day was
never intended for me because I did not expect to come
near the limit, and that a law prohibiting more than twenty-
five shots at one duck might have been *more* embarrassing
to me. But on a later visit, just before a hotel temporarily
destroyed the value of the lake as a hunting resort, I had
a streak of luck. I killed my quota of twenty-five before
sundown on the first afternoon and then killed my quota
the morning of the next day so that in the afternoon I had
to content myself with pointing out ducks to others. Next
morning I again killed my quota before noon, making
seventy-five for the three days. This was my record day,
surpassing all other hunting experiences.

My father was in the habit of impressing his views upon
me by apt illustrations or humor. I recall that during my
early boyhood I expressed a desire to take lessons on the
piano. He checked my ambitions in this direction with
the brief but firm suggestion that the girls in the family
could take lessons on the piano but that the boys would
learn to make music with the hand saw. I have only
inherited half of his views on this subject. When I hear a
song that appeals to my heart I envy those who are able to
sing. But experience has confirmed in me the views of
my father about music in general. One has only so much

time. If it is spent on instrumental music sufficient to become proficient it occupies time that must be taken from other things, as for instance, reading, from which I think more practical value is derived. It is a very pleasant thing for a man to be able to furnish music to a company, but it is sometimes done at the expense of other lines of development. If one cannot reach the maximum in both entertainment and service, service is the more important of the two.

My parents believed in the old adage, "Spare the rod and spoil the child," and as they loved me too well to risk my being spoiled, they punished me. As I look back upon these punishments, I find myself more tolerant in passing judgment upon them than I was at the time, although I recall instances where I recognized the punishment as just, and some instances where I felt that I deserved more than I received. They were quite strict with me and I sometimes considered the boys more fortunate who were given more liberty, but on reflection I am not prepared to say that I would have done better under a different system. Other kinds of discipline may be better for other children—that parents must decide for themselves. I am not only satisfied but grateful for the punishment I received.

At the age of ten I was sent to school; before that time my mother taught me at home. Grandma's room—the back sitting room—was my first schoolhouse, and a little walnut table about two feet square, as my memory reproduces it today, was the first stump from which I made a speech. I would learn my lessons until I could repeat questions and answers without the book and then I would stand up on this little table and declaim them to my mother. My first audience, therefore, was a receptive, appreciative, and enthusiastic one.

Webster's spelling book and McGuffey's reader, then a geography, whose author I cannot recall, formed the basis of my education and furnished the themes for my earliest declamations. I would like to own this table, but it has thus far eluded my search.

A difference of opinion may arise as to the inheritance of my ability as a speaker. My father's talent in this line of work may form the basis for argument in support of hereditary ability, but I am inclined to give more weight to environment than to inheritance. It is unusual for the descendants of a prominent public speaker to excel in speaking, and differences among those who inherit equally would seem to raise a doubt as to the value of ancestral abilities. The child of a public speaker has the influence of his father's example and the inspiration that comes from an ambition to be like him. If to this is added the devotion and diligence of a mother who, like my mother, encouraged the tendency, the weight of the argument may be on the side of environment rather than heredity.

I began very young to manifest an interest in speaking and received all the encouragement that a child could from both father and mother. As the profession which I liked leads up to forensic efforts, it must also be taken into consideration no child could have had an environment more favorable to a public career or stronger incentives to follow this particular line of work. As the story proceeds illustrations will be given of the continuity of purpose and the permanence of the ambition.

In School

The first public school I attended was in what we called "The Old College," a building once used for a girls' seminary. When the school was abandoned the building was turned over to the city and my first lessons from a teacher of a public school were given me there.

Mrs. Lamb was the teacher, a woman somewhat advanced in years at that time but an enthusiast on education and a strict disciplinarian.

I next attended a school in a different part of the town

and soon entered the high school, from which I went to Whipple Academy, a preparatory department of Illinois College, Jacksonville.

During these five years in the public school I do not recall much that is worth recording. I walked in to school, a distance of three-quarters of a mile to the first building and about a mile to the second and to the high school. I was regular in attendance and studious, having behind me the coercive power of parents who were determined that I should have an education. I do not recall that I ever failed in an examination, neither do I remember to have been at the head of the class in these earlier days. I might have been called an average—I was not below the average in my studies and well toward the front in deportment. In the high school I began studying Latin and also went a step forward in the art of declamation in the literary society work. We had a debating club in the high school and I recall taking a part in what we called The Senate, and I was a senator from Illinois. It may have been that this experience in a "senate" suggested to me the thought of being some time a Senator of the United States. This ambition received encouragement from my father's race for Congress in 1872 when I was twelve years old.

I early became interested in the political news in the papers and recall very distinctly the eagerness with which I searched the columns of the *Missouri Republican*, the first prominent political newspaper I ever read.

I do not remember the subjects debated, but I recall that in one debate in which the color question came up, I used a sentence which brought forth applause when in the course of a brief speech I described something under consideration as "the darkest picture ever painted upon the canvas of time."

It was during my high-school days that I made my first venture in poetry, but while the jingle was praised by the schoolmates who saw it, the success was not sufficient to turn my head or my mind in that direction.

My father, being a very devout man, lost no opportunity to impress upon me the value of the Bible. To him it was not only the Word of God but the fountain of wisdom. He was especially fond of Proverbs and was in the habit of calling me in from work a little before noon to read a chapter and comment upon it. I cannot say that I shared his enthusiasm at the time—in fact, I was at times a little restless and even wished that I might have been allowed to devote the time to work in the field rather than to the reading and comment. But when he died, soon after I was twenty, the Biblical truths that he sought to impress upon me grew in value and I took up the book of Proverbs and read it through once a month for a year. I have frequently mentioned this experience and advised young men to read Proverbs because of the accumulated wisdom to be found therein—wisdom on all moral questions and expressed with wonderful force and clearness. I have quoted from Proverbs in my political speeches more than from any other part of the Bible or from any other book. Solomon left a rare collection of epigrams and it was the reading of Proverbs that gave me my first appreciation of the value of epigram.

The moulding of public opinion is one of the greatest of the arts, and the essence of moulding public opinion lies in the ability to say much in a few words. No uninspired writer has left so much of wisdom contained in so small a compass. One of the proverbs of Solomon which I early learned and often quoted was "A prudent man forseeth the evil, and hideth himself." This cannot be improved upon so far as the sentiment is concerned or the beauty of expression, but I found that audiences—especially students—did not seem to grasp it. As the object of speaking is to impress truth, I finally took the liberty of presenting this truth in a way most familiar to the student and most

43

easily remembered. The paraphrase ran like this, "The prudent man gets the idea into his head, the foolish man 'gets it in the neck.' " The students instantly caught the idea and I felt that the impressing of the idea did more good than the slang did harm. The consolation of the reformer is that if he is right in uttering the warning and the people do not heed, they will come to him when their necks are sore.

My religious training was not neglected at any period of my life. We had family prayers—one of the sweetest recollections of my boyhood days—and I entered Sunday school early. My father being a Baptist and my mother being a Methodist, I went to both Sunday schools. The only advantage that I know of that can come from the parents belonging to the different churches is that the Sunday-school opportunities are doubled. I would not offer this as sufficient reason for encouraging a difference in church membership on the part of parents, but where there is a difference of this kind, the Sunday school may, to some extent, be an off-setting advantage—at least, in my case it gave to me the double interest in Sunday-school work, an interest which has never waned.

At the age of fourteen I reached one of the turning points in my life. I attended a revival that was being conducted in a Presbyterian church and was converted. Having been brought up in a Christian home, conversion did not mean a change in my habits of life or habits of thought. I do not know of a virtue that came into my life as a result of my joining the Church, because all the virtues had been taught me by my parents. Truthfulness had been so earnestly enjoined that in more than one case I received my parents' commendation for not misrepresenting the situation when truthfulness might bring criticism if not punishment.

I remember that one day we children were playing in the sitting room, and noticing father's pocketbook upon the bureau, it occurred to some one of us—I do not know which—to count the money, so we locked the door and proceeded to inform ourselves upon the amount in the pocketbook. When we were just finishing we heard his footfall in the hall. We hurriedly crowded the money into the pocketbook and opened the door, but not soon enough to avoid suspicion. When he found me alone he asked me what we were doing. I told him we were counting his money, whereupon he took me down town and bought me a saddle, presenting it and telling me, as he presented it, to remember I received it for telling the truth. I do not know of any similar amount of money that ever made so great an impression upon my youthful mind and heart.

As an illustration of the teaching which I received at home I cite two other instances. Before entering school at the age of ten my mother so impressed upon me her opinion of swearing—a matter in which my father also set me a valuable example—that when I entered school I felt a distinct aversion to swearing. I would find myself withdrawing from the crowd when the boys began to swear, and to this day I have not overcome an aversion which I felt in those early days.

The other subject impressed on me was that it was wrong to gamble. My father hated gambling and taught me to hate it. With him it did not matter whether the amount wagered was large or small or whether the person won or lost—gambling was gambling. Some time before I was fifteen I had an experience that almost rivaled the gift of the saddle in the impression it made. My father had bought me a forty-cent knife which I wagered against a ten-cent knife on a proposition where I felt that I could not lose. The boys had given me a number of cards, each containing a series of numbers. These numbers were so arranged that the sum of the first numbers on each card equaled the number asked for. After I had used the cards until I felt confident of their accuracy, I undertook to tell the age of a boy's mother if he would pick out the cards on

45

which the age appeared. The wager was my knife against his and I lost. Upon examination, I found that the number required was the only one which could not be determined by the adding together of the first numbers on the cards containing this number. Knowing my father's views on gambling, I was so terrified at the thought of his learning what I had done that I resolved never to gamble again, no matter how certain I might be to win. The loss of a forty-cent knife has saved me a great deal of money, if I can judge what my experience would have been from the experiences of friends who have bet on elections where I, like they, thought the result was certain.

CHAPTER II

CHURCH AND SCHOOL

IN becoming a member of the Church I entered upon an important epoch—much more important than I thought at the time. I was, of course, too young to know anything about the creeds of the different churches. I knew the names of the churches and had attended all of them at different times and had been connected with the Sunday schools of several of them. The Baptist Church in Salem had a very small congregation at that time. There was preaching there once a month and but very few young people in the Sunday school. The Methodist Church was a larger organization and I went to the Baptist Sunday school in the morning and the Methodist Sunday school in the afternoon. Besides these denominations the Presbyterian and Cumberland Presbyterian and the Catholics had congregations there. The last named ministered to but a few families. After my mother joined the Baptist Church with my father, about 1872, I began to attend the Cumberland Presbyterian Church in the afternoon. It had one of the largest congregations in the city and a great many children in that church were my companions in school. I think no other Sunday school had so large an influence upon my life.

The superintendent was the best Sunday-school superintendent I have ever known—at least, he so seems to me as I look back through the years and recall his devotion to the school, his friendly attitude toward all the children, and our intimate acquaintance with him. He seemed like one of the family; we liked to meet him on the street and enjoyed being sent to his store to make purchases. He was always on hand and the lessons that he drew from the Bible text are yet part of our thoughts and lives. If in the world beyond, he knows, as I believe he does, how affectionately the children remember him, it will be abundant reward for the time he devoted to his work—probably he felt that he received his reward as he went along from a consciousness of service rendered and from the knowledge of the affectionate regard the children had for him.

Then there was Sam Chance, who led the singing. He had one of the sweetest tenor voices I have ever heard; his notes still ring in my ears. He has only one rival among those nonprofessionals to whom I have listened. My wife's father had a tenor voice, not so strong as Mr. Chance's but fully as sweet and as expressive, but I did not hear him until considerably later in life—and then I heard him sing frequently.

There is one fact in connection with my early days that should, I think, be recorded, namely, my parents' willingness to allow me to choose at that early age a church different from their own. It was an evidence of their liberality in denominational matters, notwithstanding the deep and permanent convictions which they had on Christian fundamentals. I noted this liberality first in the attitude of each in the other's church before they became members of the same church. I noticed it also in their treatment of ministers of the various churches who were occasionally assembled at our house at family dinner. I was also impressed by the fact that when we gathered our hay my father was in habit of sending a load away to each minister, including the Catholic priest when a priest resided there.

This liberality was also proof of the deep concern about my religious life. When I asked my father whether he had any objections to my joining the Presbyterian Church— my inclination to join being based upon two facts: first, my conversion at a revival held in that Church; and second being the fact that some seventy young people of the Sunday school, my schoolmates in the day school, joined at that time—he said that he wanted me to join where I felt

I would be most at home and could do the most good. I never knew until after his death that he was disappointed that I did not become a member of his own church.

When, a year later, I entered Whipple Academy at Jacksonville, I took my letter to the Presbyterian Church at Jacksonville and remained a member of it until 1887, when I took my letter to the First Presbyterian Church at Lincoln, Nebraska. Though my connection with the Presbyterian Church at Salem was very brief, the church has had a very warm place in my heart for half a century. Six years ago I presented to the church a pulpit made after a pattern which appealed to me at Dr. Hindman's church, the Northminster Presbyterian Church at Columbus, Ohio. The pulpit was made for him by an elder whose father was an elder in the Presbyterian Church in Scotland.

In front of the pulpit was a cross and in the center was a burning bush—the cross representative of the New Testament and the bush the Old Testament. This so deeply impressed me that I had a replica of the Columbus pulpit made for the church at Salem. I spoke at its dedication in May, 1920, my subject being "Symbols of Service." Dr. Glover, pastor of the Jacksonville Church when I became a member of it, was a man who had ministered to the church for a generation. He became my personal friend as well as my pastor and I feel that he exerted a very beneficial influence on my life at that formative period. His wife, who shared in his devotion to spiritual things, invited me to her home one evening that she might appeal to me to prepare for the ministry. While I had great regard for the ministry, I did not feel that my life work lay along that line and, therefore, while I was willing to hear what she had to say, I was prepared to defend my choice of the law as a life pursuit. I recall that I had fortified myself with the third verse of the twenty-first chapter of Proverbs: "To do justice and judgment is more acceptable to the Lord than sacrifice." When I called at her home I found that sickness of a relative had taken her away from town and, as the invitation was not renewed, I never had occasion to weigh the reasons that she had intended to present.

After Dr. Glover's death, which was before my graduation, Dr. J. R. Southerland was called to the church and the attachment formed between us continued until his death a few years ago. He was succeeded by A. B. Morey. Although his pastorate was brief, it was long enough to become the basis of an attachment between us that lasted till his recent death. His successor had a personality and charm that made a deep impression on me. In one sermon he gave a graphic picture of the right way and the wrong way of doing a thing. He said that to take a tree through a little gate you must take the trunk first, then the limbs would be pressed in against the trunk. If, on the contrary, he attempted to take it through by pulling the limbs through first, the other limbs would catch against the gatepost and prevent progress.

When in 1887 we moved to Nebraska we found Dr. Curtis pastor of the First Presbyterian Church. He was called to a Chicago church and was followed by Dr. Hindman, with whom I became intimately associated, and this friendship I have cherished through years that have followed. Dr. Henry V. Swearingen, who was later Moderator, followed Dr. Hindman. He, too, became one of the inner circle of our friends.

Soon after moving to our country place, Fairview, near Lincoln, Nebraska, in 1902 we took our letters to the Westminster Presbyterian Church. I was elected elder of this church and held the position until we took our letters to the First Presbyterian Church of Miami, Florida, in 1921. But in order that we might know our neighbors better we attended the Methodist Church in Normal. In the Sunday school Mrs. Bryan assisted as teacher, and I was a teacher from time to time as my traveling would permit.

As I look back over the years, I am increasingly grateful

for the religious environment that surrounded me in my youth and the devotion of my parents and for the influence that the Church had upon me in my school days. The period through which one passes in the journey from youth to maturity is quite likely to be accompanied by some religious uncertainty. In the course of nature the child will substitute the spirit of independence for the spirit of dependence. Instead of doing things because he is told to, he must do them upon his own responsibility and from his own convictions. During this transition period the pendulum is apt to swing too far and he sometimes finds himself more self-reliant than he ought to be and less disposed to be influenced by advice of others. It is just at this time when the parental authority is weakening that usually the student begins in the study of the physical sciences. If he is fortunate enough to have teachers who are themselves Christians with a spiritual vision of life, the effect is to strengthen his faith and he advances to a normal religious life. If he is unfortunate enough to fall under the influence of mind worshipers, he may be led step by step away from faith into unbelief. It is a matter of profound gratitude to me that during these days I was associated with Christian instructors so that the doubts aroused by my studies were resolved by putting them beside a powerful and loving God. Knowledge of the experiences of students has made me very sympathetic with students in college and has led me to go from college to college in the hope of helping young men to find solid ground upon which to stand. It was this interest in young men more than anything else which led me to prepare and deliver the address entitled, "The Prince of Peace." (See Chapter XXI.)

WHIPPLE ACADEMY

At the academy I got my first taste of college life. It looked a long road ahead of me when I counted up the two years at the academy and the four years at the college before the day of graduation. And it was the classical course, too. I cannot remember when I decided to go to college—in fact, I do not recall that I ever did decide to go to college. It was decided for me by my parents and when I was too young to fix the day. All I know is that I was going to college from my earliest recollection. I was not only going to college but I was going to take the highest course the college provided, and the plan was later elaborated by the addition of a post-graduate course at Oxford, England. My father was enthused upon the subject of education and my mother fully shared with him this desire for the children. When not long before his death I sat by his bedside and in the presence of my mother took down at his dictation the words of his will, he expressed in a paragraph this ideal which had led him as a poor boy to make a successful struggle for a classical education. He directed that all of the children (I was then twenty and there were four younger than myself) should have the best education that the generation afforded. Not long before he died he bought fifty calves which were to grow until I graduated at Illinois College and then were to be turned into money, the money to be used for a year at Oxford. It so happened that when he died he owed security debts to the amount of about $15,000, the larger part represented by a note given by a man to his sister which father endorsed. In settling up the estate it seemed best to sell the cattle and pay off those security debts, so that my trip to Europe was given up. My mother took enough of the calf money to purchase for me a gold watch which I carried until it was replaced by the precious timepiece given me by the employees in the State Department.

In September after my fifteenth anniversary I was sent to Whipple Academy, Jacksonville, a preparatory school connected with Illinois College. Here again I was the beneficiary of one of the best bits of good fortune that has fallen to my lot. My father, being a Baptist, had intended to send me to William Jewell College in Liberty, Missouri, an institution of his own denomination which he had come to hold in high esteem. If I had been two or three years older I presume he would have carried out this purpose and I would have been brought into contact with other personalities and my life might have been moulded by an entirely different chain of circumstances. My father had a distant relative, a physician of prominence, Dr. Hiram K. Jones, between whom and my father a warm friendship had developed. Dr. Jones was a man of the highest character, of great learning, and lofty ideals. His wife, Cousin Lizzie, as we called her, was one of the sweetest characters which it has ever been my privilege to know. She was a woman of rare intelligence, fond of literature and music, and was possessed of temper that nothing could ruffle. She was so charitable in her attitude toward others that I do not recall having heard her say an unkind word of anyone during the six years that I made my home in the family. Even a criticism made by others would pain her as if it were directed against her and she would protest with a sincerity that was manifested in both tone of voice and in the expression of pain upon her face.

Dr. Jones was the head of the literary circle of the city and for some years a lecturer at the Concord (Massachusetts) School of Philosophy. His specialty was Plato. Possibly no scholar of his day was more thoroughly acquainted with the work of the great Greek philosopher. Dr. Jones' diversion was microscopy and he often called me in to examine the specimens upon which he was working.

Dr. and Mrs. Jones were members of the Congregational Church and he was a trustee of Illinois College, which was founded by a group of Yale graduates who came out to Jacksonville in the early years of the century. As I view in retrospect my own life in the Jones family I find it difficult to calculate the influence which association with them had upon my ideas and ideals. They had no children and

53

I was only one of a number of schoolboys to whom they had furnished a home, and these, as I came to know them, were as grateful as I became for the splendid environment furnished.

Dr. H. K. Jones had a brother, Dr. George Jones, ten years his junior, who was associated in the practice with him. He was a man of different type but one to whom I became also attached. His wife, an admirable woman, was more or less of an invalid. Their house was in the same yard as that of the elder doctor, so that my acquaintance with them was almost as intimate as with Dr. and Mrs. H. K. Jones. The families furnished a splendid illustration of the strength and tenderness of family ties. Dr. George and his wife had no children and, like the family with whom I made my home, they nearly always had students with them. These were my most intimate friends during these delightful days.

I began Greek in my first preparatory year and Latin in the second year. Like most boys, I was relatively further along in mathematics than in the languages.

When I left home for school father told me that he was able to furnish me with the money that I actually needed but that he could not afford to have me waste money, and then he suggested what I have always believed to be a good rule, that I should keep an account and report to him the use I had already made of the money when I wrote for more. This I proceeded to do and I do not recall that he ever referred to the expenditures except in one case.

I had spent ten cents for blacking, twenty cents for bay rum, and ten cents for candy. I entered the account as "forty cents for blacking, bay rum, etc.," the "etc." covering the candy. It so happened that the next entry was "to the church, five cents." He sent me the money that I asked for, merely adding by way of comment, "I notice that you spent forty cents for blacking and five cents for the church. It seems to me that that is travelling toward the Dead Sea pretty fast." I can imagine that there was a smile upon his face when he wrote this reproof, but it answered the purpose. I never covered any expenditures afterward with "etc." and I never forgot the inference that he drew from the relative size of the amount spent for improvement of my appearance and the amount spent for the church.

I hope that it will not seem to the reader too trivial if I add that this old account book fell into my wife's hands after we were married and she discovered that the first item of my college account was "five cents for a bologna sausage," spelled "ballony." Another entry was, "oysters and needles—15c."

When I first left home I was growing very rapidly. I have reason to remember, because I wrote back home for money to buy a new pair of pants, explaining to my father that my pants had become so short that I was ashamed to attend the church sociables. He wrote back saying that I would soon be home for the holidays and could then replenish my wardrobe and added, "But you might as well learn now that people will measure you by the length of your head and not by the length of your breeches."

College Years

By the fall of 1877 I entered college proper. While I was only a freshman, the two years' experience in the academy had somewhat worn off my freshness and I felt well on the road toward manhood. I had developed so rapidly during the years preceding that I had almost reached my growth. My ambition was to be six feet in height and weigh 180. That was my idea of the proper height and weight; possibly I had obtained my standard of height from my father who was a little more than six feet tall. He did not, however, give me my idea of weight, because he weighed only 154, as I had reason to know.

WILLIAM JENNINGS BRYAN

When I went home from college for a vacation we happened to weigh at the same time. He weighed 154 and I weighed 150. I was rather proud of my weight and said, "I shall soon be as heavy as you are." He replied with a twinkle of the eye, "When you have four pounds more of brains we will weigh the same." The next time we weighed I weighed more than he did and recalling his remark I attributed all the increase as "brain weight."

I did not give much attention to athletics during college. My principal exercise was walking from my boarding place on College Avenue up to my recitations and back and down town and back, as I had frequent occasions to run errands for Dr. or Mrs. Jones. While I played games to some extent, I was not an expert except at jumping. When I played baseball I was usually assigned to the right field, where my inefficiency would least embarrass the club. In my younger days I had been more conspicuous upon the diamond, but my prestige waned when the round bat was substituted for the flat bat and when the ball began to be thrown instead of pitched. The curve was always a mystery to me and I never secured sufficient control of the muscles of my face to restrain the expression of surprise called forth by the curved balls that passed me unimpeded in their flight. But when it came to the broad jump I had to be reckoned with. I was somewhat proficient in the running broad jump, but the only thing in which I excelled was what we used to call the standing jump, known technically, I believe, as the standing broad jump. I began at nine feet when I entered the academy. I gradually increased the distance until I won a prize with a record of twelve feet four inches. I would commence jumping as soon as the frost was out of the ground and jump until I was sore and then I would continue jumping until the soreness disappeared.

I entered many jumping contests, but one competitor after another fell behind. I remember one good-natured

MARY ELIZABETH BAIRD AS A STUDENT, 1880   WILLIAM JENNINGS BRYAN AS A STUDENT, 1880

At Jacksonville Academy, Illinois, where she first met William Jennings Bryan.

rival, Charlie Carter, who, when he discovered that his efforts were hopeless, vented his disappointment in the following good-natured rebuke: "Bryan, my father always told me never to speak of anyone unless I could speak well of him. Whenever I speak of you I always say you are a good jumper." I have thought of this many times since when a stranger introducing himself would say, "Mr. Bryan, I must say that you are a man of wonderful physical endurance." I know by that compliment that he is a Republican, he wants to speak kindly and he can say this much without making any political concessions.

My practice in the jumping forward led me also to practice the jump backwards, in which I left a record of nine feet. I do not recall but one man who surpassed me in the jump backward. There is more of art than strength in this jump, a good deal depending upon so balancing as to use the weight of the body without being thrown off one's feet. Very few can jump any considerable distance backward and the number of those who can jump three jumps backward without falling is still less.

I did not have much chance to hunt while I was in college, although occasionally when there was snow on the ground I went out on Saturday with a college friend. I remember one of these hunts with Oscar Kenneth, one of the members of the class who unfortunately died soon after graduation. We started out early in the morning and hunted until late in the afternoon. The dinner that his mother served to us about four o'clock stands out in my memory as one of the most refreshing meals in my life. It was not that there was great variety of unusual food, but there was plenty and we were hungry—the two necessary elements of a satisfying meal.

I early became acquainted with Glenn Hulett and was frequently his guest. He lives a few miles in the country and we became a terror to the rabbits in the neighborhood. I devote more space to this friend when I speak of my

57

college course. We were rivals and our marks were quite close together at the end of four years' race. But one of the most delightful of rivalries it was. Our friendship was never disturbed by our ambitions. I would have congratulated him as heartily as he did me; if he had been the victor I would have felt that it was an honor to be next to him.

I took the classical course, not as a matter of choice, because I had no choice in the matter. My father and mother decided that question and told me what I was to do, as they had decided for me the question of going to college. I do not know the date of the decision; I only know that from my earliest recollection I was going to college and was going to take the highest course. When I left home, father took from his library two of the largest books, a Greek lexicon and a Latin lexicon, and told me that I was to use the former for six years in the study of Greek and the latter five years in the study of Latin. I did not then know of their importance, but have since been very glad that there were others wiser than myself to decide such questions for me. I have come to place a high estimate upon the study of the dead languages because of the training they give one in the choice of words and because of the acquaintance that they give the student with the derivation of words. I liked Latin better than the Greek—possibly because it is easier. I became so attached to the Latin that I planned to read some Latin every year as a recreation. But I soon became so occupied with work which was necessary that the sentimental was crowded out.

Mathematics was my favorite study until I took up political economy. During the senior year of my preparatory work I took freshman college mathematics and was marked one hundred in geometry. I was a contestant for the freshman prize in mathematics with Sam Montgomery, a boy who was taking the scientific course. I do not know which had the highest marks, because I learned before the prize was awarded that the competition was

58

open only to those who were in the freshman class. This excluded me.

The College Literary Societies

Students of Whipple Academy were permitted to enter the literary societies of the college and I immediately availed myself of this opportunity, joining Sigma Pi (it was not the fraternity which bears this name, but merely the literary society). There was a rival society known as Phi Alpha and I soon caught the college spirit and for six years was prepared to defend my society whenever it was challenged by the "Phis." From the start I took my part in the meetings, beginning with recitations and declamations and later in essays, orations, and debates. My work in the literary societies at Salem had given me some little experience, and yet before this new body of critics I found myself embarrassed by a feeling of timidity. My first appearance called forth more applause from my trembling knees than from the audience.

I may digress for a moment here to commend the work of literary societies. They are an important factor in school life, specially if one contemplates public speaking—an experience into which an increasing number are drawn when they are young though they may have no intention of entering public life.

Of the tasks that fall to the members of literary societies I put the greatest value upon declamations, essays, orations, and debates in the order named. The essay which is often read is, of course, easier to deliver than the declamation. The declamation, on the other hand, employs the words of another and does not require as much thought as the essay. The essay is the preparatory to the oration. It compels an originality of thought which is not necessary in declamation. The oration has all the virtues of the essay and adds to those the virtues of the declamation. It carries the student a step further. The debate is the climax of good speaking.

WILLIAM JENNINGS BRYAN

A debate brings out the ability of the essayist to think and to express himself with clearness and force. It also tests his ability to think upon his feet and to express himself without the aid of manuscript. But still more, it compels him to think quickly and to construct his replies on the moment. He analyzes his opponent's speech as it is made, takes its principal points and frames a reply without time for examination of authorities or for deliberation. The debate is superior also because it is the form of public speaking that wins the largest victories and gives the greatest renown. It gives the most conclusive proof of completeness of preparation, of a thorough understanding of the subject, of earnestness in its preparation, and therefore is most effective in its impression upon an audience.

CHAPTER III

AT THE BAR

POLITICAL opponents have sometimes referred to me as an unsuccessful lawyer; one president of a great eastern university in a campaign speech delivered in my home city in 1896 argued that I was unfit for the Presidency because I had never enjoyed a large income from my profession. I will not attempt to urge in my behalf the argument that turned Disraeli from the law to politics, that is: "To succeed as an advocate, I must be a great lawyer, and to be a great lawyer, I must give up my chance of being a great man"; but I think I owe it to my friends to give them a glimpse of my career as a lawyer. From this they can form an estimate as to whether I would have succeeded had I continued in the profession.

After graduating from the law school and after admission to the bar I returned to my home at Salem to prepare for a change in residence to Jacksonville, Illinois. During the preceding vacation (1882) I made a trip to Kansas City, which I had considered as a possible location. I was impressed by the reports of the growth of the city and went upon a tour of investigation.

I was deeply impressed with the size and bustle of the city, but was disturbed by the fear that I might not have money enough to support me until I could become self-supporting. If I had known as much about law business then as I learned afterwards I would not have been so timid about starting in a city, but the more I pondered over the problem the more strongly I was inclined to start in Jacksonville, where I thought the beginning would be easier. I reasoned thus: I had spent six years as a student at Jacksonville, was acquainted with many of the literary and business people there. I had graduated as the valedictorian of my class and was also class orator. I do not know whether others were ever guilty of the same error, but I am satisfied that I overestimated the impression that my college successes had made on the general public. But, mistake or no mistake, I decided to hang out my shingle in the charming little city which had come to seem like home to me after six years of student life there. So I planned to take my departure from Salem. I have been rather inclined to observe anniversaries and so I chose the Fourth of July for the date of my entering into Jacksonville—it was an easy day to remember and it gave me an anniversary that was sure to be generally observed.

Here again good fortune attended me. The law firm of Brown, Kirby, and Russell, one of the most, if not the most prominent in the city, was made up of three splendid men. William Brown was one of the ablest lawyers I have ever personally known. He was not only a most delightful companion but his way of addressing a judge or jury came nearer being ideal than that of any other person I have known. I think he had more influence upon my style of speaking than any other person from whom I have taken lessons. The friendship that grew up between us continued until he died, and my admiration for the man grew until he became so heroic a figure that I would have offered him a place in my cabinet had I been elected President.

Judge Edward P. Kirby was an admirable partner for a lawyer like Brown. The latter was a trial lawyer without a superior and with few equals; the former was an office lawyer, a man acquainted with pleadings and precedents and authorities, a man whom everybody trusted. He was especially consulted in any matters of probate and settling of estates.

Robert D. Russell, the third member of the firm, was younger than either of the others and one of the most lovable men it has been my lot to know. He was what is often called "the rising young lawyer," ready, diligent, and the friend of all who needed friends. They were all closely identified with Illinois College and within the circle of Dr. Jones' friends and it was possibly for that reason that I received the welcome they accorded me. Some six months after entering the firm, Mr. Russell, who was a brother of the great actor, Sol Smith Russell, moved to Minneapolis, which led to the turning over of much of the collection business of the office to me.

I remember with what anxious expectations I nailed up my modest sign, "W. J. Bryan, Lawyer," on the doorpost and awaited the rush of clients. I use the word "awaited" advisedly, because waiting was the word. It was then that I experienced my first disappointment. The people whom I knew personally seemed to have very little law business or were supplied with legal representatives. The days passed wearily. There was a continuous tread upon the stairs leading up to the second floor where the firm's offices were, and I would turn to the door each time I heard a hand upon the knob, only to find that the visitor had turned into the office of Mr. Brown, Mr. Kirby, or Mr. Russell. They had clients enough and were busy all the time, but the chair that I had been careful to provide and place at my desk stared at me vacantly.

One of my earliest clients was John Sheehan. He had worked for Dr. Jones when I made my home there. He took care of the doctor's horse, looked after the furnace, mowed the lawn, etc. When I opened my office he was keeping a saloon on East State Street. Soon after I began the practice he called to renew acquaintance and to tell me that, while he had a cousin practicing law, he was going to bring me all the business that he could. The reason he gave was that I was friendly to him when I was a student. This was one of the earliest instances—they have been numerous since—where I saw the return of bread cast upon the waters. It did not cost me anything to be friendly to John when he worked for the doctor. I was amply rewarded by the friendliness that John showed in return, and my impression upon him made him one of my first clients.

He said he knew that I was not in sympathy with his business, but that he thought I might be willing to collect some small bills that men owed him for liquor they had bought. I told him that I did not drink myself nor advise drinking, but that I thought those who bought liquor ought to pay for it. I think the first bill he gave me was for $2.60 and a note from me to the debtor brought a prompt settlement. John was very much pleased when I went to the door of his saloon, called him out, and counted out his $2.60, less twenty per cent commission; but what pleased John still more was that the man from whom I made the collection returned and again became a customer. This gave John an argument that he was quick to employ, as I had reason to know he told his friends that Mr. Bryan could collect a bill without making the man mad.

I was not slow to learn the lesson that this taught. I made it a practice not to make men mad when I was collecting bills. If the man could not pay at the time, I asked him to fix a day when I should call again. If he was not ready at the second call, it never annoyed me; I fixed another time. And so I continued to call until the bill was paid, often a little at a time. This sometimes made clients of the men from whom I collected bills.

I recall that Dr. Jones put some accounts in my hands, one of them against a liveryman. After he had postponed payment until I had called half a dozen times he said, "I could pay this bill if you could collect some bills for me and apply the amount, less your commission, on Dr. Jones' bills." I said, "Certainly," and he turned over a batch of accounts. It was not long before I had collected enough to cover the bill that I held against him and had some others besides. One of the bills brought me one of the first of a series of

64

cases that gave me a good deal of satisfaction. One of the liveryman's bills was against a policeman and he wanted a credit of $25, I think it was, which the liveryman had offered as a reward for the recovery of a stolen horse. It seems that the liveryman had missed a horse one night and, thinking it had been stolen, had offered a reward. The policeman found the horse not long afterward tied not far from the livery stable and claimed the reward. The horse was so near and was found so soon that the liveryman did not think the finding came within the spirit of the offer. I looked the matter up and found that there was a city ordinance making it unlawful for a policeman to receive a reward for work done in the line of duty. I brought suit and having prepared myself on this point I plead the ordinance and defended it on the ground of public policy and won the suit. This success did not come until after the Devlin suit later referred to, but was the outgrowth of early collections.

At the end of each month I counted up my receipts—not a difficult task. I remember that at the end of one month my total receipts amounted to $2.50, and, a little discouraged, I wrote to my sweetheart something of my start in the law. After I had finished the letter and reported the meager returns a man came in and wanted an acknowledgment, for I was a notary as well as a lawyer, and I added a postscript saying that I had taken in twenty-five cents more that month. She wrote back a cheering letter saying that I should not be discouraged and that I was simply passing through the narrows. I replied that that was true if it meant that I was in straitened circumstances.

The outlook was so much less promising than I had anticipated that I entered into correspondence with Henry Trumbull, the son of Judge Lyman Trumbull, the law-school classmate I have referred to, with a view to trying my fortune in Albuquerque, New Mexico, where he had located, his choice being influenced largely by his threatened consumption. Between the Fourth of July and the first of January, nearly six months, my total receipts amounted to a little over $67, or an average of $11 a month.

With the beginning of the new year business picked up. The collections turned over to me by Brown and Kirby gave me a start. Dr. Jones found me a few clients and John Sheehan, whose enthusiasm had been increased by my success in collecting bills for him, brought me a really substantial client, out of whose business I made $200—three times my income for the first six months.

This client was Richard Larkin, an Irishman who had a little grocery store, and who, as I learned afterwards, handled liquors on a small scale. I was made assignee of Mr. Larkin's business, which included the collection of a large number of store accounts. These accounts brought me into acquaintanceship with a large percentage of the Irish who traded in Jacksonville and I made friends of his patrons. I was a persistent collector and a very patient one. It never annoyed me to have to call again and again. I may add here that I formed the practice of keeping my collections separate.

When I would collect a little bill I would take out my commission, put the balance in an envelope and put the envelopes away in a vault so that I could always pay my client the amount due him at any time. This custom of keeping clients' accounts separate was adopted upon the advice of my father. When my father last visited me—the visit which ended by his death—I was treasurer of the college paper and he noticed that I had in my bureau drawer an envelope containing money that I collected from advertisers and subscribers. When he inquired about the money I explained to him that it belonged to the college members and that I kept it by itself. He took occasion to commend and to advise me to follow that rule in regard to all money that I collected from others, saying that if I kept their money separate from my own I would not be tempted to make a temporary use of it and would always have it ready for my clients.

While Sheehan brought me the Larkin business Dr. Jones went on my bond as assignee.

My first lawsuit grew out of Mr. Larkin's business. I had an account against Mr. and Mrs. Matt Devlin. The sum was not large—somewhere between $30 and $40, I think. They objected to some items which he was not willing to omit and I brought suit. Mr. and Mrs. Devlin employed as their counsel Jerry Donahue, one of my classmates at college. When we graduated from Illinois College he studied law at Ann Arbor and I at Chicago. We returned to Jacksonville about the same time and this was his first suit as well as mine. It may seem a trifling thing to report, but a suit for that amount was not trifling to either of us at that time. Mrs. Devlin was an important member of the family and took the leading part in resisting payment. I distinctly recall the expression of disgust upon her face when I concluded my argument in support of my client's claim. She settled back in her chair and said, "Thank God, he's done." When the jury returned the verdict in my favor for the full amount it was with great difficulty that I restrained myself from giving utterance to a similar expression.

As time went on larger matters were brought to me and my clients increased in number and in business importance.

My first calendar year, January, 1884–85, showed receipts of something over seven hundred dollars. The second year something over a thousand, the third about fifteen hundred. As I removed to Nebraska at the end of nine months, the fourth calendar year was not completed. The receipts for nine months were nearly fourteen hundred dollars, making sure that that year would have shown a reasonable increase over the preceding one. I give these facts to show the growth of my practice. The beginning was about as small as it could well be, but the gain was constant and my prospects were equal at least to those of any young lawyer in the city of like age and experience. I had the confidence of the profession and the community, as one instance will illustrate. I had my small bank business with the First National Bank, whose president, Felix Ferrell, had been my Sunday-school teacher when I was in college. One day Mr. Brown came from his office to ask me to become assignee in bankruptcy for one of his clients. I responded in the affirmative. He then asked me whether Mr. Ferrell would go on my bond for $40,000. I told him that I had never asked him to go on my bond and could not answer until I had consulted him. Mr. Brown was connected with another bank and I told him that if Mr. Ferrell went on my bond I would want to give the assignee's account to his bank. This he readily assented to as fair and proper. Then he telephoned Mr. Ferrell, who immediately came to the office. I hope I will be pardoned for saying that what followed was a compliment that I have never ceased to appreciate. Mr. Ferrell was not a man of many words; neither was Mr. Brown; and the conversation was brief and to the point. Mr. Brown: "We want Mr. Bryan to act as assignee in bankruptcy for ——. Will you go on his bond for $40,000?" Mr. Ferrell: "Yes." Mr. Brown: "Thanks." Mr. Bryan: "I am much obliged."

While I was practicing I had the usual experience of young lawyers in being called upon to speak on many different occasions. The lawyer has the advantage over all others in such matters. He is the natural spokesman of those of his school of thought and he is called upon more at banquets than those of other professions, because in the course of business he has to deal with a greater variety of subjects. Every form of question comes before the court and the lawyer is really attending school all his life. Some one has said that every speech represents the sum of the man's knowledge. Consciously or unconsciously, the speaker uses all that he has learned as background for each effort.

AT THE BAR

As I look back over my life I am increasingly impressed with the important part played by little circumstances. They really shaped events. While they seemed trivial at the time, yet in retrospect we can see how the absence of any one of them would have broken the chain of causation. My removal to Nebraska and the events following it furnish numerous illustrations.

To begin with, the one thing that singled Lincoln, Nebraska, out from other Western capitals and gave me a special interest in it was the fact that Adolphus Talbot lived there. We had been in law school together from the fall of 1881 to the spring of 1883. We were members of the class of '83, Union College of Law, Chicago, Illinois. We had been meeting twice a day at recitations for some weeks when the following incident occurred. A lady who was on a visit to the family with which I boarded inquired whether I knew Dolph Talbot. Upon my replying that I knew him as one of the members of the class she proceeded to tell me about a very charming young lady to whom he was engaged. Knowing enough about Talbot to know that he was a jovial good-natured fellow, I thought I would have some fun with him, so I sat down by him when the class was assembling and before the lesson began made up a story about as follows:

"Talbot, when I came up here last fall I felt rather lonesome and advertised for unknown correspondents. A number of young ladies answered me, but after a few exchanges of letters I dropped all but one. She made such a favorable impression upon me that we continued the correspondence until we made known our real names. As she lives at Abington, where you graduated, I thought you might be able to tell me something about her." I then gave him the name of his own sweetheart.

I need not add that he was surprised. My joke was working well. He replied with evident seriousness, "If she is the Miss —— whom I know, she is a very nice girl."

WILLIAM JENNINGS BRYAN

Having obtained the information that I pretended to seek, I tried to change the subject, but he would not change it, and kept returning to the theme, much to my enjoyment. I could see that he was not taking much interest in the lesson that morning and when it was over he followed me downstairs, still returning to the young lady at Abington. I did not have the heart to leave him in suspense all day, so as we separated at the corner of Dearborn and Washington Streets I told him that it was just a joke suggested by the fact that I had that morning met a lady who told me of his engagement to Miss ——. He chased me for a block down the street until I dodged into the Rapier Building, where Judge Trumbull's office was located.

At the afternoon recitation Talbot hunted me up with a broad smile on his face and admitted to me that my joke had him "going," as they say. At the conclusion of the recitation we went out together and during our conversation I learned that we were practically of the same age, had graduated on the same day, had become engaged about the same time. Our fiancées, as we compared notes, seemed to stand out as quite superior to all other young ladies of that age. This was a beginning of a friendship which has for forty years been one of the most delightful that I have known.

I speak elsewhere of the partnership which was an outgrowth of this meeting; I refer to it here as one of numerous factors which combined to take me from Illinois to Nebraska and, in so doing, laid the foundation of my political career.

Some years later, while a member of Congress, I made a speech in Baltimore in which I referred in a humorous way to this incident and after tracing its influence up to the time that I was elected to Congress, concluded: "My election to Congress, therefore, may be regarded as a result of a joke which I played in college."

The man who followed me (I think it was Dr. Gonzales) convulsed the House by referring to my statement and adding, "To come to Congress as a result of a joke is not new; I have known men to go to Congress as a result of a joke they have played upon the whole community."

But to continue the chain of circumstances. In the spring of 1887 I still had desk room in the office of Brown and Kirby. A part of the work turned over to me by Brown and Kirby was the collection of interest on notes held by Illinois College as its endowment fund. Judge Kirby, who was treasurer of the Board of Trustees, suggested that I make a trip to Kansas to call personally on some of the makers of these notes. He explained to me that the college could not afford to do more than pay traveling expenses and a small commission on collections made. As I had never been West, the proposition appealed to me and I made plans for the trip.

When I spoke of the matter at home, my wife's father asked me whether it would be much out of my way to go to Creston, Iowa, and look at a tract of land there which he had held for many years. I examined the map and found that it was not far out of my way and decided to include Creston in the trip. Upon closer examination, I found that I could go from Kansas to Creston either by way of St. Joseph or via Lincoln. The fact that Talbot lived at Lincoln decided me to go by that route.

I reached Lincoln early on Saturday morning in July of 1887, was accorded a hearty welcome and spent that day and the Sunday following with my old law-school classmate. The joke, plus the errand upon which the college sent me, plus the fact that my father-in-law had a piece of land in Creston—the three combined to make me acquainted with Lincoln and the opportunities which it offered to a young lawyer. Here were three little circumstances, each one a necessary factor in my change of residence.

But even these would not have led to my removal to Lincoln had it not been for two other small circumstances. Just before I made the trip to Kansas I had decided to open up an office for myself and I had rented rooms next to Brown and Kirby's office—I had even gone so far as to re-paper the rooms and put them in order for my return from the West. But when I came back from Lincoln I was so deeply impressed with the advantages of the proposed change of location that I arranged for a transfer of lease and began to put my affairs in shape to leave for Nebraska in the autumn.

About the time I had rented the room and began planning for a separate office, I came near entering a partnership at Jacksonville which, if it had been formed, would have prevented my going to Nebraska and by so doing prevented the experiences which followed the change of residence. As I look back upon the little difference which prevented the formation of this partnership I am amazed at the influence that it had upon my life.

Richard Yates, son of Illinois' "war governor," who had graduated from Illinois College two years before my graduation, was the city attorney and a candidate for reëlection. We compared our incomes and found that his, including the city attorney's salary, was about the same as mine without any salary, and that therefore we could divide equally without material loss to either. But his salary constituted a considerable part of his income and he felt that it would not be fair for us to divide equally unless he should be reëlected. As the election was some considerable way off, I did not like to delay action in the matter of partnership until then and I proposed to him that I would take the nomination on the Democratic ticket so as to make sure that the salary would come into our office. To this he objected on the ground that his majority against me (I conceded that the chances were greatly in his favor) would not be as great as the majority he hoped to get against the Democrat who seemed likely to be nominated. Looking to a political life, he counted on the size of his majority to aid him in future candidacies.

AT THE BAR

As I recall this incident nearly thirty-five years ago, it seems to me that the two objections to the partnership were both trivial, my unwillingness to risk the small chance of his being defeated and his unwillingness to risk the small loss of majority that he might suffer from my candidacy; and yet these trivial objections prevented the formation of a partnership which would have kept me in Jacksonville.

Another circumstance quite as insignificant might have kept me in Illinois. After the election of President Cleveland in 1884, Mr. James Van Horbeck was appointed United States District Attorney at Springfield. He resided at Carlyle, Illinois, county seat of Clinton County, which was included in my father's judicial circuit when he was on the bench. Mr. Van Horbeck had practiced law under my father and had, I think, been admitted to the bar by him. For that reason he was personally friendly to me.

In the spring of 1887 I went to Springfield and consulted him about appointment as Assistant United States Attorney. He told me that he was not now ready to make the change, but that he would gladly give me the place when there was a vacancy but for the fact that he had promised it to a man endorsed by Congressman Springer. I returned to Jacksonville regretting that circumstances denied me the appointment.

The following September, while I was breaking up housekeeping preparatory for our departure for Nebraska, a carriage drove up to the door and the Assistant United States Attorney called to tell me that he was ready to resign and that the man to whom Mr. Van Horbeck had promised the Assistant's place had moved to Oklahoma and that I could have the position. But it was then too late. My plans had been completed and could not at that time be changed. I was sorry that the information had not come sooner, but if the appointment had been offered me before I went West I would have taken the position at Springfield and would not have gone to Nebraska.

WILLIAM JENNINGS BRYAN

Having laid before the reader the five little circumstances that had a part in my moving to Nebraska, I will only add here that I reached my new home just in time. If I had gone earlier I might have been involved in the divisions in the party and been less available at the particular time which was most favorable for my entrance into politics.

I have described how circumstances combined to take me to Lincoln, Nebraska, where I caught a vision that led to a change in residence. When I returned to Jacksonville I laid the matter before my wife, giving her the reasons for the change as they had impressed me.

First; While I was prospering in Jacksonville, it was only a question of a few years before I would reach the limit of possibilities and Lincoln was a city about four times as large as Jacksonville. Then, too, Lincoln was the capital of a state and I might expect Supreme Court business from outside counties. Illinois had passed through its period of rapid development; Nebraska was growing rapidly. I had found in Lincoln the owner of a weekly newspaper who offered to give me a column of his paper for the answer of legal questions submitted by his readers. This, I thought, would enable me to make acquaintances and become known to the people of the county. And then I had further found there my law-school friend Talbot, who offered me a partnership.

Every argument that impressed me was professional, no thought of politics ever entered my mind. How could it when Nebraska was a Republican state? The Congressional District to which I was moving was Republican; so was the county of Lancaster, the city of Lincoln, and the ward in which I expected to live.

When I had finished my argument my young wife answered in the spirit which she has always shown, "You know Jacksonville; you have seen Lincoln. If you think that the change is for the best, I am willing to go."

We had both attended school in Jacksonville and were

attached to a delightful circle of friends. It was hard to leave these and go to a new country. She was loath to leave the friends who had become so dear to us, and my regret was as deep as hers, but she left the decision to me.

Having obtained my wife's consent, I laid the matter before her father and I cannot forget the generous manner in which he met the situation. I presented to him the same arguments I had laid before my wife and told him of her answer and of my opinion. He replied, "Well, William, it does not make much difference to Lovina (his wife) and me where we live. It does make a difference to you and Mary. You do what you think is best for you and for her, and her mother and I will suit ourselves to your plans."

As a result of an impression more than as a result of clearly defined reasons the die was cast in favor of a change of residence. As I look back to that day I confess that I am somewhat bewildered. Not a single reason that led me to favor the change materialized, but reasons that I never saw and could not therefore take into account justified the change. As I shall show later, my professional success, while as great as we could reasonably expect, covered so brief a period that I could not test the opportunities which appeared to me large enough to justify beginning to practice law in a new state.

And so I arranged to leave for Nebraska on the last day of September and reached Lincoln on the first day of October, 1887, the third anniversary of our marriage. As it was too late in the fall to begin the construction of the home in Lincoln, it was decided that Mrs. Bryan would remain in Jacksonville during the winter with our child and my wife's parents and would join me when the house was completed. When we sold the Jacksonville home I found that Dr. Jones had never put on record the mortgage which I gave him when the house was built, an expression of confidence which I appreciated. The Nebraska home was built by my father-in-law, Mr. Baird, and I rented it until I was in a position to buy it sometime later.

October first, 1887, was a beautiful autumn day. Talbot was at the station to welcome me and he there introduced me to two Democrats who were the beginning of my political friends in that state. One was R. P. Millar, the station agent of the Missouri Pacific Railroad in Lincoln, and W. B. Morrison, a resident of Hickman, about twenty miles south of Lincoln. The partnership of Talbot and Bryan began at once and our offices were in the First National Bank Building. Talbot was the local attorney for the Missouri Pacific Railroad, but it was understood that his salary and fees from the railroad were individual and not covered by the partnership. All other business was the firm's. It was not large at first, because Talbot's connection with the Missouri Pacific had taken him away from the office for a considerable portion of his time and his practice had suffered for lack of a partner.

My first fee came from a man by the name of O'Mara, an Irishman who had heard my Buckhorn School House speech. Although the fee was small, it was a pleasant reminder of the speech into which I had, for professional reasons, tried to inject a reference to my being a lawyer.

When I went to Nebraska I carried with me about $300, a fee which I had just earned in a lawsuit won in the Appelate Court. I also carried with me to Lincoln a letter of introduction to the German National Bank. Joseph Boehmer, the cashier of that bank, had come from Quincy to Lincoln and the letter was from Erwin Wood, who had known him in the former city. I deposited the $300 in the German National Bank and soon became its attorney. The business I received from the bank and through its influence aided me materially in the beginning. Soon after I located in Nebraska we moved our offices to the Burr Block, a building just completed at that time. As I was alone and as I wished to make my $300 go as far as possible, I saved room rent by sleeping on a folding lounge in the office. I economized on food also by buying twenty-one meal tickets for $4.50 at O'Dell's Restaurant and using them two a day instead of three. I ate in the morning and in the evening and contented myself with a lunch at noon, usually an apple and a few gingersnaps. I can remember with great distinctness when the office receipts became sufficient to justify the use of three meal tickets a day.

When I began practice anew in Nebraska my first work was in the matter of collections. I recall one small collection which fell into my hands soon after I joined Talbot. A client who had a little grocery store in the suburbs brought in a small bill which was owed him and told me that he thought the man would pay it if I wrote him a note to stir him up.

I wrote the usual note, framing it in language as polite as I could command, and awaited the call of the debtor. He never came, but the client dropped in the office a few days later to report. As he came into the outer room I noticed a smile upon his face which I interpreted to mean that my note had been successful. When he reached the door I greeted him with,

"Well, I sent him the note. Did it stir him up?"

"Stir him up?" he replied. "I should think it did." Then he took off his hat and showed me a lump nearly as large as an egg on the side of his head, explaining that the debtor had responded to the note, but had called upon him instead of upon his attorney and had hit him on the head with a brick!

I have often thought of this incident when in a campaign I would hear some one boast that he had stirred up the enemy.

I was always interested in the establishment of important legal principles, as two illustrations will show. Not long after I located at Lincoln, Editor Emmons of our local weekly Democratic paper, called on me for advice in regard to a lawsuit. He had been circulating cards advertising his newspaper among the delegates who had come in to attend the county convention. Some of them threw the cards upon the sidewalk and a policeman attempted to arrest Emmons for violating a city ordinance which forbade the throwing of paper upon the street. Emmons resisted arrest and came out second best in the encounter. He went to the office of a justice of the peace and filed complaint against the policeman for assault and battery and the constable refused to serve the papers without fees being advanced. Emmons wanted to know whether it was necessary for him to advance the fees in order to secure redress. I looked for authorities and could find none. One statute specifically gave the constable the right to demand fees before serving papers. After careful consideration of the facts I reached the conclusion in which Judge Cassidy, who was associated with me, concurred: that while the statute made no exception of papers served in criminal cases, such an exception must be presumed, otherwise redress for criminal assault would be impossible to those without means.

Pleading the case upon what I regarded as a fundamental principle, namely, that justice could not be sold and that a remedy in a criminal case could not depend upon the financial ability of the party injured, I drew a petition for a writ of mandamus compelling the constable to serve the warrant without prepayment of his fee. When I took the petition to Judge Chapman and told him the nature of my petition he shook his head and replied:

"You will have to have a very strong case before I will make an officer serve papers without fees being advanced."

"I have a strong case," I answered, "as I think I shall be able to convince you." At the hearing I did convince him and he issued the writ, from which the defendant appealed.

AT THE BAR

When the matter came up in the Supreme Court the hearing was held in a room on the walls of which appeared the seal of the state with the state's motto, "Equality before the law." As that was the basis upon which our fight was being made, I was able to point the judges to the state's motto and it doubtless had its effect in securing a decision, the first, I think, in the United States establishing this important principle. Neither Judge Cassidy nor myself received any fee in this case, but Emmons, who afterwards moved to Oklahoma, had a little post office in his county named after me.

Another case in which I took a deep interest brought me more satisfaction than money. Some beet-sugar factories were established in Nebraska soon after I went there and those in charge of the factories secured a state statute granting a bounty and also sought bounties of counties and precincts. One day a lawyer called with a letter of introduction from J. Sterling Morton to consult me about the legality of a bond issue voted in a precinct in which he lived. My recollection is that his vote was the only vote in the precinct against the bounty. But he wanted to oppose it on the ground that it was unconstitutional. He found me sympathetic. He paid me $25 down and was to pay $25 later. But the account remains open. The fee, however, was immaterial; the case gave me an opportunity to contest the constitutionality of a bounty and I was glad of the opportunity.

We decided to contest the issue of the bonds voted when an attempt was made to issue them. Before they reached this particular precinct a suit was brought to test the validity of similar bonds issued by an adjoining precinct. It was a friendly suit brought by the interested parties against the State Auditor to compel the registering of the bonds, both parties being for an affirmative order. I appeared at the trial and asked for permission to file a brief, stating to the court that I represented a client who was

79

contesting bonds of the same kind in an adjoining precinct. Both sides objected to my request, but the court overruled the objections and allowed the brief to be filed.

When the court decided against the bonds, and in so doing disappointed both plaintiff and defendant, I had satisfaction enough to more than make up for the unpaid portion of my promised fee and was rewarded still further when as a member of Congress this experience enabled me to answer a question which was put to me by an Iowa Republican who knew of the bonds voted but did not know of the court decision nullifying them.

My first case in the Supreme Court came from Greeley County and involved a county-seat election. Those who have ever lived in a county where such elections take place need not be told that the interest in a presidential election is, in comparison, quite negligible. The question to be decided was whether the county seat should be removed from Scotia, a Union Pacific Railroad town on the edge of the county, to Greeley Center, a Burlington Railroad town near the center of the county. The railroads as well as the localities were interested and every voter in the county was at the polls, plus others.

General Barry and John Cavanaugh, two members of the election board, favored Greeley Center, where they lived, but as honest and conscientious officers they were compelled to throw out the vote of one precinct as fraudulent. After the vote was counted it gave the majority to Greeley Center, but Barry and Cavanaugh, true to their oath of office, acted against their personal interests and rejected this precinct.

When the case came up in the Supreme Court Scotia had her attorneys and Greeley Center had hers. The Scotia attorneys wanted the vote in question thrown out. Greeley Center wanted it counted in. Barry and Cavanaugh retained me to represent them as officials, explaining to me that, officially, they wanted me to defend their action, but they personally would like to have their action overruled.

It made my position a delicate one. There was no doubt in my mind about the fraudulent character of the disputed returns. I question whether any records present a case where the fraud was more transparent. The law required that the name of the voter be entered, and those who committed the fraud evidently had to act in a hurry; not having time to manufacture a list of names which would at least look honest, they put down prominent names of presidents, well-known senators, and distinguished men of other states.

In the trial I, of course, was on the side of Scotia and therefore acted with the Scotia attorneys. Before taking up the case on its merits, Scotia's attorneys moved for a delay, and at the request of my clients I joined with the Greeley Center people to oppose delay. This confused the court and one of the judges asked, "Mr. Bryan, for which side do you appear?"

I replied, "I had hoped that my argument would indicate that."

The judge said, "Your argument is clear enough, but I thought you were on the side of Scotia."

"I am," I said, "on the merits of the case, but I am with the attorneys of Greeley Center in opposing the motion." My clients had the pleasure of winning their case and the sorrow of seeing their city fail in its effort to secure the county seat.

Measured by its outcome, my removal to Nebraska was the gift of good fortune. I was most lucky in the selection of a law partner. Adolphus R. Talbot is a rare man—one of God's noblemen. In law school we had come to address each other as Dolph and Will and so when we united our energies in the practice of law, it was a very friendly union. We were about the same height and age, he nearly a year the older—from April around to March—about the same

6

size and not far from the same weight. We were as much alike as two men could be and yet we were quite dissimilar in several respects. He was of English stock, having been born in England; I was very much mixed, with the Irish predominating in my name. He was a Methodist and I a Presbyterian; he was a Republican and I a Democrat. When baldness attacked us, his hair retreated from the front and mine from the rear. In the practice he looked at our side of the case and I inquired as to the arguments that the opposition could advance. But in spite of our points of dissimilarity, no two lawyers ever worked together with less friction. On the first of each month one would take his day book into the room of the other—whichever one happened to think of it first—and we would go over the credits and debits together, each would strike his balance and whichever had the largest net receipts would give the other a check for half and then we wrote "settled" across the two books and never had any other reckoning.

I mentioned the fact that he was a Republican and I a Democrat. At one time he was chairman of the Republican City Committee and I was chairman of the Democratic City Committee.

Our offices consisted of three rooms, the reception room and two private offices. When a man came in and inquired for the chairman of the Committee the clerk would ask him "of which committee?" He was still chairman when I ran for Congress and reported an incident that occurred during the campaign.

One of the members of the city committee called on him to say that he felt that he ought to resign as a member of the committee because he was going to support Bryan for Congress. Talbot assured him that that was not necessary, that the Republican candidate for Congress was only one of many candidates on that ticket and this was only one campaign. The man was finally persuaded not to give up his committeeship and I learned later that the chairman and more than half the committee were supporting me. During my campaign of 1896 Mr. Talbot was a Republican candidate for the Nebraska State Senate and was embarrassed by seeing published in the Lincoln papers glowing eulogies of me which he had written to papers in other states in answer to inquiries.

Talbot's personal friendship was always greater than his Republicanism, despite his prominence in the party. For more than thirty years he has been one of my nearest and dearest friends. Whenever I am relieved for a moment from the pressure under which I have lived, a pressure so great as to prevent any leisurely review of the past or unhurried contemplation of the future, and I allow myself to think of the latter days, I dream of a brief period before the close of life when, my work done, I can commune with lifelong friends and recall the joint struggles of early days. I always think of Dolph as one of those with whom companionship will be most satisfying.

When I was elected to Congress, I felt that I should give my entire time to my work and therefore I turned over to Mr. Talbot the unfinished business and only appeared where it was necessary to please some particular friends among our clients. The only conflict of opinion we ever had over fees was when I went to Congress. He insisted on giving me a larger percentage of the fees which came from the left-over business than I thought I deserved and it was not without a good deal of argument that we reached a compromise of our differences.

The firm name was continued while I was in Congress and I expected to resume the practice when I returned to Lincoln in 1895, but by that time the fight over bimetallism was just beginning and I received about the same time three invitations from widely different points, one to answer John Sherman at Salem, Oregon, another to answer him at Cincinnati, Ohio, and a third to answer John G. Carlisle at Memphis, Tennessee. It soon became apparent that I must either refuse political invitations or suspend practice again. I was too much interested in the fight for which I had helped to lay the plans to disappoint those whom I had helped to enlist, and so I decided to postpone for another year my return to law.

Then came the Presidential campaign of 1896 which so completely identified me with national politics that I felt that I must keep up the fight for at least another four years. So I retired from the firm.

My last appearance as a member of the Nebraska bar was in the United States Supreme Court in a maximum rate case which arose over a law passed in Nebraska and contested by the railroads. The Attorney-General of Nebraska, Hon. C. J. Smythe, one of my closet political friends, represented the state. I was so deeply interested in the result of the trial that I volunteered to appear without pay in order to present the one point in which I was concerned.

The proposition upon which I based my argument was taken from a book written by Governor Larrabee of Iowa, who became a leader of the agriculturists of that state in their effort to secure reasonable railroad rates. I read the book soon after I entered Congress and attempted to secure the incorporation of the principle in a pooling bill that passed the House while I was a member. My amendment to that bill was defeated, but it attracted enough attention to call forth one of the earliest epithets applied to me. A Richmond, Virginia, paper quite conspicuous for its sympathetic support of the corporation side of public questions, had an editorial denunciation of my amendment which appeared under the title of "Nihilist Bryan."

INTERCOLLEGIATE DEBATING TEAM

Representing six middle western colleges. The lady is Miss Jane Addams; the tallest figure standing is that of Mr. Bryan.

CHAPTER IV

THE LURE OF THE COLLEGE PRIZE

I FELT the lure of prizes from the start and took part in every contest for which I was eligible. A prize always stirred me to activity, and a recollection of its influence upon my studies has led me in later days to stimulate students to similar activity by the establishing of prizes in a number of institutions of learning.

The principal prizes I established were in the public school at Normal, the precinct in which our country home near Lincoln was located, and in some nineteen institutions —seventeen of them state universities—in which I established a prize for the best essay on the science of government. When, some years later, Mr. Philo S. Bennett consulted me in regard to the best use of some money which he desired to leave by will, I recommended similar prizes and upon his death distributed for him funds for the establishment of such prizes in twenty state universities.

In my first year in the academy—"Junior Prep" as it was called—I entered the declamation contest, using as my theme Patrick Henry's famous speech, "Give me liberty or give me death." The judges did not seem to regard me as especially promising. At any rate, I was not near enough to even second place to give me any intense interest in the returns. The next year I entered the declamation contest again, this time taking as my subject by the advice of Mrs. Jones, "The Palmetto and the Pine." The sentiment was most excellent, but my delivery seemed to lack something— enough to enable two of the contestants to pass me. I came third in the estimate of the judges and Dr. Jones thought that my failure may have been due to indistinctness of articulation. I do not know whether that was true or not, but it spurred me up on that particular subject and distinctness of articulation became a controlling passion with me.

In the freshman year I entered the declamation contest for the third time, after having divided the second prize in Latin prose composition with a fellow student. I was gaining ground. In my first contest I came down toward the last, in my second contest I ranked third, in my third contest I won half of the second prize, in my fourth contest— freshman declamation—I rose a point higher and had the second prize all to myself. I did not like dramatic pieces, but at the earnest solicitation of my instructor in rhetoric I took Bernardo del Carpio for my freshman declamation. Of course, the matter was very much on my mind during the days immediately preceding the contest, so much so that a night or two before the declaimers were to appear in public on the stage of Strawn's Opera House I had a dream that made an indelible impression upon me because it came true. In my dream, we seemed to have finished our declamations and were awaiting the announcement of the award of the prizes—a moment of great suspense, as all will admit who have passed through the experience. Then the chairman of the committee of judges appeared and wrote upon the blackboard the names of the victors. I could see my name very distinctly occupying the second place, but I could not make out the name of the man who was awarded the first prize.

My dream not only assured me of my success in securing second prize but it even disclosed to me the books which I selected (the prizes were given in books to be selected by the students themselves. The second prize in this case was $10.00). I selected an Oxford Bible with a concordance and a volume of Shakespeare. As I am writing these words I turn to this treasure and find on the first page of the Bible the following: at the top the Greek letters Sigma Pi and my class '81 and following that these words: "Presented to W. J. Bryan, Salem, Illinois, by the faculty of Illinois

THE LURE OF THE COLLEGE PRIZE

College, May 28, 1878. Second prize in declamation."
The copy of Shakespeare bound in calf is still in my library
and on the first page is a duplicate of the first page of the
Bible above referred to.

I digress here to say that I received the usual training in
public speaking. Professor Hamilton was our instructor;
he was a large man with a strong face and a piercing eye.
He rather leaned to the dramatic and recommended dramatic pieces to us. I rather preferred the oratorical style.
He complimented me by saying that I declaimed the oratorical pieces so well that he could not be of much assistance to
me along that line. He trained us in modulation of the
voice, gesticulation, etc., and I presume that his instructions
were beneficial to me, although I have been so much more
interested in the subject matter than in the form of presentation that my use of his advice has been unconscious
rather than intentional.

As our absorption of ideals is gradual and constant, I
do not know to what extent I am indebted to him for the
settled opinions which I have formed on public speaking. I
think that instruction in gesticulation becomes valuable as
one forgets the instructions and moves his arms and body
without thought of the instructions. It is hard to be
graceful in gesticulation when one is thinking about the
movements to be made, just as it is difficult for one to speak
naturally while he is engaged in artificial effort. But the
training that one receives, both in the modulation of the
voice and in action, finally becomes a part of him—a second
nature, so to speak—and he obeys the suggestions that he
has received without a thought.

In my sophomore year I entered the contest in essay and
won the first prize—my first first prize—with an essay on
the by no means novel subject of "Labor." This pleased
my father more than the previous prizes won. He said that
he would rather have me gain prominence for my own thought
than by repeating the words of others.

WILLIAM JENNINGS BRYAN

In my junior year I entered the oratorical contest influenced by a double ambition, because the successful orator in this contest would, as a matter of custom, represent the college in the intercollegiate contest the following fall. My subject on this occasion was "Individual Power" and I left nothing undone that would contribute towards success. I had had in mind for nearly five years the honor of representing the college in the oratorical contest. It so happened that soon after my arrival in Jacksonville I had the privilege of attending a contest in which Fred Turner, the orator of Illinois College, represented our institution. From that night this vision was before me and my work as a declaimer, as an essayist, and in the delivering of orations was to this end. I was successful—securing the first honor here as in the contest in essay the year before.

Possibly another digression here may be excusable. My good wife often refers to it when someone has in later years commented as to what they have described as the ease with which I speak. She says that they do not know how hard and for how many years I worked as a college boy and as a young man when I was in training. The incident which she often related is as follows. The contest came in May, 1880, some seven months after we became acquainted. Mrs. Jones, who was very fond of Miss Baird, conceived the idea of having a May Day party out in a woods pasture belonging to Dr. Jones. It so happened that this woods pasture adjoined the grounds of an insane asylum and it also happened that a man who had formerly worked for Dr. Jones was cultivating a farm close by this spot selected for the party. I went out to the grove an hour or so ahead of the rest of the party and spent the time delivering my oration with the trees as an audience. When Miss Baird and the other members of the May Day party approached the woods pasture the former employee left his plow and ran out to the road waving his hand in warning, calling out: "Don't go in there. There is a man over there shouting and waving

88

his hands. I think he must have escaped from the asylum."
Mrs. Jones and my wife-to-be guessed at once the cause
of his alarm and entered the pasture in a mood to enjoy
the day.

In the following October (1880) I went to Galesburg,
Illinois, to represent my college in the contest to which I had
looked forward for many years. My subject was "Justice."
After the prize had been awarded, General John C. Black
of Chicago, with whom I afterwards served in Congress,
one of the judges in this contest, took me to his room in
the hotel and gave me encouragement and advice. He
told me that he had marked me one hundred on delivery
and high enough on thought and composition to make
me his first choice (the marks of the other two brought
me down to second place). He then gave me his advice
on various styles of oratory, contrasting the style of Edmund
Burke, whose sentences were long and involved, and the
style of Victor Hugo, whose sentences were short and
pithy. He said that I leaned rather to the style of the
latter and advised me to cultivate longer sentences. I have
not forgotten his advice, but have found it difficult to follow
it, possibly because I have always labored under the coercion that made me so anxious to present a subject clearly
that I could not give much attention to ornamentation and
figures of speech.

In my oration on "Justice" my introduction was, I
think, as appropriate as any that I have ever employed.
I learned quite early the wisdom of a beginning that
immediately catches the attention. I noticed this in
speeches, of which I early became an eager reader, and
observed in Wendell Phillips when he delivered his famous
lecture, "The Lost Arts," at Jacksonville during my student
days. The great orator was in the habit of commencing
with some reference to some local object of interest, which
he linked to his address. Dr. Conwell employs the same
art in his remarkable lecture on "Acres of Diamonds."

WILLIAM JENNINGS BRYAN

As it is my purpose to make my memoirs as useful as possible to the young people who read them, I am led to add that Paul has given to the public speakers of the world probably the most perfect illustration of easy and felicitous entrance on the presentation of a theme. His speech at Athens was before the most critical of his audiences and he was especially happy in selecting an opening phrase which at once enlisted the attention of his hearers:

"Ye men of Athens, I perceive that in all things ye are too superstitious.

"For as I passed by, and beheld your devotions, I found an altar with this inscription, TO THE UNKNOWN GOD. Whom therefore ye ignorantly worship, him declare I unto you.

"God that made the world and all things therein, seeing that he is Lord of heaven and earth, dwelleth not in temples made with hands;

"Neither is worshipped with men's hands, as though he needed any thing, seeing he giveth to all life, and breath, and all things;

"And hath made of one blood all nations of men for to dwell on all the face of the earth, and hath determined the times before appointed, and the bounds of their habitation;

"That they should seek the Lord, if haply they might feel after him, and find him, though he be not far from every one of us:

"For in him we live, and move, and have our being; as certain also of your poets have said, For we are also his offspring.

"Forasmuch then as we are the offspring of God, we ought not to think that the Godhead is like unto gold, or silver, or stone, graven by art and man's device.

"And the times of this ignorance God winked at; but now commandeth all men every where to repent:

THE LURE OF THE COLLEGE PRIZE

"Because he hath appointed a day, in the which he will judge the world in righteousness by that man whom he hath ordained; whereof he hath given assurance unto all men, in that he hath raised him from the dead." (Acts 17: 22-31.)

My speech on Justice began: "Plutarch tells us that men entertain three sentiments concerning the gods; they fear them for their power, respect them for their intelligence, and love them for their justice." The local paper had a complimentary account of my speech—they generally praised where they could performance of students—and these early bits of eulogy are very satisfying to participants in contests—especially those who fail to win prizes. I came second, my college backer insisting, as college boys are wont to do, that I ought to have had first place.

The fifty dollars handed me by the treasurer of the oratorical association was the largest sum that I had earned up to that time. The first draft upon me was made for the purchase of an engagement ring for my intended wife. I had waited from June until October in order to purchase the ring with money that I had myself earned. It was a modest ring—a garnet set in gold—but it was sufficient to satisfy our simple tastes, and adorn Mrs. Bryan's hand until it was lost during the campaign of 1896. It was my custom to earn the money to pay for any gifts to Miss Baird, and during a large part of my college days I added to my spending money by clerking in a hat store on Saturdays.

This contest was quite an event in college life and, as was customary, a delegation of the students went along to boost for their representatives. I had gone upon a similar expedition when Richard Yates represented our college and won the first prize at Champaign, Illinois, two years before. The successful competitors in a number of these inter-collegiate contests contested for the interstate prize at a later meeting which was at the time held in Jacksonville. By winning second prize I became the alternate and would have represented the state at the interstate contest had the winner of first prize failed to appear. Although this was a very remote contingency, I prepared myself for it, but Mr. Erskine, orator of the state at Galesburg, was there and I not only had no opportunity to enter the larger contest but was the victim of a good deal of ridicule when the man who defeated me came near the close of the list in the interstate contest. For several days I was greeted by college friends with substantially the same question: "If Erskine came last, where would you have been?"

At the Galesburg meeting, I was, because of my residence at Jacksonville, the place of the next contest, made vice-president of the interstate association. The work of arrangement fell to President Montgomery of Indiana and Secretary Howard of Iowa. In the correspondence that took place prior to the date of the contest at Jacksonville I was in correspondence with Montgomery and Howard. We had never met, but in the intimacy between us developed by the correspondence we had exchanged guesses as to each other. Howard and I discussed Montgomery, Montgomery and I discussed Howard, and Howard and Montgomery discussed me. When the time came for the meeting Montgomery and Howard arrived at Jacksonville at the same time and our acquaintance ripened into a permanent friendship. Judge Montgomery has since held a high judicial position in his state and I have frequently enjoyed the hospitality of his delightful home when I visited Seymour, Indiana. Howard afterward moved to Indianapolis and then to New York and was a Republican in his early days. He became a supporter of mine in 1896 and until his death in New York some years ago was a colaborer in the political vineyard.

I was a contestant for one prize in my senior year and there I came second, but I was even more pleased to have

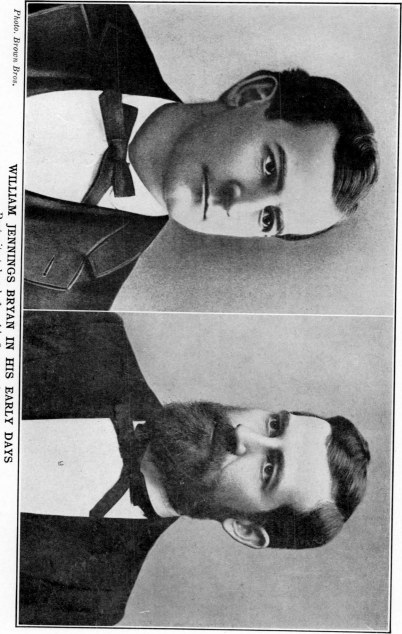

Photo, Brown Bros.

WILLIAM JENNINGS BRYAN IN HIS EARLY DAYS

Portraits taken before his first nomination.

the prize go to Sam Eveland than to have won it myself. Sam was one of the lovable members of the class and one of the most interesting men I ever knew. He was brought up in Michigan. His education was neglected and he went early into the logging camps. As a young man he tramped from section to section in search of work. He went by chance one evening into a church where a protracted meeting was in session. He was converted and decided to be a minister. With Sam it was really a new birth. His life was as completely changed as was the life of Paul. I have never known a man more completely consecrated to the service of God and to the life patterned after the example of Christ.

He went to school in spite of the embarrassment that a grown person finds in studying with children. He was fourteen years older than myself, and I graduated at about twenty-one. I was about the average age for the class. He was not a brilliant man, but no one could surpass him in industry and in patient plodding. He was as truthful as a child; everybody loved him. When the professor of political economy announced "Pauperism, Its Causes and Remedies," as the subject of the thesis and that each member was expected to write, I remarked that we might each give our experience and let the prize go to the one who knew most about the subject, and that is the way it went. Sam Eveland won the prize. Evidence, if evidence was needed, of the value of personal knowledge in the presentation of any subject.

Still another digression here. When I went home to spend the Christmas holidays I went out to the county poorhouse, thinking that I might get some information for my thesis. I acquainted the superintendent with the object of my visit and he gave me access to the inmates. The first man I met was, to my surprise, a brother of one of the most prominent citizens of the county, a man of wealth, family, and influence. I found that this inmate was an unmarried man. My questions did not bring out much information beyond the fact that he had not saved anything and found himself a pauper during his later days. The second man whom I met was also unmarried and I jotted down "celibacy" as a cause of pauperism.

I began in my mind to sketch the path of the unmarried man without responsibility, he gives free rein to his desires and pleasures, wasting his life in enjoyment, and finally comes down to old age with no provision made for the days of failing strength. I thought I had made some progress in preparing my case. Then I met the third inmate.

"Are you married?" I enquired.

"Yes, my fourth wife left me when I came here."

"Have you any children?"

"Twenty-six." And my first theory was exploded.

After time for reflection I thought that possibly there might be a golden mean—that was before the word "golden" had been made odious by bad association—between the irresponsibility of the unmarried man and the burdened spouse and father. I have not yet been able to understand how a man could raise twenty-six children without having at least one among them who could care for him in his old age!

Returning to Eveland again: I cannot resist the temptation to record facts that come to my memory when the name of this dear friend is recalled. First was one of his experiences in courtship. I was rather a patriarch among the boys during my last year in college. I reached my twenty-first anniversary less than three months before graduation and I was engaged, as they say, during my entire senior year. This was known among the boys and some of them came to me for advice—among them Sam.

He took me aside one day and with evident emotion told me that he had at last found the girl for whom he was looking. He described her to me and according to his description she would make a model wife for a pastor. He said that he had laid his claims before her the night before and that she had accepted him.

I was rather surprised at the suddenness with which he had proposed and suggested to him that it might have been better to have gone about it more gradually, but he was a very practical sort of a fellow and, having found the kind of wife for whom he was looking, he did not see why any period of romance should be injected between the discovery and the filing of his claim. I congratulated him, though I confess it was with some misgivings as to whether the agreement reached was really conclusive.

A few days afterward the poor fellow came to me distressed beyond description to tell me that he had called upon the young lady again and found that she did not understand that they were engaged. In fact, it was not long before he brought back that familiar report that while she could not marry him she would always be his friend. Later he was more successful and found an exemplary lady about his own age who was deeply religious and who became his wife.

The day before his marriage, he called on me. "Bryan," he said, "I want you to do me a favor. As I am a minister, I am afraid that the preacher who will officiate will not be willing to accept a fee from me. So I will give you the money and you can hand it to him."

Of course I responded favorably, and took the coin away with me in my pocket. Between that hour and the hour when he and his chosen one were to be united in the holy bonds of wedlock I framed a little speech to be made to the minister when it came time to act as Sam's paymaster. Everything went well. The invited guests were as happy as the bride and groom, the pastor was on hand and the ceremony was duly performed. After the congratulations I took the minister off to one side and began to deliver Sam's message. When I reached the proper point I put my hand into my pocket and to my amazement discovered that I had changed my trousers. The minister had to take my word for the fee until I could go home and get the money and hunt him up. Whenever I saw Sam afterward and we became reminiscent, this embarrassing episode was sure to be recalled. But my, what a smoke a little fire kindleth! All these recollections were unloosed when I thought of being defeated in a thesis contest by a classmate who had once been a tramp.

CHAPTER V

EARLY NATIONAL CONVENTIONS

I FORMED early the habit of attending national conventions. It so happened that the Democratic National Convention of 1876 was held in St. Louis, only seventy miles from my birthplace. My father and mother were attending the Philadelphia Exposition at the time, but my enthusiasm reached a point where I decided to go to the convention with some of the other boys—I do not recall that any of them were as young as myself. I sold enough corn to secure the small amount necessary, the railroad fare being only a few dollars and my other expenses being small. I recall that I stayed all night at East St. Louis, sleeping in a room with more than thirty others on cots.

Next day I appeared at the convention hall, but not knowing anyone from whom I could secure a ticket, I had to content myself with standing around watching the distinguished Democrats, to me unknown, go in and out of the convention. But here again my lucky star helped me out. A policeman, taking pity on me, put me in through a window and I had the pleasure of hearing John Kelly make his famous speech against Tilden. That was my initiation into national politics. Since that time I have attended every Democratic National Convention but three, and I was in close touch by wire with two of the three, those of 1900 and 1908. The Cincinnati Convention of 1880, therefore, is the only one that I have actually missed since I was sixteen years old. I was still a college boy in 1880 and Cincinnati was so far from Salem that I was able to withstand the temptation which overpowered me four years before.

When the convention of 1884 was held at Chicago I was living at Jacksonville, but my income was so meager that I decided that I could not afford a trip to Chicago, but here again fortune favored me. I was invited to deliver a Fourth of July address at Greenwood, not many miles from Jacksonville. In accepting the invitation I answered the inquiry about compensation by saying that I expected nothing more than my traveling expenses. When I was through speaking, the chairman of the committee asked me about my expenses. When I stated the amount, something less than three dollars, he handed me a twenty-dollar bill with the remark,

"That will cover your expenses."

I was so surprised that I almost forgot to thank him. I decided that I would construe my good luck as a providential provision for convention expenses and arranged to go to Chicago. On the train I fell in with Carl Epler, son of Judge Epler, one of the circuit judges presiding in the Jacksonville circuit, and we made the trip together.

At Chicago we went from one headquarters to another and listened to the arguments in favor of the various candidates. My personal preference was Senator Bayard of Delaware. In one of the senates of which I was a member when a schoolboy I represented Delaware and took the name of Senator Bayard. I was open to conviction, however, and ready to hoorah for the candidate who won the nomination.

As it is in all national conventions, it was difficult to get a ticket of admission. Finding Hon. Telas W. Merritt, of Salem, a prominent politician at the Illinois headquarters, I asked him if he could secure tickets for Epler and myself. He said he could not secure any tickets, but that he knew one of the doorkeepers, whereupon he took us to Joseph Chesterfield Mackin, a Chicago politician, and said in his stammering way—he stuttered—"Joe, pa-pa-pass these b-b-boys in." Joe passed us in and we returned to his door regularly during the sessions of the convention. I am sorry to have to remark in passing that Joe was soon after sent to the penitentiary for "ballot-box stuffing"—this was through no fault of Mr. Merritt's or of ours and I only mention it because I never think of the incident without also thinking of what befell Joseph Chesterfield after we had thus become acquainted with him.

When the 1888 convention was held in St. Louis I was a resident of Nebraska. Having helped elect Hon. J. Sterling Morton a delegate, I had no difficulty in getting a ticket to this convention. I remember being very much impressed by a nominating speech made by Senator Daniel of Virginia.

The Democratic National Convention of 1892 was held at Chicago. I was a member of Congress then and was renominated a few days before the convention, in fact, went from the Congressional Convention to the Chicago Convention. By this time I had become acquainted with a good many public men and also with a good many politicians. I spoke at Creston in the Boies Campaign the fall of 1891. Here I met a prominent Democratic politician of that section by the name of Duggan. I happened to meet him at Chicago and learned from him that he was doorkeeper. He offered to let any of my friends in and I soon found out how easily one could add to his list of friends when he could reward them with admission to the national convention. Before the sessions were over I had put a liberal number of western Democrats under obligation to me by bringing them into acquaintance with Mr. Duggan.

At the Chicago Convention I heard Bourke Cockran make his celebrated speech against the third nomination of Mr. Cleveland, but took no part in the convention's deliberations.

In 1896 I began attending Republican Conventions as well as those of my own party. The first was the McKinley Convention, which was held at St. Louis about two weeks before the Chicago Convention at which I was nominated. I was at that time editor of the *World-Herald* and attended the convention ostensibly in the character of a newspaper man. As a matter of fact, however, I was there to encourage the Silver Republicans in the fight they were making. Beginning in 1893, I had been more and more intimately acquainted with the Silver Republicans like Senators Teller, DuBois, Pettigrew, and Cannon, and Congressmen Shafroth, Towne, Hartmann, and others. I was in conference with them during the course of the fight over the platform and sent back editorial correspondence to my paper.

The convention turned out as I expected and the looked-for bolt took place. I felt sure that the action of this convention would have a large influence at Chicago.

CHAPTER VI

A Brief History of the Chicago Convention

FOR some months prior to the Chicago Convention of 1896, I had received letters from different parties in different states suggesting my candidacy. John W. Tomlinson, a delegate from Alabama, wrote me; Mr. Cassady, a delegate from Mississippi; Mr. Felix Regnier, a delegate from Monmouth, Ill.; Hon. M. A. Miller, a delegate from Oregon; Gov. J. E. Osborn, of Wyoming; Ex-Gov. Baxter, of Wyoming, and a number of others. They all presented the same arguments, and the arguments presented were the ones that led me to believe that there was a possibility of my nomination.

During the year 1895 I visited Springfield at the invitation of bimetallists and spoke at a convention which was the beginning of the organizing of the silver forces of that state. I met Governor Altgeld there and have letters which I received from him afterward suggesting the possibility of my receiving the nomination for Vice-President, he being favorable to Congressman Bland for President.

When I delivered my Tariff Speech in Congress in March, 1892, I received a telegram from a friend in Jacksonville which ran about as follows: "How old are you? Am for you for the Democratic Presidential Nomination if you are old enough."

This was one of the earliest outbursts of enthusiasm. From time to time newspapers mentioned my name in connection with the nomination. This occurred with increasing frequency after my Silver Speech in August, 1893. I had prepared the address on Bimetallism signed by some thirty-three members of Congress and had given it to the public about the fifth of March, 1895. I prepared it after consulting with Mr. Bland, whom we all recognized as the

101

leader of the silver forces in Congress. I had him sign it first, and I signed it second. No senators, as I recall it, signed it, and only about one fifth of the Democratic members. Others to whom it was presented objected on the ground that it might divide the party. A short time after that appeal was published, President Cleveland wrote a letter to a Chicago Club, in which he indicated that the fight was to be on the money question, and this aroused the silver Democrats to the realization of the fact that they would have to control the organization or be read out of the party. A conference was called for June at Memphis, Tenn. There the Democratic Bimetallic League was organized with Democratic senators as its officers. I attended this conference at Memphis—in fact, I had spoken in Memphis a month before in answer to Mr. Carlisle. He went to Memphis to deliver an address intended to line up the South in favor of the gold standard.

For the next year I traveled throughout the country, lecturing in some places and making public speeches in other places—everywhere helping, as best I could, in the organization of the silver forces. At Wilmington, Delaware, I paid the hall rent and introduced myself, and spoke to a handful of people in a small room. At one other place I helped to pay the expense of the meeting. It was through these speeches that I became acquainted with a number of the delegates who were present at Chicago. I perhaps was personally acquainted with more delegates than any other man who was mentioned as a candidate. My own state would have instructed for me if I had permitted it, but I objected on the ground that I did not want to be presented as a candidate for two reasons. First, there was no likelihood of my being instructed for in any other state, and, second because I wanted to help other men who were candidates to secure their own states.

I went to Chicago a few days before the Convention to

confer with the leaders who were making their plans for the control of the convention and was present when Senator Daniel was selected for temporary chairman. We already had a majority of the delegates instructed for bimetallism. At that time the sentiment seemed to be divided between Bland and Boies and Matthews, and as I looked over the situation, I did not think that the outlook for my candidacy was encouraging. In fact, I told Mr. Tomlinson that I did not want him to feel bound by his pledge to me if he found it to his advantage to support some one else. He gave me an insight into his political purpose when he told me that he had no interests of his own to advance, and that, as he still believed I was the most available candidate, he preferred to advocate my nomination whether there was any chance of my success or not.

I had an engagement to speak at the Chautauqua in Crete, Nebraska, between the preliminary conference at Chicago and the convening of the Convention. I was advertised for a debate there with John Irish of Iowa, one of the prominent advocates of the gold standard. I went to Nebraska to fill this engagement and then returned to Chicago with the Nebraska delegation. In the debate with Irish I used the sentence with which I closed my Chicago Speech—the sentence which refers to "the cross of gold and the crown of thorns." I had used it a few times before that time, recognizing its fitness for the conclusion of a climax, and had laid it away for a proper occasion.

Some of my friends spoke of me for temporary chairman of the Convention, but this position, as I have said, went to Senator Daniel, and a very wise selection it was. Then there was some talk of me for permanent chairman and this seemed a possibility when I made the brief trip to Nebraska. On the train I made some preparations in anticipation of an opportunity to speak at the Convention, although there was no certainty that this opportunity would come to me.

WILLIAM JENNINGS BRYAN

While I spent all my spare time in arranging the arguments for any speech that I might deliver at the Convention, I prepared only one new argument and that I have always regarded as the most important argument presented, although it has never received a great deal of attention from those who have commented upon the speech. I do not recall that it has ever received prominent attention until recently, when it was selected in England as the passage to be quoted in a description of that speech published in London. The passage reads as follows and was intended for a double purpose: first, to awaken small business men to an appreciation of their importance; and, second, to rebuke the gold advocates who were continually talking about business men but who regarded those engaged in big business as the only business men to be considered:

"We say to you that you have made the definition of a business man too limited in its application. The man who is employed for wages is as much a business man as his employer, the attorney in a country town is as much a business man as the corporation counsel in a great metropolis; the merchant at the crossroads store is as much a business man as the merchant of New York; the farmer who goes forth in the morning and toils all day—who begins in the spring and toils all summer— and who by the application of brain and muscle to the natural resources of the country creates wealth, is as much a business man as the man who goes upon the board of trade and bets upon the price of grain; the miners who go down a thousand feet into the earth, or climb two thousand feet upon the cliffs, and bring forth from their hiding places the precious metals to be poured into the channels of trade are as much business men as the few financial magnates who, in a back room, corner the money of the world. We come to speak for this broader class of business men."

When I got back to Chicago the situation, so far as my prospects were concerned, had not perceptibly improved and I found that my first fight would be to get my delegation seated, it having been shut out of the temporary organization by action of the National Committee in which the Gold Men had a considerable majority.

I might add here that the night before I made my speech in the Chicago Convention, the North Carolina delegation held a meeting, and as the majority of the delegation voted in favor of my nomination, the entire delegation was given to me by the unit rule, and I was so notified by one of the delegates, I think it was Mr. Josephus Daniels, who was national committeeman that year, and has so continued up to this day. Before the delivery of my speech I had assurances from several other states. I think that a majority of the Kansas delegation had indicated a preference for me in case Bland was not nominated. Senator Patterson has since told me of an incident that impressed him.

Senator Towne and Congressman Hartman were with Senator Patterson, and they came over to ask me to support Senator Teller. As Senator Patterson relates it, I listened to their arguments and when they were through, said to them that I did not regard Senator Teller's nomination as a possibility, that I was perfectly willing to vote for him myself because I regarded the money question as the paramount issue, but that we had won our fight in the Democratic party while the Republicans had lost their fight in the Republican party, and that it was easier to bring the disappointed Republicans over to the Democratic party than to carry the victorious Democrats over to the Republican party. Knowing that the gold Democrats would vote, I thought they could make a much stronger fight against one who, up to that time, had been identified with the Republican party, than against one who had been all his life a Democrat.

I still believe the reasoning sound, and I say this after reflection upon the ability, character, and patriotism of

105

Senator Teller, whom I then admired and for whom my admiration has grown with more intimate acquaintance. When I stated that I did not believe Senator Teller could be nominated, Senator Patterson asked me who could be nominated, and I told him that I thought I had as good a chance to be nominated as anyone, for by that time I thought I saw a considerable improvement in my chances. He asked me what strength I had in the Convention. I told him that Nebraska would be for me whenever I wanted its vote, that half of the Indian Territory would be for me on the second ballot, and I was intending to give the rest of my strength as far as I had learned it (I am not sure whether North Carolina had acted then or later in the evening); but before I could go any further, some one came up and interrupted the conversation, and Senator Patterson and his associates, not considering the matter of sufficient importance to wait longer, took their leave.

The Senator has told me with some amusement of the conversation that followed when he, Mr. Towne, and Mr. Hartman reached the street. They looked at each other and smiled at the presumption of a man who calculated on the presidential nomination with only his own state back of him and the Indian Territory on the second ballot. Had they waited longer I would have given them better evidence that my hope had a substantial foundation, but I am afraid that I could not have given them enough evidence to make them share my expectations.

The possibility of my nomination led me to urge Mrs. Bryan to attend the Convention, a precaution of which I was afterwards glad when the Convention resulted as it did. We took rooms at the Clifton House, where my delegation had headquarters.

As some comment has been made upon the fact that our delegation had rooms at the Clifton, I might explain that we tried to get rooms at the Palmer House, but all the other delegation from Nebraska had secured headquarters there, and we went to the Clifton, not so much because it was less expensive there as because it was nearer to the Palmer House than any other hotel. Our delegates were prepared to meet whatever expense was necessary, but they wanted to be near the center of political activity, and the Clifton House suited their purpose. I may add, however, that as the rates were lower at the Clifton House, I can point to a less pretentious hotel bill than I would have had at the Palmer House. I took $100 with me and after paying the hotel bill of Mrs. Bryan and myself during the Convention week I had about $40 left, a sum probably as small as anyone has spent in securing a presidential nomination. It did not, of course, include my share of the expenses of the delegates or the expenses of the preliminary contest in which the delegates were selected, but even this sum was inconsiderable, as no money whatever was spent in entertaining delegations or delegates.

My ambition had been to be chairman of the Committee on Resolutions, but I found that Senator Jones aspired to that place, and as he was a much older man, and the president of the bimetallic organization formed at Memphis, I did not care to be a candidate against him, and gave up the thought of that place. As our delegation was shut out of the temporary organization by the National Committee, it would have been impossible for me to be chairman of the Committee on Resolutions, but the committee did not act until after I had given up the idea. Then there was some talk of my being voted for as permanent chairman, but by this time the papers had begun to discuss the possibility of my being a candidate, and I was objected to by the friends of other candidates. As my time was occupied in the contest before the Credentials Committee, I did not get a chance to attend the convention during the earlier sessions, and although I was called for when others were called for, I did not have a chance to speak to the Convention.

The exclusion of my delegates was a good illustration of

107

machine politics. As has been shown elsewhere, there was not the slightest ground for the opposing delegates. There was irregularity in our Conventions and it represented more than nineteen-twentieths of the party vote in Nebraska. But the Gold and corporation faction had control of the old National Committee and the other delegation was seated, making us the contesting delegation before the Credentials Committee of the delegates. The delegates desired me to lead the fight before the committee and this kept me from attending the sessions of the Committee on Resolutions for which I was selected by our delegates.

The contest before the Credentials Committee of the Convention was one-sided, the opposition bringing in no minority report. I was more exultant over the seating of our delegation than I was over my nomination. In the former case I could rejoice with the boys, in the latter case my rejoicing was sobered by a sense of responsibility.

As soon as our delegation was seated, I went at once to the Committee on Resolutions, of which I was a member by selection of my delegation, and found the platform practically completed. I looked at a draft of it and found that the money plank was there as I had written it two weeks before. While in St. Louis, attending the Republican Convention, I had called upon Mr. Charles H. Jones, then editor of the *Post-Dispatch*. He was a very able man, entirely in sympathy with the progressive ideas of the party. I found him engaged in writing a draft of the platform to be presented at Chicago. I prepared a plank covering the money question and he inserted it in the platform which he was drawing.

I hasten to explain that the language which I employed was language which had been incorporated in many state planks beginning more than a year before. I explain elsewhere the origin of the most prominent plank in the platform. There was no part of the plank which had not been thoroughly discussed and quite unanimously approved by the advocates of bimetallism.

When that plank was adopted by the Committee on Resolutions, it is probable that the members did not know that I had written it—at least, I have no reason to believe that they did know—and they approved of it in my absence. There were two planks which, according to my recollection, I added after I joined the committee. Some one suggested that we had no plank on arbitration and, if my memory serves me well, I wrote that plank and it was accepted. And then some suggested that there was no plank on the Venezuela question, and I wrote that plank. It will be seen, therefore, that I had very little to do with the writing of the Chicago platform, although since the Convention I have been given credit for writing it.

And now came an unexpected stroke of luck. Soon after we went into the Convention to report the platform, a page came to me and said that Senator Jones wanted to see me. I went to his seat and he asked me if I would take charge of the debate. I asked him if he did not want to conduct the debate himself and he replied in the negative. The request came as a surprise, for he had never intimated to me that he wanted me to do this, and I had never suggested it to him or anyone else.

I digress for a moment to remind the readers that this was a position to which I aspired in the beginning but for which I was not willing to be a candidate after I heard of Senator Jones' aspirations. I had seen my chance of temporary chairmanship disappear and then the chance for the permanent chairmanship—which afterward had become impossible because the possibility of my nomination made the other candidates hostile to the suggestion. And now, having passed through the circle of disappointment, I found myself in the very position for which I had at first longed.

Before continuing the narrative the reader may be interested, as I was, to know why this good fortune befell me.

After the Convention was over and Senator Jones had been made chairman of the National Committee at my request, I asked him how he happened to turn the defense of the platform over to me. I know that it was not with any thought of favoring me as a candidate, because he was a supporter of Mr. Bland and too loyal to him to have knowingly given an opportunity to any possible candidate if there was any likelihood of the opportunity being used to the disadvantage of his choice. And I myself had no thought of the effect produced by the speech. While I had, before the Convention met, regarded my nomination as a possibility I had relied upon what I called the logic of the situation rather than upon the influence of a speech.

The speech that I expected to make was not different from the speeches that I had been making except in the setting, to which I had not given special consideration. My interest was in the subject and I felt that I was master of the subject and could give expression to the sentiment of the Convention as represented by a little more than two-thirds of its members. Senator Jones answered my question by saying that I was the only one of the prominent speakers who had not had an opportunity to address the Convention. He referred to the speeches made by the temporary and permanent chairman and by others who were called out by the Convention while I was attending the meeting of the Committee on Credentials. He knew of the part I had taken in the organizing of the fight and how I had traveled over the country for a year helping in many states and said that his invitation to me was due entirely to a sense of fairness, and hence I honored him more for it than I could have done had it been due to partiality for me.

But to return to his request. I asked him what members of the committee wanted to speak on the platform and he said that no one had asked for time except Senator Tillman. I then went to Senator Hill, of New York, he was the leader of the minority, and arranged with him about the time to be allotted to the discussion. We agreed to an hour and a quarter on a side. I believe that was the time named. I then went to Senator Tillman and asked him whether he wanted to open or close the debate. He said he would like to close and that he wanted fifty minutes. I told him that that was too long for a closing speech and that I hardly thought the other side would agree to our using so much of the time in closing. I went back to Senator Hill and presented Senator Tillman's request and he objected to it, as I supposed he would, and said that if Senator Tillman wanted to use as much time as that he ought to use it in opening. I then returned to Senator Tillman and stated the case, and as he, Senator Tillman, felt that he needed more time than Senator Hill was willing to use in closing, he decided to open the debate and left me to close it. This again was an advantage, but it was an advantage that came by circumstance, for I would not have felt justified in refusing to allow Senator Tillman to close the debate if he had been willing to accept a shorter time.

I had spoken long enough to know that, comparing myself with myself, I was more effective in a brief speech in conclusion than a longer speech that simply laid down propositions for another to answer.

Fortune favored me again. For some reason—I do not now recall what the reason was—the debate on the platform was put over until the next day and I had time to think over my speech during the night and to arrange my arguments in so far as one can arrange arguments for a closing speech. I fitted my definition of the business man at the place that I thought best and kept my "cross of gold and crown of thorns" for the conclusion. When it became known that I was to have charge of the debate my delegation was quite buoyant. They had known of debates in Nebraska and they were confident that my closing speech would make an impression on the Convention.

When the Convention convened I felt as I always do

just before a speech of unusual importance. I usually have a feeling of weakness at the pit of my stomach—a suggestion of faintness. I want to lie down. But this being impossible in the Convention, I got a sandwich and a cup of coffee and devoted myself to these as I waited for the debate to begin. During these moments of suspense Clarke Howell, with whom I became acquainted in 1893 and whose father was one of the leaders in the silver movement, sent me a note scribbled on an envelope. It read, "This is a great opportunity." I wrote under the words, "You will not be disappointed," and sent the envelope back to him.

Senator Tillman's speech did not present our side to the satisfaction of the friends of bimetallism. It was a strong speech—he could not make any other kind—but it presented the question as a sectional issue between the south and west with northeast states on the other side. While that division was very clearly presented in the Convention, we did not regard it as a necessary division; we believed that the restoration of bimetallism would be beneficial to the nations everywhere, not only to this country but all over the world. When Senator Tillman was through, Senator Jones took the platform and announced to the Convention that the Committee did not endorse the sectional argument by Senator Tillman. This increased my responsibility because it threw the whole burden on my closing speech.

Senator Hill followed Senator Tillman and made a very strong speech. He was at his best and presented the arguments on his side with consummate skill and adroitness. The effect upon the audience was apparent and the nervousness of our delegation increased as he proceeded.

He was followed by Senator Vilas, a man of high standing in the party, large experience in politics, and great ability as a lawyer. He pounded the advocates of free coinage without mercy.

Near the close of his speech Governor Russell of Massachusetts, who was the third and last man on the gold side, came back to Senator Hill's seat with evident excitement and protested that Senator Vilas was not going to leave him any time. My seat was so near Senator Hill's that I could hear the conversation. I immediately stepped across the aisle to Senator Hill and suggested that I was willing to have the time extended to give Governor Russell the time he wanted, the same period to be added to my time. Governor Russell was very appreciative of the suggestion and Senator Hill at once agreed to it. I cannot say that it was entirely unselfish on my side, and I think I would have made the suggestion if the extension of time had fallen to some one else, but as it was, it added about ten minutes to my time and I needed it for the speech I was to make. This was another unexpected bit of good fortune. I had never had such an opportunity before in my life and never expect to have again.

There never was such a setting for a political speech in my own experience, and so far as I know there never was such a setting for any other political speech ever made in this country, and it must be remembered that the setting has a great deal to do with a speech. Webster says that the essentials for a successful speech are eloquence, the subject, and the occasion. I felt that I had at least two-thirds of the requirements. I had a subject of transcendent importance. The demonetization of silver in 1873 had so decreased the world's supply of standard money as to bring about a shrinkage in values that covered a period of more than twenty years. This shrinkage in prices caused by the increase in the purchasing power of the dollar had led to three international conferences in which the leading nations had sought in vain for a remedy. Many prominent Republicans were on record as in favor of remonetization as the only means of fighting for the restoration of the parity between money and property. The Republican Convention had declared for the maintenance of the gold only until it was possible to restore international bimetallism by agreement and the platform pledged the party to an effort to secure international bimetallism.   The cause was great enough to bring about a revolt in the Democratic Party—a fight won by the rank and file against all the power of the administration, and of the power of the big corporations and the metropolitan press. I was to make the final speech to a Convention in sympathy with our fight.

After an unsatisfactory opening of the debate and after our side had been pounded unmercifully by the giants of the other side, all that was necessary to success was to put into words the sentiments of a majority of the delegates to the Convention—to be the voice of a triumphant majority. The occasion was there and complete in every detail.   I had no doubt that I could meet the expectations that had been aroused by this extraordinary combination of circumstances, because I had spent three years studying the question from every angle and I had time and again answered all the arguments that the other side had advanced.   All that I had to do was to analyze the speeches of Hill, Vilas, and Russell as they were made and then present the answer as effectively as I could.

The delegates had been hammered by the very able speech of Senator Hill; they had been provoked by the language of General Vilas, and still further irritated by the speech of Governor Russell, and they were in a mood to applaud.   Fortunately my voice filled the hall, and as I was perfectly familiar with the subject, I was prepared to answer in an extemporaneous speech the arguments which had been presented—that is, extemporaneous in so far as its arrangement was concerned.   No new arguments had been advanced and therefore no new answers were required.

The excitement of the moment was so intense that I hurried to the platform and began at once. My nervousness left me instantly and I felt as composed as if I had been speaking to a small audience on an unimportant occasion.

From the first sentence the audience was with me. My voice reached to the uttermost parts of the hall, which is a great advantage in speaking to an assembly like that.

I shall never forget the scene upon which I looked. I believe it unrivaled in any convention ever held in our country. The audience seemed to rise and sit down as one man. At the close of a sentence it would rise and shout, and when I began upon another sentence, the room was as still as a church. There was inspiration in the faces of the delegates. My own delegation I can never forget. No man ever had a more loyal sixteen friends than I had on that day. Their faces glowed with enthusiasm.

Two faces stand out as in memory I look over the hall. Ex-Governor Hogg, of Texas, was a large man, probably six feet two or three inches in height, and heavy. He wore no beard and his face was beaming with delight. He stood by the aisle to my left, and about in the same relative position on my right stood Ollie James, a member from Kentucky, also a large man with a smooth face. As I turned from one side of the hall to the other, these two faces impressed me, for like the rest of the audience, they were in full sympathy with the sentiments to which I gave expression. They could not have responded to the expressions of my own face more perfectly if I had been speaking a speech that they had prepared.

The audience acted like a trained choir—in fact, I thought of a choir as I noted how instantaneously and in unison they responded to each point made.

The situation was so unique and the experience so unprecedented that I have never expected to witness its counterpart.

At the conclusion of my speech the demonstration spread over nearly the entire convention. As is customary at such times, the standards of the various states were carried through the aisles followed by the delegates, the Nebraska standard at the front. During the demonstration many persons came to me to tell me of the votes in their delegations; in some cases whole states were pledged. Others came to ask questions.

I remember that one man came to report that I was accused of drinking to excess. It was easy to answer him with the assurance that I was and always had been a tee-totaler. Another man came to tell me that some one in his delegation accused me of saying that I would not support a gold candidate if one were nominated by our convention. I replied that I had stated that I would no more support a gold standard or a gold platform than I would an army marching on my home. The delegate said that he would not either and went back to carry my answer.

After the nomination Hon. Arthur Sewall, my running mate, came to tell me of an experience which in the confusion had made no impression upon me. He said that he came up and told me that they would nominate me that night if my friends would prevent adjournment. He quoted me as answering, "Should I want to be nominated tonight if they would be sorry for it tomorrow?"

To another, as he reported to me afterwards, I said, "If the desire to nominate me will not last until tomorrow, would it last during the campaign?"

The nomination came on the following day on the fifth ballot. I had been so busy all the forenoon that I had not had time to shave. When the bulletin was brought in announcing my nomination I knew that the crowd would soon turn from the Convention to my headquarters, and I hurried down to the barber for a shave. I mention this as evidence that I was not excited, but the barber was—so much so that he could hardly handle his razor.

Mr. Sewall, who became my running mate, was one of the first to call to congratulate me. When they met for the selection of Vice-President I sent for some of the leaders and told them that I had no choice for that position and did not care to advise further than to say that I had no

WINNING THE NOMINATION

William Jennings Bryan and the Chicago Convention in 1896, when he delivered his famous "Cross of Gold" Speech.

objection to the nomination of a Southern man if the Convention thought proper to do so. I did not mean to advise such a nomination, but I wanted them to know that I did not share the objection so often raised to a Southern man. I felt then, as I have felt since, that a man otherwise eligible should not be barred because he lived in the South, even though he were an ex-Confederate, as most of the men old enough to be candidates were. I had become convinced, even then, that the voters were not so much interested in the locality of the candidate or in his position during the Civil War as they were in his attitude on public questions.

Honorable Arthur Sewall was nominated, the chief argument being that I lived so far West that they should have an Eastern man to balance the ticket. Mr. Sewall had gained distinction as the only silver man on the National Committee representing eastern states. He had voted to seat the Nebraska delegation when the question was before the committee. I did not know Mr. Sewall until he was nominated, but I learned to love him as I became acquainted with him. I soon learned that he was a thorough Democrat. I sounded him along the various lines and never in a single instance did I find him holding views inconsistent with the most fundamental Democracy. He was a well-to-do man but a believer in the Income Tax; he was a national banker but preferred the Government note to the bank note. His sympathies were with the common people and he was true to their interests on every subject. Because of Mr. Watson's nomination by the Populist Convention, Mr. Sewall did not take an active part in the campaign. Had he made speeches I am sure that he would have become more popular in the West than in the East, because his views were entirely in harmony with the sentiment in those sections that dominated the Convention.

This word in behalf of Mr. Sewall is due to him. I can never forget the last time that I met him. I was speaking in the South when he happened to be near where I was to

117

speak. He wired me inquiring the time of my train, and learning that I would pass over a certain road, he met me. He appeared with me on the platform at several points where crowds were gathered, and just as he was leaving me at a place where quite an enthusiastic crowd was gathered, he said with tears in his eyes, as he bade me good-by, "Mr. Bryan, how these people love you," and I am sure that they loved me no better than Mr. Sewall did, and his affection was reciprocated by me.

The Convention closed on Saturday and Mrs. Bryan and I spent Sunday with the family of Judge Lyman Trumbull, who had died a short time before the Convention. Then came the trip to Lincoln by way of Salem, my birthplace, where we had left the children while we went to attend the Convention.

This is the story of my connection with the Convention that has had such an important influence upon my public life. I put it in writing at this time so that the story will not be lost in case my life should be ended before I have time to prepare a more detailed sketch.

In speaking of the Convention it has been my purpose to record only the incidents that were personal and of which others would have less knowledge than I. I prefer to let disinterested parties describe the impression made by the speech and the demonstration.

CHAPTER VII

LEADING UP TO MY SECOND NOMINATION

THE number of letters which I received after the election of 1896 made it certain that unless some change in conditions occurred, I would be renominated in 1900, for although defeated, the six and a half millions of voters came out of the campaign of 1896 a compact and undismayed army. The elections of 1897 indicated a growth in our party's strength and things went well until the Spanish War broke out, then attention was turned from economic matters to questions affecting the war.

I telegraphed to President McKinley on the day that the war was declared offering my services, but never received a reply. I know that the telegram was received, because the President asked Senator Allen, of Nebraska, what position I could fill, and Senator Allen communicated the question to me. I wrote the Senator that I was willing to do any work to which I might be assigned, but suggested that as I was personally acquainted with General Wheeler, it would be agreeable to be assigned to his staff if the rules permitted. Senator Allen did not receive my letter until after General Wheeler had gone South, and I afterwards learned that the rules of the army would have prevented my being assigned to his staff, as I was not a commissioned officer and had had no experience. Shortly afterwards Governor Holcomb, of Nebraska, authorized me to raise a regiment—I had already enlisted as a private in a company organized at Lincoln. I raised the regiment and served something more than five months, resigned the day that the treaty with Spain was signed, so that my military career began constructively with the offer of my services on the day that war was declared, and with the termi-

119

nation of my services on the day that the war was formally closed by treaty.

During my army life I refused all social invitations and attended strictly to the duties of the office. I also avoided any discussion of political questions, giving as an excuse that I had military lockjaw. After I began to recruit a regiment, but before I was sworn in, I had occasion to make a speech at a dinner in Omaha, where the subject of imperialism was approached, and I then announced my opposition to colonialism, and so far as I know, I was the first public man to express myself on this subject. Ex-President Cleveland and Senator Hoar, according to my recollection, made speeches, or gave interviews, a few days afterwards along the same line.

My reason for leaving the army was that I saw that the sentiment in favor of imperialism was widespread and that many Democrats had been led to join in the cry for expansion, as it was then termed. I believed imperialism to be dangerous to the country, and so believing, I resigned my position in the army in order to oppose it. It required more courage to resign than it did to enlist, for I knew that the unfriendly papers would criticise me for leaving the army just as they had criticised me for entering it. They stated that, having no military experience, I was not fit to take charge of a regiment and that it was unfair to the soldiers in my regiment to be under my command. When I resigned they stated that I had deserted my soldiers and that it was unfair to the soldiers for me to leave them while they were still in service.

When I left the army the question before the country was the ratification of the treaty, and I announced the next day after I put on citizen's clothes that I favored the ratification of the treaty and the declaration of the nation's purpose to give independence to the Filipinos. As my reason for taking this position has been explained and defended in my speech on imperialism made when I accepted the nomination in 1900 (see Chapter XXI), I need not set forth this reason here. I have never regretted the position taken; on the contrary, I never showed more statesmanship than I did when I insisted upon the termination of the war and the making of the promise embodied in the Bacon resolution.

The Democratic party was in the minority in the Senate and in the House, and a Republican President was in the White House. Our party, therefore, could not pass a resolution through either body, and it had no voice in the selection of the treaty commissioners. It required two thirds of the Senate to confirm the treaty, and a few Republicans were willing to act with the Democrats to reject it.

But the Republicans and Democrats stood in different positions. The Democrats had to furnish the bulk of the votes to reject the treaty, and had no influence with the administration. The Republicans who opposed the treaty were few in number but hoped that, through their influence with the administration, they might be able to modify the terms of the treaty. But the Democrats would have had to have borne the responsibility for the continuation of war expenditures and for any dangers that arose during the continuation of the state of war. Hostilities were feared and parents were clamoring for the return of their sons, and it was difficult for Democrats to defend an act that would continue the state of war and postpone the making of the treaty.

Then, too, several of the great nations of Europe, such as England, Germany, and Russia, were interested in the Orient and might resent the setting up of a republic there. England was not interested in the spread of the ideas of popular government in India, neither was Germany interested in having colonies take up the ideas of self-government, and Russia was at that time the most despotic of the European empires. If we had insisted upon the recognition of the independence of the Philippine republic, it might have brought us into conflict with the interests of several

European powers, and it was not necessary for us to take this risk because we could give independence to the Filipinos more easily than we could force Spain to give independence. By ratifying the treaty, we settled the question with Spain and gave to ourselves the entire control of the Philippine situation.

It then became an easy matter for us to make to the Filipinos the same promise that the treaty made to the Cubans. The ratification of the treaty did not bind us to hold the Philippine Islands; it simply severed the Philippine Islands from Spain. I felt confident that it was easier to persuade the American people to promise independence to the Filipinos in connection with the ratification of the treaty than to continue war and force Spain to recognize a republic in the Philippines. I still believe that we followed the line of least responsibility and that we are better off today for having settled the war and made the Philippine question purely an American question than we would have been had we, a minority in Congress, attempted to compel a majority to carry out a plan by which the majority would in turn be compelled to force Spain to recognize the independence of the Philippine republic.

The Bacon resolution, which was a part of my plan, came so near being adopted that it required the vote of the Vice-President to defeat it. It will be seen, therefore, that although I was a private citizen, the Senate came within one vote of carrying out a plan which I had outlined and for which I had been severely criticised. Had the plan been carried out, we would have been saved the tremendous expense which has followed our attempt at colonialism and we would have been spared the menace to which our meddling in Oriental politics has subjected us.

For a while the excitement regarding expansion, as the Republicans termed it, and imperialism, as we termed it, aroused suggestions as to other candidates. Admiral Dewey was spoken of and even went so far as to indicate his willingness to accept the nomination, although he did not indicate with which party he expected to connect himself. Admiral Schley was also spoken of as a candidate, but refused to consider the matter.

As the convention of 1900 approached, however, it became evident that no other candidate would be presented to the convention, and when the convention was held, the delegates from all of the states and territories but one, if my memory is correct, were instructed to favor my nomination. It is possible that two or three of the states instead of instructing, passed resolutions expressing a preference for me. When the convention met at Kansas City, I was not present. Mr. R. L. Metcalfe, editor of the *World-Herald*, and a delegate at large, was the Nebraska member of the Committee on Resolutions.

Mr. C. H. Jones, who prepared the draft of the Chicago platform, had prepared the draft of the Kansas City platform, using very largely the phraseology that I had employed in the discussion of the questions. About the only plank that aroused discussion was the plank restating the Chicago platform for the restoration of bimetallism and the opening of the mints to the free coinage of silver at the ratio of sixteen to one. The Eastern delegates were opposed to the restatement of this proposition, although they were willing to reaffirm the platform as a whole without any special reference to this plank. As it was intended, however, to restate nearly all the other planks of the Chicago platform, it was evident that the failure to restate this plank was equivalent to a repudiation of it, notwithstanding the general endorsement of the Chicago platform as a whole. I insisted upon the restatement of the plank because I thought that a refusal to restate it would, under the circumstances, be considered a repudiation of that plank, and while I recognized the force of the arguments made by some of our friends, namely, that the increased production of gold since 1896 had reduced the importance of the question, I was not willing to run upon a platform which either ignored the question or put me in the attitude of pretending to endorse it when the endorsement was not genuine.

I considered the matter very fully, and nothing ever distressed me more than being compelled to differ from so many of my trusted friends. A number of those who had been loyal to me in the former campaign were persuaded by the arguments of the Eastern delegates who favored the reaffirmation of the platform without a specific restatement of this plank, and but for my objection, the resolutions committee would have so acted. Even with my objection known, the vote in the committee was quite close. Several friends sent a representative to Lincoln to ask me to leave the question of the platform to the convention, and I replied that I would gladly do so, but when asked if I would be a candidate in case the convention decided to leave out that plank, I replied that I would not consent to be a candidate under those circumstances. I had fought for four years for the reaffirmation of that platform and I was not willing to go before the country on a deceptive promise, as I felt it would be a deceptive promise if the convention merely reaffirmed but refused to reiterate.

I told the friends there that I could afford to lose the nomination, that it was not necessary to my happiness, but that I could not afford to lose the confidence that the voters had in my honesty and that I would decline to be a candidate if the convention in its wisdom saw fit to write the platform as was then proposed. So unwilling was I to put my judgment against the judgment of the committee that I was on the point of sending a communication to the convention declining to be a candidate under any circumstance, for I felt that the support of the convention would not be a hearty support if it approved of a platform against its own judgment, and yet I was not willing to be a candidate under conditions that required me to apologize for the platform.

PORTRAITS OF MR. AND MRS. BRYAN, TAKEN IN 1900

Photo. Pacific & Atlantic Photos, Inc.

MY SECOND NOMINATION

I was prevented from sending this communication by the fact that the delegates were instructed for me and that it was not the fault of those who gave the instructions that the delegates were considering the propriety of yielding to the demand that came from the East. Some have thought that my refusal to consent to this change in the platform resulted in my defeat, but I have never entertained this view of the subject. I believe that the acceptance of the modified platform would have resulted in a more disastrous defeat than the one which I suffered. In fact I believe that had I consented to run on such a platform, I would have so disappointed the rank and file who made the fight for me in 1896 that I would have had something of the experience that Mr. Parker had four years later.

I did agree to the plank making imperialism the paramount issue, because I believed that with changed conditions the question of imperialism was at that time more important than the money question. The trust plank was given the second place in importance, and the money question was not discussed to any extent during the campaign. The fact that the platform reiterated the demand for independent bimetallism made it less necessary for me to discuss the question than it would have been had the platform attempted to avoid the subject. As it was, the substitution of imperialism as the paramount issue discouraged a great many of our active workers, and while I gained in the New England states and in what used to be called the middle states, those in the neighborhood of New York, I lost in the South, in the Mississippi Valley states and in the West.

A word more in regard to the contest in the committee at Kansas City. I was in telephonic communication with friends at Kansas City, and the Kansas City *Times* was being edited by a close political friend who sent a representative to Lincoln, with whom I was to confer, and it was willing to carry out editorially any suggestions that I should make. The resolutions committee harangued over the platform far into the night and as the time approached for the paper to go to press, the editor sent his representative to me to get an indication of the outcome in case the committee rejected what was known as my plank. I told him that the paper could safely have an editorial written upon the assumption that I would not be a candidate in case the convention rejected that plank. I did not tell him so, but I had no thought of letting the fight drop with a mere resolution of the committee. I would have gone to Kansas City if necessary and made a fight in the convention for an adoption of the plank; if the convention had then rejected the plank, I then would not have been a candidate.

The committee, however, by a very small majority, declared in favor of the plank, and no minority report was filed. It has sometimes been stated that the vote of the delegate from Hawaii decided the result in the committee. If so, it might be interesting to know that a Democrat passed through Lincoln years before on his way to Hawaii and asked me for a letter of introduction to President Dole. The man brought with him a letter from a friend which contained a sufficient endorsement to justify me in giving the letter desired. I saw nothing more of the man until after the Kansas City convention. When I learned that he was present at Kansas City and that he made it his business to advise the Hawaii member of the Committee on Resolutions and to fortify him against the persuasion that came from the opposition, I did not know, of course, to what extent his loyalty may have influenced the vote of the Hawaiian member, but if it did have influence, it is another evidence that bread cast upon the waters may return after many days, for it was a favorable return that this man made for the slight service that I rendered him in giving him a letter of introduction.

It ought also to be known that Mr. Richard Croker, the leader of Tammany, played an important part in this matter. Mr. Croker met with an accident a little while before the

MY SECOND NOMINATION

Kansas City Convention, and while he was laid up by the accident, he read my book entitled "The First Battle." The arguments in favor of silver convinced him of the correctness of our position, or at least removed the prejudice he had against our position. When he came back from his trip abroad he announced that he was in favor of my nomination and he sent me word that he would support the platform that I wanted. When New York's member of the resolution committee was to be selected, Mr. Croker favored Judge Van Wyck in place of Senator Hill, and he did so because he was afraid to trust Senator Hill on that question. Mr. Van Wyck voted against my plank on the committee. I have always believed that he would have voted with me had his vote been necessary—but he refused to join in any minority report. As soon as it became known that the committee had included the plank for which I asked, Senator Hill began an agitation in favor of a minority report, and I was informed at the time that Mr. Croker, upon learning of it, notified Mr. Hill that New York's votes would be cast in favor of the majority report. This ended the fight and the platform was unanimously adopted. Mr. Croker was an enthusiastic supporter during the campaign, and after the election wrote me a letter expressing his regret at my defeat and saying that he still expected me to be elected to the presidency. He was one of the few Eastern Democrats who wrote me after the election. I have appreciated Mr. Croker's support of me because I believed it entirely disinterested. He never asked a promise of me; never said anything to indicate that he had any personal reason for favoring me, and I have every reason to believe that he stated his real reason for supporting me when he gave as his reason that he believed that I was in public life because of my interest in the public and not because I had any pecuniary advantage in view.

Hon. A. E. Stephenson was nominated for Vice-President at Kansas City and his nomination was entirely satisfactory.

He is a man of splendid character and was faithful to the core in 1896 when the President and nearly all of his prominent appointees deserted the party. I explained to General Stephenson that if elected I would ask congress to enact a law to make the Vice-President ex-officio member of the cabinet in order that he might be present at all consultations and be fully informed as to all administration plans. Such a law I think would add dignity to the office of Vice-President and at the same time prepare the Vice-President for the better discharge of the duties of the office in case of the President's death. I had resolved on this recommendation as far back as 1896 and may have spoken to Mr. Sewall of it, but am not sure about it. The matter had so impressed me that the first issue of the *Commoner* contained an editorial on the subject.

CHAPTER VIII

THE BENNETT WILL CASE

THE friendship between Philo S. Bennett and myself, which began in 1896 and continued until his death, was one of my closest and dearest friendships outside of my family, and yet it brought upon me an experience which gave rise to more malicious misrepresentation than any other incident of my life. It was the only time in which I have been called upon to serve a friend at great expense to myself both in feelings and in money. I am glad to put upon permanent record the facts in connection with it. It is now possible to discuss the case with more freedom than was possible during the lifetime of Mrs. Bennett.

Philo S. Bennett was a citizen of New Haven, Connecticut, but was engaged in business in the city of New York. His firm, Bennett, Sloan & Company, were wholesale grocers, specializing in tea.

I never met Mr. Bennett until the campaign of 1896, when he was on the reception committee on the occasion of my campaign visit to New Haven.

Speaking some six hundred times during the campaign, it was of course impossible for me to recall the members of all the reception committees which took part in meetings. It so happened that at New Haven, Connecticut, Mr. Bennett rode in the carriage with me along with John B. Sargent, a prominent hardware manufacturer of that city. I had known of Mr. Sargent for some years, because he was one of the few Eastern manufacturers opposed to a protective tariff. He had made a trip around the world and on his return gained a considerable prominence by interviews in which he declared that American manufacturers could compete with the world without a tariff; basing his arguments on observations he made as a traveler. The proposition that I remember best was that American labor was so much more efficient than foreign labor that our power to compete in the markets of the world increased as the percentage of skilled labor in the manufactured articles increased. Mr. Sargent's name had therefore become known to me and I remembered the personal meeting with him and the support which he gave to our cause, but would not have been able to remember Mr. Bennett but for our correspondence which brought him to my attention just before the election. The following letter is the first which I received from him:

BENNETT, SLOAN & Co.

New York, October 30, 1896.

Hon. William J. Bryan

Lincoln, Neb.

DEAR SIR:

The betting is three to one against you in this state at the present time; but notwithstanding that, I am impressed with a feeling that you will win, and if you are *defeated*, I wish to make you a gift of $3,000; and if you will accept the same it will be a genuine pleasure to me to hand it to you any time after the 10th of next March.

You have made one of the most gallant fights on record for a principle, against the combined money power of the whole country, and if you are not successful now, you will be, in my opinion, four years later.

The solid press of the East, and all the wealth of the country have, ever since the canvass opened, concealed the truth and deceived the people regarding the whole question. They have succeeded in making 25 per cent of them believe that if you are elected the country will be governed by a lawless, disorganized mob. If you are elected I trust that you will, as soon as you can, issue a letter or make a speech, assuring them that the great body of the people are honest and can be trusted.

This letter is intended only for yourself and wife to ever see. A feeling of gratitude for what you have done in this canvass for humanity, for right and justice, prompts me to write and make this offer.

I am one of the electors at large on the silver ticket in the state of Connecticut, and accompanied you from New York to New Haven, and rode in the carriage with you and Mr. Sargent from the station to the hotel.

Hoping for your victory, and with kind regards, I am,
Sincerely yours,
P. S. BENNETT.

Mr. Bennett's first letter indicated such a sympathetic interest in our party's position on public questions that our acquaintance grew. It became more intimate as I met him from time to time on my trips to the East, and our friendship continued unbroken until his accidental death in 1903. I seldom passed through New York without seeing him. He invited Mrs. Bryan and me to spend a summer vacation with him and Mrs. Bennett at their summer home in Maine, but it was never possible to accept his invitation except as we met him for a day or two in New York or New Haven. He was so much older than I that the relationship between us was more like the relation between parent and child, he giving me the benefit of his greater experience and larger business acquaintance.

It will be noticed that this letter was written just before the election and the offer contained in it was contingent upon my defeat. The letter did not come to my attention until after the election, by which time I discovered that the campaign had brought upon me a continuing expense in the way of correspondence. The number of letters received amounted to twenty-five hundred or sometimes three thousand a day. It soon became apparent that my correspondence would cost me more than it ever cost me to live before I was nominated. Mr. Bennett's offer, coming at such a time, was quite welcome, but before accepting it I took the precaution to inquire by letter addressed directly to him whether he was pecuniarily interested in silver mining. Believing that the silver question would continue to be an issue, I was not willing to put myself under financial obligation to anyone who was in a business way interested in silver as a metal. My interest in silver was solely as a matter of the public interests; the demonetization of silver seemed at that time the only way of increasing the volume of money.

I quote from his reply dated November 20, 1896:

New York, Nov. 20, 1896.

Hon. William J. Bryan,
    Lincoln, Neb.

DEAR SIR:

I have yours dated the 13th inst. I do not now, and never have owned a dollar's interest in a silver, gold or any other mine, and do not expect to in this century.

If just as agreeable to you, I will make the gift in three different payments, sending you check for $1,000 the 15th of each March for the next three years.

I would like to have you use it all for yourself and family, and not give a penny for the cause of silver or any other political purpose.

The newspapers report that you are to enter the lecture field. If this is true, when you go to New Haven it would afford me pleasure to entertain you while there. I am confident you will have a full house and be received enthusiastically.

I am anxious to have you seen and heard on the platform in the East by the gold advocates, for I think it will help to remove from their minds some of the prejudice that now exists. To me it seems one of the best methods you have open for that purpose; it will also help hold your old friends.

You of course fully understand the *power of money and brains coupled together*. You may rest assured that both will be used lavishly to prevent you from securing the nomination for President in 1900. From now on if you mingle and keep in touch with the people, I believe they will remain true, and you can secure the nomination against the all-powerful forces named.

I hope that before 1900 you will in some manner gain the support and goodwill of part of the business element. Here in the East and middle states they were almost solid against you in November. It is important that you should have it next time in order to carry any electoral votes in this part of the country, for the money power, as it is generally understood, will be a unit against you.

I have just received the Boston *Herald*, containing a speech by Mr. F. A. Walker on bimetallism, delivered on the 7th inst.

I suppose you know that Mr. Walker has his eye on the presidency, and hopes to secure the nomination some time from the friends of bimetallism. Keep close watch on him. After reading his speech I will forward it to you.

I send you a few clippings which you will probably feel interested in reading.

With kind regards, I am,

Sincerely yours,

P. S. BENNETT.

Perhaps I ought to qualify what I have said about Gen. Walker, for I have no *positive* knowledge that he expects the nomination.

In April or May of 1900 I received a letter from Mr. Bennett asking whether I would be home at a certain time in the near future, without giving me any intimation of the object of his proposed visit. Upon receiving my answer in the affirmative, he appeared one morning at our home in Nebraska. He laid before me a will which he had made some years before, stating that he desired to make some changes in it.

He said that he felt as much interested in the reforms which I was advocating as I did myself, but that he was unable to present them to the public as I was in the habit of doing. It had occurred to him that if he made provision in his will for a sum that would be given to me at his death I would be able to make, without compensation, speeches that I delivered in the form of lectures, and he desired to set apart fifty thousand dollars for that purpose, saying that he would leave ten thousand dollars in care of Mrs. Bryan, five thousand dollars to each of my children and twenty-five thousand to myself. He felt that in this way he could share in the work and would feel that he was making a contribution that was within his means.

I inquired whether he would have that sum to spare after making provision for his wife and relatives. He told me that he was worth about three hundred thousand dollars, and that he was giving one hundred thousand to his wife, a sum which he said would furnish her a larger income than she could use during the remainder of her life. They had no children, their only child, a daughter, having died some years before. They lived comfortably but without ostentation and they had estimated the amount necessary to provide for all the wants of his wife should she be left a widow. He went further and explained that the money which he left her would at her death go to her relatives and the amount he was allotting to her was all he cared to leave them. The amount he left to his own relatives, a sister and a half brother, had been decided by him without any consultation with me.

In fact, he did not consult with me about any item of

the will except that fifty thousand dollars which he wanted to give to me and thirty thousand dollars which he desired to devote to altruistic purposes. I ventured to call his attention to the fact that after giving to his wife and his relatives the amounts he desired left them and after giving fifty thousand to me, there still remained thirty thousand dollars of his estate. We talked over the various uses which could be made of this. In the course of the conversation I told him that I had established prizes in nineteen colleges, nearly all of them state universities. These prizes were given each year for the best essay on the science of government; my plan being to give two hundred fifty dollars to the institution, the interest from which would be used to furnish annual prize money. The plan pleased him and he decided to leave ten thousand to me in trust for this purpose. I was to select twenty state universities which I had not myself endowed, giving to each five hundred dollars for the purpose outlined above. That left twenty thousand dollars and Mr. Bennett expressed a desire to use it to aid poor boys and girls to secure an education, explaining that he himself had lacked educational opportunities when he was young and that it would give him satisfaction to aid those similarly situated. I discussed with him how this might be done and he asked whether I would be willing to distribute ten thousand for the aid of boys and Mrs. Bryan a similar amount for the aid of girls. He remarked that her wide acquaintance would enable her to distribute the money over the United States to the best possible advantage. These provisions were written into the will. He had a small sum left and I told him of a plan that I had in mind to buy the ground upon which I was born and upon it build a city library.

He had so impressed me by his devotion to the political ideals and principles with which I had been identified that I told him it would be very pleasant to me to have his name linked with mine in this library. The plan appealed to him and the provision was made. The library has been built and is known as "The Bryan-Bennett Library." We contributed equally to the cost of the building, but I had previously bought the land and subsequently contributed five hundred dollars for the purchase of books.

When we came to consider the fifty thousand dollars to be left to myself, I told him that I was not an old man and was likely to live for many years and that I would not promise to accept the money at the time of his death because I might not need it at the time. There was so little opposition to my second nomination that it seemed quite certain that I would run again and I told him that if I was elected I would be in a position where I would not need any financial assistance. He thought I would need the money more in case of my election than my defeat. I had no desire to accumulate means beyond a provision against old age and I preferred to have him give the money to his wife, with instructions to give it to me if at the time of his death I desired it. He preferred to give it to me directly and asked me whether I would be willing to distribute it in case I did not desire to accept it, reminding me again that he had made what he regarded as ample provision for the members of his family and wanted this sum devoted to the public. He said it gave him pleasure to contemplate the benefit which his bequest would bring to other young people, situated as he himself had been in his youth.

He insisted that I should distribute the fifty thousand dollars among charities and educational institutions if for any reason I refused to accept it. Having no thought of the possibility of a contest, I promised to do this, and it was this promise that compelled me to oppose the breaking of the will.

The money was left to his wife in trust, the terms of which would be made known to her in a letter deposited with the will.

I have gone into this in detail because the alternative

obligation which he imposed upon me was the matter that embarrassed me at the time of his death. He explained to me that he had given to his wife all that she could use and his estimate was borne out by subsequent facts. He left his wife about one hundred thousand dollars. When she died in 1919 she left an estate of one hundred thirty-six thousand dollars. It shows an increase rather than a diminution of the amount left her.

Mrs. Bryan, who at that time used the typewriter and helped me with a considerable part of my correspondence, copied the will at Mr. Bennett's request.

When the new will was drafted, being, as I have said, a copy of the old will except as to the five bequests above mentioned, he took it back to New York with him unsigned; then, fifteen hundred miles away from Nebraska and several days after the drawing of it, he executed the will and put it in a safety deposit vault of his own selection and of which he only had the key, notifying me of what he had done. There the will lay until his death more than three years later. The will was never mentioned in any conversation between us and never referred to in any letters. And I did not know at the time of his death whether the will was in existence.

In one of his letters written upon a wedding anniversary he remarked that he was almost old enough to be my father, adding that I could not be nearer to him if I were indeed his son. I mention this because while it made no reference to the will when he thus expressed himself, he may have had in mind the provision of his will.

Between the making of the will and his death I saw him frequently and heard from him from time to time. In the fall of 1903 he made a trip to Idaho, and arranged to stop at Lincoln on his way west. It so happened that I was away from home, so that I missed an opportunity to have what would have been a farewell visit with him. He expressed himself as greatly pleased with Fairview, our country home. It was on this trip that he met his death by accident at a point near Boise, Idaho. He was riding in the open stage coach commonly used on the mountain roads when the brake broke on a hill and the team became unmanageable. He was thrown from the coach, striking against a tree, and died instantly. His widow wired me and I went to New Haven to attend the funeral. She greeted me affectionately, put the flowers which I brought on the coffin with her own flowers and invited me to speak at the grave, which I did. Below will be found my remarks.

"At another time I shall take occasion to speak of the life of Philo Sherman Bennett and to draw some lessons from his career; today I must content myself with offering a word of comfort to those who knew him as husband, brother, relative, or friend—and as a friend I need a share of this comfort for myself. It is sad enough to consign to the dust the body of one we love—how infinitely more sad if we were compelled to part with the spirit that animated this tenement of clay. But the best of man does not perish. We bury the brain that planned for others as well as for its master, the tongue that spoke words of love and encouragement, the hands that were extended to those who needed help and the feet that ran where duty directed, but the spirit that dominated and controlled all rises triumphant over the grave. We lay away the implements with which he wrought, but the gentle, modest, patient, sympathetic, loyal, brave and manly man whom we knew is not dead, and cannot die. It would be unfair to count the loss of his departure without counting the gain of his existence. The gift of his life we have and of this the tomb cannot deprive us. Separation, sudden and distressing as it is, cannot take from the companion of his life the recollection of forty years of affection, tenderness and confidence, nor from others the memory of helpful associa-

138

tion with him. If the sunshine which a baby brings into a home, even if its sojourn is brief, cannot be dimmed by its death; if a child growing to manhood or womanhood brings to the parents a development of heart and head that outweighs any grief that its demise can cause, how much more does a long life full of kindly deeds leave us indebted to the Father who both gives and takes away. The night of death makes us remember with gratitude the light of the day that has gone while we look forward to the morning.

"The impress made by the life is lasting. We think it wonderful that we can by means of the telephone or the telegraph talk to those who are many miles away, but the achievements of the heart are even more wonderful, for the heart that gives inspiration to another heart influences all the generations yet to come. What finite mind, then, can measure the influence of a life that touched so many lives as did our friend's?

"To the young, death is an appalling thing, but it ought not to be to those whose advancing years warn them of its certain approach. As we journey along life's road we must pause again and again to bid farewell to some fellow traveler. In the course of nature the father and the mother die, then brothers and sisters follow, and finally the children and the children's children cross to the unknown world beyond—one by one 'from love's shining circle the gems drop away' until the 'king of terrors' loses his power to affright us and the increasing company on the farther shore make us first willing and then anxious to join them. It is God's way. It is God's way."

After the funeral I talked with her at her home and told her about the will drawn at my house about three and a half years previously. I told her I did not know where the will was and had no knowledge of what had occurred

139

since and therefore did not know whether it was still in existence, but I told her of the bequests as I recalled them. She made no objection whatever to the bequest to me, but did express surprise and dissatisfaction with two other items in the will. The will as drawn made his partner, Mr. Sloan, and myself executors. I had an imperative engagement which took me away from New Haven for a few days and when I returned to present the will for probate I found that she and the other residuary legatees had employed a lawyer and decided to contest the fifty thousand dollars willed to myself.

I explained to her and to her attorneys that I would not receive any of the money for myself without her approval, but that having promised Mr. Bennett to distribute the sum if I did not receive it, I could not refuse to carry out his directions unless relieved by the court. The will was not contested on the ground that any improper influence had been brought to bear upon him, but merely on the technical ground that the provision to Mrs. Bennett did not sufficiently define the trust according to the Connecticut statute regulating wills. If the money had been given to me directly there would have been no contest and if I had not promised to distribute the sum in case I refused to accept it, I would have immediately relinquished all claims. However, having been taken into Mr. Bennett's confidence and having learned the disposition he wanted made of it, I did not feel at liberty to consult my own pleasure or my own interest.

My position was made plain to the probate judge, the circuit court and to the supreme court, so that it was known to all that I had no personal interest in the result of the suit but was simply carrying out the wishes of a dead friend. I received the most courteous treatment from all the officials who took part in the case. I employed Judge Henry G. Newton, a prominent member of the bar, to represent the estate in the defense of the will. At one time in the trial he interposed objections to an improper question and I asked him to make no objections to any questions that Mrs. Bennett's counsel might desire to ask, whether proper or not. I was not willing that any limit whatever should be placed upon interrogations, feeling that any objections might be open to misconstruction. At the conclusion of the hearing Judge Cleveland expressed himself very strongly as to the impression made by my testimony.

In the course of his written opinion, the judge said: "This court finds that neither the twelfth clause of the will (which was the clause in question) nor the letter therein referred to, was procured by undue influence." And the judge, in his written comment on the testimony, said:

"The testimony of Mr. Dewell, who had known him for a quarter of a century, shows that the testator was a sharp, able business man, a man of decided opinions from which he was not easily turned aside. But whatever presumption, if any, might be raised by reason of Mr. Bryan's drafting the will, has been, in the opinion of the court, abundantly overcome by the evidence. Mr. Bryan testifies that the idea of a bequest in his favor, so far from being suggested by him or Mrs. Bryan, was a complete surprise to both; a statement in which the court has entire confidence in view of Mr. Bryan's frankness on the witness stand and his evident desire to fully disclose all his relations with the testator and all the circumstances surrounding the drafting of the will.

The three $10,000 funds left in trust to me were distributed as follows:

BENNETT PRIZE FUND

Delaware College, Newark, Del..................... $400
Bowdoin College, Brunswick, Me.................. 400
A. and M. College of Kentucky, Lexington, Ky...... 400

Harvard University, Cambridge, Mass	$400
Dartmouth College, Hanover, N. H	400
University of Tennessee, Knoxville, Tenn	400
St. John's College, Annapolis, Md	400
University of Idaho, Moscow, Idaho	400
University of Montana, Missoula, Mont	400
University of Utah, Salt Lake City, Utah	400
University of Washington, Seattle, Wash	400
University of South Dakota, Vermilion, S. D	400
University of California, Berkeley, Calif	400
Nevada State University, Reno, Nev	400
University of Colorado, Boulder, Colo	400
South Carolina College, Columbia, S. C	400
Cornell University, Ithaca, N. Y	400
University of Wyoming, Laramie, Wyo	400
University of Vermont, Burlington, Vt	400
University of Oregon, Eugene, Ore	400
Yale University, New Haven, Conn	400
Brown University, Providence, R. I	400
University of North Dakota, Grand Forks, N. D	400
University of Pennsylvania, Philadelphia, Pa	400
Princeton University, Princeton, N. J	400

Each college is to invest the amount received and use the annual income for a prize for the best essay discussing the principles of free government. I had already established similar prizes in nineteen states and the twenty-five colleges selected for the Bennett prize were selected from other states so that every state but one now contains a college giving such a prize.

EDUCATIONAL FUND FOR BOYS

The fund for the aid of poor boys desiring a college education was distributed as follows:

Illinois College, Jacksonville, Ill	$1,000
Park College, Parkville, Mo	750

College of William and Mary, Williamsburg, Va..... $750
Doane College, Crete, Neb...................... 500
Howard College, East Lake (near Birmingham, Alabama)...................... 500
Hendrix College, Conway, Ark.................... 500
Tuskegee Normal and Industrial Institute, Tuskegee, Ala...................... 500
Kenyon College, Gambier, Ohio.................... 500
Muskingum College, New Concord, Ohio.......... 500
St. Olaf College, Northfield, Minn................. 500
Hillsdale College, Conway, Ark.................. 500
University of the South, Sewanee, Tenn............ 500
Trinity University, Waxahachie, Tex.............. 500
Ripon College, Ripon, Wis...................... 500
Nazareth College, Muskogee, I. T................. 500
Hope College, Holland, Mich.................... 500
Butler College, Indianapolis, Ind................. 500
Sutherland College, Sutherland, Fla.............. 500

EDUCATIONAL FUND FOR GIRLS

The fund for the aid of poor girls desiring to obtain a college education was distributed by Mrs. Bryan as follows:

Georgia Normal and Industrial College, Milledgeville, Ga......................... $500
Eureka College, Eureka, Ill...................... 500
Hastings College, Hastings, Neb.................. 500
Wesleyan University, Buchannon, W. Va.......... 500
Henry Kendall College, Muskogee, I. T........... 500
Williamsburg Institute, Williamsburg, Ky.......... 500
Wesleyan University, University Place, Neb........ 500
Baylor University, Waco, Tex.................... 500
Iowa College, Grinnell, Ia...................... 500
Tulane University of Louisiana, New Orleans, La.... 500
State Normal and Industrial College, Greensboro, N. C................................ 500

Hiram College, Hiram, Ohio...................... $500
Kingfisher College, Kingfisher, O. T................ 500
Academy of the Visitation, Dubuque, Ia............ 500
Williams Industrial College, Little Rock, Ark........ 500
Ewing College, Ewing, Ill......................... 500
Bethany College, Lindsborg, Kan................... 500
University of Arizona, Tucson, Ariz................ 500
University of New Mexico, Albuquerque, N. M...... 500
The Mississippi Industrial Institute and College,
Columbus, Miss............................... 500

CHAPTER IX

THE ST. LOUIS CONVENTION

IMMEDIATELY after the election of 1900 I announced that I would not be a candidate in 1904. Having been defeated twice, the second time by a larger majority of the popular vote and of the electoral college than the first time, I thought that it was not wise to be a candidate again until the things I had fought for were so clearly vindicated as to lead the voters of the party to demand my nomination. And having reached the conclusion that I should not be a candidate, I thought it only fair to others who might be candidates to let them know that I would not be in the field.

The result was a contest for supremacy between the radical element of the party and the conservative element. The conservative element had the advantage in that it was able to point to two defeats under my leadership. This advantage was at once seized upon and the conservative leaders promised victory if they were put in control.

Mr. Hearst announced himself as a candidate and received the support of the more radical of the radicals, but did not command the support of all who had supported me. He was especially weak in the South and when the Convention met, the conservatives had a two thirds majority.

Judge Parker, of New York, was the man on whom they had centered, but his delegates were not for the most part instructed. I recognized the difficult position which I occupied and I recognized, too, that those who had fought for me were very much discouraged by the second defeat. I was in a position to know this. After the 1896 election I received as many as 2500 letters a day, all containing promises of support and assurances of victory in 1900.

10

145

After 1900 I received very few letters that expressed hope for the future of the Democratic Party. Most of my correspondents were disappointed; they did not see how we could win after the defeats we had suffered.

As the campaign of 1904 approached, I tried through my paper and in my speeches to awaken an interest in the coming campaign and to organize the radical element of the party to resist the encroachments of the conservatives. But it was useless. I did not think it wise to support any particular man for the nomination, and this was probably a mistake, for it is difficult to attack a candidate and have no candidate to suggest in his place. A number of Democrats said to me that if I would only pick out a man, they would support him, but if I would not do so, they must select for themselves. I mentioned a number of candidates as available, Mr. Hearst among others. But no other candidate appeared with any considerable strength except Mr. Hearst. Mr. Wall had Wisconsin, and Mr. Gray had Delaware, and Mr. Cockrell had Missouri, but Mr. Hearst had the only considerable following.

I decided to go to the convention as a delegate, at least I announced my willingness to do so, but even in Nebraska a club had been organized to support Mr. Parker and an effort was made to carry the Convention for him. This effort, however, failed and we carried every county, I think, but one, in the state, and the state convention elected a set of delegates who, to a man, supported my position.

I went to the St. Louis convention from a sense of duty and not because I expected to win any victory there, or even to avoid a humiliating defeat. Remembering that the gold Democrats had left the party and by leaving had lost their influence in the party, I was afraid that if the platform was written by the conservative element it would drive a large part of the radical Democrats out of the party. My purpose, therefore, in going to the convention was to get a platform that would not sacrifice what the party had

146

been fighting for, and would, if possible, secure a candidate who could be voted for by those who had been enthusiastic in my support. I was more successful in the matter of the platform than I had hoped to be.

The first fight in the convention was over the Illinois delegation. Mr. Hearst had a considerable majority in the Illinois state convention, but the organization was against him, and the temporary chairman proceeded to run the convention with the gavel without regard to the wishes of the delegates. A crowd had been brought down from Chicago and stationed near the platform to prevent any interference with the program that had been laid down by those in charge.

While they could not prevent a resolution endorsing Mr. Hearst, they selected a delegation, a majority of which was opposed to him, and the selection was made by the most high-handed methods. The delegates from the several congressional districts made a selection of national delegates, but these were ignored and new names substituted to meet the purpose of those in charge.

When I read in the paper an account of the convention, I telegraphed M. F. Dunlap to meet me at St. Louis and I questioned him in regard to the convention. Believing that an outrage had been perpetrated upon the Democrats of Illinois, and believing that the action of the convention might have a decided influence upon the national convention, I proposed that a contest be made. I went to Chicago and laid the matter before Mr. Hearst, but he felt that it might be a reflection upon the instructions for him to attack the convention that gave the instructions. Mr. Dunlap and I then decided to make the fight ourselves, and each bearing half the expense, we proceeded to secure a petition from a majority of the delegates of the convention asking for the seating of certain men as delegates at large and of the men who had been chosen in the several districts by a majority vote.

WILLIAM JENNINGS BRYAN

Before the convention met we had a signed request of more than a majority of those who actually took part in the convention asking for the action which we suggested. Of course, this was resisted and the Parker men being in control of the convention, the contestants were overruled and the opposing delegates seated. I got a proxy from the Nebraska member of the Committee on Credentials and went into the committee and presented a minority report. I opened and closed the debate on this question and it was the first victory won in the convention, for, although I was voted down by the convention, even without the delegates, I had such an overwhelming majority of the audience with me, that their expression of opinion very much strengthened me in the contest that followed.

The *Post-Dispatch*, one of the Parker papers, had a two-column editorial entitled "The Passing of Bryan," in which the editor discussed at some length the insignificant part that I was taking in the convention. I had entered the convention the day before while some one was speaking and I took my seat unnoticed. This was commented upon as an indication that I no longer had influence in the party.

The delegates had just about had time to read that editorial when I entered the convention to make the minority report; and possibly because of the vindictive spirit that ran through the editorial, my entrance was made the occasion for a demonstration that lasted some twenty minutes. This was the first notice served upon the delegates that they were not to have things all their own way. The reception accorded my speech in behalf of the Illinois contestants increased the impression, and by the time I took up the fight in the full committee, the conservative element was aware that I had with me a large majority of the audience and a respectable minority in the convention.

I was of course a member of the Resolutions Committee, being selected for the place by my own delegation. Senator Daniel was made the chairman of the committee and he appointed a sub-committee to draft the platform. As a matter of courtesy I was put on this sub-committee, but I was the only one in the beginning who represented our side of the fight. Senator Newlands was afterwards added and he was of great assistance in the struggle which followed.

We spent one session, lasting from eight o'clock until midnight, on the tariff plank, and I was finally voted down. During the next session I was occupied in the convention in the fight over the Illinois delegation, and while I was absent the sub-committee went over the rest of the platform and was ready to report to the full committee at the evening session. At the time the committee was appointed the papers published a platform which was described as the platform agreed upon by the leaders of the party. It was not strange that I had not seen the platform, for I was not counted among the leaders by those in control of the convention, and it was not supposed that I would have any influence in the writing of the platform. I had gone over this platform and marked the planks to which I objected and had this copy with me when the full committee met to consider the work of the sub-committee. I took my place at the table not far from Senator Daniel, and we began the most memorable contest through which I have ever passed.

From eight o'clock in the evening until noon the next day—sixteen hours—the battle raged over the wording of that platform. As we took up plank after plank, I moved to strike out and to substitute, and as fortune would have it, I succeeded in securing a majority for each proposition, so that when the platform was completed, I had written a great deal more of it than I had written of the Chicago platform upon which I myself ran. I did not get into the platform all that I wanted, but with the help of a majority of the committee, I kept out of the platform everything to which I objected.

The fight over the gold plank attracted most attention, although the majority against the gold plank was larger

149

than the majority against any other plank stricken out. The vote, as I recall it, was thirty or thirty-five to fifteen. Nearly all of the Southern members voted against this plank. While I voted against it, I did not take much part in the argument, because there were plenty of Parker men to talk against it.

At one time Senator Daniel, who was urging the plank, asked if any Democrat thought that the adoption of the plank would weaken the party in his state. More than half of the committee arose, among them some of Mr. Parker's stanchest supporters.

During the course of the discussion, I asked Senator Hill when he had decided that the gold plank should be inserted in the platform. He replied that he had reached that decision only a few days before the convention. In asking the question I thought that he might answer that he had believed so for months, and I then intended to ask him why it had not been inserted in the New York platform —that platform having been silent upon the subject. His answer, however, showed that it was a newly conceived purpose. I also asked him Judge Parker's views on the subject and he said that he did not know. I asked him if he had ever talked with Judge Parker on the subject and he said that he had not. This seemed remarkable to me and it struck the convention in the same way when the conversation was reported to the convention.

I saw that it was impossible to secure the insertion of any money plank, and I did not, therefore, spend much time in urging it. I consented to a plank suggested by Senator Carmack which stated that the quantitative theory of money had been established and that the increase in the volume of money had removed the money question from the arena of politics. But that plank was objected to by Senator Hill, and seeing that the best we could do was to prevent any expression on the subject, we contented ourselves with leaving out the money question entirely.

THE ST. LOUIS CONVENTION

I urged a plank in favor of the income tax, but while nearly every member of the committee, excepting Senator Hill, expressed himself as favoring the income tax, a considerable majority opposed the insertion of the plank, some of them on the ground that it would interfere with the collection of a campaign fund. I finally agreed to withdraw the income-tax plank if the committee would agree to a stronger anti-trust plank, and when this was consented to, Senator Hill and I drew up an anti-trust plank, it being made as strong as the committee would permit. The labor planks were also inserted during the debate. There were two questions upon which there was no dispute, the election of senators by the people and the party's position on the subject of imperialism. The committee was unanimous on these questions.

The fight over the tariff question was probably the closest and most spirited fight that we had. The original proposition was strongly suggestive of protection, at least it gave very little encouragement to the tariff reformer. Several of the Parker men joined with us in strengthening this plank, among them Mr. Cable, of Illinois, who had been instructed for Mr. Hearst and was in sympathy with the Western element of the party, and Mr. Hamlin, of Massachusetts. Senator Bailey did efficient work on this plank, going so far as to threaten to bring in a minority report if they attempted to report the plank that was suggested in the original draft of the platform. During the course of the discussion I had somewhat spirited debates with several members of the committee, but while the feeling was quite intense on both sides, the debates were conducted with courtesy and no ill feeling was left when the committee adjourned.

I am not sure that I ever rendered my party more service than I did during this fight over the platform, for the platform which we adopted did not surrender the party's position on the questions which had been an issue before, it merely left out some things about which we could not agree. The convention breathed a sigh of relief when the announcement was made that the committee had agreed upon a platform, and the platform was adopted by the unanimous vote of the convention.

As soon as the platform was adopted, the presentation of candidates began, and Judge Parker, Mr. Hearst, and Senator Cockrell were presented. Then came the seconding speeches. As the time rolled on these speeches were limited to four minutes. When Nebraska was called, I arose and yielded to Wisconsin, that Wisconsin might present Mr. Wall. When Wisconsin was called the state yielded to Nebraska and I seconded the nomination of Senator Cockrell.

I was somewhat in a quandary as to what to do. My main object was to prevent the nomination of Judge Parker, who was so closely identified with the men who had defeated the party in two campaigns that I felt sure he would be so handicapped by this support as to make his election impossible.

I had no particular choice in selecting Senator Cockrell, but was governed by two considerations. First, he stood for everything that I had been fighting for and I could therefore urge his nomination without surrendering or abandoning anything. In the second place, he was an ex-Confederate soldier and I thought that there was a possibility that with him we might break the Southern support of Judge Parker, and I believed that Senator Cockrell would poll a very much larger vote than Judge Parker could possibly poll.

I had more to say than I could say in four minutes, and therefore I asked for a suspension of that rule. I announced to Congressman Clark, the presiding officer, that if allowed unlimited time, I would second the nomination of Senator Cockrell, but if the request was denied I would present the name of someone else for nomination, because in making a nominating speech there was no limit upon time.

Mr. Clark asked the convention for unanimous consent to suspend the rule, and although it was four o'clock in the morning, and the delegates were weary, no objection was made. I have always regarded this as a compliment as well as a great courtesy. Two thirds of the delegates were for Parker and they knew that I was against him; I had fought him and the platform which his leaders had urged, and yet there was no objection when I asked unanimous consent for a suspension as to the time limit, that I might address the convention against Mr. Parker's nomination.

The speech made on that occasion is a matter of record and is generally known as the "I Have Kept the Faith" speech, for what was considered the most striking passage in it was the one in which I stated, in returning the standard which had been placed in my hands, that they could dispute whether I had fought a good fight; [they could dispute whether I had finished my course, but they could not deny that I had kept the faith. (See Chapter XXI.)

My effort, however, was futile. The delegates had gone so far in their determination to nominate Judge Parker that no effort of mine could prevent it, and when the roll was called, he had the necessary two thirds. If I had been asked my opinion as to the availability of candidates, I would have decided in favor of Governor Pattison of Pennsylvania. He was the one man suggested who would have been acceptable as a compromise candidate.

Judge Parker was acceptable to the Eastern element, but not to the radical element of the party. Mr. Hearst was acceptable to the radicals, but not to the conservatives. Mr. Gray would have been more acceptable to the conservatives than to the radicals. Mr. Wall, while not for silver in 1896, supported the ticket and would have been acceptable to the radicals, but he lived too far west for the conservatives. Governor Pattison was a candidate before the Chicago convention and was a gold Democrat, but he supported the ticket that year. He lived in the East, but he had a record that commended him to the radicals, and I believed then, and still believe, that he came nearer meeting the requirements of the occasion than any other man we had, but his own delegation sided in with New York and left him no chance.

He died soon after the convention and as his death would have demoralized our campaign, it is fortunate he was not nominated. Notwithstanding the fact that I was looked upon as a disturber of harmony, I had been anxious that we should find some one upon whom the party could unite and for whom we could make a strong fight.

After being up all night for two nights—one night on the Committee on Resolutions and another at the convention (and I had only slept for a few hours for several preceding nights)—I was utterly exhausted and as soon as I concluded my speech, I returned to the hotel and retired. In fact, it was more than fatigue. I went to the convention with a severe cold and it developed so far as to threaten pneumonia. It was against the advice of my physician that I attended the convention, and the first night I attended the meeting of the Committee on Resolutions wearing a mustard plaster over my chest. As soon as I reached the hotel the doctor put a plaster of antiphlogistine on my chest and I remained in bed until night. During the day Judge Parker sent his famous telegram which threw the convention into an uproar. The delegates brought me news from time to time and no one could foresee the result. Several delegates came over and expressed themselves in very emphatic language to the effect that they "had been bunkoed." I tried to soothe them by telling them that it was no more than they might have expected and that they ought to have known from the tactics pursued that it was not a compromise which had been demanded but a surrender.

Finally the situation became so tense that I decided to

go over to the convention. Taking advantage of the absence of the physician, I dressed and hurried over, pale and worn. I went to the platform and made my last stand against the Parker element. His telegram had announced that he regarded the gold standard as irrevocably established and the Resolutions Committee brought in a resolution declaring that as the question was no longer an issue, his personal opinion was not material. I introduced an amendment calling upon him to give his opinion upon certain other phases of the money question, as he had seen fit to give it upon the gold question. But after reflection I withdrew this, not only because there was little chance of its adoption, but because I was afraid that his answers to my questions, if he answered them, would simply commit him to the wrong side of the question.

When the vote was taken the committee's resolution was adopted by about the same vote which was cast in favor of his nomination, and the resolution was not a very important one after all, because it only stated the fact which we all recognized, namely, that the money question was not an issue any longer. It would have been better, however, if the resolution had stated that it was no longer an issue because the principle contended for by the Democrats had been vindicated and because an unexpected increase of money from another source had rendered the restoration of bimetallism unnecessary.

His telegram, however, put an end to whatever hope there was of Mr. Parker's election. He had remained silent and by so doing he had alienated the rank and file of the party. If the election had occurred a week after the convention, he would scarcely have received half the votes of the party, but as time went on, the Democrats became more reconciled to the situation and recognized that he had simply expressed his own opinion and in no wise committed the party.

I took part in the campaign, justifying myself by the

fact that the Democratic platform was good as far as it went and that our candidate stood for a number of reforms, while President Roosevelt was pledged to no reforms. I offered my services to the national committee and spoke in several of the states, neglecting my own state to do so. And while I have reason to believe that I was instrumental in increasing his vote, I found it difficult to arouse enthusiasm.

I heard many amusing stories of the campaign illustrating the lack of enthusiasm. One man told me that at a ratification meeting three cheers were proposed. The chairman gave two of them and the man who told me gave one, which made the three—the remainder of the audience refused to join. At a meeting in Indiana where the Democratic candidate for governor was present, the chairman proposed three cheers for the ticket and got no response whatever, but the audience, after giving three cheers for the Republican candidate, adjourned.

I look back to the St. Louis convention as one of the best illustrations I have had of the fact that one cannot see very far ahead. I went to the convention expecting to be disregarded by a hostile majority. I never knew one hour what was coming next, but continued on my way meeting the questions as they arose and doing what seemed to me to be right at the time.

In the convention in which I expected humiliation I found victory, for I think the victory at St. Louis was really a greater personal triumph than the victory at Chicago, and did more to strengthen me in the party. My support of the ticket convinced many who had doubted my democracy that I was in fact democratic in my principles and loyal to the Democratic party as an organization.

When I went to St. Louis I could not, of course, see the outcome, and I would not promise in advance to support the nominee, but I was convinced during the course of the convention that the Democratic party was sound at heart

ACCEPTING THE NOMINATION FOR THE PRESIDENCY, 1908

and that its surrender to the conservative element was but temporary.

This encouraged me to continue the fight within the Democratic party, and the platform was such that I had something to stand on and to fight for. The platform committed our candidate to certain important reforms, while the Republican platform committed the President to no specific reforms, and I felt that if we could but get rid of imperialism and the spirit of war which the President seemed to embody, we might be better prepared to enter upon the fight for economic reforms.

Looking back upon the campaign of 1904, I think that it was probably best that Mr. Parker was nominated, because his nomination gave the conservatives a chance to test their ability to win victory, and their failure made it possible for the party to reorganize itself and become a positive and progressive force. Had we nominated a radical at that time, he would, in all probability, have been defeated, because the conservative element would not have supported him; had we nominated a compromise candidate he would also, in all probability, have been defeated, but the nomination of a man clearly identified with the Wall Street element removed, for the present at least, the fear of another conservative triumph in the party.

At the Democratic National Convention at Denver in 1908 Mr. Bryan was nominated for President for the third time. His position on the Trust question at that time is set forth in a statement and telegrams which will be found in the Appendix.

CHAPTER X

The Baltimore Convention

AFTER my third defeat in 1908 I felt that nothing but a revolutionary change in the political situation would justify a fourth nomination. Not seeing evidence of such a change and not being willing to obstruct the plans of other aspirants, I announced that I would not be a candidate in 1912. As a result of the Congressional election in 1910 the Democrats gained control of the House of Representatives and Champ Clark was elected Speaker.

Clark entered Congress in 1892, from which time my acquaintance with him began. As is the custom, he came to Washington after his election and before his term began in March of 1893. I recall our first meeting at that time. He said that he had used my record as an argument in his race for the nomination. The Democratic member of Congress from his district was serving his first term when Clark announced his candidacy. His argument against the sitting member was that he had not accomplished anything during his first term. The member replied that it was not customary for a new member to do much during his first term; that it took time for a man to secure prominence and influence in Congress. I had been made a member of the Ways and Means Committee during my first term when I was only a little past thirty.

From that time on I met Clark in the 53d Congress and afterwards at Democratic national gatherings. While I was not more intimate with him than I was with a thousand other Democrats scattered throughout the Union, I followed his record with interest and rejoiced at his growing influence.

After his election to the Speakership in 1911 I regarded him as the logical candidate and invited him to speak at my

158

birthday banquet on March 19, 1911. My purpose in inviting him was to let those who were friendly to me know that I regarded him as an available man for the nomination. Governor Wilson was being talked of more and more, but I felt that Clark was more in sympathy with the policies of the party and, therefore, better suited to lead our forces in the coming presidential campaign. Clark came, but I learned from him afterwards that it was with some reluctance. This surprised me and I was surprised still more when, as the campaign proceeded, I found that his friends were tying up with the Harmon forces wherever a combination was necessary to defeat the Wilson forces.

Wilson, on the other hand, was becoming more radical in his utterances and was gathering about him an increasing number of the progressive element of the party. He was also exciting the opposition of the reactionary element. As the campaign proceeded I received many letters from different parts of the country warning me that Harmon men were getting on Clark delegations.

Having learned from a friend who was present at the meeting that Wall Street had picked out Governor Harmon as its Democratic candidate, I at once brought the matter to the attention of the Democrats of the country and insisted that he could not expect to be the candidate of a progressive Democratic Party. I was fond of Harmon personally, but I was satisfied that his business connections and his bias made it impossible for him to be the exponent of the masses in their struggle for reforms. I had confidence in Clark personally, and, knowing that a man cannot refuse the support of those who for different reasons may favor him, continued to count Clark and Wilson as equally acceptable to the progressive element of the party.

In the Nebraska primary I announced myself as a candidate for delegate-at-large, saying that I would willingly support either Clark or Wilson according to instructions, but that I would resign as delegate in case the state instructed for Harmon, giving as a reason that I was not willing to aid in turning the party over to Wall Street. I ran about five thousand ahead of the ticket and considered my election as an endorsement of my opposition to Wall Street domination.

Some of my prominent political friends came into Nebraska and made an active canvass of the state in favor of Clark and against Wilson. George Fred Williams and Ex-Senator Pettigrew were among the number. They were both strongly against Wilson. They quoted Adrian Joline's letter and also extracts from Mr. Wilson's utterances on the money question. They urged the support of Clark on the ground that he always supported the things that I advocated and was, therefore, nearer to me in his political ideas and ideals. I favored a division of the delegation so as to avoid a fight between two progressive candidates, but Mr. Wilson's manager insisted on having two thirds of the delegation and thus prevented a joint ticket.

I was so anxious to preserve an attitude of perfect neutrality between the two that I tried to make the vote in my precinct as nearly equal as possible. There were two voters at my home and I advised them to vote one for Clark and one for Wilson. Had they done so there would have been only one vote difference between the votes of the candidates, but when the time approached they thought that one of the candidates was going to have quite a lead and so, following the spirit instead of the letter of my advice, voted together for the one they thought was weakest, but were mistaken in their calculations and their two votes thus gave the successful candidate a lead of three majority over the other.

When the returns from the state came in it was found that Clark had the instructions but that Wilson had a majority of the delegates (bound by instructions, of course, but friendly to Wilson).

Some time in the spring, Norman E. Mack, the committeeman from New York, wrote me and asked if I would like to be temporary chairman. I answered that I did not think it would be wise for me to be temporary chairman. My reason for not wanting to enter the race was that some of the metropolitan papers were construing my neutrality between the two leading candidates as evidence of a desire to be a candidate myself. I was afraid that I would be accused of trying to stampede the convention, that being the possibility upon which the unfriendly papers dwelt at greatest length.

As the convention approached it became apparent that the progressives would be in control of the convention and that Clark would have more votes, although neither would have a majority.

I wrote to Governor Wilson and suggested to him that we should have a progressive chairman and that as neither had a majority the choice would naturally fall to the candidate having the largest number of votes. I called his attention to the fact that Ollie James, the candidate of the Clark delegates, was a progressive and a fair-minded man and suggested that he accept James in case it should prove impossible to elect the man of his own choice. He answered, saying that he preferred O'Gorman. I mention this fact to combat the unfair criticism of Mr. Clark's friends directed against me after I changed my vote.

At Chicago I watched the Republican Convention select a candidate under the pressure of influence from Wall Street. What I saw there made me sensitive to the influence of Wall Street in our own convention. While I was at Chicago the Democratic National Committee met and selected Judge Parker as temporary chairman. In the contest before the committee the Clark men had supported Ollie James and the Wilson men Judge O'Gorman. Neither having a majority, Parker finally received the support of the Clark men and became the choice of the committee. Josephus Daniels, then the member of the committee for North

11

Part of Mr. Bryan's copy of his letter to Champ Clark

THE BALTIMORE CONVENTION

Ft. Wayne, Ind.

May 30

My dear Clark:—

I venture to make a suggestion for your consideration. I believe the fight over wool will prove a crisis in
your life as well as in the party's prospects. A leader
must *lead;* it is not always pleasant to oppose friends,
and one who leads takes the chances of defeat, but
these are the necessary attendants upon leadership.
Wilson is making friends because he *fights.* His fight
against Smith was heroic. He fought for the income
tax and for a primary law. The people like a fighter.
You won your position by fighting and you must continue to fight to hold it. Enter into the wool fight.
Don't be content to take polls and sit in the background.
Take one side or the other and take it *strong.* If a tax
on wool is right, lead the protectionists to victory. You
can do it and it will make you strong with that wing of
the party. If free wool is right, as I believe it is, lead
the fight for it and get the credit for the victory if
victory comes. Don't inquire about how the fight is
going to go—make it go the right way if you can. If
you fail you lay the foundation for a future victory.
The right wins in the end—don't be afraid to wait.
My opinion is that you will not have to wait long, but
whether long or not, one can better afford to be defeated
fighting for the right than to win on the wrong side.
I hope you will pardon this intrusion upon your
thoughts, but the party needs your assistance—a blast
from your bugle may save the day, and it will, in my
judgment, strengthen you personally.

Regards to the family.

Yours

Bryan

163

Carolina, called me up by telephone and asked me what I thought of the selection. I told him that I not only would criticise the selection but the committee that made the selection. I then prepared a telegram to each progressive candidate reading as follows:

"In the interest of harmony I suggested to the sub-committee of the Democratic National Committee the advisability of recommending as temporary chairman some progressive acceptable to the leading progressive candidates for the presidential nomination. I took it for granted that no committeeman interested in Democratic success would desire to offend the members of a convention overwhelmingly progressive by naming a reactionary to sound the keynote of the campaign. Eight members of the sub-committee, however, have, over the protest of the remaining eight, agreed upon not only a reactionary, but upon the one Democrat, who, among those not candidates for the presidential nomination is, in the eyes of the public, most conspicuously identified with the reactionary element of the party. I shall be pleased to join you and your friends in opposing this selection by the full committee or by the convention. Kindly answer here."

Governor Foss of Massachusetts, Governor Marshall of Indiana, and Governor Baldwin of Connecticut, all declined to join me in my fight against Parker. Governor Wilson of New Jersey and Governor Burke of North Dakota went to my support.

Woodrow Wilson sent the following reply:

"You are right. Before hearing of your message I clearly stated my position in answer to a question from the Baltimore *Evening Sun*. The Baltimore convention is to be the convention of progressives—the men who are progressive in principle and by conviction. It must, if it is not to be put in a wrong light before the country, express its convictions in its organization and its choice of the men who are to speak for it. You are to be a member of the convention and are entirely within your rights in doing everything within your power to bring that result about. No one will doubt where my sympathies lie, and you will, I am sure, find my friends in the convention acting upon a clear conviction and always in the interest of the people's cause. I am happy in the confidence that they need no suggestion from me."

Champ Clark replied as follows:

"Have consulted with committee having my interests in charge and agree with them that the supreme consideration should be to prevent any discord in the convention. Friends of mine on the sub-committee of arrangements have already presented the name of Ollie James to the sub-committee. I believe that if all join in the interest of harmony in an appeal to the entire national committee to avoid controversies in matters of organization that the committee will so arrange as to leave the platform and nomination of candidates as the only real issues on which delegates need divide."

Governor Marshall's reply was:

"You may be right, but as Judge Parker, as a member of the committee on resolutions from the state of New York at the national convention at Denver, helped to report our platform of 1908 and as he came to Indiana that year to advocate your election and mine, and as he returned in 1910 to advocate the election of Senator Kern, I do not see how his selection as temporary chairman will result in a reactionary platform in 1912."

165

WILLIAM JENNINGS BRYAN

Governor Burke of North Dakota sent the only explicit acceptance of the challenge offered by the Wall Street crowd. Governor Marshall was willing to support Parker, while Clark's answer was a straddle. Governor Wilson's telegram, while not as direct as I would have liked, began with a sentence that led the delegates to accept it as a promise to oppose the Parker candidacy, which his delegates did. The account of this incident is given by Governor Wilson's secretary, J. P. Tumulty, in his book on "Wilson as I Knew Him," page 105.

I soon afterwards left the Chicago Convention and proceeded to Baltimore, hoping all the way that the Clark delegates would oppose Parker and thus give us a progressive temporary chairman to sound the keynote of the convention. When I reached Baltimore I found the situation unchanged. A Clark delegate called on me soon after my arrival and intimated that I might have the permanent chairmanship if I did not oppose Parker. Of course, I did not entertain any such proposition, but proceeded to hunt for a candidate to put up against Parker, after having made a personal appeal to Parker himself. I had a frank talk with him on the afternoon before the convention met in which I told him that he had no part in the reforms for which the party now stood and could not possibly give expression to the thoughts and purposes of the delegates who constituted a majority of a progressive convention. I made no impression on him further than to arouse his ire, as such a protest naturally would.

I first called in Ollie James, the candidate of the Clark men when the matter was before the committee. I felt sure that he could defeat Parker. He laid the matter before Mr. Clark's managers and returned to tell me that they objected to it and that therefore he could not allow his name to be used as a candidate. I then sent for Judge O'Gorman, Mr. Wilson's candidate in the contest, but he, being a member of the New York delegation, had pledged

166

his support to Judge Parker, although he advised Judge Parker not to be a candidate.

Failing to secure a candidate from the delegates supporting Clark and Wilson, I made an appeal to Senator Kern, but found that he, too, was embarrassed by the fact that he was there as delegate supporting Governor Marshall. The Indiana delegates, following the wishes of Governor Marshall, were nearly all supporting Judge Parker. The matter was made more delicate for Senator Kern by the fact that he was already being discussed as a candidate and naturally hesitated to do anything that would divert attention from his state's candidate to himself. Senator Kern urged me to be a candidate for the place as others had, but I explained to him that my first desire was to present an argument against Judge Parker's candidacy, which I could not do if I was myself a candidate for the place.

When Senator Kern left my room the night before the opening of the Convention he did not answer positively whether he would allow me to present his name, but said he hoped I would not. I heard next morning, not from him directly but indirectly, that he had a plan, but I did not learn the details of it. Not having received from Senator Kern a positive refusal to allow his name to be presented, I placed him in nomination after the committee had offered the name of Judge Parker. My speech will be found in the Appendix.

I have regarded my use of the "pillar and cloud" of fire of the children of Israel as one of the most appropriate references that I have ever made to the Bible in a political argument, but there was so much confusion in the convention that it seemed to make but little impression and I think I saw but one reference to it in the papers. It illustrates an experience that one frequently has; a phrase upon which one sets great store is often ignored, while a sentence which is spoken on the spur of the moment and without thought of its being considered important, will attract widespread attention.

WILLIAM JENNINGS BRYAN

In the course of my speech against Parker I used a quotation from Tennyson, "He never sold the truth to serve the hour," which was printed in large letters over Jefferson's picture which hung at the right of the platform. When I used this quotation Mrs. Bryan, who was just back of the platform, heard a man near her say to another, "I told them that he would use that quotation if they put it up there."

As I look back upon the convention I have a growing appreciation of the part played by Senator Kern; it was the best piece of acting that I ever saw off the stage. In fact, I have not seen it surpassed on the stage. As soon as I had finished my speech he arose and made an appeal to Judge Parker to join him in withdrawing from the contest, that the convention might agree upon some one who could receive the united support of the convention. He made an eloquent plea for harmony and then paused for Judge Parker to answer. There was deathlike silence for a moment. Then Senator Kern appealed to Mr. Murphy, chairman of the New York delegation, to use his influence with Judge Parker to secure his withdrawal in the interest of harmony. Again a silence that was deathlike. Then Senator Kern turned to the presiding officer and in a spirit of defiance announced that if there must be a contest Mr. Bryan was the only man to lead the people's side and placed my name in nomination.

As the roll call proceeded it became apparent that Judge Parker had the support of Governor Harmon's delegates, Congressman Underwood's delegates and a considerable percentage, though not all, of Speaker Clark's delegates. (The vote stood Parker 579, Bryan 508.) Parker was elected, but the victory did not arouse the enthusiasm which might have been expected. The shadow of the vote darkened the convention, because the friends of Mr. Clark began to suspect what its effect would be on the country.

Judge Parker was conducted to the platform to deliver

168

his address as temporary chairman, but the hall was in confusion and the aisles were full of people going out. So large a percentage of the audience retired that those in charge of the convention hastily conferred and announced that Judge Parker would deliver his address at the evening session and then adjourned the convention. I have not consulted the precedents, but do not know of any similar experience. As soon as it was evident that I was defeated I went with my wife and children to the hotel. They were naturally disappointed and sympathetic, but I explained to them why I had made the fight and assured them that my purpose had been accomplished. I was satisfied that the country would be aroused when it knew that a supposedly progressive convention had selected as temporary chairman the man most conspicuously identified with the Wall Street side.

I was not disappointed. I had scarcely reached the hotel before telegrams of congratulation began to pour in. Then followed such a demonstration of the power of public opinion as has never been witnessed in a convention before or since. The effect of the contest upon the Democrats of the country was electrical. The party, sound at heart, felt that it was being betrayed by its political leaders and "the folks at home" communicated with the delegates. Many joined in one telegram, the language varying from courteous appeal to vehement denunciation.

The Montana delegation was cast for me with the exception of one vote. The result was immediately carried by bulletins throughout the country and shortly the Montana delegation received a brief telegram signed by a number of angry citizens saying, in substance, "Send us the name of the —— who voted for Parker. We want to meet him when he comes home."

These telegrams continued to pour in during the convention as each new incident gave new excuse for expression. The total number of telegrams received, according to the

169

local agents of the two telegraph companies, was estimated at one hundred and ten thousand, or an average of about one hundred to a delegate. I received 1182 telegrams and they averaged three names to a telegram. One of them, from Virginia, was signed by one hundred and forty names. I learned later as I traveled through the West that the Democrats in the agricultural section would congregate at the railroad stations, read the bulletins as they were taken from the wire, and then join in sending a telegram to the delegates whom they knew, the signers "chipping in," as they say, to pay the expense of the telegrams.

When I was given credit for having exerted an influence on the convention, I replied, that I had simply turned the faucet and allowed public sentiment to flow in upon the convention, deserving no personal credit except for knowing where the faucet was and the height of the stand-pipe from which the public opinion flowed.

But to return to my narrative; early in the evening a committee from Mr. Clark's headquarters called to offer me the permanent chairmanship of the convention. This encouraged my family and the friends about headquarters, because it was proof conclusive that Mr. Clark's managers were feeling the reaction from the victory of the afternoon. I declined the invitation, telling the messengers that those who owned a ship should furnish the crew; that when my friends controlled a convention, we never asked the minority to supply the officers. We were all kept up late that night listening to the messages that came from the various headquarters, all indicating confusion and consternation.

The next morning I was delayed in getting to the Committee on Resolutions and found when I reached the convention hall that a committee had been sent to the hotel in my absence to ask me to accept the chairmanship of the Committee on Resolutions. They soon returned and made me the offer. I expressed my appreciation of the honor done me, but suggested that the majority should furnish the chairman, as it might become necessary for me to present a minority report and it would not look well for such a report to be presented by the chairman. Mr. Kern was then chosen chairman and I was asked if I would serve on the sub-committee. This I gladly consented to do, as I desired to contribute as much as possible to the making of a progressive platform.

Before the sub-committee withdrew to begin its work I offered a resolution to the effect that the committee after agreeing upon a platform should hold it until after the nomination of a candidate for President, so that he might be consulted about the platform before it was adopted. One of the Eastern delegates arose and asked in a tone of surprise whether I thought it possible that a nominee of the convention would object to any platform that the convention had adopted. I replied, "Our candidate did in 1904." The questioner subsided amid the laughter of the committee, and the resolution was adopted.

We then had an illustration of the sensational character of reports that are sent out from conventions. The morning papers under big headlines told about my being defeated for chairman, the unfriendly papers in varying tones of gleefulness described my demise. The afternoon papers with headlines as large announced that Mr. Bryan had risen from the grave and taken charge of the Committee on Resolutions—basing the statement on the fact that the innocent resolution that I had introduced had been adopted.

My association with the other members of the sub-committee was pleasant and harmonious. I never worked with a more congenial crowd. The completeness of the harmony may be gathered from an incident. Just before the opening of the second day's session I met Judge O'Gorman, who told me that Senator Martin had stated to him that instead of being a firebrand as some of the committee feared I would be, I was the most conservative man on the committee. When the committee assembled I went up to

Senator Martin and addressing him in serious tones said, "Senator, I am sorry to hear you have been making unkind remarks about me."

The Senator assured me, with a look of honest surprise upon his face, that I had been misinformed, that he had spoken of me only in the most kind and complimentary language.

"But," I explained to him, "you told Judge O'Gorman that I was the most conservative man on this committee. What will my friends think when they hear this and know that you are on the committee?"

He enjoyed the humor of it and we went on working together as if we had always agreed on the policies of the party.

I assured the committee that I had no desire to write into the platform of another candidate any view that I had that had not already been endorsed by the party. I opposed any retreat on public questions and found the committee quite ready to endorse all that the Democrats in Congress had done since they believed, as I did, that our fight must be made upon the party's record. I was successful in reiterating in our platform many of the planks contained in previous platforms which I had helped to write, but I did not ask for the incorporation of anything new. The platform incorporated a phrase which had appeared in three previous platforms, namely, "A private monopoly is indefensible and intolerable." I first used the phrase in a speech at an Anti-Trust Conference at Chicago in 1899. The sentence used was almost identical with the sentence above quoted, and incorporated in the platform of 1900 and 1904 and 1908 and finally in 1912. I digress far enough from the narrative to say that this sentence was incorporated in President Wilson's speech of acceptance and in his message to Congress on the trust question.

I think I should mention a fact that one plank in the platform which has often been attributed to me, namely

the plank reading: "We favor a single Presidential term
and to that end urge the adoption of an amendment to the
Constitution making the President ineligible for reëlection,
and we pledge the candidate of this convention to this
principle," was proposed by Governor Beckham of Kentucky. I very gladly supported the plank, but for obvious
reasons would like to have it known that I did not offer it
at this time. I have always believed in the single term for
the President. When in Congress I introduced a resolution,
proposing the necessary amendment to the Constitution.
In each of my Presidential campaigns I made the statement
that if elected I would not be a candidate for a second term,
giving my reasons.

I will add that in every speech that I made during the
campaign following I pointed out that this pledge against
a second term enabled the President to serve the people
with singleness of purpose unembarrassed by any selfish
interest.

The platform also laid the foundation for the currency
legislation secured in President Wilson's first term. The
language employed in the discussion of banks was a distinct
departure from the language usually employed, just as the
language employed in the discussion of labor marked a new
departure. The plank on independence to the Philippines
was substantially the same as that contained in the three
previous platforms of our party. An amendment providing
for election of United States Senators by the people advocated in three preceding platforms was urged upon the
states.

While I was occupied with the work of the Resolutions
Committee most of the time Wednesday and Thursday I
was from time to time in conference with the progressive
element of the convention and learned of the activity of the
same element that had controlled the Republican Convention at Chicago. I found that the representatives of Morgan, Belmont, and Ryan were at work. Belmont and Ryan

were themselves delegates, the former from Chicago and the latter from Virginia. Being convinced of the intimate relationship between these financiers and Mr. Murphy, I became increasingly alarmed lest they should be able by the control of the New York delegation to make the nomination. The ninety delegates from New York were bound by the unit rule and Charles P. Murphy, the Tammany leader, had enough delegates to enable him to vote the entire delegation at his will.

When I returned to headquarters Wednesday night my brother, Charles W. Bryan, who had been closely associated with me in Nebraska, laid before me the information he had secured and suggested the resolution which I introduced the next night.

I took Wednesday night to think over the subject, and Thursday morning, before going to the committee room, dictated a resolution along the line he had suggested and left instructions that he call in as many of our friends as possible and get their opinion on it. The resolution, as I had prepared it, contained two paragraphs; the first was substantially the resolution as adopted by the convention; the second embodied the plan that was the outgrowth of my own experience in my three campaigns.

"*Resolved*, That in this crisis in our party's career and in our country's history this convention sends greetings to the people of the United States, and assures them that the party of Jefferson and of Jackson is still the champion of popular government and equality before the law. As proof of our fidelity to the people, we hereby declare ourselves opposed to the nomination of any candidate for President who is the representative of or under obligation to J. Pierpont Morgan, Thomas F. Ryan, August Belmont, or any other member of the privilege-hunting and favor-seeking class.

"*Be It Further Resolved*, That we demand the with-

THE BALTIMORE CONVENTION

drawal from this convention of any delegate or delegates constituting or representing the above-named interests."

I had never had a national committee entirely loyal. In the first campaign some of my committee did not attend the meetings. They were opposed to my election and yet retained their membership on the committee. The situation was so bad in 1900 that I thought that the committeemen who represented predatory wealth had little sense of political honor and should not remain on the committee when they were not in sympathy with the aims of the party. In the second paragraph, therefore, I included authority for the removal of unfriendly members of the committee.

When I returned to the hotel Thursday evening I found my brother very much discouraged, as he said that none of the men whom he consulted thought it wise to introduce the resolution, the criticism being directed mainly to the second paragraph which they thought might arouse opposition on the ground that it interfered with the rights of the states to select committeemen.

All my political friends appeared to be at the hall at the time and I suggested that I might strike out the second paragraph, whereupon he expressed a fear that the first paragraph alone might not draw the line with sufficient clearness.

He suggested a second sentence that dealt with Belmont and Ryan, who were delegates, in order to put teeth in it as he said. I framed the sentence, embodying his suggestion, and started for the convention not quite certain whether to chance the resolution or not. On the way to the convention I decided to introduce it. I felt some timidity about taking the responsibility without any encouragement from those who were nearest to me and most in sympathy with what I was trying to do, and reached the decision more from conviction that it was my duty to act than from reasons with which I could justify the act.

As I went to the platform some one pulled me aside to introduce me to Mrs. Taft. This little incident led me to change a sentence in the first paragraph referring to Mr. Taft's nomination in Chicago. I had included a few words not necessary to the resolution but comparing the attempt that was being made in our convention with the successful effort of Wall Street to control the Chicago nomination. When I found that Mrs. Taft was there I felt that it would be ungenerous to give her pain by such a reference to her husband and I therefore struck out the offensive words. President Taft afterwards learned of it, and in his characteristic way thanked me for the consideration shown his wife.

I do not recall just who took part in the debate on the Morgan-Belmont-Ryan resolution. Flood of Virginia led off with a denunciation of the resolution. He stood at one side of me a few feet away. I next met him after I became Secretary of State. He was chairman of the Foreign Relations Committee of the House and called at the Department on some matter in connection with his committee. I did not recognize him until he gave me his name and then I made him feel at home by remarking, "The last time I saw you I saw only your profile."

Honorable Cone Johnson of Texas made a speech in which he condensed a great deal in a few words. I became better acquainted with him afterwards when he came into the State Department as solicitor.

I went to Permanent Chairman Ollie James and asked for his recognition. It was necessary to suspend the rules and that required a two-thirds vote. I have many reasons to cherish the friendship of Ollie James, but he never did me a greater favor than when he recognized me on this occasion.

The resolution came as a surprise to my friends as well as to our opponents. "Dropping a bombshell into the crowd" is a phrase often used to describe the sudden precipitation of an issue. The phrase never more accurately described a situation. The explosion was immediate and vehement. The convention was in an uproar. Many were on their feet shouting denunciation. Old politicians accustomed to surprises in conventions were dazed. One member of the Congress rushed to the platform and, gesticulating violently, denounced me until he frothed at the mouth, and almost hysterical he was carried away by friends. I sat upon the platform where I could see the seething crowd. Urey Woodson, near me, was one of the Parker crowd. He was my friend in the earlier campaigns, but went off with Wall Street element in 1904 and had become prominent among the reactionaries. His apostasy had not led to any rupture in our relationship, although we understood that we were no longer co-workers. He had a box near me and was watching the proceedings as much mystified as his associates on the floor of the convention. I was near enough to him to remark, calling him by his first name, "When your machine ran over me it moved so slowly that I was able to inspect the works from the underside and I am now telling the convention what I saw."

My aim was to get a roll call, because I felt that whichever way the convention voted it would be difficult to nominate a man who had the support of the New York delegation. If they passed the resolution it excluded anyone who was the representative of Morgan, Belmont, or Ryan or under their influence; if they voted it down, the rebuke from the country would make it impossible for New York to select a candidate.

Just before the roll was called I announced that I would strike out the second paragraph of the resolution. I do not know how many in the convention understood what I had done; they were too excited to distinguish between the two paragraphs. When the roll was called the tumult reached its height. A state would be called; its chairman

12

would announce its full vote, "aye." Then half the delegation would jump to their feet and demand a poll, shaking their fists and shouting in violent language. I do not think there were ever before so many people in one hall, wildly excited and swearing at one another without someone being hurt. I heard afterwards of delegates who were loudly expressing the hope that somebody would take me out and hang me. One delegate, whom I afterward aided to a high position, stated that he would give twenty-five thousand dollars to anybody who would kill me. I have no thought that these men who poured out their threats would have carried them out. I only mention them to show the state of super-excitement.

Polls were taken in nearly all the delegations and some of them changed from a solid vote against the resolution to a solid vote in favor of it. As the roll call proceeded the opposition became frantic and delegates piled over each other to vote for the resolution, with the result that it finally carried by a vote of about 4½ to 1. Even New York voted for the resolution.

Some one reported to me afterwards that Murphy turned to Belmont and said, "August, listen and hear yourself vote yourself out of the convention." Virginia voted 23½ votes for the resolution. It was a great victory for progressive Democracy. Nearly all the Wilson delegates voted for the resolution and nearly all of the Clark delegates also, although many of the Clark leaders voted "no" and in so doing greatly lessened the political chances of their candidate. Clark's leaders are more responsible for his defeat than Clark himself, or would have been if it were possible for a candidate for President to excuse himself for allowing his managers to do what he would not do himself.

The effect of the Morgan-Belmont-Ryan resolution can hardly be overestimated. One of the London papers compared it with St. George slaying the dragon. One of

178

the Baltimore papers pictured it in a cartoon as burning the word "progressive" into the hide of the Democratic donkey. The passage of the resolution stirred the enthusiasm of the progressive Democrats and gave a new impetus to the shower of telegrams from the rank and file of the party. Having, as I thought, insured the convention against the nomination of anyone by Wall Street influence, I retired from the convention, while the delegates proceeded to place candidates in nomination.

Balloting began on Friday. Up to this time I had not taken my seat with my delegation, although I had appeared twice on the platform—Tuesday, when I made my speech against Parker, and Thursday night, when I introduced the Morgan-Belmont-Ryan resolution. My reason for absenting myself was that I did not want to risk attracting attention, having in mind the oft-repeated charge of unfriendly papers that I wanted to stampede the convention in my own favor. My intention was to keep out of the hall until the nomination was made and then appear at a time when I could make a speech in support of the candidate, whoever he might be.

On Friday night I was in the room of the Resolutions Committee when a great demonstration broke out in the convention hall. After waiting a while for it to subside, I went to the hall to inquire the cause. I found the convention in an uproar—the New York delegation had gone over to Clark on the fifth ballot. New York had started out voting for Harmon, thus verifying my predictions in regard to Wall Street's choice. I knew that New York's second choice was Underwood, but the throwing of the vote to Clark was by many believed to be evidence of an understanding between the Clark leaders and the New York delegation. I never heard anything other than circumstantial evidence to support this charge and never made it myself.

I am quite sure that Mr. Clark's leaders had calculated on using the New York delegation to give him a majority vote in the convention and that they then expected to claim his nomination on the ground that he had a majority. One of his leaders had asked me while I was at the Chicago Convention whether I thought any candidate receiving a majority could be prevented from securing two thirds. I answered that I thought there was only one instance when the two thirds rule had ever prevented a majority candidate from receiving the nomination.

I expected the nomination of a majority candidate, not only because precedent favored it but I had never taken kindly to the two thirds rule. I believe that the rule should be changed so as to allow a majority to nominate, and have advocated the change, but I have coupled with it the abolishment of the unit rule, which gives the big states an unfair advantage in the convention. New York, for instance, with a delegation of ninety, can, under the unit rule, exercise a tremendous influence and do so in spite of the protests of nearly half the delegation. If those in control have forty-six delegates of the ninety with them, they can use the other forty-four to carry out their purposes in spite of any protest that the forty-four can make. It was because the New York delegation, under the control of Mr. Murphy, was used to give Mr. Clark a majority delegation that I was not willing to help to swell the vote to two thirds. I felt that during the campaign the party would be unable to deny that Wall Street had exercised a deciding influence in the naming of our candidate. I then entered the fight to prevent not Mr. Clark's nomination only but the nomination of any person by the New York delegation.

While the demonstration was still in progress I took my seat with the Nebraska delegation and from that time until the convention adjourned never left the hall during the sessions of the convention. One of the assistants of the sergeant at arms who was stationed in our part of the hall supplied me with water, keeping a large bottle under the platform, while my brother supplied me with sandwiches. My one thought was to save the Democratic Party from defeat at the polls. I believed then, and have believed ever since, that if the nomination of our candidate was brought about in such a way that the country would regard it as a triumph for Wall Street, he would be defeated no matter who he was.

Ex-President Roosevelt, defeated at Chicago, had not yet decided whether he would enter the field. I felt sure that he would become a candidate if he could charge that Wall Street had nominated both candidates and make his appeal to the progressives of both parties and I felt sure that in such a campaign he would have been successful. I think the result proved this to be true. Mr. Roosevelt took from the Republican Party more than half its vote, polling 4,119,582 votes as against 3,485,082 votes for Mr. Taft. Mr. Taft carried but two states in the electoral college, Utah and Vermont.

As the Democratic Party was more progressive than the Republican Party, what chances would we have had to win with any candidate not free from Wall Street domination? He would have been defeated if he had had to carry in the campaign the handicap of having secured his nomination by the aid of the New York delegation dominated by one man, Charles Murphy, who had back of him the influence of the financiers of Wall Street.

My interest was not in any candidate, but in the party. I was under no personal obligation to either of the candidates. Neither one had exerted himself in my behalf in the primary at which I was chosen delegate. Mr. Wilson had never supported me in my campaigns and Mr. Clark's support, while always given to me, was given to me as thousands of Democrats give their support. Being a candidate for Congress in each of my campaigns, he could not have opposed me without injury to himself, even if he had desired to do so. While, of course, his support was not perfunctory, because he believed in the things for which I stood, still it was never given to me at a sacrifice, and I had done fully as much for him as he ever had done for me. But I digress.

The vote of our delegation was cast solidly for Clark for thirteen ballots. A number of our delegates wanted to leave him as soon as New York went to his support, but I insisted that we should continue to support him, as I expected that New York would throw its vote to Underwood and thus leave Clark to secure his nomination—if he secured it—from the progressive delegates of the convention.

I felt sure from what I had heard that New York really preferred Underwood and would leave Clark at any time its influence could aid Underwood. After the thirteenth ballot the convention adjourned until Saturday morning. Realizing that to keep the promise I had made to the Nebraska Democracy when a candidate for delegate, namely, that I would have no part in turning over the party to Wall Street, and realizing that to carry out this promise it might become necessary to change from Clark* at any moment, I prepared a written statement to be read to the convention when I changed my vote, hoping all the time that it would not be necessary.

This statement was prepared before the convention opened on Saturday morning. I had kept it in my pocket ready for use and, as a further precaution, asked Chairman James to recognize me if I asked for recognition during roll call.

When I conferred with the delegates I found a number of them in rebellion against Clark. They were afraid to risk voting for him any longer. I still pleaded with them, but when the roll was called, half or a little more voted for Wilson, but I still cast my ballot for Clark. Senator

---

* Mr. Bryan's change from Clark to Wilson was soon after endorsed by the Nebraska State Democratic Convention, showing that he was right in his interpretation of the spirit of the instructions from his constituents.

THE BALTIMORE CONVENTION

Hitchcock, who advocated instructions for Harmon in the Nebraska primary, came to me and said he would have to demand a poll of the delegation. I replied that in case a poll was taken I would take the platform and explain my vote. I was willing to continue voting for Clark if the delegation was not polled, but expecting at any time that I might be compelled to change my vote, I was not willing to announce a vote for him that I might have to take back at any time. I decided, therefore, to make the change at that time if the poll was taken. Senator Hitchcock insisted upon the poll and when my name was called I went to the platform and read the explanation of the change which I had prepared. It will be found in the Appendix.

As might have been expected, this change caused a commotion in the convention. The Clark delegates, with four ex-governors among them, sat just in front of the platform. None of them questioned me, but two other delegates, one from Mississippi and one from West Virginia, did. One asked whether I intended to support the candidate. I answered that that was a hypothetical question and that such a question was never favored in a court of law because it was difficult to put into the question all the conditions that might enter into the decision, but that I would answer his question by saying that I expected to support the nominee, whoever he was. Another asked how I could support the candidate if I was opposed to his nomination. I answered that the questioner, being a lawyer, ought to know that an attorney could defend his client after the crime was committed, but that he was not allowed to join the client in committing the crime.

Early in the afternoon Senator Stone arose in his place in the Missouri delegation. Suspecting that he intended to make some motion relating to the two thirds rule, I immediately went to the front of the platform (our delegation, while on the front row, was some distance to the left of the speaker) in order to be ready to make an objection. He asked unanimous consent to move to suspend the rules and declare Mr. Clark the nominee of the convention, basing his argument on the fact that he had received a majority of the votes cast. Some one, I think from New Jersey, objected and the roll call proceeded.

A little later in the afternoon some of the supporters of Mr. Clark brought into the convention a banner on which was reproduced a sentence that I had used in eulogizing Mr. Clark when I spoke in his district in 1910. This caused an uproar as it was carried through the aisles. It was finally brought over to our delegation and caused such a burst of feeling from some of our delegates that I feared trouble might be precipitated. I immediately returned to the platform with the intention of explaining the time and the conditions under which the words were spoken and the reasons why I did not feel that an opinion expressed then required me to support Mr. Clark under the circumstances that had developed. While Speaker James was trying to secure order I stepped down from the platform to the Missouri delegates to inquire of its leaders whether the men carrying the banner were acting under their instructions. They assured me that they were not responsible for it. Finally Chairman James, acting wisely, I think, refused to recognize me, at the same time, as I recall it, directing that the banner be removed from the hall.

This was one of the exciting moments of the convention, because it stirred up much feeling. I think in the excitement blows were exchanged in two or three instances. I know that many of my friends feared for my personal safety. The Texas delegation of forty was, I afterwards learned, ready to lend assistance in case any attack was made upon me. It was the only time in my life when I was in danger of physical harm and, therefore, the only time when my physical courage was tested, if test it could be called. The thought of danger did not occur to me as I went among those who were highly excited.

THE BALTIMORE CONVENTION

When Saturday night came the issue was still undecided. Wilson had gained enough to make Clark's nomination improbable and Clark still held enough to make the selection of Wilson uncertain.

From the time the convention met there were many delegates who favored my nomination, some under instructions for Clark and some under instructions for Wilson. I had aided in the election of many of these delegates, the anti-Harmon delegates from Ohio being under special obligation for the trip that I made through that state. One of the Ohio delegates voted for me until I asked him to refrain, pointing out that it was unfair to me to make it seem that I had only one friend in the convention when others were restrained from voting for me out of regard for my wishes. When the convention seemed to be settling down into a deadlock there were many who urged my nomination as a solution of the situation. But I felt that it was not proper for me to consider the question as long as there was any chance for any of the candidates who had been encouraged to enter by my announcement that I would not be a candidate, and I felt, too, that the action I had been compelled to take out of a sense of duty to the party had alienated some of those whose support was necessary to an election. I told all who inquired that nothing but a situation which made the whole convention regard my nomination as necessary justified my considering the nomination and that there had been no time when circumstances presented such a situation or promised it.

While hostilities were suspended during the Sabbath the messages continued to pour in from over the country and these at last crushed the opposition to Wilson and compelled his nomination.

When the convention entered upon the nomination of candidates for Vice-President a delegate from the District of Columbia presented my name for Vice-President. I had not been consulted about the matter and am not sure that the nomination was made in good faith. I did not wait to inquire or to ascertain the sentiment of the delegates. I declined to be considered, embodying my reasons in a brief speech which will be found in the Appendix. When the names were being presented I made speeches seconding the nomination of two western men, Burke of North Dakota and Chamberlain of Oregon. I had no personal objection to Governor Marshall, but his support of Judge Parker for temporary chairman, his opposition to the initiative and referendum, and his attitude toward prohibition as shown in the campaign of 1908 seemed to me to raise issues that might endanger success of the party. While his views on the initiative and referendum and prohibition had not altered, these questions did not come before him during his term as Vice-President and I have admired the manner in which he presented the Democratic side of most of the big questions at issue. He made a very popular Vice-President.

CHAPTER XI

The Grape Juice Incident

I HAVE mentioned my aversion to swearing as due to my mother's teachings, my father concurring; and of my aversion to gambling taught by my father, my mother concurring. I am indebted to both for a third moral lesson in which they joined so heartily that I am not able to emphasize the influence of either over the influence of the other. They both abstained from the use of intoxicating liquor and impressed upon me at a very early age the evils that follow from its use. Even before I had any clear understanding of the temperance question I began signing the pledge. I have no way of knowing at what age I first signed—my recollection does not run back so far— I only know that I have been signing since I can remember. I met, a few years ago, a temperance lecturer who told me that I was among the signers at his meeting when he spoke there in 1872; I was then twelve, but it had by that time become a habit with me. The formative influence of these early habits is well illustrated in this case.

My wife was brought up in the same way and the antipathy toward the use of liquor as a beverage at any time and in any form was so great that she joined me in excluding it from public dinners when I was Secretary of State as we had excluded it from our table in private life. It may be better to speak of the "Grape Juice Dinner" here than to refer to it later in recording my experiences in that office.

When President-elect Wilson invited me to Trenton I surmised the purpose of the invitation was to invite me to become a member of his Cabinet and I discussed with my wife the matter of serving liquors before meeting with the President. We were not willing to violate our custom in

187

this respect and to set such an example to others, and it was therefore understood that I should bring the matter to the attention of the President at the time in order that there might be no criticism later. After going over other matters connected with the office, I told him that there was one thing about which I felt concerned and that was whether he would regard the exclusion of intoxicating liquors from our table as an insurmountable objection to my assuming the duties of the office. He promptly responded that it was a matter upon which we could feel perfectly free to follow our own wishes. I said that we never had served it and as a matter of conscience did not wish to. The matter was never referred to again by the President in conversation with me.

Soon after I became Secretary of State we had occasion to entertain Ambassador Bryce at luncheon. In order to explain the absence of wine from the table I told him that Mrs. Bryan and I were departing from the official custom in this respect and that he was our first guest. He answered very cheerfully that he was a good person to begin on, as he did not use intoxicating liquors himself. He was preparing to leave Washington and not long after this we gave him a farewell luncheon to which all of the ambassadors were invited. Several Washington ladies were invited as luncheon companions for the ambassadors whose wives were not in the city. When Mrs. Bryan arranged the table she had a glass for grape juice, not that we thought of drawing a contrast between wine and grape juice, but because the glasses for plain and mineral water looked a little lonesome. At her suggestion, I explained to the guests very briefly the reason for our departure from the official custom, and stated that we hoped that our hospitality would be so cordial that the guests would not miss the wine. It was rather an embarrassing occasion to us, because we had no desire to emphasize our views on this subject and I felt quite relieved when the explanation was finished. To my

THE GRAPE JUICE INCIDENT

surprise, the guests applauded very heartily and we had a delightful time together. I did not mention the incident to the newspapers and it was some days before anything was said about it. When the facts were published, I was called upon for a statement, and the statement gradually found its way throughout the world.

The foreign comments were numerous and for the most part unfriendly. Some friend who had gathered a collection of these comments sent me his file. About the only friendly reference among them was from a Canadian paper which remarked that, from the criticisms made by the newspapers on the absence of wine from our table, one might suppose that the luncheon had been a bartenders' reunion.

A few months afterward when a Republican ambassador was closing up his accounts at the department before retiring from the office, he called upon me and with evident emotion thanked me for my action at the luncheon, especially referring to the harm done young men by the bad example set by the use of liquors by men in high official position.

Within two years the war had aroused so much interest in the liquor question in foreign nations that a number of the crowned heads of Europe were lining up against intoxicating drinks. Then I received my reward. The papers began to cartoon me as driving a water wagon with kings crowding each other for a seat on the vehicle.

CHAPTER XII

THE CHILDREN

WE have been fortunate in our children and grandchildren. The former are three in number, Ruth Baird, now Mrs. Reginald Owen, born October 2, 1885; William Jennings Bryan, Jr., born June 24, 1889; and Grace Dexter, now Mrs. Richard L. Hargreaves, born February 17, 1891.

Ruth came within a day of celebrating our first wedding anniversary. She was a precocious child and her parents and grandparents were kept busy expressing surprise at evidences of her early intelligence.

What a marvel a child is! It comes into the world with such perfection displayed in its mechanism, is so helpless, and yet so full of possibilities for good or for evil. It gives to one woman a sweet consciousness of motherhood and to one man a sense of responsibility otherwise never known before. Before its tiny hands can lift a featherweight, it has drawn two hearts closer together; its innocent prattle echoes through two lives and its influence upon its parents is almost as moulding as their influence upon it.

I think my wife never before looked so sweet as she did when she brought Ruth downstairs for the first time. The wrapper which she wore that day was long and flowing and she made me think of a Madonna. In fact, seeing a copy of Bodenhausen's painting of the Madonna a few weeks afterwards in an art gallery in Kansas City—the Madonna arrayed in a gown of almost the same tint as the gown my wife had worn—so impressed me by the resemblance that I took the picture home with me. It hung upon our walls until our son was married and desired to have it for his own home.

One of the distinct recollections of Ruth's babyhood was

the time when she was old enough to distinguish the different members of the family. Mrs. Bryan's father and I would often be sitting near the mother when the baby was being washed and dressed. When her night garments were removed she would hand them sometimes to the father and sometimes to the grandfather. It was an anxious moment when we were in suspense while she decided to which she would hand the garment. She was quite impartial, bestowing the favor on first one, then the other as if she thought favoritism to one might hurt the feelings of the other.

Ruth, when about three years old, delivered a prayer which we have always remembered as illustrating at that early age a keen sense of discrimination, as well as indicating a positive opinion. It was in the fall of 1888 and I was away from home campaigning. When it came time to go to bed she was irritated about some happening of the day and refused to say her usual prayer, which began, "Now I lay me down to sleep," and ended with, "God bless Papa, Mamma, Grandma, Grandpa, and all of Grandma Bryan's folks, Amen." Her mother tried persuasion along several lines, but in vain. Finally, thinking to appeal to her affections, she said, "Poor Papa is away on the train and might get hurt and his little girl will not say any prayer for him." This touched Ruth's heart. She went over to the bed, knelt down and said, "Dear Lord, take care of Papa—not Mamma nor Grandma nor anybody else, just Papa. Amen." It reminded me of Lincoln's letter to Horace Greeley in which he so specifically expressed his intentions and carefully negatived everything else.

Ruth early gave evidence of literary ability. She wrote stories which showed imagination. One day when eight or nine years old she came to her mother and asked whether it would be better to have the hero save the heroine from a fire or from drowning. Mrs. Bryan expressed a preference for a rescue from fire. In a little while Ruth had her story completed with a thrilling description of the rescue of a girl from a burning building.

It was about this time that she revealed her ambition and, at the same time, her doubts as to whether she would realize it. She was confined to her bed by an attack of measles. One morning when I took her breakfast to her room and sat by her while she ate it, I said, "Ruth, what would you like to do when you are grown?" She answered spiritedly, "I would like to write stories and books"—and then she added in a melancholy tone, "But I expect I'll get married and raise a family, like Mamma and Mrs. Schwind."

It was during this period, also, that she returned from the Sunday school one day very much disgusted and threatened not to go any more, giving as her excuse, "They don't teach righteousness; they just teach geography."

I may add here that Ruth always showed a discretion rather unusual for her years. In the campaign of 1896 when she was eleven she was, of course, often questioned by strangers. One day a man stopped her in the street and asked her whether she thought her father would be elected. She replied, "I think he will get a good many votes on D Street" (the street on which we lived), "but I do not know about the rest of the country."

After nine years in the Nebraska public school, two years at Monticello Seminary (Illinois), and two years in the State University of Nebraska, came Ruth's marriage the day following her eighteenth birthday anniversary, October 3, 1903. She had a son and a daughter by this first marriage.

In the autumn of 1907 she made her first venture on the lecture platform, filling engagements for the Extension Department of the State University of Nebraska and under other auspices.

Her second marriage occurred on the third of May, 1910. Reginald Altham Owen was a lieutenant in the Royal Engineers of the British Army at the time of their marriage.

192

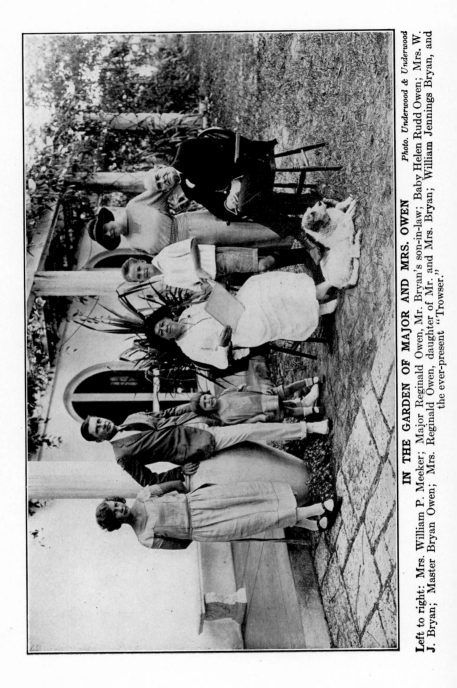

IN THE GARDEN OF MAJOR AND MRS. OWEN

Photo. *Underwood & Underwood*

Left to right: Mrs. William P. Meeker; Major Reginald Owen, Mr. Bryan's son-in-law; Baby Helen Rudd Owen; Mrs. W. J. Bryan; Master Bryan Owen; Mrs. Reginald Owen, daughter of Mr. and Mrs. Bryan; William Jennings Bryan, and the ever-present "Trowser."

THE CHILDREN

He served with distinction in the World War, throughout the entire Dardanelles Campaign and the three years of the Egypt and Palestine campaign. His health was so seriously impaired by his war service that he was retired from the service in 1924 after prolonged sick leave.

Major and Mrs. Owen's home since the conclusion of the war has been in Miami, Florida.

Ruth has during the past five years extended her lecture tours and achieved considerable success to which she has added some prominence in literary work. Her daughter Ruth, who was born September 28, 1904, grew from a bright child to a very attractive young woman. She was married June 20, 1923, to William Painter Meeker, of Baltimore, Maryland, and Miami, Florida, only son of our nearest neighbors in Miami. Their daughter Ruth, born June 30, 1924, is our only and much beloved great-grandchild.

Mrs. Owen's son, John Baird Bryan, was born November 16, 1905. He was a most interesting child and has developed talent for art and poetry, which he is disposed to cultivate. The two younger children of Major and Mrs. Owen are not yet old enough to give indication of their natural bent. Reginald Bryan, who was born in London April 14, 1913, gives evidence of a strong will, a quality of great value when well directed. Helen Rudd, born August 3, 1920, is a very precocious child with unusual poise and self-reliance.

William, our only son, was born on June 24, 1889. He was what is called "a regular fellow." He was one hundred per cent boy—never bad, but always mischievous. He could get into dirt more quickly after he was sent out washed and cleanly dressed, and into more different kinds of dirt than any boy I have ever known. This may be because I was never as well acquainted with another boy.

When Ruth was a baby she was a little thin—at least, not fat. William was quite a fat baby. Mrs. Bryan says that when Ruth was a child and rather thin I expressed a preference for thin children; but that when William came I thought he was just fat enough to look well.

Mrs. Bryan took care of the children herself. As the care of the children increased she turned over more of the domestic work to others in order that she might have entire charge of the children. She put them to bed and read to them until they went to sleep. Often after she had cleansed William of the dirt stains of the day and read him to sleep, she would lead me to the room that I might admire our young hopeful, exclaiming as she looked upon him with loving eyes, "Isn't he sweet when he is asleep?"

How a boy ever lives through the accidents of childhood is a mystery. William fell down the stairway and was insensible for several hours, but he was soon over it and ready to take another risk. One day his mother was badly frightened when she looked out and saw him working his way along the telephone wires some distance from the house. When we took him out with us on visits to friends, the conversation was often interrupted by a cry of alarm, some member of the family finding William up on the roof or in some other place of danger.

He had reached the age of eleven by the time of the second campaign in 1900. By that time he had become an excellent swimmer. I might add that Mrs. Bryan had taken upon herself the task of teaching all the children how to swim. Like all swimmers, he was fond of diving. During a few days' stay in Chicago the newspaper men, who take such an interest in every member of the family of the candidate, discovered his fondness for the water and gave a good deal of attention to his accomplishments, not diminishing in the least the sensational features. At one time he was described as hanging out of an upper window of a tall building and being rescued by General Wheeler.

A few years ago I discovered a photograph of William at this busy age. I had it framed and put on his mother's desk as a reminder of the anxiety she cheerfully endured during the superactive years of William's youth.

William was nearly seven at the time of the death of Mrs. Bryan's mother. His affection manifested itself in a bit of consolation that we have often looked back to with amusement. He went up to his mother when she was weeping and, putting his arms around her neck, said, "Mamma, when you feel sad, just think of me."

At another time when he was just recovering from a punishment for some misdemeanor, he sobbed out a warning to his mother, "If I died in the night, you would not feel so gay."

Like Ruth, he was studious enough to pass his examinations, but was not at the head of the class. I had hoped that he would early manifest an interest in public speaking as I had, but instead of showing an unusual interest in it, he manifested an aversion to speaking. Mrs. Bryan went over one day to the school to hear him speak a piece. When the teacher called on him to do his part, he sank down into his chair and clutched its arms. After his mother had waited for a few moments for her son to immortalize himself as a speaker, the teacher gave up in despair and said, "William will speak *next* Friday."

I was somewhat surprised, therefore, when my wife read me a letter from the superintendent of Culver Military School which he was attending, stating that William was studying public speaking. A few months afterwards, I met the great evangelist, Rev. J. Wilbur Chapman, and he told me that his son and mine were in the same elocution class; adding that he had promised his boy fifty dollars if he would surpass William in speaking. His boy replied that that was impossible, that not one of the boys could do better. This was the beginning of his efforts to express himself "on his feet." I found afterwards as I read his speeches and heard them that he had an analytical mind, logical arrangement of his arguments, persuasive delivery, and a sense of humor that enabled him to enliven his addresses.

Owing to the fact that his betrothed, Miss Helen Berger, with whom he fell in love when he was quite young and to whom he had been engaged for some years, found it necessary on account of her health to reside in Arizona, he was married before he finished school and continued his studies at the University of Arizona at Tucson, where he graduated. He afterwards became regent of the University by appointment by Governor Hunt and reappointed by Governor Campbell.

I was very much pleased to learn that he was made director of the Y.M.C.A. and a member of the Democratic Committee of Tucson the same week. I accepted it as an indication that he was interested in the two lines of work, religion and politics, which not only do not conflict but are entirely consistent.

After graduating he studied law at Georgetown Law School. He was elected president of his class, but in a few months he was compelled to return to Arizona on account of his wife's health and he resumed his law study there. After his admission to the bar he became assistant to the United States Attorney under United States Attorney John Flynn.

William was married in June 24, 1909, to Helen Virginia Berger, of Milwaukee, Wisconsin. They have three children —all daughters: Mary Scholes, born April 7, 1910, Helen Virginia, born August 13, 1911, and Elizabeth Baird, born December 31, 1914. They are as charming a trio as one could find, but three distinct types.

In 1920 William and his family removed to Los Angeles, California, which is their present residence.

[PUBLISHERS' NOTE. In publishing these unfinished Memoirs of Mr. Bryan, we are sure that no omission would

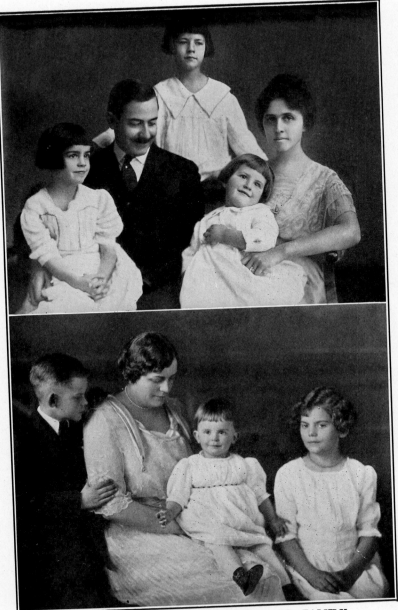

WILLIAM JENNINGS BRYAN, JR., AND FAMILY
Left to right: Helen, William Jennings Bryan, Jr., Mary, "Betty," and
Mrs. Bryan.
ANOTHER FAMILY GROUP
The younger daughter of Mr. and Mrs. Bryan, Mrs. Richard L. Hargreaves,
with her children, Bryan, Margaret, and Evelyn Mary Hargreaves.

THE CHILDREN

fill him with more regret than his failure to complete the chapter which tells of his children.

He was called from this task before he had written of his younger and much loved daughter Grace Dexter (Mrs. Richard L. Hargreaves of Berkeley Hills, California).

Herself born in the midst of a political campaign, Mrs. Hargreaves has always been deeply interested in politics. As a child she took part in all the children's parades with great zest and in later years followed her father's political work with keen interest and sympathy.

During Mr. Bryan's second term in Congress she was critically ill with pneumonia, which left her in a very weakened condition. She became a great anxiety to her parents, and several years of special care and sojourn in warm climates was required to restore her to strength.

She was educated at home by a governess and afterwards in the Lincoln, Nebraska, schools, and at Hollins Institute (Virginia).

She was married in June 7, 1911, to Richard Lewis Hargreaves, of Lincoln, Nebraska, and to them three children have been born: Margaret, born March 3, 1914; Bryan, born September 7, 1915; and Evelyn Mary, born October 16, 1920, the latter being the tenth and youngest of Mr. Bryan's grandchildren.]

CHAPTER XIII

FRIENDSHIPS

SO much is flippantly told about the fair-weather friends in politics who flock about the successful candidate and then desert him in times of trial, that I shall take this opportunity to record a few instances of heroes who came under my personal observation. I omit the names out of consideration for those who had been personally connected with the incidents and who may not regard them in the same spirit in which I regard them.

First I mention a Congressman and one of the Ways and Means Committee. He had retired from Congress in 1896 and resumed charge of a large mercantile business in the town in which he resided. He was an advocate of bimetallism when in Congress and took a large interest in my first Presidential campaign. He was one of the well-to-do men of his city and a director in the bank in which he kept his store account. Like most merchants, he enjoyed a credit in the bank and borrowed money from time to time to discount his bills.

In the midst of the campaign he was called before the directors of his own bank and informed that his interest in me was injuring the bank and then he was told that his notes could not be carried any longer if he continued to support my candidacy. He was put to a test to which I have never been subjected. There has never been a time since I was grown when my bread and butter depended upon the will or favor of any other person, and therefore never a time when I incurred any financial risk in exercising political independence. It was not so with the friend of whom I am speaking. He knew that he could not at that time secure loans elsewhere if the bank of which he was a director refused to accommodate him, but he did not hesitate for a moment.

198

He replied, "Gentlemen, you can bankrupt me, but you cannot take from me my right to vote as I please."

Of course, the directors dared not carry out their threat, but their bluff gave one friend a chance to show the mettle that was in him. Until he was called to his reward, I counted him as one of the inner circle of my friends.

Another illustration is taken from among my New York friends. I appreciate them the more because the coercion was there at its maximum and the support to be found in companionship at its minimum. As far back as 1893, the campaign of 1896 cast its shadow before it. I spoke at Cooper Union in the fall of that year, my subject being the unconditional repeal of the Sherman Law then before Congress. The hall was crowded and I learned a few days afterward the following incident relating to a man then and since prominent in the business world.

Not being able to find a seat, he was standing in the aisle near the door when an acquaintance on the platform spied him and invited him to a seat. A place on the platform did not necessarily indicate sympathy with the speaker, but one of the papers next morning gave a list of those on the platform and included the gentleman of whom I am speaking. I was about to say friend, but at the time of the incident I was not personally acquainted with him.

Upon reading the list this gentleman's banker sent for him and called his attention to the fact that he had been mentioned among those who sat on the platform. He explained the situation, assuring the banker that he was not there by pre-arrangement or for the purpose of being counted among those specially interested, but the explanation did not satisfy the banker and he notified this gentleman that they could not carry loans for those who gave the weight of their names to so disreputable a cause and insisted that he immediately pay a note of $25,000 which the bank held against him. Fortunately, he was able to do so without embarrassment and immediately complied with the request.

WILLIAM JENNINGS BRYAN

It is needless to say that the demand made a deep impression upon him and that that impression was not favorable to the bankers' side of the question. During the campaign of 1896 he took a prominent part, and Mrs. Bryan and I had the pleasure of being guests later in his beautiful home on the Hudson. From that time to this his sympathies have been with the masses on all the economic questions that have arisen.

A Massachusetts friend reported to me an experience through which he passed in the campaign of 1896. He was engaged in manufacturing upon a considerable scale and carried a credit of some $20,000 or more at his local bank. In the campaign of 1896 he was a Democrat and outspoken though not active in the support of the ticket. His banker sent for him and asked him whether he was supporting my candidacy. He answered that he expected to vote for me, but was not active beyond that. The banker informed him that they could not lend financial aid to those who were opposing the bank's policy and asked him to take up his notes. This he did and then went out and spoke for me during the rest of the campaign. He, too, has ever since that time continued his political activity.

A New York lawyer who had been a delegate to the Chicago Convention returned to the metropolis and entered the campaign. He was one of the delegates who had refused to join the New York financiers in support of the gold ticket. He was attorney for a bank, and the bank on reading of his attitude sent for him, withdrew all its cases from him and asked him to change his deposit to another bank. He complied with the request, opened his account in a bank not so illiberal in its politics and took an active part in the campaign until it closed.

This is the only case I know of where a bank compelled a depositor to withdraw his account. After the election was over the bank sent for the attorney, asked that the unpleasantness be forgotten and reëmployed him. In New Jersey he afterward became a member of Congress and became quite conspicuous in public life.

I have a very delightful recollection of a conductor on one of the railroads running into Lincoln. "Pat" was the name by which he was known and it was spoken with affection by the multitude who knew him as a man of character—the kind of man who attaches his friends to him by hooks of steel. I became acquainted with Pat in my early trips through the first district even before I became a candidate for Congress. I had no more ardent supporter than he in my races for Congress and for the Senate.

In 1896, when so much pressure was brought by corporations upon their employees, Pat was called into the office and informed that the railroad was strongly in favor of Mr. McKinley's election and that they would expect him to give the benefit of his influence.

Did they intimidate him? Not for a moment. He replied: "Your salary pays for my services as conductor, but it does not include my citizenship. That is my own. I vote as I please." Pat continued to be a Democrat and he also continued to be a conductor.

In my own city one of the banks required a business man to agree to support the Republican candidate in order to continue a loan at the bank. He told of the instance himself. Upon my return from a trip around the world a dinner was given me. This merchant, whom we had known from the time I moved to Lincoln, asked whether he could secure a ticket, adding: "I have voted for Mr. Bryan at every election except one. I voted for him for Congress twice and for the Senate and would have voted for him in 1896 but for the fact that I owed a large amount to the —— bank. Just before the election Mr. ——, the president of the bank, refused to extend the loan unless I would agree to vote for McKinley. It would have meant bankruptcy if I had refused and so I promised to vote for McKinley and, having promised, I did so, but by 1900 I had so far reduced my indebtedness that I was independent and I voted for Mr. Bryan that year."

Shortly after the election I met on the train Mr. Yost, an Omaha business man who was president of the Lincoln Telephone Company. Introducing the subject himself, he said, "I have a friend of yours working for me at Lincoln."

Guessing whom he had in mind, I said, "Do you mean Mr. ——?"

"Yes," he replied. "I went down to Lincoln just before the election and told him that we were very much interested in Mr. McKinley's election and hoped he would do what he could to help him. He said, 'Mr. Yost, your company has been very good to me and I do not want to do anything that would injure it. If you think that my support of Mr. Bryan will hurt your company, I will resign.' After hearing his answer, what do you think I told him?"

"What?" I asked.

"I told him that if he did not vote for you we would discharge him."

I have often recalled this incident because it illustrates an important truth, namely, that a frank and firm defense of one's political rights is much better at all times than an evasion of the subject or the practice of deception.

In recording my political experiences I dwell with greatest pleasure upon the friendships formed in early years. I was in no position to reward men for what they did for me, so that their acts of kindness were wholly unselfish and were prompted by a devotion which I have come to regard as the most beautiful thing in American politics. We are too prone to explain service as selfish and kind acts as prompted by a hope of reward. The prevailing opinion of political support has been put into poetry in the description of those who "crook the pregnant hinges of the knee, where thrift may follow fawning." This may be an accurate description of some self-seeking politicians, but it is a slander upon the

FRIENDSHIPS

virtuous masses to suggest that what they do is done from
other than the noblest spirit.

When George Hopkins, of Nemaha County, Nebraska,
wins a place in my memory by taking me in a sulky some
thirteen miles from Peru to Auburn after a night meeting
and then appears regularly at every meeting held in this
county for a quarter of a century and gives weeks of time
to campaigning for me no matter to what office I aspire,
it can only be accounted for by similarity of political ideals
which made him feel that my campaigns were really his
campaigns also.

When Will Glenn, of Knox County, takes me in a buggy
fifty miles in a single day and night and puts me on a departing train a little before daybreak, it is proof of his heart
interest in the issue at stake.

When a farmer in the center of the state gets out of bed
in the middle of the night when we have lost our way, rides
ten miles before us, and then when we come in sight of the
lights of our destination, turns back, refusing compensation
with the remark, spoken in a tone that indicated that even
the offer hurt his feelings: "Do you think I would do this
for money? I am a Bryan man," one catches something of
the sentiment upon which campaigns are built and can
better understand how it is possible for millions of people
to coöperate without organization but actuated by a common
impulse.

These incidents could be continued indefinitely; there
has never been a time when in Nebraska or somewhere else
in the United States I have not had occasion to be proud of
the average man and his influence in politics. The names of
the humble heroes in political battles of the United States
is legion. Their names are unrecorded, but those whom
they so faithfully support receive the glory. I cannot forget
these soldiers upon whom the brunt of the battle falls.

As I look back over the years I see the face of one of the
most loyal friends that any political leader ever had. His

name was John Ahern, a big, brawny Irishman. He was nearly, if not quite, six feet four inches in height and broad in proportion. His face was round and no beard concealed the friendliness that beamed from every feature. I met him in 1888 when I made my first trip to Richardson County, Nebraska. He lived some twenty miles from Fall City, the county seat. Partly because his size made him a conspicious figure in the crowd and partly because of the devotion which he manifested, I came to look for him in the crowd whenever I spoke in his county. And I do not recall a meeting that he did not attend.

One night I went home with him and stayed all night. It is a rare treat to drop in upon one of these country friends, a treat in which I indulge myself whenever opportunity offers, but the opportunities have been all too few. Time and again at Chautauquas as I have looked into the faces of the old men for whom the front seats are generally reserved, I have picked out one of these American sovereigns, a well-informed voter whom an army could not terrorize and whom the federal treasury could not buy, and regretted that on account of the briefness of my stay I could not step up to him and say, "May I go and spend the night with you?" These are the common people, the people to whom the Bible pays the highest compliment it ever pays to any class when it says that the common people heard Christ gladly. It is by communion with such as these that one is assured of the impregnable strength of the nation and it is from such as these that one can learn the drift of the public sentiment and best predict with certainty the things to be.

But to return to Ahern. In the fall of 1894, when I was a candidate for the United States Senate, I made my usual trip to Richardson County and spoke to a great meeting in Fall City. When the crowd had dispersed Uncle John, as he was familiarly called, came up to encourage me by a grasp of his large warm hand and went with me to the hotel not far distant. We sat down and talked a little while about the political prospects and then prepared to start out to his country home. He hesitated for a moment and then, taking me by the arm, led me out of the hotel office and into the broad hallway to the farthest corner. Speaking in an undertone, he said:

"If we carry the legislature"—this was in 1888 before the popular election of senators—"I will come to Lincoln during the session. I do not know that I can do any good, but there may be some member whom I can influence.

"And then," lowering his voice, "if we can get you into the Senate you can take care of yourself."

I do not recall a more fatherly expression that that of this dear friend. He had done all he could for me in two Congressional campaigns and now he had a chance to aid in an election, which, if successful, would give me a six-year term in the Senate, and he felt that two terms in Congress and a term in the Senate ought to put me on such secure ground that I would be assured a permanent place in public life.

Sixteen years later, in 1910—sixteen years during which his unwavering devotion had expressed itself in three Presidential campaigns—the question of prohibition became an issue in Nebraska. I came out in support of county option, as is recorded in another chapter. Mr. Ahern was not only not a prohibitionist but he lacked something of being a teetotaler. I never saw him under the influence of liquor, but he drank with some regularity and possibly, when political excitement ran high, with some freedom. The newspapers soon reported my activity on the side of county option and one of the Democrats of Richardson County brought the matter to the attention of Ahern. The conversation was reported to me as follows:

"Uncle John, have you heard that Billy has come out for county option?"

"No," Uncle John answered in surprise.

"Well, he has," said his informant.

WILLIAM JENNINGS BRYAN

"Is that so?" replied Uncle John.

"What do you think of Billy now?" continued his informant.

"I am for him, wet or dry," responded my Irish friend. And he was.

Little differences like that did not disturb his friendship; it was built upon a more solid foundation.

A few years after this Mr. Ahern passed away, as I learned during a visit in Nebraska. By this time the demands of national politics kept me away from my home state most of the time. The only offset to the pleasure that comes from a large circle of friends is the frequency with which one is called upon to mourn when "from love's shining circle the gems drop away."

In 1916 the question of state prohibition became the dominant issue in Nebraska and I made a tour of the state in support of that movement. In the course of my travels I spoke at Shubert, the nearest Richardson County town to Mr. Ahern's farm. I spoke from an auto and told the group of listeners that I was more interested in prohibition than I ever was in my own candidacy and needed their support more than I had needed it in previous campaigns. When my speech was finished four men filed up to the auto, all over six feet in height, and informed me that they were sons of John Ahern. I greeted them as cordially as I had their father, and after telling them how much I missed his presence, asked them if they were with me in my fight for prohibition. They all answered very positively in the affirmative. I was greatly pleased to find that the sons had inherited from their father the friendship that had so long existed between the elder Ahern and myself.

My last campaign in Nebraska was made in the spring of 1920 when I was a candidate for delegate for Nebraska to the convention at San Francisco. In my tour from my old first district I passed Ahern's home and detoured a mile or so to visit the family. In a very few minutes the boys had come in from the field, and the children, including the oldest daughter, who was a cripple, assured me that they would be on hand to help make me a delegate.

Possibly the reader, if he has never been in politics, may feel that I have devoted too much space to one of my million and a half political friends, but I single him out as illustrative of a very large number from whom I have received so many manifestations of confidence and affection. It is to such as these that I owe the political opportunities which have come to me, opportunities without which it would have been impossible for me to be identified in a large way with great national problems—opportunities by the improvement of which I have been able to accomplish whatever may be placed to my account in the final reckoning.

Another friend lived in Dawson, in the same county, Richardson. He gave touching evidence of his devotion. Jerry Fenton was my friend and supporter from the time I entered politics in Nebraska until he died. During my Congressional campaigns my picture was used, as is customary, in the advertisement of meetings, and either in this way or by direct request Mr. Fenton secured my likeness and had it hung on the wall of his bedroom. My trip around the world was commenced in the fall of 1905, fifteen years after my first race for Congress. Mr. Fenton had supported me, therefore, in two Congressional campaigns, one senatorial and two Presidential campaigns. He, too, was always present at my meetings and was an influential factor in our party. When I returned in 1906 his family physician told me of an incident that I have remembered as one of the sweetest expressions of that affection which is not infrequent in political life. During my absence abroad I kept in touch with intimate friends through my paper, the *Commoner*, which published altogether more than forty letters written in various countries that I visited. While I was away Mr. Fenton fell ill, so ill that at times his life was despaired of. On one occasion he had a sinking spell which it was feared would speedily end in his death. After his priest had called and administered the sacraments of the Church, the patient, sustained by his faith, calmly awaited the end. During this period of suspense, while the members of the family stood by in helpless anxiety, Mr. Fenton called the doctor to the bedside and whispered to him, pointing to the wall, "When Mr. Bryan gets back tell him that his picture was before me to the last." One incident of such devotion outweighs a multitude of cruel and unjust criticisms.

PART II

AN EARLY PORTRAIT OF MRS. BRYAN

INTRODUCTION

MR. BRYAN'S time was so interrupted that further work was impossible. His records reach to his college days. I knew him first as a college boy, so it seems appropriate for me to begin at that point and carry on the story as I may.

I undertake this work with strong purpose. I certainly know my subject and have a hope that I may be able to write a book which people will like to read; a book which will show the more personal side of his life; a book by which his career may be interpreted.

CHAPTER I

A Picture of the Times

THOUGH a young civilization is freed from the burden of custom and of precedent, an older community has the advantage which comes of permanence. A man born in a stabilized environment has a well-defined background which may be traced with clearness and accuracy. Stratford-on-Avon still gives a setting for Shakespeare. The Scottish Highlands revive again the poems and personality of Burns. One sees from the bridge of the Arno the dim figures of Beatrice and Dante. London jealously guards streets and buildings where lurk the shades of Chaucer, Johnson, Dickens, and a long procession of statesmen and scholars.

In the older part of America time has given in a less degree some permanence of background. Our New England States have not a few spots hallowed by memories of our early scholars, and near the old North Church one can almost hear again the hoof-beats of the ride of Paul Revere.

In the newer part of our country such conditions do not obtain. Landmarks of fifty years ago are gone. The trail of the pioneer has given place to paved highways; the log-built home has vanished to be replaced by structures of steel and cement; the time of Lincoln can no longer be read in the context (if one may use that expression) and the student must reconstruct the environment by research. Even to one born sixty-five years ago in the Middle West, the background grows dim, for almost within the life of a generation a vast region has been completely changed.

When my grandfather, Colonel Darius Dexter, and his two brothers, left the village of Dexterville, now a suburb of Jamestown, New York, for the great West in 1838, they built a sort of raft boat, and with their families and household goods, voyaged up the Great Lakes and down Lake Michigan to the present site of Chicago. Mother, then a child of ten, has told me that only a warehouse, standing on piles above the swamp, and three or four small houses, foreshadowed the presence of an immense city. The fertile plains of central Illinois enticed my grandfather, and thither he went and here he lived and died. My paternal grandfather, coming with his children the following year from near Easton, Pennsylvania—where the first of his family had settled in 1628—located in the same community.

This chapter is not intended to produce for inspection a leaf from my family tree, and I only mention this early migration to prove that I am not unfamiliar with the development of the West.

Illinois, assuming the responsibilities of statehood in 1818, held within her wide plains a wealth as great as any gold mine; a soil of such depth and richness that it seems inexhaustible, and fortunate are they whose ancestors bought and kept these acres.

While Illinois was receiving many settlers, and little towns began to dot the watercourses, railroads were not numerous, and the stage coach was the usual means of travel.

As I was born in 1861, my very early recollections may help to place the times. My father, second generation from the pioneer in Illinois, did a general merchandise and commission business, which, at its height, included dry goods, groceries, china and glassware, cooking utensils, boots and shoes, farming implements, hardware, a harness shop, and a millinery store filled with wonderful bonnets. I recall snow-covered ground, horses with frost-encircled nostrils and steaming coats, dragging creaking sleds, on which were piled high the neatly scraped and stiffly frozen carcasses of hogs. These were brought by the farmers to my father's pork house. We did not know about packing plants in those days, and the Swifts and Armours had not yet shown the inefficiency and wastefulness of the small concern. In this long, low building the bricklayers, carpenters, and others of the community who could not carry on their work in cold weather, found winter employment. Here the hogs were prepared for the city market. Lard was rendered in two huge kettles, side meat was salted, pickled pork, sausage, and other by-products were made ready, and once or twice I peered into the door of a brick building—mysterious and awesome—where I dimly saw long rows of hams hanging from the rafters and taking color from the smoke of hickory wood smouldering in heaps upon the earthen floor. I recall long rows of wagons loaded with these finished products and with many sacks of wheat, slowly rumbling along to the Illinois River, eight miles distant. The stern-wheel river steamer, into which this produce was loaded, chugged away down the Illinois and into the Mississippi, until it reached St. Louis, even then a city of importance. Along the river banks stretched the levees, paved with rough stone, where rows of steamers docked. There were no cranes or derricks in those days and the produce was unloaded by negro deckhands, droning their monotonous songs, and hurrying up and down the gangplanks like busy ants. The wholesale produce houses faced the river at that time and there was no great river bridge.

Belonging to this period, though perhaps five or six years earlier, is a story my father told me of the campaign methods of Douglas. During the famous Lincoln-Douglas debates, so I was told, whenever the stage coach stopped to change horses or to take on or deliver mail, Douglas would descend with his pipe filled and beg a coal to light his tobacco. This opened the way for friendly chat and banter. When he took his place again, the coal and tobacco were thrown away and the pipe returned to his pocket, where it rested until the next station was reached, when it was refilled and the request repeated. This was one of our family stories, and often when Mr. Bryan and I were driving, I have said: "Why are you stopping here? Are you going to light your pipe?" And he would reply, "Yes, I believe I'll look in and see if he has a coal."

While the Mississippi Valley States were growing steadily in population and in everything which makes for comfortable living, the farther West was untouched. Illinois was admitted to statehood in 1818; Iowa in 1846; while the next state in line, Nebraska, did not gain this distinction until 1867, a half century between Illinois and Nebraska. The act which constituted Nebraska a distinct territory and which opened her lands to settlement, was passed in 1854, but in 1861 there were less than 30,000 people in the state.

The natural barrier was the Missouri River; on the eastern bank a busy population and on the western bank the Indian and the buffalo, with here and there a trail winding toward the Western coast.

It may seem unnecessary to remind Americans of the fact that the West was peopled by the East. Immigrants, when settling in colonies, have made here and there spots of foreign influence, but for the most part the foreign element sank into the life of communities already organized and controlled by our own citizens. Not only was the West peopled by the East, but in this migration the East lost many of her best citizens. Men of energy, of education, of broad outlook, saw the possibilities in the West and joined the ranks of those who were bent upon the task of subduing a new land.

With men of vision and of education in the lead, the young civilization did not neglect the founding of churches and schools. Illinois College was the first to be established in that state, followed soon by other colleges, by state universities and young ladies' boarding schools. In Lincoln, Nebraska, almost the first act of the new capital was the founding of the State University, which has grown to be a great educational center. From the beginning the West was not only developing the material resources of the country, but was looking to the intellectual and spiritual development of her citizens. While I bore no conspicuous part, I count myself fortunate to have been born in the Mississippi Valley, and regard as a privilege my small part in this wonderful development, which has sometimes been called the "heart of our government."

I have spoken chiefly of Illinois and Nebraska, the two states which I know best, but which I hope may be regarded as typical.

The economic and political conditions surrounding western people in approximately the year 1860 may be briefly summarized in the words "unrest and discontent," with the question of debt underneath. The West was in debt and in debt to the East. The money had been used to improve their land and they were depending upon an increase in land values, upon good prices for their products and upon sufficient loanable capital to meet their obligations. None of these were forthcoming. Money grew "tight"; the farmers could not pay their interest; failures were frequent, and everyone was searching for a panacea.

The Civil War had brought industrial problems and the age-long question of the relations between capital and labor was stirring in the public mind. The railroads were at once a blessing and a curse to this generation, and were so important to the development of the country that anxious-eyed settlers were eager to have the roads upon any terms. This was particularly true of the more Western states where watercourses are fewer and where distances are so tremendous that transportation seemed impossible without the aid of the iron horse.

In this environment a dark-eyed little boy opened his eyes upon the world March 19, 1860. The political problems which existed in the United States thirty years later when, in 1890, William Jennings Bryan stood for Congress in Nebraska, are worthy of attention.

To even a casual reader of history, it is evident that conditions had not improved. The whole country had felt the stringency of money conditions, and a movement was in evidence which showed that the average citizen had less confidence in the masters of finance and was inclined to seek his own remedies. This independence took the form in the New England States of the Grange with its demand for the issuance of greenbacks by the Federal Government as opposed to paper money issued by the banks. In the West this independence was shown in the formation of the Farmers' Alliance and the Populist Party, both of which were recruited from progressive Republican ranks.

The Populist Party, while not often in office, held the balance of power in Nebraska for many years. This period, too, witnessed great activity in the development of natural resources. The achievements of American railroad builders, promoters, miners, traders, manufacturers, and financiers between 1864 and 1890 exceeded their work of the whole preceding century—another evidence of restlessness. The cotton mills of New England were disturbed by the awakening of the South. The Southern states had reached the very sensible conclusion that it was better to build mills where the cotton grows than to send it to New England. One could hear at every crossroad discussions on monopolies and combinations in restraint of trade because of the aggressions of the trusts, and the expression "tainted money" as applied to church contributions, came into common use.

Chief among the elements of discontent was the bitterness the people felt toward the railroads. It is difficult to justify the tremendous concessions given to the railroads in the Western states. I quote briefly from "The Menace of Privilege," by Henry George, Jr.:

"Besides a continuous strip of land from one to four hundred feet wide for a right of way, with additional land for sidings, stations, yards and the like, the Federal

A PICTURE OF THE TIMES

Government granted all alternate sections (a section is a square mile in United States land measurement) in a belt of land a number of miles in width running on each side of the right-of-way strip. The grant to the Southern Pacific, for instance, consisted of a belt of land 60 miles wide in California, and 100 miles wide in the Territories (now States). The grant to the Northern Pacific consisted of alternate sections in a belt of land 120 miles wide, running from the western boundary of Minnesota to Puget Sound and the Columbia River

"Besides land, the Federal, State, and municipal governments made enormous grants of money and bonds for the stimulation of railroad building, mainly in the West. The five Pacific roads received from the Federal Government alone United States bonds amounting to $64,000,000."

The settler, who had been most anxious to secure the building of a railroad, found he had invited in a relentless and apparently unmanageable power. The railroads sometimes ran the track far enough away from the old town to ruin it—the old town representing so much hard work and sacrifice on the part of the settler. The railroad selected a site and laid out the new town, having sold the lots beforehand to Eastern investors who were willing to resell these lots to the community at a neat profit. The original town had to be abandoned. As we who lived in the North never quite understood what the people suffered under "The March of General Sherman to the Sea," so the individual in the East cannot realize what was endured by the individual in the West during this period. Such incidents as these were not infrequent.

Grain elevators for the storage of wheat would be erected at intervals along the track by men who were secretly in league with the railroad officials. The farmer cut and threshed his wheat which he planned to ship. He found the freight rates had gone up and he could not afford to ship. He could not afford to hold the wheat; he had no place to store it; he needed money. At this point the owner of the elevator made an offer, lower than it should have been, but which, under the circumstances, the farmer could not refuse. The wheat was bought by the elevator man and stored in the elevator. This process was repeated until the elevator held all the wheat of that community. A little later the freight rates suddenly came down; the wheat was shipped, and the elevator man and the railroad officials shared the profits, while the inhabitants stood by in impotent rage.

I can add here a personal experience. When we went round the world, we sent back from Japan some heavy freight, a stone lantern, some bronze lions, etc. The goods were billed to Kansas City, and when we paid the account, our enterprising railroad had charged us considerably more to bring the boxes from Kansas City to Lincoln, Nebraska, then we paid from Yokohama, Japan, to Kansas City.

It is not surprising that the West urged railroad regulation.

There was, too, a frequent source of anger in the "long and short haul," that delicate bit of railroad mechanism the functioning of which was past understanding. People would see their coal hauled through their own town to a town beyond them. They would have to pay freight charges to the distant point and then back again to their own place. One town (usually the one owned by the railroads) was built up, and another ruined through discrimination in freight rates.

In this connection I might add that in 1910 Mr. Bryan advocated an enlargement of the powers of the Interstate Commerce Commission. This was the only body which was authorized to cope with the "long and short haul." In spite of tremendous opposition and outcry, the powers of the Commission were enlarged and the "long and short haul" is now more staid in its movements, and is called upon to show cause for its action, such as competing water rates.

While it is the duty of every citizen in a republic to understand political questions, there is an undercurrent of delightful possibilities in these studies. Think of the racy reading we shall have when some scholar decides to write a thesis on railroad methods in 1900, and think of the pleasing symposium which might be contributed by old gentlemen who remember these times!

I have tried to paint a picture of these times—although with clumsy fingers and inadequate colors—in order to show that the subject of this biography found his political issues ready for him. The issues were here when he was born. When we removed from Illinois in 1887, to Nebraska, we entered a younger civilization in which people were even more harassed by conditions and more determined to find a solution.

Mr. Bryan came upon this stage endowed by nature and by training for his work. He saw the problems. He recognized the needs and became the voice of an unorganized multitude which was seeking a leader.

CHAPTER II

STUDENT DAYS

I FIRST made the acquaintance of Mr. Bryan in the autumn of 1879 in Jacksonville, Illinois. I had heard from my maiden aunt rumors of a splendid young man named Bryan, but I did not meet the gentleman until he appeared at a reception at the boarding school which I had entered that year. A group of college boys entered the parlors and passed the receiving line. From an adjoining room I watched this row of students. I am sorry not to chronicle a case of love at first sight, but one boy among the number attracted my notice and I asked my companion, "Who is the tall fellow with dark hair and eyes?" and when she replied, "Will Bryan," I knew he must be the youth of whom I had been hearing. Our families had known of each other through mutual friends, but had never met.

Years ago I wrote a short biography of Mr. Bryan, and as my early impressions were probably more vivid at that time, I turn to this book for a description of his appearance:

"His face was pale and thin; a pair of keen, dark eyes looked out from beneath heavy brows; his nose was prominent—too large to look well, I thought; a broad, thin-lipped mouth and a square chin, completed the contour of his face. He was neat, though not fastidious in dress, and stood firmly and with dignity. I noted particularly his hair and his smile. The former, black in color, fine in quality, and parted with distressing straightness; the latter, expansive and expressive. In later years this smile has been the subject of considerable comment, but the well-rounded cheeks of Mr. Bryan now check its onward march, and no one has seen the real breadth of the smile who did not see

222

THE HOUSE WHERE WILLIAM JENNINGS BRYAN WAS BORN,
MARCH 19, 1860
Photo. Brown Bros.

THE BRYAN FARMHOUSE NEAR SALEM, ILLINOIS
Where William Jennings Bryan spent his boyhood.

"FAIRVIEW," THE HOME OF MR. AND MRS. BRYAN AT LINCOLN,
NEBRASKA
Photo. Brown Bros.

it in the early days. Upon one occasion, a heartless observer was heard to remark, 'That man can whisper in his own ear,' but this was a cruel exaggeration."

While I was completing my inspection of the young men, Mr. Bryan was brought to me and formally presented. I learned later that he had chosen me among all the girls present and had inquired my name.

For exercise, the schoolgirls were in the habit of walking around the square upon which the academy stood, and it was natural that Mr. Bryan, who lived with relatives just across the street, should often find it necessary to walk toward town at the same hour we were taking our promenade. I grew to expect him and could see his smile the whole length of the square. Mr. Bryan in an earlier chapter has given many details of this period and there is not a great deal to be added. My chief source of material is found in his letters, extending over our four years of engagement, for we were betrothed the following spring. We owe much to Mrs. Jones, our old friend, with whom he lived, who sang his praises in season and out of season to me, and was equally industrious in praising me to him. Dear Mrs. Jones, with her quaint primness and stiff little side curls, was the soul of goodness and entered upon the dangerous business of matchmaking without fear, and we have had no reason to question her judgment.

Another factor in bringing us together was the presence of my mother at a local sanitarium during the winter of 1879 and 1880. I went to visit her often and Mr. Bryan asked permission to call upon me there, which was granted and from there we sometimes took an afternoon drive. These drives, although taken with my mother's consent, were very wrong from the viewpoint of the head of our school, who was so horrified upon the discovery of our meetings that he punished me by not allowing me to remain at the school through commencement. After I had passed my examinations, I went home.   But, as was then arranged, I returned the following term and won the first honors of my class.

I dreaded to leave school a few days early, dreaded to tell my father, and dreaded what he might think of Mr. Bryan, whom I was beginning to regard as a most admirable and mature man.   The morning I left Jacksonville, the irate principal put me on the train for my thirty-mile journey, not knowing that a young man was concealed in the baggage car.   When the train was under way, Mr. Bryan came and joined me, and we planned for him to make an early visit to my home and for him to ask my father's consent to our engagement at that time.   Father was what is known as a gentleman of the old school, tall, dignified, and very reserved.   But to my surprise and great relief, he had no fault to find with this young man, and the pleasant relations then established continued without a break until my father's death.

While I have never regarded Mr. Bryan as a great letter writer—a little too absent-minded, a little too didactic— glimpses of his character may be gathered from the following extracts:

Upon a Withered Bouquet

"May 12, 1880.

". . . Beauty, how changing!   That lovely bouquet whose beauty charmed while its fragrance enchanted, is falling a victim to the cruel tooth of time.   Its form still remains, but its freshness has gone forever.   Yet why should we wonder?   Like the flowers we have grown, and like them we also must decay.   Yes, its beauty is gone, but the memory of her who gave it still lives, and like the dew, refreshes by its presence.   Those who rejoice in the memory of noble actions and heroic deeds look back.   Those who live only in the present are concerned neither with the past nor the future.   There is still another class of people who anticipate events.

To those the writer belongs. The first object which now meets his eye is commencement week."

Upon Receiving a Letter

"May 12, 1880.

". . . You know well both how to sadden and how to gladden as the first page of your kind letter proved:

" 'W. J. B.', how icy! I went home and built a fire, sharpened my skates, and then took up your letter again. Imagine the change in temperature, if you can. Behold the new address!"

Upon Receiving a Prize

"October 17, 1880.

". . . The prize is won—at least, received. That is the second, and I do not feel as I thought I would. I prayed that humility might be given with success. My prayer is answered, for I cannot feel that I am anything more than I was before, and as I look over the possibilities of life, I can honestly ask in the language of Lincoln's favorite hymn, 'Why should the spirit of mortal be proud?' If one obtains the highest position to which an American can aspire, he can return thanks to God, for He gives both talents and favorable circumstances, and commands that both should be used. What honor then if one does all that he possibly can! He only does his duty."

Upon Reading a Life of Lincoln

"April 3, 1881.

". . . Have been reading 'The Life of Abe Lincoln.' It is quite interesting. He was ambitious and is the most humble statesman we have ever had. He had an eloquence which seemed born of inspiration. He spoke the truth and with it won the hearts of his hearers. As a lawyer he was a perfect model. He only wished justice for his clients and always got it. He was scrupulously honest, once walking three miles to return six and a half cents he had taken by mistake. He is a good character for study."

Upon a Gold Thimble
"December 3, 1883.

". . . How much did you say a gold thimble costs, and what size do you wear? If I have the money, I will get you one for Christmas. That statement 'if I have the money' does not sound very well, but I do not hide even my poverty from you." [He always earned the money with which he bought gifts for me.]

"So you have learned to make waffles. I am so fond of them."

On Shaving His Mustache
"April 17, 1881.

". . . How do you think I look without my mustache? As I shaved off that long-petted and delicately fondled evidence of manhood, I was deeply impressed with that awful truth that it is easier to destroy than to create. The result of weeks of patient, weary watching gone in a moment. Did I say gone? No, not gone, for the remains of that capillaceous production still live and will bear to future ages testimony of the beauty they bestowed as well as the care and trouble which they gave."

On the Principal of My Boarding School
"March 27, 1881.

". . . I cannot blame you for being angry. It is difficult to control one's temper *always*. It is a life work to become able to govern oneself. Two or three times since I have been here at school I have been angry," [he had been in school for six years at that time] "but I am always sorry for it as soon as it is over.

". . . You must not let such prevarications on the professor's part give you a dislike for the religion which he professes. He is not, I think, a perfect example, but the religion which he pretends to live up to, is perfect. Look at Christ instead of B."

THOUGHTS ON PUBLIC OFFICE

Referring to himself, Mr. Bryan writes, under date of May 17, 1880:

". . . But since he belongs to you, perhaps he should not speak lightly of your possessions. He has no past except that spent with you, upon which he delights to look. He has taken four prizes in college, but who could not with his surroundings? Of his dear, honored father you have read. All that son could say of mother, he can say of his. His future I cannot tell. Law will be his profession; his aim, to mete out justice to every creature, whether he be rich or poor, bond or free. His great desire is to honor God and please mankind. He does not desire to be wealthy, believing that money fails to bring happiness as soon as it is made the object of pursuit. Yet by willing labor he hopes and expects to be able to provide for himself and one more. Do not laugh when he tells you that he desires to stand with Webster and Clay. Noble aims make noble men, and his father, who still lives to aid him, often said that one could by diligence, make himself just what he wished to be, and that our duty was to make ourselves worthy of any office within the gift of the people. Such are his parents and such his aspiration."

TRIBUTE TO MEMORY

"Chicago, November 30, 1882.
(Thanksgiving Day)
". . . Oh, memory, God given garden of the soul, where flowers once planted will forever bloom. May

we scatter on thy sacred soil only seeds of kindness, truth, and love. Seeds watered by the dews of Heaven which may blossom and bear fruit through eternal years."

FIRST JURY SERVICE

"Chicago, January 29, 1882.

". . . I notified you last week of my success, or rather, misfortune. I was a little surprised at being elected on the first ballot; came near missing the oratorship by being put on as debater. I preferred to be orator and could not be both. Trumbull and Kagy were with me and helped me to the position for which I think I am best fitted. My subject for oration is 'Vigilance.' I have been deeply moved by the lethargy of our people. The perpetuity of a nation I think depends more upon the character of its people than upon the principles which underlie its government, and observing the inaction of our people, the carelessness with which they elect their representatives and neglect the administration of justice, I am wrought up to such a pitch that I cannot hold in. There are reports of recent jury packing in this city and they only indicate how criminally negligent and selfish we as a people are becoming.

"And just here let me relate a novel incident. I had been writing on my oration and had reached the corruption of the jury system, attributing it to the fact that our better class of citizens would excuse themselves from serving the public because their private affairs were so pressing. Feeling tired, I went over to the gymnasium, and after I had refreshed myself, was starting away when I was met by a man with a small open notebook in his hand. He was a constable looking for a juror to try a case before a justice of the peace near by. He told me his business and wanted me to go with him.

"Remembering that my oration was unfinished, I tried to excuse myself, but he said he wanted to get some good, honest man and was unwilling to let me go. I told him that I was studying law and I believed lawyers were excused.

" 'Not until they are admitted to practice,' he said.

"Then I remembered the point I was trying to make in my oration, and the preciousness of consistency occurred to me in a new light, and this, together with the assurance that the law allowed jurors 50 cents for serving, overcame my objection. I went and did my best to prove to the world that the jury system which Blackstone says 'is the bulwark of English liberties' is also the palladium of our safety.

"The facts of the case in brief were as follows:

"A policeman received word that certain parties were stealing potatoes from John Murphy. The policeman went to the men and claimed to have a search warrant, but did not read it. He asked them to go to a justice near by and settle the matter. They all started, but soon the men with the potatoes whipped up their horses and tried to get away. This aroused the policeman's suspicions and he arrested them and took them to a justice, where the matter was examined into and the parties released. The arrest, however, made one of the parties angry and he appeared as a prosecuting witness in a case of assault and battery. It was claimed that the arrest was without authority and hence became an assault. After the witnesses were examined, the lawyers rose to tell us our duty. One told us that the policeman had no right to make the arrest, and that by fining him, we would teach him that he should regard the rights of free men and their immunity from arrest on groundless suspicions. The other explained to us the discretionary power of officers of the law; how they were compelled to act on the spur of the moment lest the criminals should escape; how they watched while we slept, and having to deal so often with the lower classes, they were necessarily suspicious and liable to error, even when most conscientious in the discharge of their duty.

"The jury was then sent out to agree upon a verdict, and as the papers were handed to me, some one suggested that I act as foreman. On the first ballot four voted not guilty and two guilty. We who were for acquittal were young men, and the two who voted guilty were about forty years old. After about three minutes' discussion, we signed our verdict which read 'that the jury finds the defendant not guilty,' signed, etc. Then it was announced that in people's cases where the verdict is for the defendant, the jurors receive no pay!"

Last Letter Before Marriage

"Jacksonville, September 28, 1884.

". . . Your ring is bought and engraved with the strange device 'Won, 1880. One, 1884.' I think my 'regulation black' will be all that could be desired. If you can boast of wearing the finest wedding dress ever worn there, I think I may be the first to wear a swallow tail. . . ."

"Professor T. [president of the college] yesterday informed me that he and his wife had received their invitation and that he was preparing himself for the ring ceremony. I am practicing on 'and with all my worldly goods I thee endow' so as to make it duly impressive. If you dare laugh when I say that, I won't kiss you when he tells me to salute my bride.

". . . I trust no angry words will ever pass between us and nothing must ever be allowed to shake our confidence in each other. If we keep no secrets from each other, we cannot wander far from the right path."

The first official document signed by Mr. Bryan in the first office he ever held, that of notary public.
(His deposition before himself declaring his love for Mary E. Baird. Dated May 21, 1883.)

CHAPTER III

OUR FIRST DECADE TOGETHER

THE next three years after the wedding day were spent in our little home on College Hill, Jacksonville, Illinois. This home had been built before our marriage and contained a suite of rooms for my parents, who needed my care and who made their home with us until their death.

Very early in our married life Mr. Bryan and I discussed together the best use to make of our leisure hours. Young friends had asked us to join the tennis and social clubs, but after considering the matter carefully, we decided to study instead. Mr. Bryan read a great many books, chiefly on the tariff, railroad problems, political economy, and the science of government. When the family wished to give him a little present, we bought a book along these lines. I joined a German Conversation club, took a course in early English in Illinois College, and worked at night on the same course of law which Mr. Bryan had pursued in Chicago—a busy and a happy time.

Mr. Bryan's law practice grew slowly but steadily and each year we added to our savings. Mr. Bryan's ideals as a lawyer are well illustrated by his answer to a letter of a young attorney who had asked him for advice. He said:

"Remember that a lawyer is an officer of the court and, as such, is sworn to assist the court in the administration of justice. That being true, no lawyer can afford to make an argument he does not believe to be sound, or try to mislead either the judge or jury. It is better to refuse a case that you believe to be unjust than to risk, for any amount of compensation, the strain upon your morals involved in the attempt to deceive the court or jury. One who repeatedly attempts to prove that 'black is white' in time becomes color blind and cannot himself distinguish between right and wrong.

"Besides this effect upon himself, he must consider the effect upon the court and also his reputation, which will have an effect upon the jury. If a judge has been deceived by a lawyer, he spends his time watching for deceptions when the lawyer is speaking before him. There is nothing so valuable to a lawyer as the confidence of the judge and jury in his integrity. When a lawyer has secured for his client all that the client is entitled to, he has done all that the law requires, all that any honest client would desire, and all that an honest lawyer would do."

Mr. Bryan has dwelt on the causes which led us to remove to the West in June, 1887—leaving one school center for another. We had both in Jacksonville, Illinois, and in Lincoln, Nebraska, delightful association with college faculties, and found the new friends quite as satisfying as the old ones.

During our first years in Lincoln we were instrumental in the organization of the Sorosis Club for women and the Round Table for men. These clubs are particularly valuable because they discuss only current questions and keep the members in touch with the times. Both those organizations, now more than thirty-five years old, are vigorous and influential in the life of the city.

After two and a half years of diligent work accomplished in addition to the care of my parents and my baby girl, I passed the examination and was admitted to the bar in Lincoln, in 1887, being the only woman in the class and ranking third in a class of seventeen.

Mr. Bryan had an increasing reputation as a speaker and during these years we went to many public gatherings. I hold the theory that if a wife does not show an interest in her husband's work and does not go with him when he

asks her, the time may come when he will cease to ask her.
I pass this idea on to young wives for whatever it may be
worth.

One seventeenth day of March we went to a St. Patrick's
Day celebration in Lincoln where Mr. Bryan was to speak,
and he greatly enjoyed an incident of the evening. I feel
sure he would want this story to find place here.

The meeting was presided over by the rather pompous
Nebraska governor against whom Mr. Bryan had made
fifty speeches during the previous autumn. In Mr. Bryan's
words:

"I was a little nervous when I saw the Governor in
the chair, for I felt he might be annoyed because of the
fifty speeches I had made against him.

"The program was a varied one—an instrumental
selection, a declamation, a song, etc. The Governor
rose and read from the list prepared for him, 'The next
number is by Mr. W. J. Bryan.' As I stepped forward
the Governor advanced and extended his hand. It ran
through my mind that he was a kind old fellow to forgive my opposition. Then the Governor drew me
toward him and said in a hoarse whisper, 'Do you speak
or sing?' He did not know I had spoken against him
and had not even heard of me. The sudden revulsion
of feeling was almost too much for me. I could hardly
control my laughter and began to speak with great
effort. I have always regarded this as one of the best
jokes which Fate has played upon me."

I find also one of his early post-prandial efforts which
shows so clearly his views on the separation of Church and
State, that I venture to reproduce it:

"Mr. Chairman, Ladies and Gentlemen: It is rather
by accident than by design that this sentiment has fallen

234

to me. Had not my law partner been called unexpectedly from the State he would have responded with more propriety and more ability to 'The Law and the Gospel.'

"These are important words; each covers a wide field by itself and together they include all government. There is not between them, as some suppose, a wide gulf fixed. Many have commenced with us only to be called to a higher sphere, and a few ministers have come to us when they were convinced that they had answered to another's call.

"In the earlier days the prophet was also the lawgiver. He who wore the priestly robe held in his hands the scales of justice. But times are changed. For the good of the State and for the welfare of the Church, the moral and the civil law have been separated. Today we owe a double allegiance, and 'render unto Cæsar the things that are Cæsar's, and unto God the things that are God's.' Their governments are concentric circles and can never interfere. Between what religion commands and what the law compels there is, and ever must be, a wide margin, as there is also between what religion forbids and what the law prohibits. In many things we are left to obey or disobey the instructions of the Divine Ruler, answerable to Him only for our conduct. The Gospel deals with the secret purposes of the heart as well as with the outward life, while the civil law must content itself with restraining the arm outstretched for another's hurt or with punishing the actor after the injury is done.

"Next to the ministry I know of no more noble profession than the law. The object aimed at is justice, equal and exact, and if it does not reach that end at once it is because the stream is diverted by selfishness or checked by ignorance. Its principles ennoble and its practice elevates. If you point to the pettifogger,

I will answer that he is as much out of place in the temple of justice as is the hypocrite in the house of God. You will find the 'book on tricks' in the library of the legal bankrupt—nowhere else. In no business in life do honesty, truthfulness, and uprightness of conduct pay a larger dividend upon the investment than in the law. He is not only blind to his highest welfare and to his greatest good, but also treading upon dangerous ground, who fancies that mendacity, loquacity, and pertinacity are the only accomplishments of a successful lawyer.

"You cannot judge a man's life by the success of a moment, by the victory of an hour, or even by the results of a year. You must view his life as a whole. You must stand where you can see the man as he treads the entire path that leads from the cradle to the grave —now crossing the plain, now climbing the steeps, now passing through pleasant fields, now wending his way with difficulty between rugged rocks—tempted, tried, tested, triumphant. The completed life of every lawyer, either by its success or failure, emphasizes the words of Solomon—'The path of the just is as the shining light, that shineth more and more unto the perfect day.'

"By practicing upon the highest plane the lawyer may not win the greatest wealth, but he wins that which wealth cannot purchase and is content to know and feel that 'a good name is rather to be chosen than great riches, and loving favour rather than silver and gold.'

"There are pioneers of the Gospel whose names you speak with reverence, Calvin, Knox, the Wesleys and Asbury, besides many still living, and you love them not without cause. There are those in our profession whom we delight to honor. Justinian and Coke, Blackstone and Jay, Marshall and Kent, Story and Lincoln, men who have stood in the thickest of the fight, have met every temptation peculiar to our profession, and yet maintained their integrity.

"It is a fact to which we point with no little pride, that with a history of an hundred years no member of the Supreme Court of the United States has ever been charged with corrupt action, although untold millions have been involved in the litigation before the court. Nor do I recall any member of the Supreme Court of any State who has been convicted of misusing his office.

" 'The Law and the Gospel.' Great in their honored names, great in their history, great in their influence. To a certain extent they supplement each other. The law asks of the Gospel counsel, not commands. The Gospel goes far beyond the reach of law, for while the law must cease to operate when its subject dies, the Gospel crosses the dark river of death and lightens up the world which lies beyond the tomb. The law is negative, the Gospel positive; the laws say, 'do not unto others that which you would not have others do unto you,' while the Gospel declares that we should 'do to others that which we would that others should do unto us.'

" 'The Law and the Gospel.' They form an exception to the rule that in union there is strength, for each is strongest when alone. And I believe that the greatest prosperity of the State and greatest growth of the Church will be found when the law and the Gospel walk, not hand in hand, but side by side."

December, 1891, found us en route to Washington, where Mr. Bryan took up his duties as Congressman. Our children then numbered three, the youngest being nine months old, and we broke our journey by a few days in Jacksonville, Illinois. Dr. Jones, our host, owned a particularly fine microscope with many carefully prepared slides. Under his supervision our daughter Ruth, age six, was standing on a chair squinting down the barrels of the microscope when her brother came in, watched her a moment, and said, "Sister, get down from there; I want to smell that too." Honesty compels me to admit that our children were not always infallible.

Even at that remote date the hotel and apartment owners of Washington had declared against children, and Mr. Bryan had a long search to find a home for us. At one time we regarded the drowning of our entire family as a necessary prelude to establishing ourselves. We saw race suicide from a new angle, and experienced great relief when we had secured pleasant quarters opposite the National Library on Capitol Hill. Our good friends, the Brides, gave us, their first lodgers, a home for four years.

In the House of Representatives the organization of Committees occupied first attention, and among these the Committee on Ways and Means is regarded as most important.

During the rivalry between Congressman William M. Springer, whom we had known in Illinois, and Speaker Charles F. Crisp, of Georgia, for the Chairmanship of this committee, Mr. Bryan supported Springer with that tenacity which he always showed in a fight. When Springer won and the smoke of battle cleared, Mr. Bryan was given a place on this important committee. I have been told that no other new member has been thus honored. This gave him a standing at once and prepared the way for his Congressional work. His first extended speech, March 16, 1892, was in support of the Wilson Tariff Bill. Here Mr. Bryan received the reward of his patient study in our first home. He knew his subject and was able to take the lead because of that knowledge. I was exceedingly anxious about this first speech in Congress and sat in the gallery of the House of Representatives with my hand clasping the arm of the seat so tensely that my glove was split across the palm. That he affected his listeners was shown by a conversation which I heard in the gallery.

OUR FIRST DECADE TOGETHER

Soon after Mr. Bryan began to speak a lady came in and said to a earlier arrival, "Who is speaking?"

The first lady replied, "A young man from Nebraska who is said to consider himself a great orator."

When his speech was nearing its close, a third lady entered and asked the first one the same question, "Who is speaking?"

Her changed reply was, "Congressman Bryan of Nebraska, and he has been making a wonderful speech."

In his second term Mr. Bryan took up the matter of monetary legislation and favored free coinage of silver. His speech, August 15, 1893, upon this subject, attracted great attention, and again his charm of speech was aided by his thorough knowledge of the subject. He spoke in January, 1894, upon the income tax, boldly standing for a most unpopular measure. The full text of these speeches cannot be given here, but may be found in supplementary volumes.

After four years in Congress he became a candidate for the United States Senate, but the landslide of 1894 gave the Republicans a great majority in the Legislature and Thurston was elected. The following extract from a letter was written to friends after the Senatorial defeat:

"The Legislature is Republican, and a Republican Senator will now be elected to represent Nebraska. This may be mortifying to the numerous chairmen who have introduced me to audiences as 'the next Senator from Nebraska,' but it illustrates the uncertainty of prophecies.

"I appreciate more than words can express the cordial good will and the loyal support of the friends to whom I am indebted for the political honors which I have received. I am especially grateful to those who bear without humiliation the name of the common people, for they have been my friends when others have

239

deserted me. I appreciate also the kind words of many who have been restrained by party ties from giving me their votes. I have been a hired man for four years, and, now that the campaign is closed, I may be pardoned for saying that as a public servant I have performed my duty to the best of my ability, and am not ashamed of the record made.

"I stepped from private life into national politics at the bidding of my countrymen; at their bidding I again take my place in the ranks and resume without sorrow the work from which they called me. It is the glory of our institutions that public officials exercise authority by the consent of the governed rather than by divine or hereditary right. Paraphrasing the language of Job, each public servant can say of departing honors: The people gave and the people have taken away, blessed be the name of the people.

"Speaking of my own experience in politics, I may again borrow an idea from the great sufferer and say: What, shall we receive good at the hands of the people, and shall we not receive evil? I have received good even beyond my deserts, and I accept defeat without complaint. I ask my friends not to cherish resentment against any one who may have contributed to the result.

.   .   .   .

"The friends of these reforms have fought a good fight; they have kept the faith, and they will not have finished their course until the reforms are accomplished. Let us be grateful for the progress made, and 'with malice toward none and charity for all' begin the work of the next campaign."

CHAPTER IV

GROWTH OF ORATORICAL POWER

MUCH valuable time has been spent in discussing whether or not an acquired trait may be transmitted to descendants. As one moves along in life, he grows less and less sure of a conclusion. One instance clearly supports one side of the controversy—only to be flatly contradicted by a later instance.

Therefore I do not attempt to say how far a certain slender, dark-eyed boy was influenced by the fact that his father had a great interest in oratory and was himself a forceful speaker. Judge Bryan took his son with him to court, and the boy from his seat on the steps of the platform, listened to the arguments of the counsel and to the decisions of the bench.

The first recorded efforts of declamation show that at the age of seven or eight he committed to memory his geography lesson, and then was placed on a little table where he declaimed the same.

Looking through our letters, I find light upon the feeling which he had for his father.

"Our church has no pastor, so we had a kind of prayer meeting in the forenoon on Sunday. I spoke. Afterwards Mr. Chance (Jakie's father) said: 'While our young brother was speaking, I thought of his good old father. How he used to encourage us by repeating the promises of the Bible, and my heart went up in silent prayer that the mantle of Elijah might fall on Elisha, and then I prayed that he might become a shining light and that his influence might be felt far and wide for good.' I tell you, I could not help weeping, nor was I alone, for I felt so unworthy to take my father's place." (Letter dated August 29, 1880.)

"Later in reading over an address delivered by father to the grand jury as he left the bench after a term of twelve years service as circuit judge, I find this, which you will pardon me for quoting. 'I have not grown rich from the spoils of office. During the whole term of twelve years I have received not more than a living. I have nevertheless succeeded reasonably well in the affairs of life and have of the world's goods a reasonable competency, but it has not come to me from office. It has been the result of rigid economy, long and patient professional labor, and the sweat of the face in agricultural pursuits, aided and supported by Heaven's greatest bestowment—an affectionate, confiding, and prudential companion—and finally, gentlemen of the jury, I add that the experience of public life has tended to confirm in me the convictions of my early education —that the more we conform our lives and actions, both in private and public relations, to the demands of honor, truth, sincerity, justice, and Christianity, the greater will be our happiness and prosperity, and the better we shall enjoy this present world, and the broader will be our foundation for the enjoyment of the world to come.'

"Such is the example set me by my venerated father. I have been reading several of his speeches today."

Mr. Bryan gives a list of the prizes he took in college under the caption "The Lure of the College Prize." If one refers to this list, it is quite apparent that failure did not discourage him. He entered the next contest with his best effort. Some samples of his youthful style may be of interest. The reader will note that he began to run true to type at an early age. Below appears a speech, "A Defense of Democracy," which was written for delivery in chapel,

A PRIZE WINNING ORATOR
An early portrait of Wm. Jennings Bryan

January, 1880. He was evidently smarting under the defeat of Hancock.

"It was the custom in ancient warfare, when the battle was over, to follow the vanquished and put each individual enemy to the sword. Advanced civilization, however, denounces the practice as barbarous in the extreme, and hails with joy the dawn of a brighter period, when charity, instead of revenge, will characterize the conduct of victors toward the conquered.

"The result of the last Presidential election has caused those who hoped for a more enlightened age, to despair, and has deferred for some years at least, the day when true bravery will appear in the conflict, rather than in despoiling the slain. Since the wires flashed the startling news of our defeat; since that pompous funeral demonstration, when, with beating of drums and sounds of mingled shouts and rejoicings, one of America's greatest generals was laid to rest in his political grave; since 'requiescat in pace' was written over the silent tomb of 'The Superb,' pure in character, and great by name and nature; we have been the object upon which the *cruel* mercies of a party, driven to desperation before the election, have been exercised.

"But such a devotion to their cause does not prove its righteousness; on the contrary, a devotion which overreaches its bounds, more often defeats than promotes its object. We, who have exhibited a patience of twenty years duration" (the speaker was twenty years old at this time) "can well afford to wait until the Republican party finds its death from suicide; but *duty* calls upon us to defend by word and act the principles which we believe.

"Before advancing to the statement of principles, it is necessary to free ourselves from the charge of slander. It has been urged from this platform by those flushed with unexpected victory, that the Democratic leaders and even the stump speakers, as they are contemptuously called, have been guilty of making false accusations against the good and the great. How fortune changes the fate of man! Success finds an eraser of crimes, for which party managers had sought in vain; and the noise of triumph too often drowns the voice that cries out against corruption in high places. Let it be remembered by our accusers that all the charges made against Mr. Garfield were found among the records of their own investigations. Do they distrust them? An unfortunate reflection upon their party! All the charges we have made remain upon the records, and there they will remain forever. They accuse us of slander. Let them prove, not by witty evasions, not by ridicule, but by facts that the charges are false; then, and not till then, will those who expose corruption, deserve the names, 'vile slanderers and calumniators.'

"They tell us we are dead. *In memoriam* has appeared in every Republican journal throughout the land. How they long to plant the cypress over our final resting place! But, gentlemen, they sing their solemn dirges too soon. The Democrats may have been slaughtered, but like the oxen of the sun, which the companions of Ulysses butchered, the hides crawl after their tormentors.

"But what are the principles for adherence to which we are so denounced? Look at the word democracy itself, 'the rule of the people.' That is the fundamental idea of the party, and a government by the people is the form which we desire. Contrast this with the form proposed by Hamilton, that aristocrat who has been represented, during the last campaign, as the embodiment of sagacity, wisdom, and statesmanship. His plan was that the president should hold office for life, or during good behavior, and that the governors of the states should be appointed by him. He feared and distrusted the people, chose for his model the English government, and once declared that Cæsar, who had the courage to take and destroy the power of the people, was the greatest man who had ever lived. Against Hamilton and the followers of Hamilton the Democratic party has raised and will forever raise, its voice.

"We want no one-man power. The people are equal before the law and are *supreme*. They waked this new world from its sleep of ages; they drove the savage red man toward the setting sun and turned his fertile hunting grounds into fields of waving grain; they made the mountain torrents turn the mighty mill wheels; back and forth, the busy shuttles flew to do their bidding. Armed with the strength of conscious right, they freed themselves from English oppression. France trembled before them, and Mexico acknowledges their power. A civil war has been put down by their arms. Their history covers an hundred years of unparalleled progress; why should we distrust them now or take from them the power they have so nobly used?

"Again, we believe in the superiority of civil law to military rule. Hancock, acting upon this principle, won the admiration of all who were not blinded by party zeal or sectional hatred. We believe in a free press and free speech—twin guardians of liberty.

"We believe in the entire separation of Church and State for the benefit of both. Read, by the light of the fagot and the torch, the history of the bloody deeds perpetrated during those long years when Church and State joined forces and crushed opposition by the heel of power. Hear, in the agonizing cries of martyred heroes, as they come with mournful cadence from the darkness of the middle ages, that solemn voice warning us against the dangers of so terrible a union. We stand upon the Constitution. The general government has powers delegated to it, and the powers not delegated to it are reserved to the states and to the people. Thus reads the Constitution. Who can doubt the wisdom of the provision?

"We believe in free schools, fostered and protected. Are you proud of the school laws of Illinois? They were made before the Republican party was born, and will still live when weeping willows shade the sod which hides its lifeless form. Education is necessary to self-government. The schoolhouse is the dearest friend of a free people. Intellectual and moral development is the only safeguard against corruption. God speed the day when education shall banish bigotry from every mind, when the man of learning will stoop to help the man less fortunate and confess himself superior only in his ability to do greater good.

"These are some of the principles which the Democratic party cherishes, and these are the pillars upon which our government stands. Behold these massive columns fashioned by the hands of those who built more wisely than they knew, as, unimpaired, they continue to give stability and permanence to the grand structure that rises above them. Is the party dead? No, it still lives; and standing, Samson-like with its arms around these mighty columns, it will die only when this governmental fabric shall fall, involving parties, freedom, and human hopes in one common ruin."

While others of this period will be reproduced in his collection of speeches to be published later, I venture to add a few paragraphs from one of the orations which he prepared during his school life. This oration we found in an old purple-backed notebook written in a cramped, boyish hand.

"We may not, my fellow classmates, be able to declare like a Whitefield or a Beecher, the 'glad tidings

of great joy.' We may not, as did Washington and Lincoln, receive the nation's highest honor. We may not equal in eloquence Webster, Calhoun, and Clay. The Muses may not lead us to those lofty heights of poetry and song which Bryant and Longfellow were able to reach. Our names may not be written with those of Choate and Prentiss as the champion defenders of justice, yet in our humble calling, whatever it may be, we can stand in the protection of our country's trust.
* * *

" 'To some we find the
  Ploughshare's annual toil assigned;
  Some at the sounding anvil glow;
  Some the swift sliding shuttle throw;
  Some, studious of the wind and tide,
  From pole to pole our commerce guide;
  While some, with genius more refined,
  With head and tongue assist mankind.'

"No class of man can cease from labor. There is a place for all, there is a work for all. No drones are needed in the human hive. The idle are not only unnecessary, but dangerous to society. * * *

"Nature has given the material. Man must shape it. It is possible to grow in size, but strength comes only with exercise. No one can become strong in body without much patient, and we may say, continued labor, for no sooner does he relax his efforts than the receding tide bears him back whence he started. Intelligence is necessary to direct physical force, and the training of the mind, like that of the body, is accomplished slowly and steadily. Success, glory, and honor have been placed as the reward of the diligent; defeat, misery, and shame are the lot of the idle.

"We value that most which has cost us most of toil. Gold is more precious than silver because it is more difficult to procure. Marble brings a higher price when polished than in the crude state because labor is necessary to bring it to perfection. Natural talent does not remove the necessity for labor. Even the flame of genius burns more brightly when fanned by busy hands. Indeed, it would cease to exist if not employed.

> " 'The lamp of genius, though by nature lit,
>   If not protected, pruned and fed with care,
>   Soon dies, or runs to waste with fitful glare.' * * *

"We are so bound together in the relationship of life that each one exerts an influence upon those about him, and is in turn affected by their actions. Nor is influence ended by the confines of the tomb. History is made up of the words and deeds of men. We must employ our every talent and quicken our every energy, or yield our places to others more willing to toil than ourselves. Cities have been built; magnificent structures speak of the powers of man; moving palaces plough the ocean; the iron horse speeds over the prairies, hills, and valleys; nations and continents converse through whispering wires; colleges and universities of learning are scattered through the land; wise men are rising to take the lead in law, in science, and in the ministry. * * *

"An infinity of the unknown lies before us. It stands open and invitingly to all."

An epoch in his career as a speaker came at the age of twenty-seven, shortly after we went to Nebraska. He had spoken in a town in the western part of the state, came home on a night train, and arrived at daybreak. I was sleeping when he came in, and he awakened me. Sitting on the edge of the bed, he began: "Mary, I have had a strange experience. Last night I found that I had power over the audience. I could move them as I chose. I have more than usual power as a speaker. I know it. God grant I may use it wisely." And as it was his custom all through life to carry to his Heavenly Father any new development, he prayed.

This was the beginning of that power which was his— explain it as you like. I speak positively of his power, for I have seen proofs. For years I attended political meetings. Social functions might be crowded out, but political meetings went on forever, and from the platform I saw it all. If conditions were favorable, his mood was transmitted to his listeners. He smiled, and the smile rippled away over his audience; he frowned, and so did they; he grew tense with emotion, they bent forward and sat upon the very edge of the seats.

Nor was the power over an audience shown only in these moods. An unusual instance may be cited at a meeting in the summer following the campaign of 1896. Mr. Bryan spoke in a little Utah mining town. The surrounding mountains were so high that the valley in early afternoon was already in shadow. He spoke from the second-story balcony of the railway station to a great audience of miners with mine lamps on their caps. Mr. Bryan had just suffered a defeat. He was speaking to them after an unsuccessful struggle. But his youth and his deep earnestness rang to his audience on every clear note of his voice. While he was speaking, the shadows had deepened. It was twilight when he closed his speech with the statement that "all his life, whether in victory or defeat, he would fight the battles of the common people. His life was pledged to their cause through all the years to come."

With his closing phrase, there came the moment when applause conventionally follows, but none came. There was a deep silence, and one miner after another took off his cap, until that great crowd was standing with bared and bowed heads. His mood of consecration had carried to them.

After a tense pause such a roar of cheers filled the valley as sent echoes rattling back from the hills; a clamor of applause.

When Mr. Bryan and our little girl and I came down to enter our carriage, the miners crowded forward to shake his hand, but again the crowd had grown still, and so full of emotion were they that they could scarcely speak their words of gratitude and affection, and those who could not reach his hand, put out their hands to touch him.

A phase of his oratory which is not well known is his debating. In his campaigns for Congress formal challenges to debate were sent to his opponents and accepted. These debates were held in the larger towns of the district and attended by thousands.

He used the same plan in debate which he used in the discussion of any issue, namely, to study both sides of the question. He was quite as familiar with the arguments he expected to combat as with those he expected to advance.

These debates interested me more than any form of discussion. Knowing both sides, Mr. Bryan was able to set little traps for his opponents. When he had the opening speech, he would deliberately seem to leave open a loophole; the enemy would seize upon the weakness only to find a danger lurking within, for his closing speech would clamp down the argument like the teeth of a steel trap.

The neatness of his work may be shown in the closing speech of his first Congressional campaign, the last of a series of debates with Mr. Connell.

"Mr. Connell: We now bring to a close this series of debates which was arranged by our committees. I am glad that we have been able to conduct these discussions in a courteous and friendly manner. If I have in any way offended you in word or deed I offer apology and express regret and as freely forgive. I desire to present to you in remembrance of these pleasant meetings this little volume, because it contains 'Gray's Elegy,' in perusing which I trust you will find as much pleasure and profit as I have. It is one of the most beautiful and touching tributes to humble life that literature contains. Grand in its sentiment and sublime in its simplicity, we may both find in it a solace in victory or defeat. If success should crown your efforts in this campaign, and it should be your lot 'Th' applause of list'ning senates to command,' and I am left

    " 'A youth to fortune and to fame unknown,'

forget not us who in the common walks of life perform our part, but in the hour of your triumph recall the lines:

    " 'Let not ambition mock their useful toil,
       Their homely joys and destiny obscure;
    Nor grandeur hear, with a disdainful smile,
       The short and simple annals of the poor.'

"If, on the other hand, by the verdict of my countrymen, I shall be made your successor, let it not be said of you:

    " 'And melancholy marked him for her own,'

but find sweet consolation in the thought:

    " 'Full many a gem of purest ray serene,
       The dark unfathomed caves of ocean bear;
    Full many a flower is born to blush unseen,
       And waste its sweetness on the desert air.'

"But whether the palm of victory is given to you or to me, let us remember those of whom the poet says.'

WILLIAM JENNINGS BRYAN

" 'Far from the madding crowd's ignoble strife,
Their sober wishes never learn'd to stray;
Along the cool sequester'd vale of life
They kept the noiseless tenor of their way.'

"These are the ones most likely to be forgotten by
the government. When the poor and the weak cry out
for relief they, too, often hear no answer but 'the echo
of their cry,' while the rich, the strong, the powerful
are given an attentive ear. For this reason is class
legislation dangerous and deadly; it takes from those
least able to lose and gives to those who are least in
need. The safety of our farmers and our laborers is
not in special legislation, but in equal and just laws
that bear alike on every man. The great masses of our
people are interested, not in getting their hands into
other people's pockets, but in keeping the hands of
other people out of their pockets.

"Let me in parting express the hope that you and
I may be instrumental in bringing our government back
to better laws which will give equal treatment without
regard to creed or condition. I bid you a friendly
farewell."

From writing and committing speeches to memory, Mr.
Bryan passed to speaking from notes and wrote nothing
unless the speech was of official importance.

In any story of his oratorical equipment, his voice must
find a place. A wife may be considered an incompetent
witness and on this point I confess enthusiasm.

Among the losses the world has suffered by Mr. Bryan's
going, the stilling of his voice is to me most irreparable.
I speak now of his voice, not of what he said. When he
had attained sufficient skill to dispense with manuscripts
and really speak, the beauty of his voice was revealed.
There was in it a reverberating quality—vibratory hardly

expresses it. Upon occasions when he was especially moved I have heard his tones ring out with bell-like clearness and resound far beyond the circle of his hearers. As years passed, this quality grew less, but never was entirely lost. Few voices have ever equaled his in carrying power. Many instances might be cited. I mention one.

During the winter of 1898–99 Mr. Bryan spoke in Corpus Christi, Texas. I was tired and did not go to the meeting. I was reading in my upstairs room when I heard some one speak. I went to the open window and found that Mr. Bryan was talking. I listened several minutes, hearing every word quite clearly. Next morning I asked how far the meeting had been from the house and found that it was three long blocks distant.

The skill with which he used his voice was natural, no forcing or straining. When in school he had a few lessons in so-called elocution, but not enough to change his methods. His intonation and emphasis were excellent and his gestures simple and effective. His speeches were free from any stumbling or hesitating for words. His words flowed along like the steady current of a stream and always fitted the subject. Although a good Greek and Latin scholar, and appreciating the finer shades of meaning, he used the simple words and the more colloquial expressions. Uneducated people caught his meaning and understood as clearly as the learned.

Among debates, the one I remember best is the closing debate of his second Congressional campaign. To begin with, I felt more interest in this than in any other campaign, presidential not excepted. It seemed to me most necessary that he should win, as he was not sufficiently established in national affairs to withstand a defeat.

The district had been gerrymandered and was more hopelessly Republican than ever. Lincoln, then a town of sixty thousand, furnished the opposing candidate. He was a judge and had lived there longer than we. Interest became so intense that when the time came for the last debate no place could be found large enough for the crowd except the ball park—a huge place with a semicircle of bleachers facing east and a platform built for speakers in the space in front.

That year the tariff was the main question. Anticipating this campaign the winter before, when in Old Mexico, Mr. Bryan and I had made a tour of the hardware shops of Mexico City, and as we had suspected, we found American cutlery selling for much less there than it sold for in the United States, some articles costing fifty per cent less. This fact seemed to prove to the friends of tariff reduction that the tariff wall enabled the manufacturers to charge the American consumer any price he chose, and then dump the surplus on the foreign market, and still make money on a twenty-five to fifty per cent reduction. We bought several articles—particularly pocketknives and butcher knives of different sizes—put them into a neat handbag, and Mr. Bryan produced his wares at the first debate. The effect was good. People saw the point, with the result that our opponent shortly appeared with cutlery too—although to Democratic ears his arguments were not convincing.

The night of the debate found everything in readiness. Bleachers were filled with eager people; arc lights turned night into day; ice water was put on a table for the speakers. Thomas Stinson Allen (stanch Democrat and Chairman of the Congressional Campaign) was concealed under the platform with a large floral pillow mounted upon a standard. Stretching diagonally across the pillow was the word "Eloquence." This floral piece was to be presented to Mr. Bryan at the close of the evening.

The two debaters arrived, each with his handbag of cutlery. Mr. Bryan had the opening speech and was getting under way when the wind freshened a bit, and from the southeast advanced the vanguard of a dust storm. A low-hung brownish cloud swept through the park, enveloped everything, and passed on. At intervals cloud after cloud came and went. At times we could not see the speakers or the platform. Sometimes shouts were in order and we shouted, swallowing our quota of dust without a murmur. Did anyone leave? As far as I know, not one.

Mr. Bryan spoke with his usual fire, and his opponent advanced to the fray in good form except that he was at times a little confused. When he rounded a period with "Germany and the other islands of the sea," the Democrats jeered exultingly.

And, after refuting Mr. Bryan's statements on wire nails, when he wished to enlarge the field and was evidently trying to mention "wire bed springs," he said, "And wire-wire-wire bed *quilts!*" The delight of the great unwashed (a most appropriate expression for a dust storm) knew no bounds. The loyal Republicans stood firm for their man and cheered again and again.

The last speech by Mr. Bryan was the usual summing up of arguments with clearness, rapidity, and rapier-like thrusts. The close was a scene of cheers and counter cheers, clapping, stamping, whistling, confusion and clamoring, but no riotous disorder. There may have been one or two policemen present, but I cannot now recall one. Democrats, so long in the minority and rejoicing that they now had some one to voice their feeling, hurried to the platform, crowding the aisles, to shake hands with their defender.

After several minutes a voice issued from under the platform: "Say, make room there! Let me out!" And then emerged our good T. S. Allen with the floral tribute. The psychological moment had passed. Few people saw the word "Eloquence," but we carried the piece home with the accompanying thought that even if they had not seen the word, they had felt the power.

As I am making a picture of that time, I venture to finish the story.

Election came the following Tuesday. The vote was

so close that the result was in doubt. Outlying counties must settle the matter. Wednesday found both headquarters crowded. A telegram came which elected the Republican by 116 votes—out marched the Republicans, and with hurrahs and horns celebrated the victory, while gloom settled upon the other headquarters. Perhaps before they had finished their march, the returns came from another county electing the Democrat by 54 votes. The Republicans slunk back and the Democrats marched proudly out and a new set of hurrahs arose. No one could settle down to work. This swinging back and forth continued all day Wednesday and all night. I went down town Thursday and men came to speak to me, so hoarse they could only whisper; all showed lack of sleep, but were resolute. Men took turns at night guarding the ballot boxes.

On Wednesday noon more than a hundred women were to give a parting luncheon to a friend who was leaving Lincoln. I was to toast the guest. That morning things looked dark for us. The Republicans seemed to have it. I knew the wife of our opponent would be there, and the majority of the women were Republicans. I felt at first I could not go—am afraid I cried a little—but my pride led me to dry my eyes, dress as nicely as I could, and go to congratulate our enemy. I had a little speech ready. The successful candidate's wife was there, surrounded by friends, all happy and smiling.

Shortly after I came I was called from the room. Word had been telephoned up from headquarters that later returns gave the election to Mr. Bryan by 75 votes. What a load off my heart! I could smile too. The Republicans, not having the latest news, were jubilant and so was I. I did not make my speech of congratulation.

On Thursday it was decided that an official count must be taken, and Friday afternoon the result made Mr. Bryan the winner by 140 majority.

Perhaps I have given too much space to this campaign, but it may be justified by the hope that this book may live, and that readers fifty years hence may find interest in a picture of the time when people took a personal interest in their policies and in their candidates.

The great Ecumenical Conference was held in Edinburgh in May, 1911. Perhaps a more distinguished body of clergy never was assembled, leaders in mission work coming from all over the world. Mr. Bryan was in England and cabled me to meet him in Edinburgh. I had not intended making this journey and seemed to be needed at home, but decided to go. I was rather proud of the fact that I went, attended the conference, motored about in Scotland, returned, and reached Fairview, our Nebraska home, in exactly four weeks.

So many notable people were present at the Conference that the mornings were given over to speeches limited to three minutes. I was interested to watch what the different people were able to accomplish in so short a time, and was particularly proud of the American delegates. These eliminated all introductions and preliminaries, and beginning, "I wish to say, first—second—third," and in three minutes had stated their position quite fully. Some could not condense and wasted time on nonessentials. Of course I was pleased when Mr. Bryan was asked to take an evening service and make an address in the great Cathedral, and the following Sunday was asked to speak in the leading church in Glasgow, which he did.

We went to the Cathedral—that solemn pile whose walls have echoed the voices of so many prominent divines. The edifice was crowded. We were met in the vestry by several clergymen, and Mr. Bryan went to the pulpit while I sat in one of the front seats with those who had joined us. Dr. James Stalker, known the world over for his clear ideas on theology, sat beside me. Because I had read two or three of his books, his name meant something to me. He was

17

evidently not quite sure about Mr. Bryan and looked him over indifferently. Mr. Bryan's subject was "The Fruits of the Tree." He had put the address in shape while crossing the ocean. He read his text from the last chapter of Revelation, second verse: "In the midst of the street of it, and on either side of the river, was there the tree of life, which bare twelve manner of fruits, and yielded her fruit every month; and the leaves of the tree were for the healing of the nations," and remarked that his subject naturally divided itself into twelve heads. A chill ran down my spine. Twelve! Even the driest and most hardened seldom went beyond *sixthly*. It was a question whether an audience even of Scots would tolerate a *twelfthly*.

But I had no reason to be anxious. Mr. Bryan began to discuss the "twelve manner of fruits," the interest grew, and a rumbling sound, deep and inarticulate, rose from Dr. Stalker, which proved to be his first, "Hear, hear!" Shortly another, more clear and emphatic, "Hear, hear!" Then he hastily exchanged his spectacles for a pair of more distant vision and gazed at the speaker. Soon he augmented his applause by stamping with his cane, and until the end of the speech, no old political friend could have been more enthusiastic.

His attitude was typical. If prejudice existed in the audience, it disappeared. Indifference was changed to interest; suspicion gave place to confidence, and a critical spirit became one of hearty approval.

The same eloquence which had held his hearers in the dust storm echoed through the Cathedral and the concourse of critical scholars paid him the highest honor.

When he became an older man he received many letters from young speakers asking for advice and suggestions. Below is his reply.

"Webster, the great orator, said of eloquence that it must exist 'in the man, in the subject, and in the occasion.' And then he proceeded to elaborate the statement, showing that it was a combination of high purpose, firm resolve, and dauntless spirit, speaking from every feature and reaching the heart of the hearer. There are two things absolutely essential to eloquence. First, the speaker must know what he is talking about, and, second, he must mean what he says. Nothing can take the place of knowledge of the subject and earnestness. To these other things can be added, such as clearness of statement, felicity of expression, aptness in illustration, beauty in ornamentation and grace in delivery.

"Eloquence is heart speaking to heart. There is no mistaking the cry of terror or the shout of joy, and so there is no misunderstanding the sincere message that passes from heart to heart.

"The young man who would fit himself for real influence in the forum must himself feel deeply upon the subjects which he discusses, and he cannot feel deeply without being in full sympathy with those whom he addresses. He must also be able to give them information which they do not possess or to state what they know more forcibly than they can state it themselves.

"The young man ambitious to stand as the representative of his people—not as an official nominally speaking for them, but as a man actually voicing their aspirations and giving utterance to their hopes—such a young man is advised to read the address entitled, 'The People in Art, Government and Religion,' delivered by George Bancroft at Williams College in 1835. (It will be found in Volume VII of Modern Eloquence, known as Reed's Collection of Speeches.) This oration is one of the greatest tributes ever paid to the common people, and it will furnish not only thought, but inspiration to young men. It defends not only the rights of the people, but the capacity of the people for self-government, and declares not that 'the people can make right,' but that 'the people can discern right.' This admirable address is referred to because of the sound advice that it gives to young men, advice that is pertinent in this connection.

"Bancroft says: 'Let the young aspirants after glory scatter seeds of truth broadcast on the wide bosom of humanity, in the deep fertile soil of the public mind. There it will strike root and spring up and bear a hundred-fold and bloom for ages and ripen fruit through remote generations.'

"The difference between a demagogue and a statesman is that the former advocates what he thinks will be popular, regardless of the effect that it may ultimately have upon the people to whom he appeals; the statesman advocates what he believes to be the best for the country regardless of the immediate effect which it may have upon himself. One is willing to sacrifice the permanent interests of others to advance his own temporary interests, while the other is willing to sacrifice his own temporary interests to advance the public welfare. While the conduct of the statesman may seem unselfish, and is unselfish in the usual acceptation of that term, yet it is really an enlightened selfishness, for no man, when he takes a broad view of his own interests, can afford to accept an advantage which comes to him at the expense of his country. The statesman is building upon a firmer foundation than the demagogue, and in the end will find a more substantial reward for his self-denial than the demagogue will be able to secure for himself.

"It has been said that the orator, more than anyone else, needs information upon all subjects, for questions that are no longer matters of controversy can be used as matters of argument, and no one can speak so well of the future as he who is well acquainted with the past.

GROWTH OF ORATORICAL POWER

"A knowledge of human nature is necessary to the orator. Pope has said that the proper study of mankind is man, and in the study of man the heart is the most interesting as well as the most important subject of investigation. He who would succeed in public speaking must understand that a sense of justice is to be found in every heart, and that that sense of justice is the safest foundation upon which to build a government. Bancroft, in the address above referred to, declares that popular government is the strongest government in the world, because 'discarding the implements of terror, it dares to rule by moral force and has its citadel in the heart.'

"Moral courage is indispensable to the orator. A man cannot speak eloquently while he is running from the enemy; neither can he inspire courage if his knees smite each other, and there is a tremor in his voice. Courage rests upon conviction; a man has no convictions to speak of, who is not willing to endure suffering in support of them.

"The orator must have faith—faith in God, faith in the righteousness of his cause, and faith in the ultimate triumph of the truth. Believing that right makes might, believing that every word spoken for truth and every act done in behalf of truth contributes to the final victory, he does his duty, more anxious to help the cause which he espouses than to enjoy the fruits of victory.

"And, finally, let the ambitious young man understand that he is in duty bound to discard everything which in the least weakens his strength, and under obligation to do everything that in any degree increases his power to do good. Good habits, therefore, are always important, and may become vitally so. He can well afford to leave liquor to those who desire to tickle the throat or to please the appetite; it will be no help to him in his effort to advance the welfare of his fellows. He can even afford to put into books what others put into tobacco. The volumes purchased will adorn his shelves for a lifetime, while smoke from a cigar is soon lost to sight forever. He does not need to swear; logic is more convincing than oaths. Let him feed his body with food convenient for it, remembering that food is only useful in so far as it strengthens man for his work; let him train his mind to search for the truth, remembering that his power to discern the truth will increase with the effort to find it. Let him keep his heart diligently, for 'out of it are the issues of life.' Let him recognize service as the measure of greatness, and estimate life by its outgo rather than by its income. Let him to himself be true, 'and it follows as the night the day, he cannot then be false to any man.' "

CHAPTER V

PRIVATE LIFE OF A CANDIDATE

MR. BRYAN in his Memoirs has dealt at length with the Chicago Convention and the circumstances which led up to his nomination for the Presidency in 1896. But while his record ceases with the fact of his nomination, and while history records the balloting which gave the election to his opponent, William McKinley, the following November, nothing is recorded on that peculiar subject, the private life of a candidate, if, indeed, a candidate can be said to possess a private life.

Up to the time of his first nomination a few pages will suffice to record the outline of our busy, quiet days.

In our new home in Nebraska and in Washington, during Mr. Bryan's years as Congressman, we lived serenely. The care of my father, who, by that time, had become totally blind, and of my mother, an invalid, and of my three young children, together with my close participation in all of Mr. Bryan's legal and political work, filled my years. Mr. Bryan had applied himself unremittingly, and though we were progressing steadily up the ladder which ambitious youth may ascend, the first nomination found Mr. Bryan and me, at thirty-six and thirty-five years of age, a very serious, quietly prosperous, closely congenial couple.

Upon our small household suddenly shone the white light which is said to beat upon the throne. Our very house had altered its appearance when we returned home to it from the Chicago Convention. Streamers of bunting festooned it from porch to eaves; small boys sat in rows along the roof; the crowd which filled the front yard overflowed into the house; flowers and smilax decorated the crowded rooms. It was a symbolic atmosphere. The public had invaded our lives.

WILLIAM JENNINGS BRYAN

There must be certain features which are common to the lives of all Presidential candidates. I think Mr. Bryan's conscientious desire to reply personally to every correspondent and to admit the inquiring reporter into every recess of his life, may have intensified some of these features in his case. The mail poured in upon us and inundated our little home. Letters of congratulation, commendation, and abuse; inquiries on every known and unknown subject, and much advice generously bestowed by the public. It is indeed a humble citizen who cannot advise a political leader. While it is recognized that technical training is necessary to produce a doctor, a lawyer, or a clergyman, a multitude will rise up, apparently without study or even thought, to shower advice upon a political candidate. But while giving the candidate advice upon his own business, the public do not fail to ask his counsel upon their most intimate concerns. The candidate is asked to advise on domestic relations, to furnish material for debates and essays, and to give his judgment on innumerable manuscripts of varying length. Some manuscripts, which would have required from a week to a month of careful study, were submitted during a busy campaign, and the senders would indignantly protest if the candidate did not give their efforts his mature consideration.

The demands for autographs were not so difficult to satisfy, even though these were numerous. Occasionally their form was varied to include writing the autograph on a sofa pillow, a tablecloth, or a piece of material to be later embroidered and incorporated in that sort of bed covering so fittingly termed a "crazy quilt." Often such sofa pillow tops or table covers would be lost in the mails, and we would receive a series of abusive and threatening letters demanding their return.

Then there were the prophets and the seers who had predicted Mr. Bryan's nomination by the position of the stars, or tea leaves, or sand, or other mysterious methods,

PRIVATE LIFE OF A CANDIDATE

and having predicted his nomination, offered also to forecast the election. There were thousands who had had dreams and visions of prophetic content. One man, I remember, wrote a letter telling Mr. Bryan that he had seen in a dream Mr. Bryan's election. He offered furthermore, if the candidate should request it, to dream again and find out what the statistical majority would be. The number of our prophets in America is surprising and bewildering.

It is natural that a public man should be the storm center for requests of benevolence and charity, and that the petitions for aid should run the entire gamut from the request from a total stranger for a pink silk dress or a bicycle, to a petition for a new church building—requests equally beyond the means of a young lawyer struggling to adjust his finances to the new demands.

Great numbers of churches augmented their finances in 1896 by doll and handkerchief sales: "We hope you will dress a doll for us. It will not mean much to you," they would write, to the harassed wife of the candidate, who had in the same mail received several identical requests. We bought and dispatched dolls by the dozen and handkerchiefs by the gross. There were a number of devices for raising church funds which required time and science as well as benevolence. There were cards to which had been attached a little pair of overalls, with the request that the victim measure his own waist and then place in the little breeches pocket one penny for each inch of his girth. In other similar devices the candidate was penalized for each pound of his weight or each inch of his stature. Many churches and schools issued cookbooks compiled from the favorite recipes of well-known people, and I paid for the honor of a place among their number by broadcasting my culinary methods through the pages of these volumes.

But while we were struggling to satisfy the demands made upon us, we were in our turn receiving gifts. A stuffed alligator of tremendous size, so long that its tail protruded its scaly length from the back of the express wagon, and also from every room in our house where we tried to place it, and four live eagles of prodigious size and strength, were among the largest gifts. After trying in vain to place the alligator in the house, we were obliged to lodge him in our back yard until the University Museum came to our aid and housed him amongst its treasures.

I recently found amongst our papers a small notebook in which we recorded, as they arrived, the gifts received at our home during the first Presidential campaign. This book awakens vivid memories of those days, when waves of friendly delegations inundated our garden and, receding, left in their wake demolished flower beds and shattered trellises. Here follow a few items from our notebook:

One set of harness.
One pair of suspenders.
One cane.
One band wagon.
One mule.
One silk bed quilt.
A large watermelon in a gilded laundry basket (this was enthusiastically received by the children).
One dog.
Four volumes of Thomas Jefferson's works.
One ostrich egg.
One cane.
One picture frame made from cigar boxes.
One frosted cake.
One silver plate with presentation inscription.
One cane.
One cane.
One cane.

As canes were, perhaps, our most frequent gift, some of these deserve very special mention. It takes ingenuity to make a walking stick from the vertebræ of a fish, or from petrified wood, or from the horns of the antelope. And we must add to this list a cane made from macerated newspaper editorials. This strange material was then pressed into the shape of a cane and lacquered on the outside. There were canes made of bone with loaded heads; made of the pith of the cactus plant; of rattan, and of rings of pressed leather; canes of bogwood from Ireland; canes made of hickory from Andrew Jackson's birthplace, and of cherry, presumably from George Washington's cherry tree; canes with silver heads, decorated with a daisy with sixteen silver petals and one gold, and in some cases canes with gold heads, voted by church fairs to the most popular candidate. I remember one of these canes, the head of which represented an eagle whose eyes were made of diamonds, until after a large public reception, when we found that his eyes had mysteriously disappeared.

Then there were the natural phenomena; fungi with the strange resemblance to the candidate, and the egg with the curious conformation of shell which suggested his initials, etc.

The term "sixteen to one" took hold upon the popular imagination, and we would receive a potato with sixteen sprouts to one potato; an ancient Phœnician vase with sixteen handles to one vase. I recall seeing in a political parade an ingenious development of the idea of bimetallism. Borne high on a standard was a huge replica of the silver dollar (the dollar at that time contained 53 cents in silver bullion). High upon the standard was the inscription "In God we trust for the other forty-seven cents."

In no subsequent campaign has Mr. Bryan received such quantities of mascots as in the campaign of 1896. I cannot vouch for the fact that this explains his tremendous popular vote in that campaign, but for want of a more suitable place, I may as well set it down at this point.

Mr. Bryan received the largest Democratic vote ever

cast in the history of the country up to that time and exceeded by 946,007 the vote of Cleveland, who had been elected four years before. His vote in 1896 exceeded by 1,425,014 the Democratic vote cast for Parker eight years later, and his vote in 1908 exceeded by 116,984 the vote of Wilson, elected four years later.

If there be virtue in the hind foot of a rabbit procured under the most favorable circumstances, Mr. Bryan should have won this election. It is difficult to imagine that his opponent was more adequately supplied with rabbits' feet; plain, furry little feet, feet mounted in every ingenious form; horseshoes, plain, gilded, wrapped in tinfoil and in ribbon, came to us with such frequency that they are not included in the notebook record.

The bizarre election bets also seem to have become less frequent in succeeding campaigns, but in 1896 there were large numbers of men who had been so certain of a Democratic victory that they wagered recklessly, and after election found themselves pledged to abstain from shaving for the term of their natural life, to hauling their Republican friends around the town in a wheelbarrow, to rolling a peanut interminable distances, or riding a donkey from New York to San Francisco. I recall the day when the last-named individual called at our house in Lincoln in the course of his donkey pilgrimage. He was maintaining himself by selling photographs of his beast and its trappings and patent medicines. We felt in a sense personally responsible for his weary journey.

Several men wrote to Mr. Bryan and indignantly demanded reimbursement for the loss of money and time occasioned by their election bets. One man, I recall, wrote and told us that he had lost in an election bet on Mr. Bryan the money which he had intended to use to mend his roof. "My house is leaking badly," he wrote. "Please send the money at once." Another man said that he had bet his cow on the election and wrung the heart of the candidate by a story of his children left without milk by this reversal of fortune.

If these seem unusual demands upon the purse of a candidate, we had even more tenuous claims to consider. During a trip into the far West, Mr. Bryan's approach to a city had been heralded by a volley of loud explosions. On our return to Nebraska Mr. Bryan received a bill for $87.00, as nearly as I can recall it, the amount computed by a chicken raiser as the sum he had lost when the eggs which he had placed in an incubator had been prevented from hatching by the concussion of the gunpowder.

The kindness and good will which was represented in the gifts and other evidences of friendliness received by Mr. Bryan during a campaign warmed his heart and amply compensated him for incidents which were trying and discouraging. The mementoes of the early political days were always treasured by him and are now treasured by his family.

One of the most valued gifts, and one which bespeaks unmistakably the faith and devotion of the sender, is the photograph of a namesake baby. In 1896 our daughter Ruth made the namesake babies her particular charge and pride. When a letter was received telling of a new little "William Jennings," or another little "Bryan," Ruth claimed him proudly and recorded his arrival. Those were special days when we received the three photographs of three sets of triplets having been given respectively the names "William," "Jennings," and "Bryan." One mother wrote a letter saying she had heard that Mr. Bryan's family treasured the liknesses of the namesake babies, but that her baby had not lived long and they had no photograph of the little boy to whom they had given the name of "Bryan," but she enclosed in her letter two pieces of cloth, one from the baby's christening dress and one from his shroud, and asked that these be kept along with the pictures of the living babies who bore Mr. Bryan's name, and there they have remained during the years.

269

CHAPTER VI

SOLDIER AND EDITOR

WHEN, after a vigorous campaign for the Presidency, Mr. Bryan received news, on November 5, 1896, that his opponent had been elected, his first act was to send the following telegram:

> Lincoln, Nebraska
> November 5

Honorable William McKinley,
  Canton, Ohio

Senator Jones has just informed me that the returns indicate your election, and I hasten to extend my congratulations. We have submitted the issue to the American people and their will is law.

> W. J. BRYAN.

President-elect McKinley wired the following response:

> Canton, Ohio
> November 6

Honorable W. J. Bryan
  Lincoln, Nebraska

I acknowledge the receipt of your courteous message of congratulation with thanks and beg you will receive my best wishes for your health and happiness.

> WILLIAM McKINLEY.

This exchange of courtesies received much comment at the time, but Mr. Bryan, in his book, "The First Battle," wrote of it:

"Our contest aroused no personal feeling on the part of either. I have no doubt that had I been elected, he would as promptly have sent his congratulations."

270

WILLIAM J. BRYAN.
LINCOLN NEBRASKA

April 25 = 1898

Hon William McKinley
President

My Dear Sir —

I hereby place my services at your command during the war with Spain and assure you of my willingness to perform to the best of my ability any duty to which you, as the commander in chief of the army and navy, may see fit to assign me

Respectfully yours
W. J. Bryan

Letter from Mr. Bryan to President McKinley volunteering his personal services in the Spanish-American War.

WILLIAM JENNINGS BRYAN

In 1894, after Mr. Bryan's defeat for the United States Senate, he became chief of the editorial staff of the Omaha *World-Herald*, which position he held until his first nomination for the Presidency, and he contributed various political articles to the *World-Herald* and other newspapers after he had given up his position as editor-in-chief; but in 1898 circumstances arose which directed Mr. Bryan's life for a while into unforeseen paths. America had become involved

THE WESTERN UNION TELEGRAPH COMPANY.
INCORPORATED
21,000 OFFICES IN AMERICA. CABLE SERVICE TO ALL THE WORLD.

This Company TRANSMITS and DELIVERS messages only on conditions limiting its liability, which have been assented to by the sender of the following message. Errors can be guarded against only by repeating a message back to the sending station for comparison, and the Company will not hold itself liable for errors or delays in transmission or delivery of Unrepeated Messages, beyond the amount of tolls paid thereon, nor in any case where the claim is not presented in writing within sixty days after the message is filed with the Company for transmission. This is an UNREPEATED MESSAGE, and is delivered by request of the sender, under the conditions named above.

THOS. T. ECKERT, President and General Manager.

RECEIVED at 1035 N STREET, LINCOLN, NEB.   Standard Time.

36 OM E B 122 Paid Govt May 31
JEFFERSON CITY MO. 31'st
Hon.Wm.J.Bryan-Lincoln, Neb.
Seeing that your State, under the second call for 75000 volunteers may not be requested to furnish a full regiment and knowing of your patriotism and anxiety to go to the front in the service of your country during the present War, I hereby tender you, if under the second call I am empowered by the Secretary of war to make such an appointment, the Colonel of a Missouri Volunteer regiment. Presuming to speak for my State, I will say that our people will be as loyal to you personally as you are to our country and they will feel honored to fight under your leadership.

Lon.V.Stephens, Governor of Missouri
9:36 Am

in the war with Spain and on April 25, 1898, Mr. Bryan sent to President McKinley the offer of his services in any capacity. Mr. Bryan had been authorized by the Governor of Nebraska to take all necessary steps looking to the speedy formation of a provisional regiment, and in less than a week from the announcement of his intention, Mr. Bryan received applications from over thirty organizations for a place in his command. From these he selected twelve, recognizing each of the six Congressional districts of his State. The Governor of Missouri had telegraphed, asking Mr. Bryan to serve as colonel of a Missouri regiment, but Mr. Bryan replied in the following telegram;

SOLDIER AND EDITOR

Honorable Lon V. Stephens

Jefferson City, Missouri

I am deeply indebted to you for the great honor you do me. I should be pleased to be associated in any capacity with the Missouri volunteers, but it is quite certain that all or a considerable portion of my regiment will be accepted, and I feel that my first duty is to the Nebraska boys.

W. J. BRYAN.

On July 13, 1898, the Third Nebraska Volunteer Regiment, under Colonel William Jennings Bryan, was mustered into service at Fort Omaha, Nebraska. I had taken the children with me to see their father take command of his regiment for the first time, and we watched as he rode out on *Governor*, his shiny black Kentucky horse, which we all loved as one of the family, into the hollow square formed by his waiting regiment. As he gave his first order and his sword flashed for a moment in the sun, the motionless lines of men began to move at his command, and we felt proud of the regiment and its colonel—so proud that our hearts were pounding anxiously. Memories of those days are so vivid and the intervening time has passed so swiftly, it is difficult to realize that a stretch of years lies between the present and those tense days. We could not know when we sewed the insignia of rank on Colonel Bryan's uniform overcoat and found the tears blurring our stitches that the regiment which he raised would be stationed for months in Florida, awaiting its turn to cross the channel to active service, and that the grim enemy he would face was fever in a southern camp.

I found a yellowed newspaper clipping with date of twenty-seven years ago, which gives recognition to the soldiers who waited.

WILLIAM JENNINGS BRYAN

LET US NOT FORGET THE HEROES WHO ARE READY FOR THE FRONT

While we cry aloud the praises
Of the heroes at the front;
Tell of deeds of valiant soldiers
Who have borne the battle's brunt.

While we love to speak of Dewey,
And of Sampson, and of Schley;
And we cheer the name of Hobson,
Who was not afraid to die.

While with pride we speak of Shafter,
And of Wheeler, and of Miles,
Who have fought so well for country
In the proud Castilian Isles.

Then there's William Jennings Bryan,
Just as eager now is he
For the Cuban Independence
As that silver should be free!

While we cheer the distant soldiers,
Who have borne the battle's brunt,
Let us not forget the heroes
Who are ready for the front.

J. FRED DE BERRY.

To W. V. Allen, Senator from Nebraska, Mr. Bryan sent the following telegram, lest the well-intentioned efforts of friends might make request for preferential treatment of his regiment:

274

Photo. Underwood & Underwood, N. Y.

COLONEL WILLIAM JENNINGS BRYAN AND THE THIRD NEBRASKA VOLUNTEERS
A regiment recruited and commanded by him during the Spanish American War.

SOLDIER AND EDITOR

Senator W. V. Allen:

Please do not make any requests or suggestions as to destination of third regiment. I have no preference. If the War Department asks my wishes I shall expect to leave matters entirely with my superior officers and go wherever they see fit to send me. Confidential.

W. J. BRYAN.

The regiment was assigned to the 7th Army Corps under General Fitzhugh Lee, and their journey from Fort Omaha to Jacksonville, Florida, was one continued ovation. As one newspaper stated, "No other regiment is led by a man who has received six and a half million votes for the presidency."

As the regiment passed through Illinois, en route to Florida, Mr. Bryan's native state did honor to its son. I quote from a press account of the welcome at Bloomington, Ill.

A WELCOME TO BRYAN

"Colonel William Jennings Bryan, former candidate for President, and the greatest of American orators and statesmen, received just as heartfelt a reception today as he did when he visited this city during the memorable campaign of 1896. There were thousands to see him that day and his ringing words at Franklin Park were cheered to the echo as he stood before the assembled masses defending a great cause. Then he was a private citizen; today he belongs to the defenders of this country in the capacity of a commanding officer. . . .

"The occasion of his brief visit in the city today was a lucky chance for Bloomington. Colonel Bryan is on his way to the front with his regiment from Nebraska to Camp Cuba Libre, at Jacksonville, Fla. The four trains bearing the patriot leader and the boys in blue from Nebraska transferred from the Burlington at La Salle to the Illinois Central. The first section of the train passed through this city at three o'clock and the train bearing Colonel Bryan about a half hour later. The excessive heat of the day prevented an elaborate celebration, but the booming of a cannon told of the coming of the great leader and his followers. . . .

"Amid the booming of cannon and the cheering of several thousand people the first section of six coaches loaded to the guards came in. The men looked both happy and hot. The train arrived at 3.22, and after stopping a few minutes for water, pulled out. Colonel Bryan was on the second train in the last coach with his staff. When this announcement was made the excitement grew, the cannon became louder and everything in general became animated. The prominent citizens of Bloomington were all there.

"As Bryan's train rolled in a mighty cheer went up from the multitude. It was the event of the afternoon. Bryan himself, with his smiling yet commanding face, appeared at the rear platform, followed by his officers, all his regimental staff. The vociferous cheering continued and on the appearance of the great leader the enthusiasm broke all bounds. Hats went up in the air and everyone tried to outdo his fellow enthusiast in making a demonstration.

"The hands went up faster than Colonel Bryan could grasp them. He had a pleasant word for all and when

276

quiet was restored he began speaking. He did not touch any of the political issues, but spoke principally of the soldiers. He said:

" 'Ladies and Gentlemen: I had the pleasure of speaking here two years ago and I am glad to speak and meet you now. I am proud of my regiment of sturdy, healthy fellows, as only one of them out of the 1300 men was not well enough to leave Omaha. I am very glad to know that you take a great interest in them and me. I had a letter from an Illinois man who could not get here, asking to join my Nebraska regiment. In time of peace you can all help fight your country's battles.' (Prolonged applause.) When Bryan finished the handshaking began again, and women, boys, and men fought for a chance to grasp the colonel's hand."

That Colonel Bryan's regiment did not lack for food is indicated by a clipping from a Nashville newspaper:

"Information was received by Superintendent M. C. Wrenne, of the Nashville, Chattanooga & St. Louis Railroad, last night that the first section of the train bearing Col. William Jennings Bryan's regiment of Nebraskans would arrive in Nashville this morning about eleven o'clock. . . .

"The committee made arrangements with the Tea Room to prepare 2000 sandwiches and about a thousand lunch boxes. Mr. Hancock has charge of the coffee and will have over a thousand gallons ready. This is all in addition to the voluntary contributions."

[This generous provision indicates one gallon of coffee for each of the brave soldier boys.]

"The boxes prepared by the Tea Room give some idea of the good things in store for the Westerners.

These boxes contain two sandwiches, two hard-boiled eggs, two tomatoes, two beaten biscuits, and a lemon. It is supposed that most of the boxes will contain about the same articles, though some enthusiastic ladies may have disobeyed the order with regard to cake and pickles."

The Third Nebraska Regiment were encamped at Panama Park and later at Pablo Beach, Florida. As evidence that Mr. Bryan's life in camp was no less energetic than civilian life, I quote from his letter to me dated September 12:

"Let me imitate your plan and tell you what I did Sunday and I am sure you will accept my apology for not writing yesterday. The hotel is about a mile from camp. I went out to camp before breakfast and put things in shape to leave, then ate breakfast and took the 8.45 train for Jacksonville. I hired a buggy at J'ville, went to the telegraph office to see if any messages had been rec'd (we have no telegraph office at Pablo). Just in front of the office I met Col. and Mrs. Montgomery and gave her one of my spurs as a memento. (She says she is going to wear it—suspended from a necklace—when she visits us at the White House!)

"Then I went to the hotel to find Col. Maus and met Robert Ellis of Macon, Ga.—who had charge of my meeting there last spring. I took him with me and got an order for 25 barrels of lime and one barrel of carbolic acid for disinfectant purposes. Then went to corps headquarters and got an order for some water pipes; then found the chaplain was sick and called on him and arranged for him to leave last night on a furlough; then went to the ferry to meet some invalids on their way to the hospitals (they did not come at that time, but I was afraid they might). While waiting there I got a glass of iced tea and a piece of pie. Then went to the Third Div. Hospital (six miles), stopping at 4th Ill. to inquire about a boy Ex-Congressman Lane wrote me about.

"I visited a part of the wards and found Hartquist about the same. Pinto has fever now. While at Panama I learned that 16 patients were coming from Pablo to the Hospital and I got six men to arrange the cots, secured an order for three ambulances and hurried to the ferry, arriving just in time to meet the patients (returned the horse and buggy after six hours' use and paid $4.00 for same). Helped the 16 men off the boat and into the ambulances, which came soon, and went out to Panama with them. Went from the hospital to Gen. Hubbard's tent to report our doings and got to bed about 10 o'clock. Got up at 5, visited the hospital from 5.30 to 6.45. Went to breakfast. Went to J'ville via 2nd Ill. reg. and made inquiry about another man. Got a life line for the beach, sent some telegrams, and came to Pablo, arriving just before noon. I have omitted a number of minor details, but this will show what I did."

Colonel Bryan threw himself into the duties of camp with a personal solicitude about every detail. In early September, 1898, he writes me:

"The boys are busy preparing for inspection and are anxious to make as good a showing as possible. I have been drilling the regiment more of late, and am doing it quite well, I thank you. Won't you be proud of your husband when he gains a reputation as a drill master! We had only 19 men in hospital yesterday; 10 of these had measles; only 9 with other diseases out of 1300. Isn't that good? One man is threatened with typhoid fever—the first case we have had."

This was the first indication of the scourge which was to take its heavy toll of the regiment a little later.

By October 29, in spite of all his efforts at sanitation, the Colonel found his hospital filling with his sick "boys"— and himself struggling with a fever.

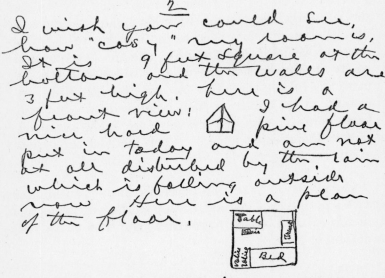

Part of letter from Colonel Bryan to his wife, describing camp life.

"I am lying here in bed," he wrote to me on October 26, "eating nothing but milk and soup. My temperature was almost normal early yesterday morning, but then it ran up to over 100. It seems to linger along, and I cannot tell when I will be strong enough to go back to camp."

Lying in bed, with the anxiety of the camp in his mind, he writes further:

"If I consulted my own happiness I would forsake public life forever, but I am not free to please myself. I have consecrated whatever talents I may have to the service of my fellow men. To aid in making the government better and existence more tolerable to the producer of wealth, is my ambition, and the one question which I am considering now is whether I can be more useful in the army or out of it. Unhappy woman to be yoked to such a companion! But you have borne the burden bravely for eight years—I might almost say twelve." (This includes the period of our engagement.)

Colonel Bryan made no speeches during his military service and applied his every energy to the care of his men. A review printed by the regiment at the time of his resignation says:

"That he is loved and respected by his soldiers goes without saying. Scarcely a day passes without some pleasing act, some good deed looking to the welfare and the bettering of his soldier boys. Indeed, so far has this particular trait in his generous nature been carried that there are those who look upon his intimacy with the boys of the rank and file as demoralizing and injurious to proper army discipline. There are others, however, who take another view, and these give the Colonel his proper meed of credit for the care he takes of his soldiers, and for the personal efforts he is constantly making for their health, their comfort, and their contentment, under the extraordinary circumstances of war and the ever occurring perils and uncertainties of camp life."

WILLIAM JENNINGS BRYAN

When the war with Spain was ended Colonel Bryan resigned his commission—not without an affectionate parting from his brother officers and enlisted men.

One day when Mr. Bryan was at home on furlough, a Japanese boy, valise in hand, appeared at our door. As I saw him, I recalled how two years previously a boy had written from Japan announcing that he wished to join Mr. Bryan's family and be educated by him. We had written at once stating that we had three children of our own to educate and could not undertake the responsibility of a Japanese student in addition.

Some weeks later a second letter arrived, this time announcing that Yamashita had reached San Francisco. In no wise deterred by our communication, he had crossed the ocean and was planning to come to Nebraska.

This time Mr. Bryan had written to one of the Democratic committee men in San Francisco explaining the matter and urging him to make it clear to the young man that Mr. Bryan could not educate him.

Our next news of the ambitious young Japanese was his appearance at our front door.

He knew almost no English and was so manifestly homeless that we took him in for the night, intending to struggle with his problem on the day following, but his eagerness won our attention and our respect and Yamashita made his home with us for five and a half years. He studied in the public schools and the state university before he returned to his own country in 1903.

Through this association our family gained an abiding interest in the Oriental peoples and made a number of friendships in Japan which were charmingly strengthened when we visited that country in 1904.

Political work filled his time during the second presidential campaign of 1900. Following his defeat by Mr. Roosevelt, Mr. Bryan commenced, on January 23, 1901, the publication of his weekly periodical *The Commoner*. It is probably unique in
282

the history of newspapers that the advance subscription to *The Commoner* entirely defrayed the cost of its initial publication.

Mr. Bryan announced his intention of publishing a sheet which would reflect his views on public questions, and 17,000 subscriptions at $1.00 per year were in hand before the presses began to revolve.

The purpose of the publication as stated in its first editorial was "to aid the common people in the protection of their rights, the advancement of their interests, and the realization of their aspirations." In the term "common people" the editor included the "rich man who has honestly acquired his wealth and is not afraid to entrust its care to laws made by his fellows," but excluded the poor man, "if he fawns before a plutocrat and has no higher ambition than to be a courtier or a sycophant."

The Commoner found its way into tens of thousands of American homes. In it the issues of the day were discussed in no uncertain terms. Mr. Bryan laid bare his political philosophy and his position on men and measures. A hostile press often took up his writings and pursued his editorial utterances with merciless criticisms. The columns of *The Commoner* contain a faithful history of the politics of the times and here the student may find a discussion of the political issues which divided men and parties for the first quarter of the twentieth century.

When Mr. Bryan entered the cabinet he found it necessary to change *The Commoner* from a weekly to a monthly publication. In the last few years of its publication many columns were given to the discussion of religious topics in which Mr. Bryan had become increasingly interested.

In the conduct of the paper Mr. Bryan found an able coworker in his brother, Charles W. Bryan, who, after becoming Governor of Nebraska, could no longer give his time to the publication, and Mr. Bryan, who had removed his permanent residence to Florida, was engrossed with other matters. Therefore *The Commoner* suspended publication in April, 1923.

CHAPTER VII

CHAUTAUQUA AND TEMPERANCE SPEAKER

AN American President once made this statement as he stood on the platform of the Mother Chautauqua at Chautauqua Lake, New York: "This is the most American thing in America." He would have had frequent cause to repeat this observation had he been as closely identified as was Mr. Bryan for many years with the great circuit and independent Chautauqua systems of this country.

"Chautauqua" had its origin in a Camp Assembly for Bible Study under the leadership of good Bishop John H. Vincent and Lewis Miller on the shore of the lake bearing that name. This assembly developed into a summer forum and a national reading course which gave to thousands of students "the college outlook." To Chautauqua Lake came a cosmopolitan throng from the north and south, east and west, and each summer hundreds of graduates passed through the gates of "the Hall in the Grove." America came to Chautauqua. It remained to carry Chautauqua to America.

Imitators of the Chautauqua Lake assembly arose on other camp grounds. Independent managers started lecture and concert courses at other summer assemblies. Mr. Bryan took part in such courses as one of the earliest and most popular Chautauqua speakers. He could testify to the hardships met in reaching these widely scattered points. I quote from a letter written to me by Mr. Bryan several years ago:

"What a night I had last night! I left Watertown on the 5 P. M. train for Sioux Falls, 103 miles away. When we got to Badger, about thirty miles out, we found a car off the track, and not knowing when the

284

train could go on, we got out at 6.30 and started for Sioux Falls, wiring to Sioux Falls to send a fast car to meet us. We made pretty fair time for 42 miles. (We found the distance by wagon road some 85 or 90 miles.) Once we got off the road and lost half an hour and then stuck in the mud. We waked up a farmer and were going to have him haul us out of the mud, but by the time he had dressed, the Sioux Falls car arrived and took us about 45 miles in two hours, i. e.: 10.30 to 12.30. *But the Chautauqua audience was still there and shouting,* and I spoke from 12.40 midnight to 2.08 A. M. That is the record for Chautauquas—it almost equals my political meetings. I am approaching my last town. Then I drive 15 miles and catch a train for Chicago."

He had experience in addressing crowds which had gathered in inadequate shelters in those pioneer days of the movement. But America has the organizing mind, and by and by the great Chautauqua managements developed. Chautauquas developed a system of standardized circuits; they owned their own tents, chairs, pianos, and equipment, and Chautauqua created a new profession. It not only provided a hearing for musicians and speakers, but it provided them with an extraordinarily large audience. I cannot give accurate statistics on this point, but it is my impression that there are now more than ten thousand towns which hold their annual Chautauqua assembly, and that these Chautauquas are attended each summer by more than ten million people.

These enlarged Chautauquas retain two original features which are most wholesome. In each instance the movement is supported and guaranteed by a large local committee, unsectarian and nonpartisan. Although the financial obligation for the week of Chautauqua programs is considerable, it is not beyond the reach of any earnest crowd of citizens. To thousands of small towns Chautauqua has not only been a means of bringing the best music and the best lecturers, but it has been the occasion for town unity and village improvement. The town and surrounding countryside unite their interests under the great brown tent or beneath the roof of the auditorium, and these gatherings have built for a friendliness between urban and rural America. The other feature which has continued is the free forum. Every current viewpoint of interest has a hearing at Chautauqua. Distinguished foreigners, military heroes, great travelers and explorers, politicians, and statesmen—all are heard at Chautauqua, and often informal discussions follow the lectures and the audience is brought into the closest touch with the platform. From Chautauqua platforms went forth impassioned pleas before our entry into the World War. From the same platforms went patriotic calls to war when America had entered the conflict. Upon Chautauqua platforms millions of dollars were pledged for victory loans. And now, from these same platforms, to that vast audience of thinking Americans, comes the constructive study of the principles of international arbitration. The study of international relations and the principles which underlie international understanding, have found a place in the Chautauqua programs of these later years, and our daughter Ruth has been working through this medium which her father loved, to help present the ideals of arbitration which he held dear.

Upon the Chautauqua platform Mr. Bryan was always perfectly at home. He met the perpetual heat, the restlessness of the great throngs which usually overspread the adjoining grove, with genial ease and command. His leisurely approach, his humanity and humor soon won the audiences and continued to hold them to the end.

Mr. Bryan usually spoke at length fortified by the ever-present pitcher of ice water. His message was so simple, so passionate, so keyed to lofty issues, it never failed to find an eager response. A delightful magazine article, published several years ago, treated Mr. Bryan's Chautauqua lectures with pleasant satire. The writer pointed out how for the hour or two that they listened, his audiences had caught a glimpse of nobility and civic virtue. Their breasts had swelled with the goodness and they had been lifted, for a while, upon a very cloud of lofty aspirations, and, he concluded, "But when the audience got back to earth sufficiently to inquire what practical means they could employ to produce the millennium; lo: Mr. Bryan was on the train again hurrying off to his next lecture." But whether or not there is a kernel of truth in the satire and the exaltation of the audience was not always a permanent condition, there is no doubt as to the purity and loftiness of the conceptions of government and character which he presented, and his audiences under Chautauqua tents showed no flagging in numbers or in enthusiasm in all the years.

Chautauqua in the main is a small town affair, although many larger towns have their Chautauquas, the average has a population of less than 5000. This is probably the reason why the metropolitan press has always ignored or misunderstood it.

But Chautauqua is something deeper than concerts or inspirational lectures. It is more than the gathering together of great crowds in the interest of civic progress.

When Mr. Bryan stood in the Chautauqua tent at night under the electric lights and the starlight, with practically every adult and most of the children from miles around within sound of his voice, he could forget the hardships and weariness of travel. His voice would grow deep and solemn, for he knew he was speaking to the heart of America.

It is not too much to say that Mr. Bryan has remained the most popular Chautauqua lecturer in this country for thirty years. Each year when he returned from his tours he had not only spoken to, but had listened to, the mind of America. He had had an opportunity to know what America was thinking and he had helped America to make up her mind. On his lecture tours Mr. Bryan usually spoke twice daily, and was often asked to remain in the town of his Saturday engagement and speak on the Sunday that followed. Indeed, in the later years, it has seemed to me that he was preaching every day, for his lecture on "The Prince of Peace" had become a favorite, and that was a sermon.

As I have said, Mr. Bryan recognized Chautauqua as an opportunity for listening to and speaking to the mind of his country, but he also saw in his lecturing an honorable way to make a living. Mr. Bryan's public life did not mean perpetual office-holding, and the exactions of his political work prevented him from devoting himself to the legal profession. The lecture platform furnished him with a means of livelihood as well as a medium for presenting his thoughts and ideals to the public. The week after his death the editor of *The Lyceum* magazine, who knew his Chautauqua career intimately, endorsed this quotation from Russell Bridges:

"He did not make as much money on his lecture tours as was generally thought," says Mr. Bridges, "because about half of his speeches were given free or for charity, and when he was booked for a stipulated fee, he made it a rule never to let a local committee lose anything on his lecture, and he always kept the price of admission very low, usually twenty-five or fifty cents, never more than $1.00 for reserved seats, in easy reach of the masses.

"Then Mr. Bryan was always very generous in his settlement with his managers, nearly always paying more commissions than the agreement called for. My association with Mr. Bryan as his platform manager at various times during the last twenty years, was one of the greatest pleasures of my life. I always found him the same rugged, honest, sincere champion of the masses, and the right as he understood it."

To the criticisms which were leveled at Mr. Bryan for

lecturing while he was Secretary of State, I am fortunate in being able to give his own reply. He had been asked to read and revise a statement concerning his career, which had been prepared by the editor of a modern encyclopedia, and he replied as follows:

August 1, 1924.

My dear Sir:

I hope that delay in reply to your letter of May twenty-ninth—due to absence from home—has not made it impossible to make the corrections indicated. The article is written in such a friendly spirit that I conclude the errors into which you have fallen have been due to your trusting the unfriendly newspapers of New York which have made a business of misrepresenting me for about twenty-eight years.

What you say in regard to Chautauqua lectures dignifies a very unjust criticism engaged in by a very small portion of the public. The President approved of my Chautauqua work—which, by the way, occupied fifteen days in two years. I had less vacation than any clerk in my department; other secretaries were able to travel without criticism. I lectured at Chautauqua before I was nominated for the Presidency and afterwards. President Taft lectured at Chautauqua after he was elected; Vice President Marshall and Speaker Clark while they were in office. Nobody ever criticised them. It cost me over ten thousand dollars to serve the Government a little over two years. I would have gladly spent more if it had been necessary. There was no reason why I should be criticised for putting in a part of my vacation time lecturing. . . . However, it is not a matter of importance to me. . . .

Although Mr. Bryan's Chautauqua lectures were usually entirely non-partisan, much of his time was devoted to aiding, by his speeches, the various causes which he advocated, as they came, one by one, to be issues of national interest.

Although Mr. Bryan was a total abstainer from his youth, he was slow to take up the cause of national prohibition.

The same feeling which led him to hold elections in the towns of his Congressional districts, instead of appointing postmasters himself, caused him to consider carefully the liquor question. He stood for "equal rights for all and special privileges for none" and was for a time uncertain that such a drastic measure was desirable. He did not want to confuse the mind of the voter with too many issues and was unwilling to approve this reform until it was ripe for action.

He was deeply grieved over the sorrow and misery directly traceable to intemperance. Numbers of his acquaintances —often men of fine mentality and high purpose—died of excessive drink. He saw women and children cold and hungry because the head of the house was a drunkard, and an exceedingly sore point with Mr. Bryan was the temptation placed before the young men by the saloon.

High license he did not like, as it seemed to be a permission to lower the morals of the community if the city officials were paid a sufficient sum. He felt that the people themselves had a right to decide, and in 1904 began to advocate local option. Communities voted whether their saloons should stay or go. Soon it became evident that the community could not control the situation. Outlying neighborhoods brought liquors into the "dry" districts. The unit was enlarged and in 1908 he sponsored county option, but not without the loss of supporters. In our state, Nebraska, there were counties, settled entirely by those from other countries, who opposed the measure. And to their credit let me add that most of these people knew how to use intoxicants. Few drank to excess. Americans seem unable to do anything in moderation. County option

290

proved ineffectual. County lines were too easily crossed. In the meantime other states had voted. Maine and Kansas "had gone dry" several years before.

Digressing a moment: One often hears that the public had no warning of the coming of national prohibition; that the prohibitionists stole a march upon the voters. These statements only prove that some people are so absorbed in their own affairs that they do not know their country. These state campaigns were wonderful. I went through a number with Mr. Bryan. As I recall, Ohio had five state campaigns before the dry forces won. The brewing interests of Cincinnati died hard. One feature deserves especial mention, namely, the great processions of school children. At county seats all the children in the county would be in line, thousands of them, the girls in white with gay sashes, each child carrying a flag, and marching proudly with their banners. "When we can vote, the saloon will go." "Aren't we worth protecting?" etc. A most impressive sight and the work of women. Women are largely responsible for national prohibition, which was secured without equal suffrage. Is it reasonable to expect a repeal of the amendment when women now can vote as well as work?

State prohibition suffered from adjoining wet territory, and again it seemed necessary to enlarge the scope. One recalls devices for law violation which show bright minds behind the schemes.

A certain grocer in the southwest dealt in eggs, as most grocers do, but for some reasons his trade increased until men were standing in line to buy eggs. The enforcement officer became interested, put a plain-clothes man in line, and a case of neatly packed eggs was purchased. Each shell had been opened, the contents removed, a tiny bottle of whiskey substituted, and the two halves joined. The egg trade suddenly diminished.

Again, funeral processions moved across country. Here and there one saw a hearse, a car filled with pallbearers, followed in due course by mourners, both men and women. Though seldom taking the same route, these funeral processions increased in number until it dawned upon the public that these dear ones all had passed to their reward in wet territory, and the relatives were consigning them to their final resting place in dry territory. Unpleasant investigations ensued, and the hearses gave up case after case of death-dealing liquid, but no bodies of the slain.

Pursued by cries of invasion of state rights and of personal liberty, Mr. Bryan saw his following dividing, and a new alignment probable. Once more he took a stand apparently against his own interests. His argument ran like this: "It is true a man has a right to drink if he chooses and if he considers himself alone, but there are duties which he owes to society which cannot be ignored. Personal liberty is often curbed for a greater good. Laws are made to protect society against burglary, which run counter to a man's right to enjoy a burglar's kit and a dark lantern; laws against arson deprive the citizen of the right to strike a match and burn his neighbor's house. A drunken chauffeur has a right to drive a car, but when he kills people on the highway, he becomes a public menace and must be arrested, and his personal liberty is bounded by the local jail. How willingly should the people give up the right to drink when they can, by that act, reclaim thousands of men and bring comfort to countless miserable homes. I am sure the nation will do this when it understands. It is sound at heart."

Convinced that he was right, he was ready to fight. He announced to his close friends that he intended to take up national prohibition. He found small encouragement. They feared the consequences. Paying no attention to advice, he said: "If they do not want to support me, they needn't. I have no desire to implicate any one, and I shall announce a speech in Omaha, and hire the hall myself." I could not go with him, but on the day advertised, he

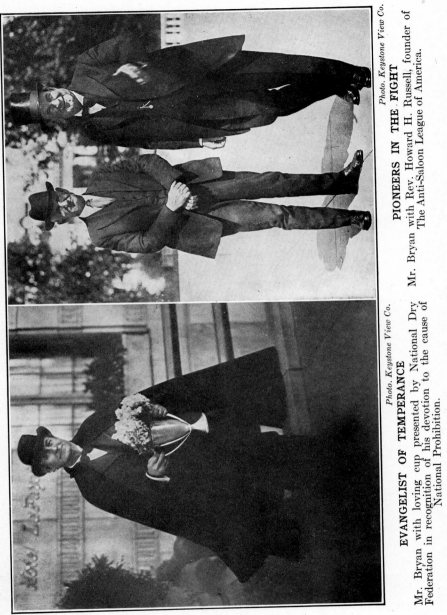

Photo. Keystone View Co.

EVANGELIST OF TEMPERANCE

Mr. Bryan with loving cup presented by National Dry
Federation in recognition of his devotion to the cause of
National Prohibition.

Photo. Keystone View Co.

PIONEERS IN THE FIGHT

Mr. Bryan with Rev. Howard H. Russell, founder of
The Anti-Saloon League of America.

appeared before a packed audience in the hall he had hired. Without a single companion he placed his coat and hat on a chair, and stepping forward, made a graceful bow to his hat and coat and said: "Mr. Chairman, Ladies and Gentlemen." The audience was delighted and the speech a success.

From that day until the passage of the Amendment in November, 1919, he worked ceaselessly. The liquor interests became alarmed and formed an organization with the avowed purpose of crushing Mr. Bryan.

He had no fear of the final result, but he knew the power of the brewers and he foresaw a long fight. Remember, this was back in 1908, long before nation-wide prohibition had become a political issue. His retort to the liquor people in a published statement is worth quoting. Said he:

"If the liquor interests can make good their threat to destroy me politically, my death will be a warning to the fathers and mothers of the power of this foe to the home and to American life."

The Amendment, which has caused so much comment, was adopted by the Senate August 1, 1917, and by the House of Representatives December 18, 1917, and ran as follows:

TEXT OF THE EIGHTEENTH (PROHIBITION) AMENDMENT

"Article 1. After one year from the ratification of this article the manufacture, sale, or transportation of intoxicating liquors within, the importation thereof into, or the exportation thereof from the United States and all territory subject to the jurisdiction thereof for beverage purposes is hereby prohibited.

"Article 2. The Congress and the several States shall have concurrent power to enforce this article by appropriate legislation.

"Article 3. This article shall be inoperative unless it shall have been ratified as an amendment to the Constitution by the legislatures of the several States, as provided in the Constitution, within seven years from the date of the submission hereof to the States by the Congress."

The Amendment was ratified by three fourths of the states, January 16, 1919; effective at midnight January 16, 1920.

Mr. Bryan felt a strong affection for all young people and particularly for college students, and helping one of these to make a good start in life seemed more to him than anything else. "Stars in his diadem," I called them.

Among his books may be found a volume containing 8831 signatures, collected during one tour to the Northwest, all signed below a pledge to abstain from intoxicating liquors as a beverage, which Mr. Bryan himself has first signed on the first page. A prominent man of —— went to hear Mr. Bryan speak on temperance and later his grown son, a college boy, was roused by the father passing through the room. "What is it, father? What are you doing?" "I am going to empty a bottle of brandy into the bath. I have finished with it. Nothing of that kind shall ever find a place in my house again." To his surprise the boy sat up in bed and said: "Dad, let me in on that too. I join you." And the two clasped hands. I can see Mr. Bryan now as he told me this story, his face glowing with enthusiasm and his eyes shining. "How wonderful, Mary, that the very first one he influenced should be his own son."

The time of Mr. Bryan's work for temperance was enlivened as usual by the press. With a clamor of indignation, they asserted that Mr. Bryan was receiving pay from the Anti-Saloon League. Reviewing the Temperance Campaign, Mr. Bryan made a dozen free speeches for every one for which he received pay, and our income was less than usual. The Anti-Saloon League gave Mr. Bryan the equivalent of his lecture salary for a few months of the time he spoke in their aid which was necessary because his only source of livelihood was his individual work on the platform.

Out of his temperance work the usual crop of anecdotes grew. Every subject seemed to develop its own illustrations. Mr. Bryan never forgot them and used them with unerring skill in his speeches. Space is precious, but I venture to tell one or two stories which he enjoyed using for illustration.

A drunken man was staggering home, and pausing before a moving picture theatre, read: "Home Sweet Home" (in three reels). "I tell you, it can't be done," he commented.

A temperance worker said to a woman whose husband had been reclaimed: "My good woman, I suppose your home life is much happier since your husband quit drinking."

"Oh, Lor', sir, it certainly is fine. My husband is so kind. He seems more like a friend than a husband."

While his temperance speeches were lightened by anecdote, they contained many passages of serious logic and haunting beauty. His apostrophe to water, which follows, will illustrate the grace of some of these phrases.

"Water, the daily need of every living thing. It ascends from the seas, obedient to the summons of the sun, and, descending, showers blessing upon the earth; it gives of its sparkling beauty to the fragrant flower; its alchemy transmutes base clay into golden grain; it is the canvas upon which the finger of the Infinite traces the radiant bow of promise. It is the drink that refreshes and adds no sorrow with it—Jehovah looked upon it at creation's dawn and said—'It is good.'"

CHAPTER VIII

ANALYSIS OF MR. BRYAN'S CHARACTER

WHEN a man is in public life, the searchlight of publicity shows only his dominant traits, these often overemphasized and out of proportion to other qualities.

It remains for those who knew him best to give, by the addition of more intimate knowledge, a well-rounded estimate of his character.

Perhaps the dominant note which has been sounded by the recent obituary notices in the press is a belief in Mr. Bryan's personal sincerity and integrity. "Even though we do not agree with some of his doctrines," they said repeatedly, "we can pay tribute to his honesty and sincerity." Under this qualifying phrase was often the shadow of years of bitter opposition.

Willis J. Abbot closes an editorial with these words: "To paraphrase the words of Henley, he may not have been the master of his fate—few men are that—but he was at all times and under all circumstances the captain of his soul."

Public opinion, as expressed by the press, has also recognized Mr. Bryan's deep religious faith. The attention which focused on the latter days of his life when that faith was made a matter of court record and subjected to the harassing ordeal of cross examination, brought the simplicity and fervor of his religious convictions into sharp notice.

But it was not in the unsympathetic atmosphere of a court room or even in those words which were placed at the beginning of his will: "In the name of God, farewell," that the quality of his religious nature made itself most plain.

296

ANALYSIS OF CHARACTER

It was in his instinctive turning to prayer in his hours of trial and indecision, as at the New York Convention when he feared that the introduction of a certain resolution might be the spark to light a thousand torches of intolerance, he asked his committee to turn with him to God for guidance. And at his bedside at night, with the Bible close at hand, he sought his Maker's counsel before he slept. His was a faith which took firm hold of the promise of Divine guidance, and which felt in the assurance of Divine approval an armor and sword, against which no foe could stand.

Moral courage, too, ranks high in this list. After the Baltimore Convention, Cardinal Gibbons said to me: "Madam, your husband stepped out like a great lion." And like a great lion he was. Without a tremor he would face a hostile gathering and force them to listen. More than once from the platform I have seen a front row of noisy enemies lose their assurance and cower lower and lower under the lash of his scorn.

Through the stress of a political campaign more than once he was warned of danger, more than once friends brought to him devices for protection (well I remember a coat of steel mail which hung for years unused in our attic), but his reply was always the same: "Mary, if my death is necessary to further this cause, I am ready to go." He knew no fear.

But as a balance to this moral courage he had great caution in small things. He drew the curtains when we sat together in the evening; he preferred a bedroom on the second floor; he never wore a valuable watch or carried much money when going out at night; if the walk were a lonely one, he selected a heavy walking-stick.

Most prominent in the letters which his death called forth from his friends, both personal and political, was the repeated statement: "He was my friend."

In the faces of the thousands who paid their last tribute of respect as the train bearing his body traveled from Ten-

297

nessee to Washington, there was written as clearly as any words, "He was our friend." His was a genius for friendship composed of a warm interest in his fellowmen and an impulse for generous affection which always met the stranger more than halfway.

His interest was inherent and genuine. Those self-seeking politicians who went about shaking hands and kissing the babies from motives of policy, did not deceive the rank and file. They knew their own.

An illustration may be in point. When he was a pale, slender youth of twenty, he came to visit in my home. I asked my father's permission to take him to the station in my phaeton. At the foot of a particularly bad hill there was a man trying to repair a broken harness. Mr. Bryan said, "Wait a minute. I had better help that man." I said, "Don't bother with him. I know the family. They are shiftless. You would only waste your time." We drove on a little way, but he was uneasy. "Stop, please, I must go back. He needs me," he said. He went back and while he repaired the dilapidated harness, the all too short hours of our visit passed.

This might serve as an epitome of his life—"I must go back. He needs my help."

So warm was his sense of friendliness that he was sometimes slow to judge the real qualities of an individual. He could gauge the probable action of the public more accurately than he could gauge the probable conduct of any one man. His universal friendliness implied a trust which was at times misplaced, and his patience and forbearance sometimes tolerated unworthy men about him.

The fact of his prolonged political leadership has been explained with varying degrees of accuracy, but his oratorical power was by no means the sole factor.

A prominent newspaper man, long since dead, who traveled with us during a campaign on our special train, saw the truth. He said to me: "Bryan and I are both leaders. I watch which way the people are going and run around the corner and get in front of them. Bryan takes a place in advance and the people follow him."

Whenever a new political issue arose, Mr. Bryan and I always discussed it fully, and the following was a typical conversation:

The Wife: "But isn't that an extreme position? The question is new. People don't understand too well. If you stand for that, they will call you a fanatic, a wild-eyed reformer, and a few other choice things."

Mr. Bryan: "But I must stand there. Don't you see, my dear, that a leader must be well in advance. All progress comes through compromise; not a compromise of principle, but an adjustment between the more radical and the less radical positions. If I begin far in advance, when the compromise is made, our position will be much ahead of the place I would have secured by a less advanced standpoint."

The Wife: "Do be more moderate. I cannot bear to have you so abused."

Mr. Bryan: "Don't mind about me. These questions are more important than my personal fortunes."

And he would take the extreme stand, submitting to misunderstanding and ridicule for the sake of the compromise which would be most advantageous to the cause.

I am hoping that light upon this point may explain to friends and enemies alike the positions that he took which at the time seemed unreasonable.

A quality seldom mentioned by his reviewers is that of political foresight. He saw the trend of public opinion and could measure the relative strength of opposing forces. He was nominated for Congress first in 1890. Fully two years before the nomination he told me in strictest confidence that he would be the candidate in 1890 and would win. He said that in a district so Republican no Democrat could hope to win, and so he could easily get the nomination; that the growth of Populism would by that time cause a

WILLIAM JENNINGS BRYAN

split in Republican ranks and make possible the election of
a Democrat, all of which came true. Again, while the
nomination in Chicago is often declared to be altogether
the result of his speech, he had told me several months
before that the logic of the situation was in his favor; that
he regarded it as a possibility, not as a probability; that
geographically he was properly situated.

He was never entirely sure of the result in great
Presidential campaigns. The field was too vast, the
forces at work were too varied and numerous; and being
always surrounded by friends, his vision was necessarily
limited.

But although he was keen-minded in his observation of
political forces, he always hesitated to turn them to his
personal advantage. After the first election of Wilson and
before his selection of his Cabinet, Mr. Bryan was dining
with warm friends in Richmond, Virginia. One of the
gentlemen said in the course of the conversation: "Mr.
Bryan, I want to see you President of the United States,
and therefore I hope that if Mr. Wilson should offer you a
place in his Cabinet, you will decline, because your presence
in his official family will be an embarrassment to you in
seeking the next nomination." Mr. Bryan paused for a
moment and then said with great feeling: "My friend, I
am not wise enough to know what is best for my political
future. But of one thing I am certain, and that is, if Mr.
Wilson invites me into his Cabinet, and I think I can be of
service to the country, it will be my duty to serve." And
then he added impressively, "Whosoever will save his life
shall lose it."

I grant he was disorderly about his desk. This came
from the fact that Mr. Bryan never answered a letter upon
the first reading. No one could change this habit. He
read his mail through, sorted it into rather irregular piles,
and answered it later. I have thought he did this to be
sure he answered dispassionately and justly. A large part

300

Photo. Kadel & Herbert, N. Y.

THE BRYAN SMILE HANDED DOWN TO THE FOURTH GENERATION

of his mail was irritating and exacting and he wished to be calm and fair.

A friend who had a large oak tree near his library window once told me that in the winter when the snow was deep, he often saw a squirrel run down the tree trunk, hesitate a moment, jump over into the snow, dig, and bring up an acorn. Each time he came, he found his food. He seemed to know exactly where to dig. I have been reminded of this squirrel when Mr. Bryan approached his desk, apparently confused and without system, to find a certain letter. His eye would roam over the different piles. Then suddenly he would dig down and he very seldom failed to bring up the required document.

What if he did fill his pockets with wadded-up telegrams? He never lost any. What if he occasionally stepped into his Gladstone bag and trod down the contents until he was able to get in every necessary thing? He got them all in and was satisfied. While disorder reigned in some minor matters, his mind was exacting and methodical to the last degree. His was the most orderly mind into which I have had opportunity to look.

The most remarkable thing was his ability to get an idea, a quotation, a story, or whatnot at the time it was needed. Ordinarily one brings forth the bright thought or the brilliant repartee—an hour or two too late. Some see the light the next day. I do not exaggerate when I say that Mr. Bryan's mind resembled a great number of pigeon-holes, with the contents all classified and labeled and ready for call.

In extemporaneous speaking, this accumulation of material was extremely valuable. Several times I have heard him use facts and figures which had been tucked away for years. An excellent illustration occurred about a year ago. I went to hear Mr. Bryan speak and he gave a long quotation which fitted the subject exactly. On the way home I said, "How did you happen to use that long quotation? I remember that from the tariff days." He replied, "It was nine years ago the seventeenth of November that I last used it." "But how did you happen to think of it?" "I don't know. I saw it fitted in that particular place, so I used it."

A mind like that was worth working with and working for. His wife was willing to plod through heavy books in order to give him the leading thoughts, and help form for him a background of erudition which he was too busy to acquire unaided.

With a generous spirit was combined an almost ascetic self-denial, or perhaps we had better say an extreme simplicity of taste. His needs were few. If he had a box of particularly fine handkerchiefs with cleverly embroidered autographs, he was pleased, but speedily lost them. When his stock ran low, he purchased anything anywhere, and was equally content with a bit of cotton hemmed on a sewing machine. He had no rings. He wore no scarf pin. Shoes were made to order and of the best leather, but simple and always the same style. His string tie and turndown collar, his alpaca coat, became a part of himself.

Though he was so simple in his tastes, he found the greatest pleasure in any evidences of affection. A gift of an apple, a picture, a cane—no matter how small—would touch his emotions. The gift which he prized most of all was a watch given him by members of the Department of State at the time of his resignation. The amount given by each was small (twenty-five cents), with the result that everyone from the assistant secretary to the youngest messenger bore a part. He wore this watch until his death and showed it to friends with the greatest pride, as no other Secretary of State had received a similar tribute of affection.

His birthday celebrations were an especial joy. And it may please the hundreds of friends who have helped to make these yearly celebrations so delightful, to know how they really gladdened his heart.

WILLIAM JENNINGS BRYAN

RULE THREE

"The chief duty of governments, in so far as they are coercive, is to restrain those who would interfere with the inalienable rights of the individual, among which are the right to life, the right to liberty, the right to the pursuit of happiness, and the right to worship God according to the dictates of one's conscience."

RULE FOUR

"In so far as governments are coöperative, they approach perfection in proportion as they adjust with justice the joint burdens which it is necessary to impose and distribute with equity the incidental benefits which come from the disbursement of the money raised by taxation."

RULE FIVE

" 'Absolute acquiescence in the decision of the majority' is, as Jefferson declares, 'the vital principle of republics, from which is no appeal but to force, the vital principle and immediate parent of despotism.' "

RULE SIX

"As acquiescence in the existence of a wrong is not to be expected among an intelligent people entrusted with participation in government, it is the duty of every citizen to exert himself to the utmost to reform every abuse of government and to eradicate every evil in government, remembering that abuses and evils are more easily corrected in their beginning than when they have become fully established."

RULE SEVEN

"In his incomparable speech at Gettysburg, President Lincoln appealed to his countrymen to consecrate harm. So far as I know, I have never been guilty of striking a man when he is down or of criticising him after he is dead. But pardon me if this seems to be self-praise; I am simply trying to justify your favorable judgment of my position."

Much of Mr. Bryan's life was spent in teaching the principles of government and the obligations of citizenship. Few men of his time have done as much to make clear these principles, and one of the great accomplishments of his life was the raising of the standard of the obligation of the citizen to the government under which he lives. He taught that this obligation was as great in peace as in war and that a man's patriotism in times of peace is measured by his unselfish interest in the public welfare. These thoughts run through all of his public utterances, but in his speech "To New Voters," delivered before the City Club of Baltimore April 25, 1915, he undertook to reduce his conception to ten propositions which he would have the voters of the country remember. They were as follows:

RULE ONE

"The social ideal towards which the world is moving requires that human institutions shall approximate towards the Divine measure of rewards and this can only be realized when each individual is able to draw from society a reward proportionate to his contribution to society."

RULE TWO

"The form of government which gives the best assurance of attaining to this ideal is the form in which the people rule—a government deriving its just powers from the consent of the governed."

20   305

of opinion on religion to blot out the pleasant memory of earlier days.

I am glad, however, that something deters you from appearing in the Tennessee case—I only wish it were something less serious than advancing years. Among the people of Colorado who have honored you in the past, there are many who believe in revealed religion and who would be as much distressed at your appearance on the side of those who attack revealed religion as you are at my connection with the other side of the case—only, still respecting you, they could not feel as bitterly toward you as you do toward me. I have passed through so many controversies that caused realignment among friends that I have become accustomed to both losses and accretions. In this controversy, I have a larger majority on my side than in any previous controversy, and I have more intolerant opponents than I ever had in politics.

Very truly yours,

WILLIAM J. BRYAN.

The following quotation from a letter to Mr. Ed. Howe, June 30, 1925, shows how completely he disassociated principles from personalities:

"You have brought out one point which I think is often overlooked, namely, the fact that my fight is on principles, policies, and doctrines, not upon men. I think Lincoln gives us one of the best illustrations of that virtue, if it can be called a virtue. It was said he hated slavery but loved the slaveholders. I want to believe that I imitate him in this respect, for there is not a person in the world for whom I have any enmity, and the number of persons whom I have singled out for criticism is few and I have only criticised them when I thought them in a position to use their position for

ANALYSIS OF CHARACTER

Another notable trait was the forgiving nature of Mr. Bryan. True to his legal training, he always believed a man innocent until he was clearly proven guilty. He did not nurse a wound or hold a grudge. Many illustrations might be given, but one will suffice.

During his service in Congress a faithful worker wished to have his father appointed postmaster in a Lincoln suburb. Mr. Bryan entered the father's name upon the list and, as was his custom, held a local election. The old gentleman received only two votes. Under the circumstances Mr. Bryan could not appoint him. The son became very angry and day after day when he passed our house, he failed even to notice Mr. Bryan's pleasant "Good morning." After he had failed to recognize Mr. Bryan's greetings, I interposed and told Mr. Bryan that I did not see why he continued to speak to him. "Why not let him alone when he acts as he does?" He replied, "His ungentlemanly behavior does not justify me in acting the same way." Mr Bryan continued his courteous greetings, and in two or three years the political wheel took another turn, and this man became a friend.

He encountered many irritating instances of ingratitude and prejudice, but Mr. Bryan bore no malice. "Ignorance," he said, "is usually the basis of misunderstanding. We have a standard set for us in those words, 'Father, forgive them, for they know not what they do.'"

During the last week of his life he received a long and particularly cruel letter written by a man whom he had for years regarded as a valued friend.

His reply to the abuse is characteristic of the way Mr. Bryan always bore such wounds.

July 1, 1925.

My dear Mr. ——:

I am not able to terminate our long friendship as cheerfully as you do, and I shall not allow a difference

303

themselves to the unfinished task that lay before them, that a 'government of the people, by the people, and for the people, might not perish from the earth.' That task is still unfinished and it is the duty of every citizen to carefully study the principles of government, the methods of government, and issues as they arise, and then give to his country the benefit of his judgment and his conscience. To this end he should not only express himself at elections but faithfully attend primaries and conventions where candidates are chosen and policies enunciated."

RULE EIGHT

"The government being the people's business, it necessarily follows that its operations should be at all times open to the public view. Publicity is therefore as essential to honest administration as freedom of speech is to representative government. 'Equal rights to all and special privileges to none' is the maxim which should control all departments of government."

RULE NINE

"Each individual finds his greatest security in the intelligence and happiness of his fellows—the welfare of each being the concern of all, and he should therefore exert himself to the utmost to improve conditions and to elevate the level upon which all stand."

RULE TEN

"While scrupulously careful to live up to his responsibilities, the citizen should never forget that the larger part of every human life is lived outside of the domain of government, and that he renders the largest service to others when he brings himself into harmony with the law of God, who has made service the measure of greatness."

CHAPTER IX

MR. BRYAN AS A TRAVELER

HAVING curbed my wifely enthusiasm during several chapters, I assert my right to praise Mr. Bryan as a traveler. Whenever I could get him beyond the reach of newspapers; when he had really bidden his country farewell, he became an ideal traveling companion, interested in everything, alert, cheerful and unmindful of the discomforts of travel.

One can imagine with what joy I hailed these intervals of rest from the grind of mail and of absorbing work. We went several times to Europe, twice to Canada, three times to Old Mexico, three times to the West Indies. We spent a year going around the world and a winter traveling in South America. During all our journeys Mr. Bryan's chief concern was the operation of governments, and it is interesting to note the political changes that have taken place during the twenty years which have elapsed since our world tour.

Leaving home on September 21, 1905, we sailed from San Francisco on September 27, and did not return to New York until the end of August in the following year. Our first stop was Hawaii, which had been organized as a territory of the United States only five years earlier. These charming islands left three memories—the exquisite color of the ocean, the beauty of the tropical fish in the aquarium, and the thrill of riding the surf in native canoes. We had often hoped and planned to return to Hawaii.

Crossing to Japan, we arrived at the time when the eyes of the world were on that island empire. At no time in her history had Japan enjoyed greater prestige. She had successfully concluded a war with Russia. Almost simultaneously with our arrival Baron Komura returned from

308

MR. BRYAN AT THE INTER-PARLIAMENTARY CONFERENCE IN LONDON, 1906

Left to right: Mr. Bryan, Count Albert Apponyi (Hungary), and Baron D'Estournelles de Constant (France).

MR. BRYAN MET BY A COMMITTEE FROM HIS HOME TOWN

On a tug in New York Harbor upon his return from Europe in 1906.

the peace conference; the naval review celebrating the new Anglo-Japanese alliance took place in Yokohama Harbor a week afterward, and this was followed next day by the reception of Admiral Togo at Tokio, which Mr. Bryan attended. Those were great days in Japan, and we could not but feel the exhilaration of the moment.

This was the occasion of Mr. Bryan's much discussed toast which he drank to Admiral Togo. Everyone at the banquet table drank the toast in champagne, while Mr. Bryan, teetotaler as he was, used water. Some one said: "You should drink to the Admiral in champagne. Why do you use water?" To which Mr. Bryan replied: "Admiral Togo won his great victory on water, so I drink to him in water. When he wins a great victory on champagne, then I will drink to him in champagne." This pleased the Japanese people very much.

Mr. Bryan was received by the Emperor, and of this meeting he wrote the following account:

"Our minister, to whom I am indebted for much assistance and many kindnesses during my stay at the capital, accompanied me to the palace and instructed me, as they say in the fraternities, 'in the secret work of the order.' Except where the caller wears a uniform, he is expected to appear in evening dress, even though the hour fixed is in the daytime. At the outer door of the palace stand men in livery; one of whom conducts the callers through long halls, beautifully decorated on ceilings and walls, to a spacious reception room, where a halt is made until the summons comes from the emperor's room. The emperor stands in the middle of the receiving room with an interpreter at his side. The caller, on reaching the threshold, bows; he then advances halfway to the emperor, pauses and bows again; he then proceeds and bows a third time as he takes the extended hand of the sovereign.

"The conversation is brief and formal, consisting of answers to the questions asked by his majesty. The emperor is fifty-three years old, about five feet six inches in height, well built and wears a beard, although, as is the case with most Japanese, the growth is not heavy. On retiring, the caller repeats the three bows.

"We were shown through the palace, and having seen the old palace at Kyoto, which was the capital until the date of the restoration (1868), I was struck with the difference. The former was severely plain; the latter represents the best that Japanese art can produce."

Another pleasant visit was to Kagoshima, of which he wrote:

"In the country, fifteen miles from Kagoshima, I was a guest at the home of Mr. Yamashita, the father of the young man who, when a student in America, made his home with us for more than five years. Mr. Yamashita was of the samurai class, and since the abolition of feudalism has been engaged in farming. He had invited his relatives and also the postmaster and the principal of the district school to the noon meal. He could not have been more thoughtful of my comfort or more kindly in his manner.

"Along our way at more than one crossroad, groups of people had gathered, bringing me gifts. Some of the choicest pieces of satsuma which we possess came from these wayside groups, and were given in appreciation of the help we had rendered to young Yamashita.

"The little country school which stood near by turned out to bid us welcome. The children were massed at a bridge over which large flags of the two nations floated from bamboo poles. Each child also held a flag, the Japanese and American flags alternating. As young Yamashita and I rode between the lines very primitive living. Amazing progress has been made by the Filipino people since that time. English was then only used by the few; now it is the language of the country. Education has become widespread, founded upon American systems, and aided largely by American schoolbooks. The time should not be far distant when the Philippines arrive at complete independence.

The charming island of Java remains in my memory. The Dutch who own the Island had a system of forced native labor which produced wonderful results. Nowhere did we see more perfect irrigation and better tillage of the soil. The wonders of the botanical gardens at Buitenzorg have few equals in the whole world.

The tremendous temple ruins at Boro Boedoer were alone worth the journey to the South Seas.

If I were able to return to one country, and to only one of the Oriental countries, I should without hesitation choose India. No other land has so fascinated and interested me. Here one sees the monuments of a glorious past, the problems of a bewildering present, and the uncertainties of the future. During our weeks in India, no city interested us more than the holy city of Benares. I quote from Mr. Bryan's book, "The Old World and Its Ways":

"Benares is built upon the north bank of the Ganges, and it is estimated that each year it is visited by a million pilgrims. When more than three hundred miles from the city, we saw the caravan of a Maharaja on its way to the river. There were five elephants, a dozen camels, and twenty or thirty bull carts, besides numerous pack animals and horses. The journey of the caravan would require probably two months, and all this for the sake of a bath in the waters of the sacred river.

"The bank of the Ganges is lined for a long distance with bathing ghats (as the steps leading to the river are called), and at one point there is a burning ghat, where examinations for rank in scholarship had been abandoned. Rows of hundreds of little stalls, three by six feet, were deserted where for centuries before the candidates had been confined while they wrote endless quotations which they had committed to memory. As I recall, none of this work covered the sciences which we regard as so important.

Perhaps the most unusual part of our stay in China was our journey by railroad from Pekin to Hankow. Americans who complain of our own train service should take note that we bought our regular railroad tickets, bought the use of a so-called sleeping car for $90.00, and then paid $10.00 each night for the privilege of sleeping in it. We provided (with the aid of missionaries in Pekin) our own bedding, towels, table linen, china, silver, food, cook, and cook stove—the latter a brazier which burned charcoal. The railroad was new and the company was evidently feeling its way, but with instincts which may be recognized even at this distance.

The inscrutability of the low class of Chinese troubled me. The face seemed no index to the thought and one was never quite sure what might be stirring behind this immobile exterior. In contrast to the coolie class, Chinese gentlemen were alert and used very well-chosen English. While those of the old order did not recognize the presence of my daughter and myself, we enjoyed watching the distinguished mandarins who called upon Mr. Bryan and our son. These visitors wore robes stiff with embroidery, and carried fans, parasols, and long bright red calling cards with black lettering. They were most ceremonious.

When we reached the Philippines, we found the leaven of American ideas spreading. A trip across Mindanao (under military escort) and by boat through the Southern Islands of the group, revealed a people far from our own standards. We were given audience by Datu Piang, a native prince of considerable influence, and received a visit from the Sultan of Sulu, later returning his call. We found that high-sounding titles are sometimes accompanied by

313

Japan had taken the country and the Emperor was on the eve of abdication. When we arrived the hotel was filled with Japanese waiting to take over the government. We had the distinction of being the last visitors received by the royal family, a family which had reigned for about five hundred years, and whose government lost its power through the dishonesty and low standards of its high officials. We were given an audience in the afternoon. A tray of gifts, the last made by the emperor, was brought to us—a large incense burner, a silver box, several fans, and rolls of silk and linen. We sympathized with the helpless little Emperor and his family, but the astounding tales of graft about which we heard easily explained the downfall. The Japanese assumed charge the following morning.

We were told that years ago Korea had been skilled in the making of pottery, but had been robbed of her finer arts by Japan; that her workmen were transported and the industries perished. Last year, when visiting the Freer collection in Washington, I discovered a case of early Korean pottery, most charming in design, like very old and very choice satsuma. I spent much time admiring these pieces and realized then that the Koreans of twenty years ago had spoken the truth.

China, too, when we visited that great country, was an empire. The nation was just awakening from the sleep of twenty centuries. Increasing contact with Europe and America was having its influence, and the example of Japan was even more potent. So it was China awakening that we saw. She was groping her way to the establishment of a republic, which came in 1911. We landed in north China, grounding on the bar which lies in front of Tien Tsin. I am wondering if the bar is still there. At that time we were told the Chinese government refused to remove the bar on the ground that such an obstruction was a protection to the harbor.

Shortly before our arrival in Pekin the old order of

they waved their flags and shouted 'Banzai.' And so it was at other schools. Older people may be diplomatic and feign good will, but children speak from their hearts. There is no mistaking their meaning, and in my memory the echo of the voices of the children, mingling with the assurances of the men and women, convinces me that Japan entertains nothing but good will toward our nation."

Knowing of our interest in young men, we had during our visit in Japan, letters from thirty-two young Japanese who gave us opportunity to adopt them for our very own. I recall one letter whose author was a little confused as to Mr. Bryan's rank, and addressed him as "My Lord, His Grace the Duke."

As this is a history of Mr. Bryan rather than a dissertation upon the Japanese government, the waiting public should know that as it is customary for all shoes to be removed at the front door and as the weather was cold, the Bryan family (Mr. and Mrs. Bryan and two younger children) all caught cold, and our Japanese protégé advised the purchase of heavy felt slippers. We were duly supplied, excepting Mr. Bryan, who being built on a larger scale than the Japanese, could get no slippers long enough. Upon consultation with Japanese authorities, my hero appeared at several elaborate functions, complete with top hat and frock coat, and with his sock-clad toes peeping out from the open ends of too-short slippers—and it might be added he was everywhere received with highest honor, in spite of this detail.

We found great joy in being in Japan at the time of the chrysanthemum. The gentle courtesy of the people, placing their flowers on display and arranging benches upon which visitors might sit and enjoy this beauty, friends going and coming quite independently of the host, was delightful.

While our stay in Korea was brief, it was full of interest.

311

the bodies of the dead are cremated. Cremation is universal among the Hindus, sandalwood being used where relatives of the deceased can afford it. Taking a boat, as is customary, we rowed up and down the Ganges in the early morning. Down the steps along the river as far as the eye could reach, came the bathers, men, women, and children, and up the steps went a constant stream of those who had finished their ablutions. Most of them carried upon their heads water pots of shining brass, and some carried bundles of wearing apparel. The bathing is leisurely as if according to ritual, with frequent dippings; water is poured out to the sun and prayers are said. The lame, the halt, and the blind are there, some picking their way with painful steps, others assisted by friends. Here, a leper seeks healing in the stream; near him a man with emaciated form mixes his medicine with the holy water, and not far off a fakir with matted hair prays beneath his big umbrella.

"Dressing and undressing is a simple matter with the mass of the people. Men and women emerging from the water throw a clean robe around themselves, and then unloosing the wet garment, wring it out and are ready to depart. Those who bring water pots fill them from the stream, out of which they have recently come, and carry them away as if some divinity protected the water from pollution. As the river contains countless dead and receives the filth of the city as well as the flowers cast into it by worshipers, it requires a strong faith to believe it free from lurking disease and seeds of pestilence.

"When we reached the burning ghat, we found one body on the funeral pyre and another soaking in the water as a preparation for burning. So highly is the Ganges revered that aged people are brought there that they may die, if possible, in the water. While we watched, a third body was prepared for the burning, and it was so limp that death could not have occurred long before. While the flames were consuming these three corpses, we saw a man carrying the body of a child, apparently about two years old, wrapped in a piece of thin cotton cloth. The children of the poor are buried in the stream because of the cost of wood. The man bore his lifeless burden to a little barge and made the corpse fast to a heavy stone slab. The boatman then pushed out from the shore, and when the middle of the stream was reached the man in charge of the body dropped it overboard, and the burial was over.

"No one has seen India until he has seen the Ganges; no one has seen the Ganges until he has seen it at Benares; and no one who has seen the Ganges at Benares will ever forget it."

It is astonishing that these same waters of the Ganges, polluted as they are, are regarded as excellent drinking water. I was told that at the time of King Edward's coronation, a Maharaja, who went from India to the ceremonies, took with him sufficient Ganges water to supply him with drinking water during his absence!

In India and elsewhere every opportunity was afforded Mr. Bryan for investigating conditions. The government placed its blue book and documents at his disposal. The natives, feeling they could put their trust in Mr. Bryan, sent committees to show conditions from their point of view.

For more than twenty years an Indian national congress has been pleading for a modified form of representative government and is still far from attaining it, in spite of the efforts of Ghandi and others.

We journeyed in Egypt, Syria, Turkey and the other Mediterranean countries until the summer heat drove us to Europe, where we spent several weeks taking what Mr.

Photo. Brown Bros., N. Y.

MR. BRYAN WITH COUNT LEO TOLSTOI IN RUSSIA

Bryan called "a bird's-eye view," which means a mad rush over that part of the world.

Learning of the probable dissolving of the first Duma, we hurried from Berlin through Moscow to St. Petersburg (later called Petrograd, and now styled Leningrad) and arrived before that remarkable body was prorogued. This was by far the most representative body ever assembled in Russia under the authority of the Czar. The breadth of the franchise was very apparent. Groups of peasants in high boots and full-skirted coats, of mountain men in gayer dress, of pale clergy in long robes, of lawyers, business men, officers, politicians, made a sight never to be forgotten. The peasants were eager to break up the great estates and be freed from the petty tyranny under which they lived. But the great Tolstoy would do nothing. Believing that reformation comes only through the individual, and that legislation is powerless, he would not lend a hand at this crisis, though he might have given valuable advisory aid to the peasant group.

In this connection I recall Mr. Bryan's visit to Russia several years before, when he was received by the Czar. After the audience I asked Mr. Bryan:

"What did you talk about?"

"Free speech."

"Free speech to the Czar! Surely not."

"Yes, free speech. I thought he needed to hear about it, and he seemed quite interested."

This first Duma absorbed the interest of Mr. Bryan. He could not foresee that in a few years the Czar, Nicholas II, would be assassinated, and a republic, or union of republics, established throughout the broad domain.

But he looked into the future, and prophesied:

"That Russia has a great future is not open to doubt. What experiences she may pass through before she emerges a free, self-governing, and prosperous nation, no one is wise enough to foresee, but the people who have sacrificed as much for liberty as have the Russian patriots have in them the material of which mighty nations are made."

Russia has not yet reached the status of a republic, as we understand the word, but she has taken a long step in the right direction, and in time the Bolshevik dictatorship will give place to more representative government.

Another interesting experience was our arrival in Norway at the time of the coronation of King Haakon VII. The old cathedral at Trondhjem was restored for the occasion. Though we arrived unannounced, when the American Minister spoke of our presence, all formalities were arranged, and Mr. Bryan and I were given seats quite near the throne. The robes of crimson and ermine, the clergy, the soft light of the old cathedral, the chanting of old, old coronation hymns by the people, make a wonderful memory.

But how vastly different is the Europe of today from the Europe which Mr. Bryan and I visited in 1906. Democratic ideals were just beginning to be dimly understood by the peoples. Government by a monarchy seemed the only possible type of government. Republics were few and were generally derided. Practically every nation with the exception of France and Switzerland clung to the "King" idea. What a marvelous spread of republican ideals has been witnessed since then! Greece had its petty king; today it is a republic. Turkey had its Abdul Hamid II, who was not only an absolute monarch throughout the dominion of Turkey but the spiritual head of the Moslem Church. Today Turkey has not only joined the great company of republics but has banished the spiritual head of the Church. While in Syria, where the family was exiled, we called on Abbas Effendi, who was then the head of the reform movement. Like Ghandi of India, he believed in moral suasion rather than force. The reform movement

318

grew in Turkey, but it is doubtful if a republic could have been established in that land had it not been for the World War.

At the time we visited Germany "parlor socialism" was the principal theme of conversation. The fatherland was a-swarm with grand dukes and petty dukes and big and little kings headed by his august majesty Kaiser Wilhelm. All these representatives of monarchy have passed and the kaiser is exiled in Doorn. Every state in Germany is a republic, and instead of the German Emperor, it has a president.

The Austria-Hungary which we visited no longer exists as such. The great dual monarchy passed with the war; and instead there are the republics of Czechoslovakia, Austria, and Hungary, with the republican idea firmly embedded in the first-named state if not in the others. Writing at the time, Mr. Bryan made this significant statement:

"The tie which holds Canada, Australia, and New Zealand to England is infinitely stronger than that which binds Hungary and Bohemia (Czechoslovakia) to the Austria-Hungary throne. And why? Canada, Australia, and New Zealand are loyal to England because England allows them to do as they please. If a British parliament acted toward these colonies as the imperial government acts toward Hungary and Bohemia, even a common language and a common history could not prevent a separation. 'There is that scattereth, yet increaseth,' says Solomon, 'and there is that withholdeth more than is meet, but it tendeth to poverty.' The proverb can be applied to governments, and Francis Joseph might consider it with profit."

Today the great empire is broken up and the monarchy abolished.

WILLIAM JENNINGS BRYAN

Sensing something of the changes that must shortly take place, Mr. Bryan wrote at the close of his world tour:

"The democratic idea is growing—the term is not used in a partisan sense, but in that broader sense in which it describes government by the people. There is not a civilized nation in which the idea of popular government is not growing, and in all the semi-civilized nations there are reformers who are urging an extension of the influence of the people in government. So universal is this growth of democratic ideas that there can be no doubt of their final triumph. The advocates of the American theory of government can, therefore, labor with the confident assurance that the principles planted upon American soil a century and a quarter ago are destined to grow here and everywhere until arbitrary power will nowhere be known, and until the voice of the people shall be recognized, if not as the voice of God, at least as Bancroft defines it, as the best expression of the divine will to be found upon the earth."

Thus, with his eyes upon the future, wrote Mr. Bryan some twenty years ago.

It was not only studies of foreign governments and sightseeing in alien lands which filled our journeys. There were moments of stress and danger which also had their part. I quote this incident from my diary:

Jan. 11, 1912.

Before the impressions fade I wish to record the facts concerning our first, and I trust only shipwreck.

We left New York on the *Prinz Joachim*, bound for Jamaica, in cloudy weather and a heavy sea. The next day the clouds became very dense and for forty-eight hours there was neither sun by day nor star by night from which observations might be taken. At 3.45 A. M.

320

on November 23, 1911, I was awakened by a shock and a grinding sound—a shiver ran through the ship and I felt something had happened.

Going to Mr. Bryan's room, I said, "We are on the rocks."

"No," he said, "you heard the anchor dragging. We must have reached Fortune Islands."

I begged him to go out and see. He went, and in a very short time returned, saying the order had gone out for everyone to dress. Outside, orders were being shouted; we could hear the lowering of lifeboats and the ceaseless whir of the wireless. Luckily the electric light plant was working—so we could see to pack.

We dressed as quickly as possible, for the ship began to settle—she "listed," in nautical language, and our stateroom sloped so that it was difficult to walk without slipping. This suggested the by no means pleasant idea that we were going down.

The idea of death so near did not alarm. I had a feeling of satisfaction that Mr. Bryan and I were going together and of regret that our little grandson, John, must go too. I felt, too, the smallness of man and the uselessness of a struggle against the inevitable. These thoughts did not deter me from getting out the heavy wraps that might add to our comfort in an open boat.

The last thing was to waken our boy, who had slept soundly thus far. When I told him we must dress and that the ship was on a rock, his first words were, " 'Chattie', didn't I tell you we would have an accident?"—as indeed he had. He did not cry, though he saw the danger and asked if we were going to drown.

When we went on deck it was to be met by appalling darkness—one of those inky black nights that are in themselves terrifying.

By this time soundings had been taken and the ship examined—one great blessing we had, i. e., a smooth

sea; without it our condition must have been much worse. It was found that we were on a reef of sunken rock. It proved to be the most easterly of the Bahama group (Atwood's Key). The ship had gone up on the long way of the rocks—had torn out her prow and the first compartment of the hull and then rested upon the reef. Everyone gathered on deck to watch for the dawn. Life preservers were brought out and all lifeboats put in readiness. There was no confusion among either passengers or crew. The only passengers who wept and prayed aloud were Spanish women. They seemed to have more sins for which to answer or were of a more excitable temperament.

While it was yet dark the hot water was turned out of the ship's boiler and struck full into one of the lifeboats below, in which two men were busy. One man was badly scalded and both jumped overboard to escape the heat. The darkness made it difficult to rescue them and not until lifebuoys that carried a red light were thrown over were they saved. These buoys were curious to me. Each one had a receptacle of some sort that was filled with red fire exactly like the red fire of Fourth of July fireworks. These lights "made the darkness visible" for a long way 'round.

Also, while it was yet dark rockets were sent up. I had read of signals of distress, but now we saw them —we saw, but no one else. Powerful skyrockets arched up into the night, burst and fell, and darkness swallowed us again.

The calls for help from wireless began to bring responses. The first station to answer was New York, eleven hundred miles away. Then six other stations along the coast answered—but no ship!

This developed one fact we had not known before— viz., that wireless operators on ships sleep between the hours of 1.30 and 6.00 A. M., and no one is at the key.

MR. BRYAN AS A TRAVELER

Everyone felt indignant—we had ample time to sink several times between 4.45 and 6.00 A. M., and a ship quite near would be none the wiser. Everyone saw this must be changed, and each ship be forced to carry two operators.

A real prayer of thanksgiving was in all hearts, I am sure, when a faint gray horizon line could be seen. Everyone took courage. As light grew we saw a little barren island about two miles away: "a stern and rockbound coast," but *land* nevertheless.

About nine o'clock a ship was hailed some eighty miles distant. She refused to come to us—which was discouraging. Not long after, another appeared, and then came definite plans for relief. How we did watch for smoke on the horizon line! The wind had risen and we dreaded a rough sea—it would be so easy to beat the ship to pieces.

Breakfast and luncheon were served in good order and shortly after 2.00 P. M. we saw, with glasses, a little film of smoke. The ship belonged to the Ward line— the *Vigilancia*—bound for New York with only four passengers on board. Her captain refused to come near because of the rising sea and the possibility of other rocks, and anchored between five and six miles away.

Then began the loading of the boats. The sea was rough by this time; a fine mist falling. Our company of eighty-nine persons was transferred in seven boats. We had three invalids on board: a tall dark woman who seemed partially paralyzed in her lower limbs; she spoke no English. No. 2, a man who appeared to have locomotor ataxia; and No. 3, a man terribly crippled with rheumatism—arms, hands, and legs. He went on crutches; and his wife, a short-bodied, short-haired, and short-tempered person, was traveling with a canary bird! The wife was greatly distressed about the bird, and in an unguarded moment I offered to carry it for her.

The gangway was wet and slippery and the boats now rocking badly. Anyone who has landed in small boats will understand the difficulties. We went in the third boat. We had our hand baggage and I got down safely with the bird cage. A passenger when near the bottom of the gangway lost her footing and knocked the feet from under the sailor who was helping her. They both swung out under the ropes—we held our breath— but after a scramble and a pull from another sailor they got on their feet again. Our boat also contained the tall, dark paralytic.

Blankets were given to each passenger. The passage across was very slow. The crew was not accustomed to rowing—the waves high and the current against us. The men smoked. The motion of the ship and the tobacco combined made Will and me deathly ill. He was very pale. Two or three people leaned over the boat's side, and shortly before we reached the ship we followed their example.

When we were being brought up to the gangway a passenger fell over on the bird cage—there was a splintering of wire and the bottom was broken out of the cage! Amid the swash of waves and rattling of chains I shrieked to all men on the gangway: "Hold on to the bottom of the cage! Don't let out the bird!" and at last saw him safely deposited on deck.

When at last we stood in the dining-room awaiting our assignments, our paralytic grew rigid and had an epileptic seizure. While people were running with ice water and smelling salts, I sank into a chair and said under my breath, "Dear Lord, what will it be next!" I soon found out what was next. The very next was to see three of our seven boats drift farther and farther out to the open sea. The men were too tired to get back to the wreck and the sea was even more rough. We thought these twenty-one men were doomed—that they had really given their lives to save us, and the thought was not pleasant. They were all picked up the second day and carried into Cuba.

The next thing was a storm through which we passed during the night. The wind was terrifying to hear and the ship plunged and rolled and shivered till sleep was impossible. It was one of the very worst storms I have experienced. We were taken to a bay not far from Nassau and there transferred to another Ward liner—the *Liguarancia*—this transfer was easily made in quiet water and by the aid of a tug boat. I again carried the bird. Will saw the owner of said bird calmly walking up the gangplank without a bag or parcel of any sort. He was indignant and called the lady back and had her take a couple of her handbags which she had put down for the public to look after. (N.B. When we landed at Port Antonio I did not carry the bird.) All this time our baggage was on the wreck.

We kept the wireless busy; found a ship bound for New York had come to the wreck the night we left, but the sea was so rough it was not possible to transfer baggage. Our captain then decided to see what he could do. We reached the wreck (about two miles distant) at twilight—starlight for the first time since we left New York, but a heavy bank of clouds in the west. Little John saw the clouds and said, "Well, I think if God is getting up another storm, it isn't very nice of him." But God did not get up another.

The water remained calm. The baggage was already loaded in the lifeboats, which were towed over. The trunks were hauled up the ship's side by a chain and an iron hook fixed through the trunk handles! I thought every handle would certainly break! You can imagine how anxious we were! I had had new handles put on one trunk just before leaving home and was duly thankful. We got all our trunks. The unloading went on until 2.00 A. M. The last load of twelve or fifteen pieces overbalanced in some way and capsized. I heard shouts of "man overboard!" of running and confused orders. (I had gone to bed.)

In the morning I learned that two men had gone over with the capsized boat, and to add to the excitement, sharks suddenly rose in the water. In the efforts to frighten the sharks and save the men, no one thought to fish out the trunks and they sank. We reached Port Antonio without further adventure. I have failed to mention the various purses which were made up for our three captains, for the crews, etc. There was also a service of thanksgiving held on our third ship. We all repeated the Twenty-third Psalm. Will made a beautiful little talk and we closed with The Lord's Prayer. Out of the entire experience has come one very satisfying fact—that one may face Death without flinching. He is not so terrible after all.

Upon our return to New York in the spring, Mr. Bryan went at once to Washington, and appeared before the proper committee. A bill was drafted compelling ships to carry two wireless operators and, as I recall, this bill passed both Houses without opposition. Those who now cross the ocean in comparative safety and with two wireless operators on board instead of one, may be interested to know that they owe this measure to Mr. Bryan.

CHAPTER X

BRYAN AND WILSON—A COMPARISON AND A CONTRAST

I REALIZE that in speaking of Mr. Bryan's work as Secretary of State, I am dealing with matters about which there has been much discussion and much disagreement. The reason which may justify me in undertaking this work is that I was always Mr. Bryan's confidante. From our marriage in October, 1884, until his death in July, 1925, he found in me a sort of mental safety valve. We discussed men, questions, and events with a freedom which relieved his mind. Without boasting, I am sure I understand and know him better than anyone in the world, and that I owe it to his work to leave an accurate record.

Whether or not I am wise enough, whether or not I may say too much or too little, there is one thing I must make clear. No one but myself is responsible. I have consulted no one; none of Mr. Bryan's family, no members of the Wilson Cabinet, none of his friends. The entire responsibility is my own.

President Wilson and Mr. Bryan in some particulars resembled each other. The same races had mingled their blood in the veins of both—Scotch and Irish—with perhaps more Scotch than Irish in the first, and more Irish than Scotch in the second. Both were of clean blood; as far back as the family is traced—through three or four generations—on either side there was industry, sobriety, and religious zeal; apparently no black sheep in either flock. Each man remembered his father with profound veneration, and each attributed to the father a large share in whatever success the son may have attained.

Another point of likeness is their connection with Virginia. Mr. Wilson's father lived in Steubenville, Ohio, and removed to Staunton, Virginia, in 1849. Here, seven years

327

later, Woodrow Wilson was born   Mr. Bryan's father was born in Virginia near Sperryville, Culpeper County, where his father had long lived and where his relatives still live. The names of Lillard, O'Bannon, Browning, and Grimsley belong to his people.   As a boy of sixteen, he went West.

They shared in common an interest in literary and debating societies which both attended faithfully, and in which both were prize winners.   See Mr. Bryan's chapter entitled "The Lure of the College Prize."   Both men became lawyers, and in the Presbyterian Church both men were elders, Mr. Bryan being a ruling elder at the time of his death.   The year before his passing he held the position of Vice Moderator in the General Assembly.

In religious training the parallel continued.   The Wilson family had family prayers both morning and evening. The Bryan family had prayers in the morning only, but the balance swings back to equilibrium when we feel safe in saying that Woodrow went to Sunday school once on Sunday, while William J. went Sunday morning and again in the afternoon.   Both boys received much instruction from their fathers on religious matters and both imbibed a strong faith in the goodness and justice of God, which they kept throughout their lives.

Both men regarded public office as a trust and responsibility.

In his second inaugural President Wilson said: "I stand here and have taken the high and solemn oath to which you have been audience because the people of the United States have chosen me for this august delegation of power and have by their gracious judgment named me their leader in affairs.   I know now what the task means.   I realize to the full the responsibility which it involves.   I pray God I may be given the wisdom and the prudence to do my duty in the true spirit of this great people.   I am their servant and can succeed only as they sustain and guide me by their confidence and their counsel."

BRYAN AND WILSON

I quote from a statement made by Mr. Bryan upon this subject:

"The most important requisite in a President, as in other officials, is that his sympathy shall be with the whole people, rather than with any fraction of the population. He is constantly called upon to act in the capacity of a judge—deciding between the importunities of those who seek favors and the rights and interests of the public. Unless his sympathies are right, the few are sure to have an advantage over the many, for the masses have no one to present their claims. They act only at elections, and must trust to their representatives to protect them from all their foes.

"The President must have a knowledge of public questions and the ability to discern between the true and the false

"He must possess the moral courage to stand against the influences that are brought to bear in favor of special interests. In fact, the quality of moral courage is as essential in a public official as either right sympathies or a trained mind.

"A President must have counselors, and to make wise use of counselors, he must be open to convictions."

But in spite of these resemblances, the difference between these men is inherent and the line of cleavage easily traced. President Wilson's ancestors were printers, editors, and preachers. Mr. Bryan's ancestors were lawyers, doctors, bankers, and farmers, more of the last. Mr. Wilson's grandfather came to this country a printer and acquired a newspaper. His seven sons were all trained to set type. The trend of the family seems to have been to reach the world through the printed page. Mr. Bryan's ancestors, though for the most part of less scholarly attainment, were reaching their fellows by direct contact. May not these facts

329

explain Mr. Wilson's reserve and Mr. Bryan's approach-ableness?

Nor did their education tend to lessen this breach. President Wilson studied in the austere atmosphere of Davidson and Princeton. Mr. Bryan, born in the Middle West, lived during his college life in the family of a physician who each summer lectured on Plato in the Concord School of Philosophy, and gave his young relative access to the social life of the Illinois town. Although his studies came first, Mr. Bryan enjoyed the companionship of a large circle of friends.

In contrast to this early geniality is Mr. Wilson's attitude. I quote from Secretary Daniels' "Life of Woodrow Wilson"

"Wilmington society opened its doors, but his (Wilson's) mind was on mastering the science of government. He did not fit in with its social life. He did not want to fit in. He was not unfriendly about it, but just calmly interested and absorbed in other things. He never argued about it."

Being fair, I must record that Mr. Bryan was the better student of the two. President Wilson in a class of 122, ranked forty-first, while Mr. Bryan was first in his class and delivered the valedictory oration with degree of Bachelor of Arts. President Wilson received his degree of Doctor of Philosophy at the hands of Johns Hopkins in June, 1886, and his thesis was "Congressional Government." Mr. Bryan, after two years' work in Union College of Law in Chicago, received his degree of Master of Arts at the hands of his Alma Mater in 1883, and the subject of his thesis was "American Citizenship."

The early reading of the two is significant. A biographer of Woodrow Wilson says that the theory of government was his hobby. His reading and his writing are in harmony

330

BRYAN AND WILSON

with that statement. His interest was in the mechanism, in the cogs and wheels, by means of which government is administered, and a part of the machine which had stood the test of time in a way was sacred. Mr. Bryan was looking at the work done by the machine and how this work affected the people; for instance, government ownership, with its implied radical changes, held no fears for him. Mr. Wilson instinctively recoiled from so drastic a measure.

While Mr. Wilson was reading on the science of government, upon political economy and the interpretation of the Constitution of the United States, Mr. Bryan was buying from the bookstalls secondhand sets of Burke, Pitt, Erskine, Elliott's debates, Lincoln and Douglas debates, collections of great orations of England and America, etc., and was studying models of oratory. He never used the money received from home for such purposes. He earned this money; hence his rigid economy and secondhand purchases.

The first articles President Wilson wrote seem to have been largely upon the machinery of government. Mr. Bryan's subjects were justice, labor, industry, individual power, and kindred themes. Though studying law, Wilson became a college professor and was absorbed in his books and his classroom. Bryan became a lawyer and was interested in outside matters. His first political campaign speaking was done while still in school at the age of twenty.

The first time I ever heard Mr. Bryan mention Dr. Wilson's name was during the latter's fight to democratize Princeton, when he expressed a belief that in colleges there was "a strong tendency to glorify money," and with the increasing wealth of our country, the tendency would be to "drift into plutocracy." Mr. Bryan was much pleased. The next time Dr. Wilson attracted Mr. Bryan's attention was during the Smith-Martine Senatorial fight when Dr. Wilson was Governor. Though Dr. Wilson was surrounded by reactionaries, and though Smith had worked for his election, he stood by Martine. Mr. Bryan interpreted this to mean that Wilson had a real sympathy for the progressive wing and was correspondingly interested.

All well-regulated biographies of these two men include the Joline letter and I hereby prove my regularity. This letter was published at an embarrassing time for the Wilson men, then organizing to nominate him for President. Plans were in progress for the Jackson Day banquet in January, 1912, and prominent Democrats from all parts of the country had been invited. The letter mentioned was written by Mr. Wilson to Mr. Adrian Joline at the time of the split of the Democratic party over the money question. The letter follows:

Princeton, New Jersey
April 29, 1907

MY DEAR MR. JOLINE:

Thank you very much for sending me your address at Parsons, Kan., before the board of directors of the Missouri, Kansas & Texas Railway Company. I have read it with relish and entire agreement. Would that we could do something, at once dignified and effective, to knock Mr. Bryan once for all into a cocked hat!

Cordially and sincerely yours,

WOODROW WILSON.

Whatever Mr. Bryan's personal feelings were, an explanation of the letter seemed necessary. It was not too easy to explain—the letter had been written and there it was. Mr. Tumulty, in his book, "Woodrow Wilson As I Knew Him," tells of a conference, and that the Hon. Josephus Daniels, "a friend and associate of Mr. Bryan, was sent to confer with Mr. Bryan in order that Mr. Wilson might have a close friend at hand who could interpret the motives which lay back of the Joline letter and impress upon Mr. Bryan the present favorable attitude of Mr. Wilson toward him." Note the phrase "could interpret the motives which lay back of the Joline letter." Skilful Josephus! With his honesty, his admiration for Wilson, and his love for Bryan. So far as I know he did not try to interpret, though interpretation was eagerly sought. It was decided that Wilson should pay Mr. Bryan a handsome tribute in his Jackson Day banquet speech. "In the very beginning of his speech, in the most tactful way," writes Tumulty, "Governor Wilson paid a tribute to the Great Commoner by saying, as he turned to Mr. Bryan, 'When others were faint-hearted, Colonel Bryan carried the Democratic standard. He kept the fires burning which have heartened and encouraged the democracy of the country.'

"On his return from Washington to Trenton, Governor Wilson told me that Mr. Bryan had bidden him not to worry about the publication of the Joline letter, saying: 'I, of course, knew that you were not with me in my position on the currency,' and Woodrow Wilson replied: 'All I can say, Mr. Bryan, is that you are a great, big man.'"

One can see with half an eye that at this stage Dr. Wilson did not approve of Mr. Bryan, as evidenced not only in the Joline letter but also in his refusal to sit on the platform when Mr. Bryan spoke in New Jersey. This was quite natural. Mr. Bryan was annoying to men like Dr. Wilson, who probably were not interested to learn his real ideals and purposes, and who drew their opinions from the Eastern press which published Bryan as a meddler and a disturber of the peace.

While Mr. Bryan understood the construction of the English language, his colloquial expressions with occasional lapses must have been most discordant to the trained ear of Dr. Wilson.

David Lawrence, in his "True Story of Woodrow Wilson," says:

"Mr. Wilson's choice of words was without fault. He was precise in punctuation. 'When I was a boy,'

333

explained President Wilson, 'my father would not permit me to blurt things out, or stammer a half-way job of telling whatever I had to tell. . . . As a young boy, therefore, even at the age of four or five, I was taught to think about what I was going to say, and then I was required to say it correctly. Before I was grown, it became a habit."

Mr. Bryan regarded language as simply the vehicle by which ideas are conveyed. I have known him to repeat mistakes in English rather than hurt the feelings of some old man who had had no early opportunities. In speaking, he often used an ordinary expression when it fitted the audience rather than the more correct and polished phrase, all of which was irritating; not to mention his advanced ideas.

The time preceding the Baltimore Convention was full of work. This seems the natural place to settle one question —the oft-repeated accusation that Mr. Bryan was trying to get the nomination for himself at Baltimore. He had made no effort to get it—if he had, the nomination would have been his. The Democratic Progressive organization was his work. It was different from an ordinary political machine. It was a personal following. Mr. Bryan was a poor organizer, and he could not be induced to calculate how many votes it was necessary to change in each ward or township in order to overcome an adverse majority; to "figger" and scheme. Any semblance of party machinery came from the work of his brother Charlie, from his brother-in-law, T. S. Allen, and from his loyal and loving friends stationed here and there at strategic points.

I know the feeling of the body of Democrats because of my connection with Mr. Bryan's mail, his brother attended to matters of correspondence at *The Commoner* office, while I was working at Fairview, our country home. Months before the convention many, many letters came urging him again to be a candidate. We talked it over fully. Mr.

BRYAN AND WILSON

Bryan said in effect: "I have had this nomination three times. It is not fair to others for me to take it again. Besides, the same powers of entrenched wealth which have defeated me each time are likely to have power to do it again. I believe another man will be better for the party." And so he discouraged the organization of local clubs.

As time wore on and Taft and Roosevelt began to quarrel, when a split between them seemed likely, and in consequence Democratic chances were brighter, I spoke to him again. I wanted him to take the nomination; I wanted him to be President; I wanted him to conquer his enemies. We had worked so long and so hard   But he said: "This may be the year for a Democrat to win. The other boys have been making their plans. I would not step in now." And he went to Baltimore with only the future of "the other boys" in his mind.

After the deadlock in the convention when he was holding on and waiting for the people of the country at large to express themselves and to force their delegations into line, I spoke to him again. He said: "There is only one condition under which I could take this nomination, and that would be if the deadlock becomes so fixed that no one is able to break it, and they turn to me as one upon whom the different factions can unite. This condition is not probable. This thing will work out somehow. The Lord does not mean to shorten my life by putting this burden upon me."

Among the "other boys" who were making plans, Mr. Bryan's first choice was Champ Clark. He felt that Clark was the best man, reliable and thoroughly progressive, if he could only get him to work. Clark was too easy-going. The following letter shows his feeling:

Ft. Wayne, Ind.
May 30, 1911

My dear Clark:

꙼ I venture to make a suggestion for your consideration. I believe the fight over wool will prove a crisis in your life as well as in the party's prospects. A leader must *lead:* it is not always pleasant to oppose friends, and one who leads takes the chances of defeat, but these are the necessary attendants upon leadership. Wilson is making friends because he *fights.* His fight against Smith was heroic. He fought for the income tax and for a primary law. The people like a fighter. You won your position by fighting and you must continue to fight to hold it. Enter into the wool fight. Don't be content to take polls and sit in the background. Take one side or the other and take it *strong.* If a tax on wool is right, lead the protectionists to victory. You can do it and it will make you strong with that wing of the party. If free wool is right, as I believe it is, lead the fight for it and get the credit for the victory, if victory comes. Don't inquire about how the fight is going to go—make it go the right way, if you can. If you fail you lay the foundation for a future victory. The right wins in the end—don't be afraid to wait. My opinion is that you will not have to wait long, but whether long or not, one can better afford to be defeated fighting for the right than to win on the wrong side.

I hope you will pardon this intrusion upon your thoughts, but the party needs your assistance. A blast from your bugle may save the day, and it will, in my judgment, strengthen you personally.

Regards to the family.

> Yours,
>
> BRYAN.

He often said: "Why doesn't Clark do something aggressive? People will not follow unless he leads."

At Baltimore, when he saw how evasive was Clark's reply to the Bryan-Parker telegram, he felt the fault was again Clark's sluggish failure to control his managers.

"His managers show no judgment and he is letting them run things. If Clark cannot manage his managers, how can he manage the government?"

At no time did he have any ill-feelings toward Clark and was sorry when later he had to oppose him in order to keep the party free from the influence of Wall Street, and we have both deplored the bitter resentment which was occasioned by Mr. Bryan's action.

Mr. Bryan has given a full account of the Baltimore Convention, but it may be of interest to add that I have never known Mr. Bryan to be less clear as to his course. Usually he saw and planned in advance. Here he moved, one step at a time, and waited to see what should be the next development. He said, "I believe the people of the country will settle this thing if I can only get word to them what is going on." His idea in submitting to defeat as temporary chairman was to use a hostile press to notify his friends of conditions. His friends understood and gave answer.

We have been taught: *vox populi, vox Dei,* but most of us live and die without realizing the truth of this statement. Those in attendance at Baltimore had the privilege of actually hearing the voice of the people. It spoke with no uncertain sound and for a time at least held a great party true to its traditions.

Mr. Wilson began to soften toward Mr. Bryan. David Lawrence speaks of Governor Wilson's first Bryan meeting on March 13, 1911. He says:

"It was the first time he had heard Mr. Bryan speak and he was deeply impressed by the Bryan personality, his sincerity and forcefulness. Mr. Bryan dined that evening with Mr. Wilson and his family and Thomas H. Birch of Burlington, New Jersey, who later became American Minister to Portugal in the first Wilson administration."

22

WILLIAM JENNINGS BRYAN

After the Convention his friendship was still more apparent, as the following correspondence shows.

June 6, 1912

My dear Mr. Bryan:

Your position about the temporary chairmanship is altogether fair and is indicative of the wise position you are taking with regard to the whole arrangement for the Convention.

I agree with you that the temporary chairman should be acceptable to the leading candidates, and I shall certainly lend myself to any arrangement which can bring about a thoroughly satisfactory solution of the question. My own opinion is that the temporary chairman should come from one of the uninstructed delegations. My own thought had been centering upon Senator O'Gorman of New York, a man of admirable poise and capable of making a speech that would be absolutely fair to all concerned, and at the same time ring true and clear with regard to progressive policies.

"Please present Mrs. Wilson's warm regard, as well as my own, to Mrs. Bryan and say to her that it was a genuine disappointment to Mrs. Wilson not to be able to go to Washington to the Dolly Madison breakfast. Only a very painful accident prevented her being there.

Cordially and sincerely yours,

WOODROW WILSON.

Honorable W. J. Bryan,
Lincoln,
Nebr.

July 8, 1912

My dear Mr. Bryan:

I have not seen the full text of it as I hope I shall, but your "valedictory," spoken in the last hours of the Convention at Baltimore, seems to me a peculiarly

338

noble thing and constituting a fitting close to a convention in which you played a part which the whole country now recognizes and assesses at its true significance.

Will you not let me send you this additional cordial message of regard with the hope that as soon as convenient to you, when you come East again, I may have the pleasure and profit of a talk with you?

Cordially yours,

WOODROW WILSON.

Honorable William Jennings Bryan,
Lincoln,
Nebr.

July 16, 1912

MY DEAR MR. BRYAN:

Thank you for your note about Mr. Osborn and Senator O'Gorman. I am very much pleased indeed that your judgment is what it is of Senator O'Gorman, and I shall greatly rely upon his judgment in matters concerning New York.

I wish you could hear what I hear on every hand with regard to your action in the Convention. By your stand there you have made yourself what would have seemed impossible—a bigger man than ever in the estimation of the people of the country.

I warmly appreciate your generous notes.

Cordially and sincerely yours,

WOODROW WILSON.

Honorable William Jennings Bryan,
Lincoln,
Nebr.

November 9, 1912.

MY DEAR MR. BRYAN:

I must give myself the pleasure of adding a more extended line than I could send you by telegraph.

I have thought of you very constantly throughout the campaign and have felt every day strengthened and heartened by your active and generous support. I was greatly refreshed also by my little visit to you in Lincoln.

We have won a great victory, and it is now our privilege to show that we can live up to it. It is delightful to see the forces of the party united, and their union should now bring fruit of richest sort.

Mrs. Wilson was greatly distressed that illness should have prevented Mrs. Bryan from coming to Princeton. I sincerely hope that she is entirely herself again. Mrs. Wilson enjoyed so much meeting her in New York. She joins me in sending most cordial messages of regard to you both.

Faithfully yours,

WOODROW WILSON

Thank you warmly for the account of the Convention.

W. W.

Hon. William Jennings Bryan,
Lincoln, Nebraska.

The time between the Convention and the election may be covered by an extract from my journal, dated August, 1912:

"The days in the mountains went all too swiftly. They did us both a tremendous amount of good. Then came a return to Denver in a blinding snowstorm, the first of the season. A banquet at Denver, and then John and I came home to Fairview. Will entered at once into the campaign. He spoke every day for seven weeks. He told me afterwards he thought he had averaged ten speeches (long and short) per day. I have never seen him go through a campaign in better condition. His voice was excellent to the last.

"Before the election, late in October, I left for Washington in order to see Ruth, Reggie, and Kitty before they sailed for England. Went with them to New York and we spent three very pleasant days together there. After they left, I was invited to meet Mrs. Woodrow Wilson at the home of Mrs. E. M. House. I met there Mrs. James Parker, with whom we traveled in India. Was delighted to meet her again. Found Mrs. Wilson a sweet, nice woman. I liked her. She asked me to spend Friday with her in Trenton. I had not been well for several days. On rising Friday morning, found myself much worse, so without further ado, I left New York for Washington, and went at once to the Providence Hospital. After I was safely settled there, I telephoned my son, who was then living in Washington, and told him of the step I had taken. (I feared the family would not consent if I consulted them first.) The doctor advised an operation. I knew that Will was in the heat of the campaign.

"The only complication was the condition of my heart. It had not acted normally all summer and I felt uncertain about the effect of an anesthetic. I thought about it overnight and then resolved to submit to the operation. Saturday morning early the work was done. I remember looking out of the window and wondering if I would see the day come again.

"Election day came as I lay in bed. I heard the boys calling extras. Wilson elected! Wilson elected! And the next morning I read the returns. The nurses were very nice about getting me the papers. This doing without Will when I was sick and leaving him in ignorance of my condition so that he could speak without any anxieties was my little personal contribution to the campaign."

CHAPTER XI

LIFE IN WASHINGTON

[From my Journal]

April 1, 1913.

MONDAY morning I rose early and went to our rooms in the New Willard. We had the best rooms in the house, but quite by accident. We had taken much more modest ones, but the man who had engaged the so-called "Presidential suite" became ill and the management turned it over to us.

Then began the stream of callers, friends from all parts of the country. I stood all day, shaking hands. In the afternoon we reviewed the suffrage parade from our balcony, a really great demonstration. I was interested to see men marching, particularly members of the House and Senate. The crowd on the Avenue was wonderful; said to be the greatest parade ever known in Washington. As one looked up the Avenue from the New Willard, the street seemed a solid mass of people for blocks. I do not wonder the parade could scarcely get through and that the poor policemen are now being investigated.

The morning of the inauguration was cloudy; we all feared it might storm, but as the day advanced the skies brightened, although the sun was overcast all day, which was more pleasant for the onlookers than bright sunlight. When we left the hotel the reviewing stands along the Avenue were filling rapidly. The streets were being cleared for the passage of the carriage of President Taft and President-elect Wilson, and their escort, and we had some difficulty in getting to the door of the Senate. Our daughter Grace could not get a seat with me and was assigned to another which proved to be in the row with the Wilsons. This gave her an opportunity to meet them. The ladies of

342

the prospective Cabinet were in the gallery on the right of the desk, a point from which we saw the door perfectly, but from which we were unable to see the various Senators and the Vice President sworn in. We listened to the work of the Senate for some time; heard one bill talked to death at the last moment; saw the clock set back. Then the dignitaries began to arrive. The Diplomatic Corps, resplendent in gold braid and medals—an imposing sight. The Supreme Court in their robes; the members of the House; then the Vice President took his oath and made a short speech. It was simple in style and expression, but forceful and I think it made a good impression. The new Senators then took their oaths, each one being led to the desk by the man whom he had defeated. In some instances I should think the relations must have been a little strained. The President and President-elect then proceeded to the stand in front of the Capitol where thousands of people had been waiting for hours. The new Cabinet followed and were given places near President-elect Wilson. We, in the galleries, did not reach our seats outside the Capitol for some minutes, but I have been told that Will was greeted by a great roar of applause. The oath was taken. President Wilson made his address. It was brief and a splendid call to all patriotic citizens to rally to his support.

After the address the President and Ex-President passed out first, then the Supreme Court and Cabinet. I waited for Will at the end of a seat and we went out together—the people patted his shoulders as he passed and shook his hand. "There he goes!" was repeated many times. It was like leaving a huge political meeting.

When we reached the Senate entrance we found many people waiting for their carriages. We gave our number but without result. At last a gentleman evidently in charge of affairs, said, "This way, Mr. Bryan." We followed him and stepped into an auto and were very happy to be provided for. As soon as we turned into the open, we discovered we were in the procession, and not far from the front.

It had not been customary for wives to accompany their husbands in the inaugural procession, but Will insisted on my presence, saying, "You have helped me win this and I want you with me." As far as I know I was the only woman in the official carriages.

Then began an embarrassing experience. Will said he felt as he did in Tokyo when the rickshaw men took him down the street which had been cleared for Admiral Togo. We could hear the applause for President Wilson from the thousands who lined the streets and sat upon the stands. The whole distance from the Capitol to the White House was solidly banked with people. When the cheers for the President were over, our carriage would pass and as the people recognized Will a simultaneous outburst would arise; women shouting and waving, men waving their hats and shouting, hundreds clapping their hands. I never expect to see such an ovation again. I felt it was something to have the people pay such homage to my boy when he was not the President. Will could not help being pleased and touched, too. He said, "It is worth sixteen years of hard work to have devotion like this, isn't it?"

Before entering the White House grounds, I wish to clear up one small matter. As one newspaper wittily remarked, "President Wilson instead of 'knocking Mr. Bryan into a cocked hat,' knocked him into a silk hat." I wish our descendants to know that this was by no means the first silk hat in our family. When I first met Mr. Bryan when he was nineteen years old, he was wearing a silk hat as a college boy, and he has had one ever since. When we traveled abroad, he always had his silk hat. At the present writing we have one hat in Japan, one in Old Mexico, and two in London. I make mention of this that all may know that he is not lacking in this emblem of official dignity.

We were invited to lunch at the White House with a

344

company of about two hundred, most of them intimate friends of the President.

The dining room looked very pretty. The lunch was served from the table to the guests as they stood around the room. I am told that the last official act of President Taft had been to order this luncheon for his successor. This may be the usual custom, but it is a gracious one.

I met there Admiral Dewey and his wife. Mr. and Mrs. House were there as amiable as ever, all the members of the new Cabinet, all the Wilson relatives and friends. After lunch we went at once to the reviewing stand and sat there until after dark reviewing the parade. I recall particularly Governor Sulzer at the head of New York's marchers, flourishing his hat and bowing right and left; the fine appearance made by the cadets, particularly those from Culver, our son's school; the college students marching and giving their college yells in front of the reviewing stand; Indians in their beads and feathers, the chiefs of several tribes, and soldiers, soldiers, soldiers.—We stayed till the parade ended, even though it was dark. It seemed too bad not to stay when the poor men in line had waited so long.

We walked from the White House to the hotel, the New Willard, as it was impossible to get a cab. Mr. and Mrs. Edward Goltra of St. Louis walked with us. A crowd of people followed, and by the time we reached the hotel we had a by no means small bodyguard. The city was in a plight. Bushels of waste paper and all sorts of débris attested the presence of a multitude.

It was a matter of great satisfaction to me to see democracy so powerful. After all, a wonderful party! Through all these years of defeat she has been undaunted, militant, courageous, never faltering—a proof to me that the principles of democracy are right. Truth lives.

Our rooms were filled all day Wednesday. I spent the time making notes of the wishes of various office seekers and lists of their qualifications. One point which seemed particularly in evidence was that they had "been with Bryan from the beginning." "How different from the days of '96!" "How I grieved over his first defeat! But I have never lost faith in him!" etc., etc. It suddenly became the acme of respectability to have supported him in 1896. I saw the undercurrent, of course, and was not always impressed. I wanted to go to the Senate when the Cabinet members were confirmed, but was not able to get away. I did close my branch office long enough to go to the State Department and see Will sworn in. I told him I had never heard him swear before and was interested to know how he would do it. As he had told no one of the hour, only a few were there. The retiring Secretary left a large bouquet of American beauties on the desk for the new Secretary.

The other members of the Department were present. Will signed his name and gave the pen to Richard, our son-in-law. I inspected the gallery of former Secretaries. The portraits do credit to the office, but the place where they hang does not. It is a dingy room. The ceiling has been patched and not retinted in one place. The backs of chairs have marred the walls and some of the upholstery is positively shabby! I hope this room may be put in order during the present régime.

Our first official function was at the White House when the President and Mrs. Wilson received the Diplomatic Corps and we were asked to receive with them. I wore my grey embroidered crêpe. The diplomats filed past with their wives—a confusing array of faces and names—they went at once to the dining room. A little later "His Excellency, the French Ambassador and Madame Jusserand" were led in to converse three minutes with the President and Mrs. Wilson, then were passed on for three minutes with us. They were followed by "His Excellency, the German Ambassador and the Countess Bernstorff," and so forth.

The Secretary and I received the Diplomats at the New

LIFE IN WASHINGTON

Willard on Saturday in the large parlor. Mr. Hale, of the State Department, presented the guests.

The most elaborate entertainment was that given at the Pan-American Republic building by Mr. Barrett, the director. My absent-minded husband had forgotten to tell me that a reception followed, so I was not dressed as I would have been. The banquet table was beautiful with a profusion of spring flowers. Mr. Bryan was welcomed by the Brazilian Minister (by whom I sat at dinner, and whom I enjoyed). Will responded in a beautiful speech which pleased them all very much. It is a great advantage to us to have traveled as much as we have. The winter we spent in South America is most valuable.

The First Assistant Secretary of State and Mrs. Huntington Wilson gave a very beautiful dinner in our honor. I sat by Count Bernstorff, the German Ambassador, and found that he lives in the Tyrol near the villages of Garmish and Partenkirchen, where we spent some happy days seven years ago. We had a very pleasant chat.

The two Sundays before we left for Lincoln found us at the Presbyterian Church. The minister has been a friend of Mr. Bryan's for many years. What he says is good, but he shouts in a most annoying way. I am trying to get Will to speak to him about it. I cannot understand why his wife does not train him a little. If she would give him just one illustration of his style, the work would be done.

We came West for Will's birthday dinner, stopping en route at Springfield, where he had been invited to address the Legislature. He made a fine speech, was in a gay humor, and full of sparkle.

Will's birthday banquet in Lincoln was large and enthusiastic. Speakers, Rev. Scoville, an evangelist, who told of the reputation Will has in foreign countries; Governor Dunne of Illinois; Governor Hodges of Kansas; Jerry Sullivan of Des Moines, Governor Morehead of Nebraska, and Will. Fourteen hundred men were at the tables.

We arrived in Lincoln on the morning of the nineteenth. It began to storm about noon and the weather gave one a continuous performance for a week. This may be nature's means of weaning me from Nebraska. I certainly feel more resigned about leaving than I would had the weather been finer. Sorosis and Fortnightly united in a luncheon for me at Mrs. Miller's. Mesdames Miller and Barbour were hostesses. I do regret parting from these club friends. A more bright-minded, clear-headed lot of women does not exist. I delight in our discussions and shall miss them sadly when I return to Washington.

I have been gathering my household goods for shipment to Washington. They are at this moment packed in a baggage car. We are taking some characteristic possessions. Our bronze Korean lions are going to guard our doorway in Washington as they did in Nebraska. The painting of Thomas Jefferson goes to preside in the front hall, the Trentanove bust, my beautiful Beatrice, our Bronze Diogenes, my "Hollandishe Dame," and many other little treasures. I think we are to have a really "homey home" in Washington. The stormy weather which I mentioned culminated in a tornado on Sunday which passed over Lincoln and devastated Omaha.

When I arrived in Washington I found a very smiling gentleman at the station. Will had reached Washington two days before. We went to our new quarters in the Willard, on the F Street side and six stories up, a corner sitting room with a bedroom and bath across the way and a nice little hall between. We were very comfortable here and could sleep much better. There was so much less noise.

The days following have been very full. Luncheons, teas, and dinners, some music and one play. I am trying to strike a pace which I can maintain. I would like if possible to dress well enough and at the same time help, by an example of simplicity, the many people here who are tempted to live beyond their means. The statement that

PRINCETON, NEW JERSEY

23 Feby, 1913

My dear Mr. Bryan;

Now contemplate the efforts of the papers are, the last few days, to make trouble for us and between us, — and how delightful it is — to me, as I hope it is to you — to know, all the while, how perfect an understanding exists between us! It has been to me, since I saw you, a constant source of strength and confidence.

I had nothing in particular to write to you about to-day. I have written these few lines merely by impulse from the heart.

Mr. Wilson joins me in warmest messages to Mrs. Bryan and yourself.

Your sincere friend,

Woodrow Wilson

Mr. Wm. J. Bryan

President-Elect Wilson speaks of "perfect understanding" with Mr. Bryan.

WILLIAM JENNINGS BRYAN

I once read that a wife is the bulletin board upon which her husband hangs the evidences of his prosperity, has come to my mind many times. A few jewels are beautiful—if they are—but wearing too many seems to me both vulgar and barbaric.

One thing which pleases me is the constantly increasing cordiality between the President and Mr. Bryan. They work together so well. Will finds him so firm and courageous and so truly progressive. The newspapers (opposition) are still trying to make trouble between them, saying all sorts of hateful things, but without avail. A circumstance which shows President Wilson's strength must be recorded. I want it to go down in history and fear it may not be recorded elsewhere.

Tumulty (the President's secretary) told Will about it. During the Baltimore Convention, when the nomination of Wilson hung in the balance, when Will was holding the bosses and combines by the throat and waiting for help, McCombs telephoned from Baltimore to Sea Girt that he could get the nomination for Wilson if Wilson would promise *not* to appoint Bryan to a Cabinet position.

Will came home and told me about it. I said anxiously, "And *what* did Wilson say?" Will answered, "Tumulty said, 'Wilson came into the room from the telephone very pale and said, "I have just refused the nomination," and then told me what McCombs had proposed. I asked him what he said to McCombs and Wilson replied, "I told him to go to h—." ' "

When Will told me about this his eyes filled with tears and he could hardly control his voice. He said, "Doesn't that show the man? Wasn't that fine?" I hope this intimacy will grow stronger and deeper. It means so much for the country and for the administration—the Cabinet and the Department are working together beautifully.

To us, the most important social function was our first Diplomatic luncheon. We gave a farewell luncheon to

Ambassador and Mrs. Bryce, whom we had known so pleasantly in England.

The other ambassadors were our guests with their wives. Four ambassadors' wives were out of town, so we asked Mrs. Burton Harrison, Mrs. Henry Dimmock, Mrs. Marshall Field, and Mrs. Senator Walsh to fill their places. The table was laid for eighteen in the parlor of the so-called "Presidential suite," at the Willard Hotel. The table looked very pretty with white roses and maidenhair ferns for decorations and little candlesticks with green and white shades.

As this luncheon has received so much comment, I had better record it accurately. Mr. Bryan and I had discussed wines at table several times and decided there was but one thing for us to do. When the guests were all seated, Will rose at his place, looking decidedly pale, but handsome (I had told the waiters not to begin serving until he had finished speaking), and asked the guests' indulgence for a few moments. He then told them how when President Wilson had asked him to be Secretary of State, he had asked him whether taking the office would necessitate the serving of liquors, and had been given permission to use his own judgment. He told them that we had always been teetotalers, that our fathers were both teetotalers, and that we could not depart from this custom without contradicting all our past. He hoped we might show our hospitality in other ways and that they would pardon us if we omitted wines. When he had finished, the guests applauded and the meal proceeded. We served white rock water and grape juice and everyone at least seemed contented. The Russian Ambassador told his dinner partner, Mrs. Harrison, that he had not tasted water for years, but as he had been forewarned (Will had told him when we dined there), he had taken his claret before he came and so all was well. At the close of the meal Will proposed a toast to Ambassador Bryce and asked the Dean of the Corps, Jusserand, to voice the sentiment. Jusserand made a charming speech to which Bryce responded with considerable feeling. He spoke so well that everyone was delighted. When we left the table, I believe they were as gay under the stimulus of the speeches as they would have been had we served wine. In any case, we have broken the ice. Some of the newspapers have made caustic comments, those in England being particularly uncomplimentary. On the other hand, we are getting hundred of letters of approval from all over the country. I hope the example may do good. It is hard to stand against prevailing customs.

Will is now in California working on the Japanese legislation. The task is difficult; I hope he may succeed.

July 16, 1913.

The summer has been upon us for several weeks, a humid, sticky heat which is very enervating and oppressive. The city is deserted; all the legations have gone into summer quarters. Newport seems to be the favorite resort and the average citizen has gone out of town.

The intervening weeks have been filled with engagements of various kinds. The ambassadors, each in the order of his rank, gave us a dinner. These are formal and it is somewhat tiresome to go so many times. However, out of it all I am beginning to feel a little acquainted and to make a few friends. I had an interesting evening with Justice Holmes, son of the author. He is now an old man, seventy or more, but very erect and alert mentally. He says he does a certain amount of reading each year because of the Day of Judgment. If St. Peter were to ask him, "Have you ever read Gibbon's Rome?" he would be very much embarrassed to admit that he had not. I thought this rather a good idea.

A very enjoyable occasion was the luncheon given by Colonel and Mrs. Thompson for the Peace Delegation. There was quite a large company from England, Canada, and

Australia. Lord Weardale was one of the number, also Moreton Frewen. I was so glad to see them both. Lord Primrose was also of the party. He is a very good-looking young fellow. He told Will, "I heard it with my own ears," that if he could do exactly as he wished, he would come here, become an American and vote for him (Will) for President, which pleased me. The Thompsons had three musicians, sisters, I think from Wales, who sang old English songs, were very quaintly dressed and made a pretty picture, besides singing nicely. One played accompaniments on an old-time harp. Andrew Carnegie graced the occasion, but had nothing to say. He is certainly little; believe it is better to look at his picture than to see him. He was greatly pleased with Will's speeches and expressed a wish that Will's life might be spared for many years.

I wish to record a strange turn in the wheel of fate. J. Pierpont Morgan, whose financial power has been used so persistently against Will, died in Rome, and Will, as Secretary of State, cabled in regard to the ceremonies which should be held at the Embassy over his body. If Mr. Morgan knew that Mr. Bryan was dallying with his funeral arrangements . . . The papers took notice of the circumstance.

Another item worthy of record was the signing of the seventeenth amendment. I went down to the State Department and saw it signed. Will was certainly delighted. It seemed so fine that he could sign it after working for it for so many years.

I discovered early in the game that many of the invitations received are for a purpose; many times a desire for an appointment is lurking beneath. Many of the attentions I do not regard as a personal tribute. The office of my husband is greater than any charms of his wife.

Official dining is a particular and serious business. Eight o'clock is the hour. Everything moves according to rule. Precedence is rigidly observed. I understand dreadful complications have arisen because Mrs. Smith went in to dinner in advance of Mrs. Jones.

As official rank decides the seating at table, one does not always have too good luck in table companions. For instance, one evening I sat with the Japanese Ambassador on my right. He is a nice little man, but his avenues of thought all end in blind alleys. One subject never leads into another. Upon my left was the Turkish Ambassador, who stubbornly refused to speak any language. I served him with a conglomerate composed of equal parts of English and German, to which he returned a linguistic pudding of German, English, and French, in a very mumbling manner.

We have dined out practically every night all winter, Sundays excepted, and are up early every morning. Working people cannot lie in bed.

Every Wednesday during the season we are officially at home. We are now occupying the house in Calumet Place which was the home of General Logan. The number of visitors each week varies from one hundred to four or five hundred.

For many years returning calls has been the *bête noir* of every woman in Washington whose husband is in office. I am hoping for easier work next winter, as the rules have been recently simplified. It has taken my best thought and planning to keep pace with demands.

The whole performance has its own charm. Sometimes the afternoon glides along most successfully, the acme being reached when everyone is out. Other days it works like this. Call No. 1—Representative moved; obliging maid gives the new address, several blocks distant; great haste. Second address, every window filled with placards, "For Rent" and the trail is lost. (Muttered remarks, annoyance.) Call No. 2—No such number. Consultation with men on box. Light breaks. It is northeast instead of southwest. Great relief. Hurried drive to northeast.

354

Entire block being torn down for new buildings. Ah, yes. We are not far from the Capitol. Will go and look up address at Senate post office. Find address and also that wife has gone home and will not return until next year. (Mutterings of increased violence.)

Call No. 3—No Senator at that number. Are sure secretary has made mistake. Try same number on next street. Same result. Being not far from home, drive around to house and look up address. Find secretary has copied it correctly. Go back again. Footman quarrels with maid. Find Senator is there. Lives upstairs, yes, of course. No, has no wife. Died two years ago. (Mutterings positively sulphurous), etc., etc., ad infinitum. These samples may be the more exaggerated cases, but will show some of the trials to which one's patience is subjected.

August 6, 1913.

July fifteenth is worthy of note for two reasons. First it was the fiftieth birthday of Secretary Lane, for whom we have such high regard, and also the day on which Huerta left Mexico.

Mrs. Lane planned a little birthday dinner for her husband at Pierce's Mill in Rock Creek Park. The table was spread under the trees quite near the water. Those present were Secretary and Mrs. Lane, Secretary and Mrs. McAdoo, Miss Bones and Miss Smith of the President's household, Senator Lewis of Illinois, Charles Hamlin of the Treasury, Senator and Mrs. Newlands, Secretary and Mrs. Bryan, and late in the evening when dinner was half over, the President came. Mr. and Mrs. Newlands brought the birthday cake, which was ornamented with a brown teddy bear (the emblem of California, from which state Secretary Lane came). The cake also bore the legend, "For a good boy," which the confectioner had volunteered in pink frosting without consulting Mrs. Newlands. Furthermore, the cake bore fifty little white candles.

When Secretary McAdoo came, Will told him of the retirement of Huerta. They embraced and danced about like a pair of boys. Every one was in lively mood. Senator Lewis told a great many stories, chiefly in negro dialect, he tells them well. We shall not soon forget the day Huerta left Mexico or the joy which his going occasioned.

MR. BRYAN AT HIS DESK IN STATE DEPARTMENT

CHAPTER XII

SECRETARY OF STATE

WHEN the Wilson administration took charge of the State Department, it found a number of questions left as a legacy by the preceding administration. Mexico was a problem of long standing. After several years of political ferment, another insurrection arose in February, 1913. During the turmoil, Huerta, the head of the Mexican army, took his commander in chief prisoner, and not long after, both the president and vice president were put to death. Then followed the insurrection of the Constitutionalists.

Knowing that Huerta had obtained his office by force, the United States Government refused to give him recognition, and made every effort for the restoration of peace. Our government was particularly anxious about the protection of Americans residing in Mexico, and so far as was possible during a state of war, protected American property interests.

Secretary Bryan was not illy prepared for this work, as in our three visits to Mexico he had learned to know the leading men; he understood the conditions of the country and the temperament of its inhabitants.

The following statement was dictated to me by Secretary Bryan in 1913:

MEXICO

"In dealing with the Mexican situation, we had a number of important questions to consider. The first was whether Huerta should be recognized. A great deal of pressure was brought to bear on the administration by American business interests in Mexico, and much of my time during the first few months was occupied in hearing delegations which came to urge Huerta's recognition. None of them attempted to defend either the character of the man or the methods by which he had secured his office. The pleas were all along the same line and ran in substance as follows:

" 'We do not care to say anything about Huerta individually nor about the way in which he obtained office, but a strong man is necessary to preserve order in Mexico, and he is the only strong man in sight. If the United States recognizes him, he can get money, and with money, he can put down the insurrection.'

"The speeches to which I listened were so similar that I finally adopted a stereotyped reply, namely:

" 'You believe, do you, that Diaz was the kind of man needed to preserve order in Mexico?' They always answered, 'Yes.'

" 'Do you think that Huerta would imitate the methods and reëstablish his régime?'

" 'Yes.'

" 'If, after thirty years of experiment with his policy, Diaz, with world-wide prestige and splendid credit, could not maintain himself against Madero, but saw his government crushed like an eggshell, what reason have you to believe that Huerta, not only without prestige and credit, but guilty of high treason and blamed for the death of Madero, will be able to succeed where Diaz failed?'

"No answer was attempted.

"The American ambassador at Mexico was very insistent upon the recognition of Huerta, but the records seemed to show that he was too intimately associated with the change in government to be in a position to speak without bias. There were in the beginning some officials in Washington who took the position that we could not properly inquire into the ethics of the methods employed, or as to whether the Huerta government represented the people of Mexico.

"My answer was, first, that I was so unaccustomed to the consideration of public questions separated from both morals and the principle of popular government that I was not able to endorse the position of those who favored the recognition of Huerta.

"Second, The question of intervention was broached from time to time, and we had to meet a dangerous form of argument which has many times led nations into war. It begins with an assumption and upon that assumption predicates an act which results in hostilities. In this case the argument ran as follows:

"First. We must intervene sooner or later.

"Second. Since we must intervene some time, the sooner, the better.

"After several conferences with the President on the subject of intervention, I presented my views on the subject in a letter, which reads as follows:

" 'October 28, 1913.

" 'My dear Mr. President:

" 'From your speeches at Swarthmore and Mobile, I take it that you are revolving in your mind the statement which you are soon to make of your Mexican policy. I take the liberty, therefore, of presenting for your consideration, the conclusions that have been running through my mind.

" 'I was in doubt as to how our country's position could be so stated as to link the new position with the earlier statements of the Monroe Doctrine, and did not see daylight until the publication of that statement then attributed to Huerta, but now believed to be entirely false.

" 'The first announcement of the Monroe Doctrine was intended to protect the republics of America from the political power of European nations—to protect them in their right to work out their own destiny along the lines of self-government. The next application of that doctrine was made by Cleveland when this Government insisted that European governments should submit their controversies with American republics to arbitration, even in the matter of boundary lines.

" 'A new necessity for the application of the principle has arisen, and the application is entirely in keeping with the spirit of the doctrine and carries out the real purpose of that doctrine. The right of American republics to work out their own destiny along lines consistent with popular government, is just as much menaced today by foreign financial interests as it was a century ago by the political aspirations of foreign governments. If the people of an American republic are left free to attend to their own affairs, no despot can long keep them in subjection; but when a local despot is held in authority by powerful financial interests, and is furnished money for the employment of soldiers, the people are as helpless as if a foreign army had landed on their shores. This, we have reason to believe, is the situation in Mexico, and I cannot see that our obligation is any less now than it was then. We must protect the people of these republics in their right to attend to their own business, free from external coercion, no matter what form that external coercion may take.

" 'Your utterance in regard to conquest was timely. We must be relieved of suspicion as to our motives. We must be bound in advance not to turn to our own advantage any power we employ. It will be impossible for us to win the confidence of the people of Latin America, unless they know that we do not seek their territory or ourselves desire to exercise political authority over them. If we have occasion to go into any country, it must be as we went into Cuba, at the invitation of the Government, or with assurances that will leave no doubt as to the temporary character of our intervention. Our only object must be to secure to the people an opportunity to vote, that they may themselves select their rulers and establish their government. . . .

" 'I shall be at your command tomorrow and hold myself in readiness to call at the White House upon a moment's notice, but I thought best to put these suggestions in writing and have them ready for you on your return.

" 'With assurances of my great respect, I am,
" 'My dear Mr. President,
" 'Very sincerely yours,
" 'W. J. BRYAN.
" 'The President.
" 'The White House.'

"I was gratified to find the President resolutely opposed to intervention except as a last resort, and I regarded his refusal to yield to pressure on this subject as one of the most meritorious acts of his administration. Intervention was avoided with its indefinite cost of blood and money, and its incalculable penalty of incurring the ill will of all Spanish people in America."

RECOGNITION OF CHINA

The recognition of China as a republic early in May, 1913, was one of the pleasant duties of this administration. While other nations held back, our nation extended the hand of welcome to the new republic.

CHINESE LOAN

The Chinese loan was another question for consideration. It was settled at an early date by the administration refusing to renew the request made to the New York syndicate by the Taft administration. The matter is fully explained in the following statement dictated to me by Secretary Bryan:

"Soon after Wilson's administration began, word was received from the Morgan group, which was the American firm interested in the six-power loan to China, asking that a date be set for the consideration of the loan. A day in March, 1913, was chosen, and on that day a committee including Mr. S. P. Davidson, of J. Pierpont Morgan Company, and Mr. Willard Straight called at the State Department and presented their case. I called into the conference counsel Anderson, and first assistant secretary Huntington Wilson.

"The position taken by the bankers was that they had interested themselves in this loan at the request of the government and that they were not willing to continue their connection with the loan unless the request was renewed by this administration.

"During the conference, inquiry brought out four important facts. First, that no American financiers, except those in this group, could participate in the loan. Second, that the financiers interested in this loan expected to control future loans. Third, that the loan was to be secured by control of revenues. Fourth, that the six groups of financiers expected their governments to furnish such support as might be necessary, even to the use of force, to compel China to live up to the stipulations of the loan contract.

"I reported the conference to the President at a Cabinet meeting and expressed the opinion that the loan was objectionable, first, because it gave the monopoly of this nation's interests in China's finances to a small group of American bankers to the exclusion of all other American financiers. Second, because it gave to the six groups interested in this loan a monopoly of China's financial affairs. Third, the security contemplated might interfere seriously with the political independence of China. Fourth, it linked our country with other countries and deprived it of any independence in dealing with China. The American group, being only one of six groups, could not have a controlling voice in matters connected with the collection of the loan, and this government, being only one of six governments interested through representatives, could not have a controlling voice in determining methods to be employed in enforcing the loan.

"The President and members of the Cabinet, after considering my report, reached the same conclusion, and the President issued a statement declining to ask the group to participate further in the loan. In the discussion of the subject before cabinet meeting, it was suggested that the refusal to approve the loan should be accompanied by a strong declaration favorable to the extension of our commerce in the Orient, and the President's statement, issued in April, 1913, contains such a statement.

"The refusal of the government to encourage this loan strengthened this nation's position in China, the Chinese people being opposed to the loan because of the harshness of its terms and because of the further fact that it endangered the sovereignty of the Chinese government, but they had felt obliged to accept this loan because they had not been able to receive more favorable terms."

Another instance in which Secretary Bryan applied the Monroe Doctrine to the settlement of affairs of State was found in his attitude toward the republics of Central and South America. The following statement was dictated to me by Secretary Bryan in 1913:

WILLIAM JENNINGS BRYAN

CENTRAL AND SOUTH AMERICA

"Another problem was found in the formulation of a reason for opposing the machinations and political intrigues of foreign concessionaires in the republics of Central and South America.

"The Monroe Doctrine, as interpreted and applied, gave us a sufficient reason for objecting to interference by foreign governments, but it had never been so interpreted as to justify an objection to the conduct of foreign residents and private corporations owned by foreign residents.

"It had long been obvious that foreign influence exerted through private individuals and private corporations can as effectively overthrow popular government in the Latin American republics as when that influence is exerted directly by foreign governments. I laid the matter before the President and was pleased to have my suggestion favorably received.

"In his Mobile speech, made a few days after, he said, 'I want to take this occasion to say that the United States will never again seek one additional foot of territory by conquest.' Continuing, he declared that the American government frowned upon efforts by any American citizens to exploit the peoples to the south of us. He denounced concessionaires who interfered with the processes of orderly government and who intrigued to overthrow one administration in Latin America so that it might be succeeded by another more favorable to these privileged interests.

"No exception has been taken to this interpretation in this country or abroad.

"Honduras has been gratified by our refusal to support as reasonable a certain loan proposition. Although this was much more favorable to Honduras than the proposition urged upon her under previous administrations, it still did not seem equable.

FOUR FAMOUS MEN WHO HAVE SERVED AND GONE ON
Left to right: Andrew Carnegie, William Jennings Bryan, James J. Hill, and
John Mitchell. © *Underwood & Underwood, N. Y.*

MR. BRYAN WITH THE CHINESE CHAMBER OF COMMERCE
Photographed in front of the State Department, Washington, D. C.
© *Harris & Ewing, Wash., D. C.*

SECRETARY OF STATE

"Colombia has been conciliated by a treaty adjusting all differences, and Chili has been pleased by the just recognition given her by raising our legation there to an embassy."

DOLLAR DIPLOMACY

At the very threshold of the new administration stood the question of so-called "Dollar Diplomacy."

While the United States has been very earnest in protecting the countries of South America from political domination at the hands of European powers, she has not always been zealous in protecting these countries from enterprising Americans whose business policies do not bear scrutiny.

Secretary Bryan dictated the following statement to me in 1913:

"The phrase 'Dollar Diplomacy' has been used to describe a policy under which this government, on the excuse of representing American industry in Spanish America, used its diplomatic influence to advance the interests of American investors and promoters without a scrupulous regard to the merits of the claim. As a result of this policy in the past the Wilson administration found a number of sore spots amongst the Southern Republics.

"Chili had been irritated by the Alsop claim; Honduras had been angered by the terms of a proposed loan; Ecuador was at war with an American railroad, and Colombia had for ten years been asking for arbitration of the differences which arose out of the establishment of the Panama Republic.

"The first case with which the Department had to deal was the controversy between the government of Ecuador and a railroad running from Guayaquil to Quito. Under the terms of the charter, disputes were to be settled by arbitration, and an arbitrator had been named to represent this government, when it was found that his name had already been suggested by the railroad. He was withdrawn and a new man, Judge Miller, to whom no exception could be taken, was appointed. Unofficial objections had been made to the retaining of the American minister to Ecuador on the ground that having been appointed by the previous administration, he labored under the suspicion of being identified with the transactions of which they complained. He was recalled and a new representative sent for the special purpose of improving the relations between the two governments."

ALIEN LAND LEGISLATION

The Alien land legislation in California involved the administration in a prolonged and delicate controversy with Japan. The President did everything in his power to persuade the California legislature to leave the matter to diplomacy, but failed. The exchange of views was prolonged, but the discussion was carried on in an admirable spirit.

In April, 1913, Secretary Bryan was sent to California to present the views of the administration.

After consultation with local leaders, the legislature went into executive session and the message was delivered behind closed doors.

A report which was made at the time follows:

"After Bryan had finished his first statement, the meeting was thrown open to a sort of questions-and-answers affair. The questions were showered at Bryan at a rapid rate, and Bryan shot back the answers equally fast.

"There was no confusion, no bitterness, and no disorder. Bryan held attention from the first to the last minute. He was prepared at every angle, and when the conference adjourned until a late hour in the afternoon the legislators departed satisfied that the Secretary of State came to California to consult with and to confer with the legislators, not to wield the club.

" 'We feel that he is a big man who thoroughly understands his errand,' was the declaration of several Senators and Assemblymen of both Democratic and Republican persuasion in attendance at the first part of the executive conference."

During the discussion in Washington of the California Alien Land Law, relations were at times quite strained, and earnest conferences were held between the Japanese Ambassador and the Secretary of State, as shown in the following incident:

Ambassador Chinda called and knotty questions were discussed without any conclusion being reached. The Ambassador arose and said, "I suppose, Mr. Secretary, this decision is final."

The Secretary advanced, extended his hand, and with his winning smile, said,"There is nothing final between friends."

The Ambassador was touched, resumed his seat, and an agreement was reached.

CURRENCY REFORM

Another important measure of domestic policy was the passing of the Currency Bill of June, 1913. The need was particularly urgent in the case of President Wilson's administration, because for sixteen years no unholy Democratic hands had been permitted to steady the ark.

The following notes on this subject were dictated to me by Secretary Bryan:

"After the discussion of a currency bill had gone on for some time and it was generally understood that the

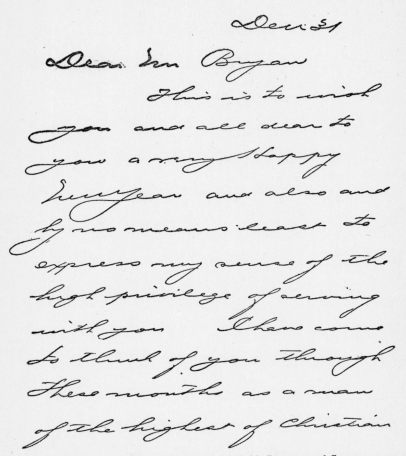

Congratulatory letter from William C. Redfield, Secretary of Commerce.

Dec. 31

DEAR MR. BRYAN

This is to wish you and all dear to you a very Happy New Year and also and by no means least to express my sense of the high privilege of serving with you. I have come to think of you through these months as a man of the highest of Christian

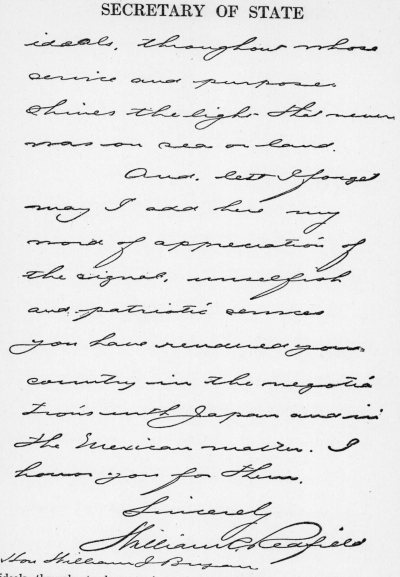

ideals, throughout whose service and purposes shines the light that never
was on sea or land.

And, lest I forget may I add here my word of appreciation of the signal,
unselfish and patriotic services you have rendered your country in the negotiations with Japan and in the Mexican matter. I honor you for them.

Sincerely

WILLIAM C. REDFIELD

Hon. William J. Bryan

24

President favored the passage of a currency bill at this session, he invited me to the White House to confer on the subject.

"He presented the plan then under consideration and expressed the hope that I would be able to support it.

"The plan was substantially that now embodied in the Owen-Glass bill, with two exceptions: First, that the emergency notes were to be issued by the regional reserve banks as bank notes are now issued; and second, that the central board of control was to be composed in part of representatives appointed by the banks, the government's representatives being in the majority.

"After hearing the proposed plan I advised against any attempt to pass such a bill at this session and against its introduction until after the tariff bill was signed. The reason being, as I stated to him, that such a currency plan would be sure to arouse great opposition in the Democratic party and might jeopardize the passage of the tariff bill through the Senate, in which the party has a small margin and in which some senators are greatly opposed to free wool and free sugar.

"I called his attention to the fact that our party had been committed by Jefferson and Jackson and by recent platforms to the doctrine that the issue of money is a function of government and should not be surrendered to banks, and that I was so committed to the doctrine that I could not consistently indorse the authorization of more bank notes and that to do so would forfeit the confidence of those who trusted me—this confidence being my only political asset, the loss of which would deprive me of any power to assist him.

"I also pointed out my objection to a divided control and argued in favor of making the entire board of control appointive by the President, so that the government would have complete and undisputed authority over the issue of the government notes which, in my

judgment, should be substituted for the contemplated bank notes.

"After presenting my views as clearly and forcibly as I could, I assured him of my entire confidence in his desire to do what was best for the people and of my deep regret that we could not view these two phases of the subject in the same light.

"He shared in the regret and expressed a willingness to have me state my position, if, when the plan was finally ready, there were any parts of it which I could not indorse, and I assured him that if I felt compelled to dissent from any part of the plan I would accompany the dissent with an explicit statement of confidence in the disinterestedness of his intention and make my dissent as mild as conditions would permit.

"In conversation with Secretary McAdoo and Private Secretary Tumulty I went over much the same ground and expressed my distress at not being able to agree with the President on these points and my fear that the plan under consideration would divide our party and make any currency reform impossible.

"I did not confer with the President again until the bill was completed, but received from Tumulty some encouragement to hope that the bill in its final form might be satisfactory.

"When I was again invited to the White House to confer on this subject, the President informed me that it had been found possible to substitute federal reserve treasury notes for regional bank notes and to give the government entire control of the central governing board.

"I was greatly relieved that the two difficulties which had seemed insurmountable had been removed.

"I expressed the opinion that the bill in its final form would be acceptable to the party and, being acceptable, its immediate introduction would no longer

WILLIAM JENNINGS BRYAN

March 19, 1914

Secretary of State
MAR 20 1914

My dear Mr. Secretary:

May I not congratulate you on your
birthday and wish you many, many happy returns?
It makes me very glad to think what happiness
it must have brought you to render the public
services you have rendered and to look back upon
years devoted to the interests of the people.
I wish you Godspeed with all my heart, and want
you to know what a deep pleasure I have derived
from association with you.

Always

Cordially and faithfully yours,

Woodrow Wilson

Hon. William Jennings Bryan,
Secretary of State.

Letter from President Wilson congratulating Secretary Bryan on his achievements.

menace the tariff bill. I offered to give him any assistance in my power and with his approval gave out an interview which was published on Monday morning—his message to Congress being delivered at noon of the same day. The manner in which he conducted the preparation of the currency bill is conclusive proof of the President's openmindedness.

"President Wilson felt it his duty to the public to urge a reform of the currency and he took up the matter with the same conscientiousness that has characterized his work along other lines.

"The first persons called into consultation were impressed with the idea that no currency reform was possible except along the lines proposed by financiers, and these financiers, viewing the subject from their own standpoint, naturally favored bank paper and a control in which the banks would participate.

"When, however, the President had pursued his investigation far enough to learn of the deep-seated objection entertained by the rank and file of the Democratic party to any extension of the note-issuing privilege enjoyed by the banks, he at once threw the weight of his powerful influence on the side of the party."

And here perhaps I might insert an enthusiastic letter which Mr. Bryan received from Carter Glass applauding his work for the Federal Reserve Act:

HOUSE OF REPRESENTATIVES
WASHINGTON
September 25, 1913.

MY DEAR MR. BRYAN:

Looking back over the remarkable campaign for currency reform just ended in the House, one thing stands out, conspicuous in the retrospect, and that is that we are immensely indebted to you for effective aid

in critical periods of the contest in committee and in caucus. I desire to thank you for your great assistance to me and to the cause, and also to express my personal gratification at the manner in which you have disappointed your enemies and pleased your friends by standing firmly with the President for sound legislation in behalf of the American people. The country and your party are greatly obliged to you for the skill and discernment with which you have helped along the fight, and I am particularly grateful.

Sincerely yours,

CARTER GLASS.

Hon. Wm. J. Bryan,
Secretary of State,
Washington, D. C.

POPULAR ELECTION OF SENATORS

Another bit of work which gave the Secretary great satisfaction was the signing, in April, 1913, of the document which made effective the popular election of United States Senators. After eighteen years of work for this measure, it seemed particularly fitting that his hand should sign the document.

PEACE TREATIES

The peace treaties with thirty nations formed so important a part of his record as Secretary of State that I have devoted a separate chapter to this topic.

Concerning these treaties, James Brown Scott, head of the Carnegie Peace Foundation, writes:

"Only the services of an international nature which he rendered as Secretary of State can properly be considered here, and they will probably be found to be much more important than commonly supposed; so important,

indeed, that Mr. Bryan is likely to hold a more prominent place among those who have striven for peace among nations, than among political leaders in the United States, who have held the attention of their countrymen, and aspired to the highest offices of State. . . .

"Secretary Bryan regarded these treaties as bis greatest achievement, and the official portrait painted for the Diplomatic Room of the Department of State represents him in standing posture, holding in his hand a copy of the treaties. He was right. At least, in the opinion of many, they constitute the greatest contribution of an official nature made at any time, by any one man."

Loans to Belligerents

With the breaking out of war in Europe, the question of loans to belligerents became urgent, and I submit the following statement dictated to me by Secretary Bryan at that time:

"Assistant Secretary Lansing and I discussed the possibility of other loans being negotiated if this plan was approved, by which the country would be divided up into groups, each group engaged in negotiating loans to the belligerent countries with which it sympathized. Before leaving the State Department that evening, I wrote a letter to the President, and a day or two later I conferred with him on the subject at the White House. He approved of the proposition not to loan belligerents, and at my suggestion wrote out a sentence stating the Government's position very concisely and strongly, and this sentence I incorporated in an announcement which he asked me to make.

"This, I believe, is the first time any great nation ever took this position. It had been discussed at peace

375

congresses and I remember having supported the doctrines some six or seven years ago at a peace congress held in New York, but I am not sure that any convention or Congress of any importance ever endorsed it. It may be regarded as setting a new standard—as establishing a new precedent, and this precedent, in my judgment, will be sooner or later followed by other nations.

"Soon after the breaking out of war in Europe in August, 1914, Mr. Davidson, of the J. Pierpont Morgan Company, telephoned the State Department to inquire what the attitude of the Government would be in regard to the making of loans to belligerent nations. He said that they had had inquiries in regard to loans which he thought were intended for the French government. I replied that I would confer with the President and would let him know.

"I at once consulted counselor Lansing and learned that precedents were all in favor of such loans, they not being regarded as a violation of neutrality. I said to him that I thought they violated the spirit of neutrality because money, being able to purchase all other contraband materials, was in effect the worst of contraband. He at once endorsed the position as sound in principle, even though not supported by precedent, and later came back to suggest an illustration which appealed to me as a very forcible one, namely, that as the government discourages its citizens from enlisting in foreign armies and withdraws the protection of citizenship from them as long as they serve under another flag, it should discourage the money of this country from taking a part in foreign wars. It is another step in the direction of peace, for the inability of belligerent nations to secure foreign loans must exert a strong restraining influence upon them."

SECRETARY OF STATE

THE DUMBA INCIDENT

Statement prepared by Mr. Bryan:

"The most maliciously misrepresented of my experiences in the State Department was what is known as the Dumba Incident. After the German Ambassador had been withdrawn at the request of the United States, the Austrian diplomat, Ambassador Dumba, took over the representation of Germany.

"While the second note was being prepared, Ambassador Dumba called at the Department and submitted several requests, which I answered according to the report of the conversation which will be found at the end of this chapter, this interview being reported to the President, as I did all other interviews of importance. The President returned the interview with his approval.

"In the course of the conversation a question was asked and answered which gave rise to the misrepresentation to which reference is made. The question was so commonplace that it seemed trivial and the answer, being the same that was being given in all the newspapers, did not impress me as of any importance.

"He asked me why we treated Germany's offense in sinking the *Lusitania* so differently from the offense of which Great Britain was guilty. I answered at once, 'Because the American people cannot regard the holding up of merchandise by Great Britain in the same light that they regard the taking of life by the sinking of the *Lusitania.*'

"There was hardly a prominent newspaper that had not brought out this distinction with greater or less clearness. It never occurred to me that the language could be misunderstood or misinterpreted; in fact, the matter was so trivial that it was not included in the report which covered the questions and answers which seemed to me important.

"To my surprise, a message came a few days later from Berlin informing us that Minister Zimmerman had reported to Ambassador Gerard that Ambassador Dumba sent a telegram saying in substance that the *Lusitania* note was 'not meant in earnest and was only sent as sop to public opinion.'

"I immediately sent for Ambassador Dumba and told him of the word I had received from the ambassador in Berlin. He expressed great surprise that such a misconstruction could have been placed upon his language and assured me that he had used no words that could by any reasonable interpretation convey any such thought.

"I had him cable the German government immediately, correcting any such misconstruction. The reader can see whether my words were objectionable, and yet this is the one incident of my administration of the State Department that unscrupulous enemies have employed when they wanted to discredit my work. The first that I recall appeared in the *New York Times* soon after my resignation. I at once gave out an interview correcting it. After that I corrected it from time to time, the most prominent occasion being at Lake Mohonk at a meeting over which Ex-President Taft presided. It was a peace meeting to which a delegate before my arrival made a reference to the Dumba Incident, misrepresenting it all along the line described above. I made the correction then that I make now and that I have made innumerable times since. I am glad to have an opportunity to put the correction in the form of a permanent record.

"A year or two later some newspaper correspondent, in writing a book on his experiences in Germany, referred to this incident and giving the usual hostile interpretation. I brought the matter to the attention of the President, and through his Secretary, Tumulty, he gave out the following denial:

SECRETARY OF STATE

"THE WHITE HOUSE
"WASHINGTON
"December 11, 1917
"MY DEAR MR. BRYAN:
"I have brought your letter of December 8th to the attention of the President, who is perfectly willing that you should say as from him that Mr. Ackerman's statements, or rather, his implications, are entirely false. Of course the President did not request or desire your resignation, and your resignation had no connection whatever with the so-called Dumba Incident.
"Sincerely yours,
"J. P. Tumulty
"Secretary to the President
"Hon. William J. Bryan
"Hotel Lafayette
"Washington, D. C."

Following is Mr. Bryan's report of his conversation with Ambassador Dumba:

"May 17, 1915
"MY DEAR MR. PRESIDENT:
"As you will not return until Wednesday morning, I think I ought to let you know at once of a conversation which I had this morning with Ambassador Dumba, of Austria. I am therefore sending this by special messenger.
"The Ambassador first expressed appreciation of your letter to the Czar and then asked me to say to you that he would be pleased to give you any assistance he could in the negotiation with Germany. He said he knew that Germany had no desire for war, but on the contrary, was anxious to maintain friendly relations with the United States and asked whether if assurances were given for the future it would not be possible to

arbitrate the question so far as past transactions are concerned. I told him I would not feel authorized to discuss the subject without first getting your views, but suggested that he might say to the German government that he felt sure there was no desire for war in this country and that we expected Germany to answer the note in the same spirit of friendship that prompted ours. He then suggested it might make it easier for Germany if she could, in her reply, say that she expected us to insist in the same spirit upon freedom of trade with the neutrals. I pointed out to him that such an expression in the answer might embarrass us and also make it more difficult to deal with the Allies along that line and that I thought Germany ought to assume that we would live up to the position taken in our answer to the Orders in Council. He asked whether we could give any confidential assurances of that kind and I told him it ought not to be necessary and suggested to him that if Germany desired to justify, before her own people, her acceptance of the doctrine set forth in our note she could publish her views in a statement—not to us, but to the German people, and say that she took it for granted that we would maintain the position taken in that statement and would insist upon our right to trade with neutrals. I told him if this statement was made to the German people instead of to us it would not require any answer from us and would not embarrass us, but if her answer contained any expression of opinion as to how we would deal with Great Britain it would seemingly link the two cases together and put us in the attitude of acting at Germany's suggestion instead of acting upon our own initiative and for the protection of our own interests, and it might also be construed as a sort of trade whereby we would settle an account with Germany by opening an account with the Allies.

"He saw the force of the objection. I emphasized the two points—first, that it was important that Germany should answer in the same spirit in which we had addressed her; and second, that there should be no attempted connection between our dealings with Germany and our dealings with Great Britain.

"He asked whether we could not refuse clearance to ships that carried explosives and ammunition. He said that in Germany passenger trains were not allowed to carry explosives and that the regulation was made for the protection of the lives of passengers; he suggested we might, on the same ground, refuse to allow ship owners to carry explosives on passenger boats. I told him that Germany was, of course, at liberty to make any suggestions that she thought proper in her reply, but that we could not consider these suggestions in advance.

"I think the call of the Ambassador was rather significant, especially as I learned from Villard that he had received some of the same suggestions from von Bernstorff. I believe that it would have a splendid effect if our note to Great Britain can go at once. It will give Germany an excuse, and I think she is looking for something that will serve as an excuse. There is much discussion of the idea suggested by Dumba—in fact, mentioned in the first explanation received from Germany, namely, that passengers and ammunition should not travel together. I have no doubt Germany would be willing to so change the rule in regard to submarines as to exempt from danger all passenger ships that did not carry munitions of war.

"I am also enclosing a statement from Page. The closing sentence is interesting. Am glad to note that it will not take a generation to regain the respect with the loss of which we were threatened.

"With assurances of high respect, I am, my dear Mr. President,
                    "Yours very sincerely,
                              "W. J. BRYAN.

"P. S.   The bearer of this letter, Mr. Yardley, will bring it to the Mayflower tonight and await instructions from you.   If you have any answer to send back tonight, he will return on the twelve-thirty train—if not, he will return early tomorrow afternoon.   If you do not send an answer tonight but desire to send one tomorrow, you can instruct him whether he is to call at the Mayflower for it or whether you can send it to the Holland House, Fifth Avenue near 28th Street, where he will stop.
"The Honorable

"Woodrow Wilson,
    "Now at New York City."

CHAPTER XIII

Peace Treaties

IN reviewing the life of Mr. Bryan, an interesting truth is brought to light, namely, the principles which he advocated were born in him and were a part of his being. None of his work gave him more pleasure than his peace treaties, which he regarded as his greatest constructive achievement.

The first instance of his peace sentiment which we can produce is a letter written by Mr. Bryan December 8, 1879, to his cousin, Thomas Marshall, of Salem, Illinois, whom he addresses as "Dear Tommie." The writer was then a lad of eighteen, writing a stiff hand and with purple ink:

'O, would that some demon might infuse into my peaceful mind a love for martial array! How unfortunate! I repeat it, alas! how unfortunate that the sound of armor, glittering steel and the gory field of battle have no claims for me! Were my disposition otherwise, I might have longed to have gazed upon the 'reunion.' But, Tom, do you know that the time is swiftly passing by when armies rule? The dawn of a brighter day is at hand. Right is beginning to rule in the place of might. I rejoice that in a few years it will not be necessary to shoot a man to convince him that you are right and to blot out a nation to prove to them that their principles are false. But we will argue this more at length when we are together Christmas."

This thread of peace may be traced through the years. Whenever the question of war was raised, he sided against it. He spoke in foreign countries on this subject. I recall his stirring address in Westminster Hall in London, July,

1906.   But it is unnecessary for me to multiply words when I am able to insert an account of his peace treaties written by Mr. Bryan himself:

"THE THIRTY TREATIES

"The above title is used because the plan under consideration was embodied in thirty treaties with governments (hereafter to be named) which exercise authority over three quarters of the world's population.

"The plan was first suggested in an editorial which appeared in my paper, *The Commoner*, February 17, 1905, and was further elaborated in a second editorial that appeared in the same paper a week later, February 24.

"I had for some years before this advocated a similar plan for the settlement of labor disputes.   Compulsory arbitration has, in a recent decision of the United States Supreme Court, been declared unconstitutional; it is also contrary to the spirit of our institutions.   To compel an employer to pay excessive wages would be confiscatory; to compel wage earners to labor for insufficient wages would be involuntary servitude. But investigation of all industrial disputes is not open to the same objection because the parties are left free to act according to their pleasure at the conclusion of the investigation.   It is eminently proper that the general public, which is necessarily the chief sufferer from any industrial disturbance, should know the cause of the dispute in order to assist in the formation of that public opinion which, in the end, controls all action in a republic.

"During the war between Russia and Japan, it occurred to me that the same principle and the same reasons would apply to international disputes, hence the editorials to which reference has been made.

PEACE TREATIES

"The proposed plan provided for the submission of all international disputes of every kind and character to a permanent tribunal for investigation, when not by other treaties submitted for arbitration. (Our Arbitration Treaties contain four exceptions; viz., Questions of Honor, Questions of Independence, Vital Interests, and the Interests of Third Parties—the very questions that give rise to wars.) The proposed tribunal was to be chosen as follows: one by each country from among its own citizens, one by each country from another country, and the fifth by agreement between them.

"Second, it provided for a year's time for investigation and report, during which time there should be no resort to hostilities.

"Third, it reserved to each party the right of independence of action at the conclusion of the investigation.

"On the 20th of October, 1905, I presented the plan to a company of Japanese statesmen and business men at a dinner given by the Bankers' Club at Tokyo, Japan, but the response was not encouraging.

"In July, 1906, I again presented the plan at a meeting of the Interparliamentary Union held in London. The plan was cordially endorsed by Sir Henry Campbell Bannerman, then the British premier. It was approved unanimously by the Interparliamentary Union as an alternative to mediation.

"After this, I lost no opportunity to lay the plan before Peace Advocates wherever they assembled. It was endorsed in 1898 by an International Peace Conference in New York, and in 1910 at a Peace Meeting in Edinburgh, Scotland.

"I explained the plan to President Taft and he incorporated a part of it in his treaties with Great Britain and France. The rejection of these treaties was due to other provisions.

25

"Upon being invited into the Cabinet of President Wilson, I secured his hearty approval of the plan. Soon after the inauguration, it was put into diplomatic form and laid before him and by him submitted to his Cabinet. Before it was offered to the foreign representatives at Washington, it was submitted to the Senate Committee on Foreign Relations and approved by that committee. It was in April, 1913, submitted to the diplomatic representatives at Washington.

"Salvador, the smallest republic (in area) in Central America, was the first government to conclude a treaty with the United States according to this plan. Four other Central American governments, Guatemala, Nicaragua, Panama, and Honduras, in the order named, entered into similar treaties with our nation before any European government was ready to accept its terms. Netherlands was the first European nation to sign one of these treaties with us, and Bolivia was the first government of South America. July 24, 1914, was made memorable by the simultaneous signing of three of these treaties with Brazil, Argentine Republic, and Chile.

"September 15, following, was made even more memorable by the simultaneous signing of four of these treaties with Great Britain, France, Spain, and China. More than half of the population of the world was represented by the five officials who sat around a table in our State Department and affixed their signatures to four treaties on that occasion.

"The following are the nations with whose governments these treaties were made; they are given in the order in which the treaties were executed: Salvador, Guatemala, Panama, Honduras, Nicaragua, Netherlands, Bolivia, Persia, Portugal, Costa Rica, Switzerland, Dominican Republic, Venezuela, Denmark, Italy, Norway, Peru, Uruguay, Brazil, Argentine Republic,

Chile, Paraguay, China, France, Great Britain, Spain, Russia, Ecuador, Greece, Sweden.

"The United States Senate advised the ratification of all these treaties except those with Panama and the Dominican Republic. Ratification has been exchanged with twenty of these, as follows: Guatemala, Norway, Portugal, Great Britain, Costa Rica, Spain, Bolivia, Sweden, Denmark, France, Uruguay, Peru, Paraguay, Italy, Russia, China, Chile, Ecuador, Honduras, Brazil.

"The plan of these treaties, with the exception of the provision reserving the right of independent action, was embodied in the Covenant of the League of Nations. It is worthy of notice that in the discussion in the United States Senate no objection was made to this plan so far as it was endorsed in the Covenant.

"The Four Power Treaty, relative to disputes that may arise in the Pacific, embodied the same principles as the Thirty Treaties, but because of ambiguity in the wording of that treaty an amendment was adopted by a vote of 90 to 2 declaring that the findings of the tribunal for investigation would impose no legal or moral obligation upon the parties.

"The latest Hague provisions for mediation and conciliation follow the plan of the Thirty Treaties and leave the nations free to accept or reject the suggestions offered.

"It is believed that the plan goes as far as public sentiment is willing to go and completes the machinery necessary for the substitution of reason for force in the settlement of all international disputes. The arbitration treaties make provision for the adjustment of all differences that can be submitted to arbitration; the Permanent Tribunal for Investigation, provided for in the Thirty Treaty plan, deals with all other disputes and allows time for passion to subside, for questions of fact to be separated from questions of honor, and for the mobilization of the Peace sentiment of the world.

"WILLIAM JENNINGS BRYAN.

"Coconut Grove, Florida.

"May 1, 1925"

These treaties have been published by the Carnegie Endowment for International Peace and will form a volume in Mr. Bryan's complete works.

In sending Mr. Bryan a copy of his article on "War Abolished—Peace Enthroned," Andrew Carnegie added a postscript, which is reproduced here:

With his whole heart wedded to these treaty principles, his appeals to President Wilson for continuous offers of mediation from the first rumblings of the war in Europe until the day we joined the Allies, may be easily understood. He could not have done otherwise and have been true to his convictions.

In order to show how early in the World War he began this work, I append a letter of September 19, 1914.

Asheville, N. C.
Sept. 19, 1914

MY DEAR MR. PRESIDENT:

The European situation distresses me. The slaughter goes on and each day makes it more apparent that

HIS CROWNING ACHIEVEMENT

Signing the Peace Treaties with Great Britain, France, Spain and China, September 15, 1914. Mrs. Bryan, seated at end of table, witnessed this event at the special invitation of her husband.

Asheville N.C.

Sept 19
1914

My Dear Mr President —

The European situation distresses me. The slaughter goes on and each day makes it more *apparent* that it is to be a prolonged struggle. All parties to the conflict declare that they did not <u>want</u> war, that they are not <u>responsible</u>

Mr. Bryan's copy of first page of his letter appealing to Wilson for offer of mediation.

it is to be a prolonged struggle. All parties to the conflict declare that they did not want war, that they were not responsible for it and that they desire peace—and to make their positions more nearly identical they desire an enduring peace.

I cannot but feel that this nation, being the only great nation on friendly terms with all, should urge mediation, since none of the nations engaged are willing to take the initiative. The responsibility for continuing the war is just as grave as the responsibility for beginning it, and this responsibility, if pressed upon the consideration of the belligerent nations, might lead them to consent to mediation—no nation can afford to refuse. Of course, each one would like to have the war stop at such a time as to give it the prestige of having the advantage, but war necessarily has in it an element of uncertainty; successes may alternate, as, for instance, recently when the Germans almost reached Paris and then were driven back. It is a gamble, even when no natural cause intervenes—and natural causes have ofttimes turned the tide of battle, as when the Spanish Armada was scattered (and, if you will not consider it irreverent, the Lord never had a better opportunity or reason than now to show His power). The world looks to us to lead the way, and I know your deep desire to render every possible assistance. Both sides seem to entertain the old idea that fear is the only basis upon which peace can rest. This idea was boldly stated by the Turkish Ambassador when opposing the sale of ships to Greece. He said that the only way to insure peace in that part of Europe was for Turkey to dominate the situation. And so the Kaiser sees peace in a victory which will insure the supremacy of Germany, while the Allies see peace only in a success so signal as to crush the German war machine.

It is not likely that either side will win so complete

a victory as to be able to dictate terms, and if either side does win such a victory it will probably mean preparation for another war. It would seem better to look for a more rational basis of peace. Your suggestion, namely, that the manufacture and sale of arms and ammunition shall be a government monopoly, is most excellent. It has also been suggested that armaments should be diminished, that all armies should be reduced in size with a view to reserving them for internal use in preserving order, and that the nations should enter into an agreement to respect present boundaries, etc.

I believe that a compulsory investigation of disputes before hostilities begin, such as our treaties provide for, would go far toward preventing war, but the most potent of all influences for the promotion of peace is the substitution of friendship for hatred, and your plan of taking away the pecuniary interest which private corporations now have in war will make it easier to cultivate friendship. Mediation would give opportunity for the consideration of all plans, and I see no other way in which these plans can be considered or even proposed, for complete success by either side will make that side feel that it is in a position to compel peace by the exercise of superior force.

Would it not be worth while for you to address a note to all the combatants reciting the awful horrors of this conflict, and pointing out—

First, that all deny responsibility for the war and that all express a desire for peace;

Second, that responsibility for a continuance of such a war is as undesirable as responsibility for beginning it, and that as such responsibility attaches to this nation as well as to participants, my suggestion is that you earnestly appeal to them to meet together and exchange views as to the terms upon which permanent peace can be insured.

They could be reminded that, while mediation can not be asked or accepted with conditions, the parties are under no compulsion to accept unsatisfactory terms; also that while an armistice during mediation would, on general principles, be desirable, it might operate unequally upon the combatants and is not therefore essential to mediation.

From the answers received there is reason to believe that such an offer would not be refused, and if it succeeded you would have the satisfaction of knowing that you had rendered an international service almost if not quite without parallel.

I feel so deeply that this is worth trying that I desire to confer with you about it on my return; but I send this letter in advance, that you may have time to consider the reasons herein submitted. Even if it fails— and that cannot be known until the offer is made—you will have the consciousness of having made the attempt.

With assurances of respect,

I am, my dear Mr. President,

Very truly yours,

W. J. Bryan.

Another letter of March 22, 1917, shows the depth of his feeling and the strong foundation upon which it rested.

March 22, 1917

Mr. W. P. Trent,
Columbia University,
New York, N. Y.

My dear Mr. Trent:

I thank you for sending me the speech by Mr. Lambert. I am not surprised that he fails to understand the proposition which I tried to present, for it seems that a great many of our preachers do not understand it. I quoted to him from the New Testament where Christ said, "Love your enemies," and pointed out to him that love comes before justice—is, in fact, necessary to the understanding of justice. It is easy to love those who are good to us. It is to love those who despitefully use us that tests our religion.

The nations of Europe all contend that they are fighting for justice and that when they establish justice, friendship will follow. That is, in my opinion, the delusion that has kept the world at war, and will continue to make permanent peace impossible as long as the philosophy is followed.

As long as there is hatred in the heart, one cannot understand what justice is. If I understand our religion, love is presented as the greatest compelling force and forgiveness as its manifestation. The President's appeal to the nations to come together in a peace without victory was rejected by both sides because European governments are not built upon that theory, and now we are asked to enter into the war on the European plan.

"If preachers who have dedicated their lives to the interpretation of the Gospel can see no higher standard of honor than the standard of war, it is hard to expect a man from Belgium whose heart is bleeding for his countrymen to be dispassionate enough to understand the philosophy of love and the fruit it is expected to produce.

Thanking you again for bringing Mr. Lambert's argument to my attention, I am,

Very truly yours,

W. J. BRYAN.

Although the fact received no recognition, Mr. Bryan had the satisfaction of seeing the idea which is prominent in all his treaties, namely, the submission of all disputes to arbitration, embodied in the Covenant of the League of Nations. Article 12 reads as follows:

"The members of the League agree that if there should arise between them any dispute likely to lead to a rupture, they will submit the matter either to arbitration or to inquiry by the council, and they agree in no case to resort to war until three months after the award by the arbitrators or the report by the council.

"In any case, under this article the award of the arbitrators shall be made within a reasonable time, and the report of the council shall be made within six months after the submission of the dispute."

At the San Francisco Convention in 1920, in speaking on the League of Nations, and his willingness to accept reservations, after it became apparent that the United States would not enter the League unconditionally, Mr. Bryan said: "You cannot call me an enemy of Woodrow Wilson; it was my treaty plan that he took to Paris. I have helped him to become immortal. If I could secure ratification without reservations, and could give to Woodrow Wilson the honor of securing it, I would walk up to the scaffold today and die with a smile upon my face."

CHAPTER XIV

WAR IS DECLARED IN EUROPE

IN 1913 when war was declared in Europe, all ordinary negotiations ceased. Nations the world over were divided into belligerents and neutrals. Our country was the greatest amongst the latter class, and as such was expected to lead. In several instances we took charge of neutral embassies or legations in belligerent territory. On foreign policies the first real disagreement between the Chief Executive and the Secretary of State came on the question of neutrality. The Secretary took the position that if we are neutral, all belligerents should receive exactly the same treatment at our hands. If we are to take place with either warring faction, let us do it—but if we are to pose as being neutral, let us be neutral.

For some time before the sinking of the *Lusitania*, many complaints were received against England; that she was holding up our shipping in her own ports until cargo owners were willing to take anything they could get for their wares; that she was using our flag to protect her munitions; that she had established a blockade which cut off food supplies from Germany and also from neighboring neutrals and was starving women and children.

The Secretary found it easy to be absolutely neutral, as he felt in a struggle of such intensity, no participants were capable of calm reasoning and all would do anything which seemed likely to help their cause. The Secretary reasoned that when occasion demanded a note of protest against Germany, it should be sent; likewise when occasion demanded a note of protest against England, it should be sent.

Germany was inhuman in her submarine attacks— inhuman to the last degree, but was England less culpable

395

when she cut off food supplies from innocent women and children, and should her unauthorized use of our flag go without protest?

The sinking of the *Lusitania* raised the question of keeping Americans from traveling on ships passing through the danger zone, the Secretary taking the position that while these people had a right to go where they pleased, there was a duty which a citizen owed not to become embroiled in any needless controversies. In the background lurked the ever-present difference, the Secretary standing for an effort to effect mediation, and taking the position that we should at least try. I insert here some of the correspondence of this period.

April 23, 1915.

MY DEAR MR. PRESIDENT:

In a note to you this afternoon I stated that Mr. Lansing would take your instructions to Old Point Comfort and prepare a tentative draft or note in the Thrasher case, during his stay there.

As I have not been able to reach the same conclusion to which you have arrived in this case, I feel it my duty to set forth the situation as I see it. The note which you propose will, I fear, very much inflame the already hostile feeling against us in Germany, not entirely because of our protest against Germany's action in this case, but in part because of its contrast with our attitude toward the Allies. If we oppose the use of the submarine against merchantmen we will lay down a law for ourselves as well as for Germany. If we admit the right of the submarine to attack merchantmen but condemn their particular act or class of acts as inhuman we will be embarrassed by the fact that we have not protested against Great Britain's defense of the right to prevent foods reaching non-combatant enemies.

©*Underwood & Underwood, N. Y.*

MR. BRYAN AS SECRETARY OF STATE IN THE CABINET OF PRESIDENT WILSON

WAR IN EUROPE

We suggested the admission of food and the abandonment of torpedo attacks upon merchant vessels. Germany seemed willing to negotiate, but Great Britain refused to consider the proposition. I fear that denunciation of one and silence as to the other will be construed by some as partiality. You do not make allowance for the fact that we were notified of the intended use of the submarine, or for the fact that the deceased knowingly took the risk of traveling on an enemy ship. I cannot see that he is differently situated from those who by remaining in a belligerent country assume risk of injury. Our people will, I believe, be slow to admit the right of a citizen to involve his country in war when by exercising ordinary care he could have avoided danger.

The fact that we have not contested Great Britain's assertion of the right to use our flag has still further aggravated Germany and we cannot overlook the fact that the sale of arms and ammunition, while it could not be forbidden under neutrality, has worked so entirely for the benefit of one side as to give to Germany—not justification but an excuse for charging that we are favoring the Allies. I have mentioned these things to show the atmosphere through which the Thrasher note will be received by Germany.

Believing that such a note as you propose is, under the conditions that now exist, likely to bring on a crisis, I venture to suggest an alternative, namely, an appeal to the nations at war to consider terms of peace. We cannot justify waiting until both sides, or even one side, asks for mediation. As a neutral we cannot have in mind the wishes of one side more than the wishes of the other side. . . .

With assurances, etc., I am, my dear Mr. President,
Very truly yours,
W. J. BRYAN.

397

While the following letter is not dated, the expression in paragraph three of the preceding letter, "but Great Britain refused to consider the proposition," seems to give it place here.

DAVID LLOYD GEORGE:
As a friend of all the nations at war, as a Christian and a lover of humanity, I respectfully but most earnestly appeal to you to use your great influence to secure your Government's consent to negotiations.

There is no dispute that must necessarily be settled by force. All international disputes are capable of adjustment by peaceful means. Every guarantee that can possibly be secured by war can be stated as a condition precedent to peace. Do not, I pray you, by refusing an exchange of views, assume responsibility for a continuation of the unspeakable horrors of this unparalleled conflict. Your decision may mean life or death to millions.

WILLIAM JENNINGS BRYAN.

THE SECRETARY OF STATE
WASHINGTON
May 9, 1915

MY DEAR MR. PRESIDENT:
As you do not read the *Post*, I am taking the liberty of enclosing an editorial that appeared in it this morning. You will notice that it calls attention to Germany's action in endorsing the requirement of notice to passengers. But my special reason for calling attention to this editorial is that it makes a suggestion for which I ask your consideration, namely, that ships carrying contraband should be prohibited from carrying passengers. The idea occurred to me last night (it was *not*, of course, communicated to the *Post*) that some such should be adopted. Germany has a right to prevent

contraband going to the Allies, and a ship carrying contraband should not rely upon passengers to protect her from attack—it would be like putting women and children in front of an army.

You will notice from another clipping enclosed that the manifest shows 4200 cases of cartridges and ammunition valued at $152,400. I learned from Mr. Lansing last night that the *Lusitania* carried ammunition, and this information suggested to me the rule which seems to have suggested itself to the editor of the *Post* also.

You will notice that Germany refers to this war material in the *Lusitania's* cargo. One result will be to make the world realize more fully the horrors of war and pray more earnestly for peace.

Ridder's comments, which I enclose, are suggestive. Our people will, I think, be the more thankful that a believer in peace is in the White House at this time.

With assurances, etc.

W. J. BRYAN.

THE SECRETARY OF STATE
WASHINGTON

May 12, 1915

MY DEAR MR. PRESIDENT:

I am so fearful of the embarrassment which the Jingoes will cause by assuming that your note means war, an interpretation which might affect the tone of Germany's reply as well as make it more difficult to postpone final settlement, that I venture to suggest the propriety of meeting the issue *now* by a statement given out at the time the protest is published or before.

To explain what I mean I give the following—not as a draft of such notice or interview, but as an illustration: The words "strict accountability" having been construed by some of the newspapers to mean an immediate settlement of the matter, I deem it fitting to say

399

that that construction is not a necessary one. In individual matters friends sometimes find it wise to postpone the settlement of disputes until such differences can be considered calmly and on their merits. So it may be with nations. The United States and Germany, between whom there exists a long standing friendship, may find it advisable to postpone until peace is restored any disputes which do not yield to diplomatic treatment.

Germany has endorsed the principle of investigation embodied in the thirty treaties signed with as many nations. These treaties give a year's time for the investigation and apply to all disputes of every character. From this nation's standpoint, there is no reason why this policy should not control as between the United States and Germany. I believe such a statement would do great good.

With assurances,

Yours truly,

W. J. BRYAN.

THE WHITE HOUSE
WASHINGTON

May 13, 1915

MY DEAR MR. SECRETARY,

After sleeping over your suggestion, I have this to propose: It would not be wise, I think, to give out a direct statement; but I think the same purpose would be served by such a "tip" as the enclosed, accompanying the publication of the note. And it would be best that this tip should be given out from the Executive Office, while the note was given out by the Department of State. What do you think?

If you will return the paper in the course of the morning, I will make the necessary arrangements.

Faithfully yours,   W. W.

The Secretary of State.

WAR IN EUROPE

TYPEWRITTEN MEMORANDUM

"There is a good deal of confidence in Administration circles that Germany will respond to this note in a spirit of accommodation. It is pointed out that, while Germany is not one of the many nations which have recently signed treaties of deliberation and inquiry with the United States upon all points of serious difficulty, as a means of supplementing ordinary diplomatic methods and preventing, so far as feasible, the possibility of conflict, she has assented to the principle of such a treaty; and it is believed that she will act in this instance in the spirit of that assent. A frank issue is now made, and it is expected that it will be met in good temper and with a desire to reach an agreement, despite the passions of the hour,—passions in which the United States does not share,—or else submit the whole matter to such processes of discussion as will result in a permanent settlement."

THE WHITE HOUSE
WASHINGTON

May 13, 1915

MY DEAR MR. SECRETARY,

Since I expressed my approval of the statement you suggested for the press, I have heard something, indirectly, from the German Embassy, which convinces me that we would lose all chance of bringing Germany to reason if we in any way or degree indicated to them, or to our own public, that this note was merely the first word in a prolonged debate. I will tell you what I have in mind when I do not have to write it.

In the meantime, I beg that you will pardon me for changing my mind thus. I am sure that it is the safer course, the one more likely to produce the results we are all praying for. Please withdraw the message (the supplementary statement) altogether. If we say anything of the kind it must be a little later, after the **not** has had its first effect.

Faithfully yours,

W. W.

The Secretary of State.

DEPARTMENT OF STATE
WASHINGTON

May 14, 1915

MY DEAR MR. PRESIDENT:

I am sending you a letter from Mr. Lansing. You will notice that he cannot possibly prepare the note to Great Britain before Monday. At my request he prepared a notice such as we discussed, warning passengers against taking these ships pending negotiations. He is doubtful about the wisdom of issuing the notice, fearing that it may raise the question as to why we did not issue an earlier notice. While this question may be asked, I think it is better for us to have the question asked and answered, rather than run the risk of any more attacks. I believe that the issuance of such a notice would not only be likely to protect the lives of some Americans and thus lessen the chances of another calamity, but would have its effect upon the tone of the German reply and might point the way to an understanding. At least it would probably prevent anything like a summary dismissal of our protest. I beg to submit the idea for your consideration and the tentative notice for your criticism in case the idea commends itself to you.

With assurances of high respect, I am, my dear Mr. President,

Yours very sincerely,

W. J. BRYAN.

The Honorable
Woodrow Wilson
The White House

WAR IN EUROPE

THE WHITE HOUSE
WASHINGTON

May 14, 1915

MY DEAR MR. SECRETARY,

I quite understand why a note about the detained ships cannot be made ready before the beginning of next week.

As to the request to Americans not to take passage on belligerent ships (for I agree with Mr. Lansing that it could be nothing more than a request), my feeling is this: the request is unnecessary, if the object is to save lives, because the danger is already fully known and those who do not refrain because of the danger will not, in all probability, refrain because we request them to do so; and this is not the time to make it, not only for the reason Mr. Lansing suggests, but also because, as I urged this morning, it weakens the effect of our saying to Germany that we mean to support our citizens in the exercise of their right to travel both on our ships and on belligerent. If I thought the notice necessary, or effective, to save lives, the second objection might be waived, but since I do not, I think the second objection ought to prevail.

Faithfully yours,

W. W.

The Secretary of State.

It will be noticed that the Chief Executive was able to see objections to any efforts at mediation, objections to warning citizens, and objections to sending a protest to England.

While I realize this is a life of the Secretary of State and not of the President, it seems necessary to give the President's views at this point. Apparently the vital reason for his position is not found in these statements. Secretary Tumulty throws a flood of light on the matter in his book, "Woodrow Wilson As I Know Him."

WILLIAM JENNINGS BRYAN

"Turning to me, the President said: . . . . England is fighting our fight and you may well understand that I shall not, in the present state of the world's affairs, place obstacles in her way. Many of our critics suggest war with England in order to force reparation in these matters. War with England would result in a German triumph. No matter what may happen to me personally in the next election, I will not take any action to embarrass England when she is fighting for her life and the life of the world. Let those who clamour for radical action against England understand this!' "

While the personal views of the President are here set forth, it does not follow that the diplomatic notes of the Department were not strictly neutral. The work was done with great care to keep the correspondence well within the bounds of the international laws of neutrality. So skilful was this work that after his resignation, Secretary Bryan commented more than once upon the neutrality of the administration. This was true. No technical flaw could be found. But I submit the thought that the administration was lacking in neutrality—not in commission, but in omission; not the notes which were written, but the notes which were not written, threw the delicate machinery out of balance and made the work of the Secretary of State increasingly difficult. It will be seen that the final break, which came on the second note, was not a sudden rupture, but was the result of long and accumulated strain.

While Secretary Bryan was bearing the heavy responsibility of the Department of State, there arose the curious conditions surrounding Mr. E. M. House's unofficial connection with the President and his voyages abroad on affairs of State, which were not communicated to Secretary Bryan, but which vitally concerned his department.

Earl Grey's memoirs, recently published, are illuminating, showing, as they do, that as early as February, 1916, the affairs of the Department of State were being unofficially conducted over the head of the Secretary and that, without consultation with him, the President was unofficially dealing with foreign governments.

Lord Grey records that in February, 1916, he and Mr. House collaborated upon a memorandum defining, as definitely as possible, the steps President Wilson would be prepared to take.

A copy of the memorandum was left with Lord Grey, while Mr. House later cabled from Washington that the text had been confirmed by the President, without the knowledge of the Secretary of State.

The memorandum from Lord Grey's memoirs follows:

"Colonel House told me that President Wilson was ready, on hearing from France and England that the moment was opportune, to propose that a conference should be summoned to put an end to the war. Should the Allies accept this proposal, and should Germany refuse it, the United States would probably enter the war against Germany.

"Colonel House expressed the opinion that, if such a conference met it would secure peace on terms not unfavorable to the Allies; and if it failed to secure peace, the United States would leave the Conference as a belligerent on the side of the Allies, if Germany was unreasonable. Colonel House expressed an opinion decidedly favorable to the restoration of Belgium, the transfer of Alsace and Lorraine to France, and the acquisition by Russia of an outlet to the sea, though he thought that the loss of territory incurred by Germany in one place would have to be compensated to her by concessions to her in other places outside Europe. If the Allies delayed accepting the offer of President Wilson, and if, later on, the course of the war was so unfavorable to them that the intervention of the United States would not be effective, the United States would probably disinterest themselves in Europe and look to their own protection in their own way.

"I said that I felt the statement, coming from the President of the United States, to be a matter of such importance that I must inform the Prime Minister and my colleagues; but that I could say nothing until it had received their consideration. The British government could, under no circumstances, accept or make any proposal except in consultation and agreement with the Allies. I thought that the Cabinet would probably feel that the present situation would not justify them in approaching their Allies on this subject at the present moment; but, as Colonel House had had an intimate conversation with M. Briand and M. Jules Cambon in Paris, I should think it right to tell M. Briand privately, through the French ambassador in London, what Colonel House had said to us; and I should, of course, whenever there was an opportunity, be ready to talk the matter over with M. Briand, if he desired it.

(Initialled) "E. G.

"Foreign Office,
   "February 22, 1916."

Obviously these conditions made the position of the Secretary of State extraordinarily difficult. Appended is his letter of resignation:

MY DEAR MR. PRESIDENT:
It is with sincere regret that I have reached the conclusion that I should return to you the commission of Secretary of State with which you honored me at the beginning of your administration.

Obedient to your sense of duty and actuated by the highest motives, you have prepared for transmission to the German Government a note in which I cannot join without violating what I deem to be an obligation to my country, and the issue involved is of such moment that to remain a member of the Cabinet would be as unfair to you as it would be to the cause which is nearest my heart, namely, the prevention of war.

I, therefore, respectfully tender my resignation, to take effect when the note is sent, unless you prefer an earlier hour. Alike desirous of reaching a peaceful solution of the problems arising out of the use of the submarines against merchantmen, we find ourselves differing irreconcilably as to the methods which should be employed.

It falls to your lot to speak officially for the nation; I consider it to be none the less my duty to endeavor as a private citizen to promote the end which you have in view by means which you do not feel at liberty to use.

In severing the intimate and pleasant relations which have existed between us during the past two years, permit me to acknowledge the profound satisfaction which it has given me to be associated with you in the important work which has come before the State Department, and to thank you for the courtesies extended.

With the heartiest good wishes for your personal welfare and for the success of your administration, I am, my dear Mr. President,

Very truly yours,

W. J. BRYAN.

Washington, June 8, 1915.

RESIGNATION ACCEPTED

MY DEAR MR. BRYAN:

I accept your resignation only because you insist upon its acceptance; and I accept it with much more than deep regret, with a feeling of personal sorrow. Our two years of close association have been very delightful to me. Our judgments have accorded in practically every matter of official duty and of public policy until now; your support of the work and purposes of the administration has been generous and loyal beyond praise; your devotion to the duties of your great office and your eagerness to take advantage of every great opportunity for service it offered has been an example to the rest of us; you have earned our affectionate admiration and friendship. Even now we are not separated in the object we seek but only in the method by which we seek it.

It is for these reasons my feeling about your retirement from the Secretaryship of State goes so much deeper than regret. I sincerely deplore it. Our objects are the same and we ought to pursue them together. I yield to your desire only because I must and wish to bid you Godspeed in the parting. We shall continue to work for the same causes even when we do not work in the same way.

With affectionate regard, sincerely yours,

WOODROW WILSON.

Washington, June 8, 1915.

THE REVISED NOTE TO GERMANY

Secretary Bryan, who resigned his portfolio rather than sign the second note to Germany, issued a statement on June 12, 1915, declaring that the note to Germany had been materially revised following the presentation of his resignation.

He stated that he had seen the final draft of the note just before his resignation *took effect* but that it contained an important change. *He had no knowledge of this change at the time his resignation was tendered and accepted.* The clause inserted follows:

"If the Imperial German Government should deem itself to be in possession of convincing evidence that the officials of the Government of the United States did not perform these duties with thoroughness the Government of the United States sincerely hopes that it will submit that evidence for consideration."

This change, while very much softening the note, was not, however, sufficient, in his judgment, to justify him in asking permission to withdraw his resignation.

As Germany had suggested arbitration, he felt that America could not do less than reply to this offer by expressing a willingness to apply in this case the principle contained in his peace treaties.

Secretary Bryan refused to discuss the change which had been made in the note, preserving an attitude of loyalty to the Administration, although when the altered note was made public it called down the most violent abuse upon the ex-Secretary. The public failed to find in the altered note "an ultimatum to Germany" and Mr. Bryan was vilified for leaving his post and for claiming the note was harsher than, in its final form, it proved to be.

A frank statement from the White House would have given the facts which Mr. Bryan in loyalty withheld, and would have made his position clear to the public, but that statement was not forthcoming and Mr. Bryan was subjected to the harshest criticism.

MR. BRYAN'S FIRST STATEMENT
(Published June 10, 1915)

My reason for resigning is clearly stated in my letter of resignation, namely, that I may employ as a private citizen the means which the President does not feel at liberty to employ. I honor him for doing what he believes to be right, and I am sure that he desires, as I do, to find a peaceful solution of the problem which has been created by the action of the submarines.

Two of the points on which we differ, each conscientious in conviction, are:

First, as to the suggestion of investigation by an international commission, and,

Second, as to warning Americans against traveling on belligerent vessels or with cargoes of ammunition.

I believe that this nation should frankly state to Germany that we are willing to apply in this case the principle which we are bound by treaty to apply to disputes between the United States and thirty countries with which we have made treaties providing for investigation of all disputes of every character and nature.

These treaties, negotiated under this administration, make war practically impossible between this country and these thirty governments, representing nearly three-fourths of all the people of the world.

Among the nations with which we have these treaties are Great Britain, France, and Russia. No matter what disputes may arise between us and these treaty nations, we agree that there shall be no declaration of war and no commencement of hostilities until the matters in dispute have been investigated by an international commission and a year's time is allowed for investigation and report. This plan was offered to all the nations without any exception whatever, and Germany was one of the nations that accepted the principle, being the twelfth, I think, to accept. No treaty was actually entered into with Germany, but I cannot see that that should stand in the way when both nations endorsed the principle. I do not know whether Germany would accept the offer, but our country should, in my judgment, make the offer.

Such an offer, if accepted, would at once relieve the tension and silence all the jingoes who are demanding war. Germany has always been a friendly nation, and a great many of our people are of German ancestry.

WAR IN EUROPE

Why should we not deal with Germany according to this plan to which the nation has pledged its support?

The second point of difference is as to the course which should be pursued in regard to Americans traveling on belligerent ships or with cargoes of ammunition.

Why should an American citizen be permitted to involve his country in war by traveling upon a belligerent ship when he knows that the ship will pass through a danger zone? The question is not whether an American citizen has a right under international law to travel on a belligerent ship; the question is whether he ought not, out of consideration for his country, if not for his own safety, avoid danger when avoidance is possible.

It is a very one-sided citizenship that compels a government to go to war over a citizen's rights, and yet relieves the citizen of all obligations to consider his nation's welfare. I do not know just how far the President can go legally in actually preventing Americans from traveling on belligerent ships, but I believe the Government should go as far as it can, and that in case of doubt it should give the benefit of the doubt to the Government.

But even if the Government could not legally prevent citizens from traveling on belligerent ships, it could, and in my judgment should, earnestly advise American citizens not to risk themselves or the peace of their country, and I have no doubt that these warnings would be heeded.

President Taft advised Americans to leave Mexico when insurrection broke out there, and President Wilson has repeated the advice. This advice, in my judgment, was eminently wise, and I think the same course should be followed in regard to warning Americans to keep off vessels subject to attack.

I think, too, that American passenger ships should be prohibited from carrying ammunition. The lives of passengers ought not to be endangered by cargoes of ammunition, whether that danger comes from possible explosions within or from possible attacks from without. Passengers and ammunition should not travel together. The attempt to prevent American citizens from incurring these risks is entirely consistent with the effort which our Government is making to prevent attacks from submarines.

The use of one remedy does not exclude the use of the other. The most familiar illustration is to be found in the action taken by municipal authorities during a riot. It is the duty of the mayor to suppress the mob and to prevent violence, but he does not hesitate to warn citizens to keep off the streets, but, for their own protection and in the interest of order, he warns them not to incur the risks involved in going upon the streets when men are shooting at each other.

The President does not feel justified in taking the action above suggested. That is, he does not feel justified, first, in suggesting the submission of the controversy to investigation, or, second, in warning the people not to incur the extra hazards in traveling on belligerent ships or on ships carrying ammunition. And he may be right in the position he has taken, but as a private citizen I am free to urge both of these propositions and to call public attention to these remedies in the hope of securing such an expression of public sentiment as will support the President in employing these remedies if in the future he finds it consistent with his sense of duty to favor them.

W. J. BRYAN.

INTERVIEW GIVEN BY MR. BRYAN TO THE PRESS

"The President still hopes for peace and I pray, as earnestly as he, that Germany may do nothing to aggravate further the situation.

WAR IN EUROPE

"Because it is the duty of the patriot to support his government with all his heart in time of war, he has a right in time of peace to try to prevent war.

"I shall live up to a patriot's duty if war comes—until that time I shall do what I can to save my country from its horrors."

It seems his great hope was to arouse the people to support more strongly the President in offers of mediation. This was not accomplished, but if this failure caused him disappointment, if the lashing of the press wounded his spirit, no one was the wiser. He calmly did his duty as he saw it, and when war was declared, ceased all warnings and offered his services to his country.

Here may I record that President Wilson was a great war president? When one thinks of the other candidates before the Baltimore Convention, any one of whom might have been elected President, one feels thankful that the position came to President Wilson. The very qualities which are difficult to understand and which are so admirably grouped in David Lawrence's book, "The True Story of Woodrow Wilson," fitted him for the work. I quote one paragraph:

"Stern and impassive, yet emotional; calm and patient, yet quick-tempered and impulsive; forgetful of those who had served him, yet devoted to many who had rendered but minor service; unforgiving and fierce in his contempt for some who had dared to disagree with him, yet generous with others even to the extent of appointing them to high office; precise and business-like, and yet, upon occasion, illogical without more reason than intuition itself; seclusive, yet a crusader for democracy—thus might his characteristic contradictions be grouped incoherently in a series of paradoxes."

These seemingly contradictory qualities gave him a core of hardness and inflexibility which enabled him to stand firm in the face of appalling possibilities and command the attention and respect of the whole world.

CHAPTER XV

MR. BRYAN'S RESIGNATION

[From my Journal]

August 6, 1914.

WE had planned for some weeks to go to Asheville on August 2, last Monday. Mr. Bryan has worked faithfully to get his twenty peace treaties through the Senate. Our house in Asheville was ready, but as usual something happened to delay us. It seems we are fore-ordained (if there is such a thing) to spend the rest of our term of office in Washington. War has been declared in Europe. There is no use writing details of what now promises to be the greatest war in history. The immediate effect is to increase greatly the work of the Department. With the withdrawal of steamers, thousands of tourists are in Europe with little chance of getting passage home. Hundreds of telegrams are pouring into the Department from friends asking for aid and transportation for these people. Will was obliged to recall Secretary Osborne and Secretary Phillips, who were away on vacation. Several countries have asked our government to take charge of their embassies in hostile territory. The Department has undertaken all these friendly offices and the President has sent a note offering to assist in any efforts at mediation or arbitration.

The war conditions in Europe grow worse and worse. I try not to read the papers, but can't help getting more or less of it. I have only been really wrought up once and that was this week when Germany dropped bombs from a Zeppelin airship upon the innocent inhabitants of Antwerp, *in the night*. I can respect honest warfare, when foe meets foe, and he who has most skill and strength is victor, but this cowardly way of sneaking up under cover of darkness and dropping death down upon sleeping people is too much.

Public sentiment in this country is strong against such methods and if adverse thought can bring defeat, the Kaiser is doomed. I cannot see how he can hold out against the Allies.

The Russians are marching steadily through Prussia, headed for Berlin. They have a great army. The English and French are fighting for Belgium. It is too horrible! Will says that the poor little minister for Belgium has returned to the city and came to see him. He is so moved and troubled by the condition of his country that he can hardly talk about it.

The British Ambassador, Sir Cecil Spring Rice, gave Will the printed official correspondence that preceded the outbreak of war. I have been reading it. The so-called "Powers" all tried to bring about a conference which would settle the dispute between Austria and Servia, but Germany, while "approving the principle of mediation," would not join, nor would she indicate any line upon which she would be willing to aid in bringing peace. What a crime for which to answer! The criticism of the administration's peace policy has died away. I believe many are thankful that the peace-loving Mr. Bryan is at the helm.

The relief work is moving. The office force has been increased here and at our embassies abroad. More than 30,000 inquiries for friends have been received. Will is sleeping better this week.

December 30, 1914.

We had taken a house not far from Grove Park Inn, Asheville, N. C., for the summer, but were unable to occupy it. It seemed foolish to open the house for so brief a stay, so we were guests at the Inn. We settled down, after two or three days, to the following régime.

We had breakfast at 7.30 and left promptly on the dot of eight for the mountains by automobile. We took Will's axes and our book, some fruit, and heavy gloves, etc., and a pitcher of water and a kitchen chair from Mr. Seeley's house on Sunset Mountain. We left the car at an unfrequented spot where the view down the valley is particularly lovely. Mr. Bryan then laid "aside every weight" in the form of coat and vest and began to cut down a tree. I sat near and read aloud from Trevelyan's "Life of John Bright." When he stopped to rest, we discussed John Bright and the Corn Laws, the conditions of the working people at that time, etc. While Will was dragging away the brush which he threw into the ravine, I worked on my hemstitching, which I kept on my lap. At noon a lunch was brought up to us from the hotel; sometimes we ate it on Mr. Seeley's porch, sometimes in "Blue Briar," the house we had rented. In the afternoon we chopped and read, or else took a long walk, once or twice walking all the way back to the hotel. I remember we walked down the trail from the top of Sunset Mountain. The path is charming, the grade excellent, and the woods wonderful. The first frost had touched the foliage. The sour wood was a brilliant red; the red berries and bronze leaves of the dogwood; the strong green of the oak with its first tints of brown and crimson; the golden rod; the purple aster; the fine white flowers of which no one seemed to know the name; all lent their beauty to our path.

Another day we spent much time gathering chestnuts which were just beginning to drop. We laid in a store of them which gave us refreshment on our drives by car. We usually reached the hotel at dark, slipped quietly to our rooms, had a good dinner served there, sent telegrams, read the papers, and went to bed. In this way we had complete relaxation and rest. It did Mr. Bryan much good.

One incident may be worthy of record. It might have been a serious accident. Mr. Bryan one morning decided to improve the appearance of the high bank on the mountain side of our roadway. At this point the bank is about fifteen feet high and had on its edge three unsightly stumps. Will took ax and mattock and climbed to the top of the bank to loosen these stumps. I sat in the roadway below and read our book. Two of the stumps were safely dislodged and rolled down. The third was a very large one. When he had located the main root, which held it to the bank, Will proceeded to cut away the other roots. He was standing with one foot on the bank, the other foot on the stump, chopping vigorously between his feet. At a particularly strong stroke the root parted, the stump broke loose, and came rolling down the bank accompanied by a very astonished chopper with an ax in his hand. Pell mell they came! Showers of dust and dirt enveloped them. I screamed, as any normal woman should, grabbed my chair and ran. A very dirty but smiling gentleman came forth from the débris, absolutely unharmed. The stump had not rolled upon him nor the ax cut him. The weight of the stump may be estimated by the fact that it took three men to carry it out of the road and drop it into the ravine.

That was the last day of our vacation. We returned to Washington with rested bodies and minds.

In October I went for a few days' campaigning with Mr. Bryan. We spent two days in Ohio and one in Indiana before returning to Washington. Then Will started for a three weeks' tour of the west. All the Cabinet members went to different parts of the country to speak for the administration. I joined Mr. Bryan at Kansas City and went through Kansas and Colorado with him. It warmed our hearts to see the loving good will extended to us in these states. The people certainly love him. He had a wonderful meeting in Denver. Our son William came from Arizona and joined us at La Junta. We went with Mr. Bryan as far as Cheyenne, Wyoming, but when he left to go into the Dakotas, William and I returned to Denver. William went South and I east as far as Lincoln.

In Denver we dined with the Shaffroths. In the afternoon we went to hear Harry Lauder. He was most entertaining. He was on his way home to Scotland from Australia. There was a terrific snowstorm in Denver, a genuine blizzard.

In Lincoln I spent two sad weeks dismantling poor Fairview. I packed everything in certain rooms. I hope we may be able to let it during the summer months. The trees are handsomer every year. I felt particularly sad at leaving the evergreen trees and my poor flower garden. I was too busy to go to many social affairs.

On Saturday night before the Congressional election Mr. Bryan spoke in Omaha. I made my first speech for suffrage in Lincoln when introducing Dr. Anna Shaw. The meeting was in the auditorium, which was filled. I did not feel embarrassed and everyone heard me. The same night William made his first political speech at Casa Granda, Arizona. At least three of the family were on the platform at one time! I have not heard whether or not Ruth was speaking in London that night.

The autumn in Washington has been pleasant; the weather clear most of the time. The war and Mrs. Wilson's death made social life much more quiet. We went to more plays and concerts than ever before. I have enjoyed them so much. The moving picture of Damon and Pythias is beautiful. There are tremendous possibilities for good in these "movies" if they are only properly used.

June 21, 1915.

Mr. Bryan resigned his office two weeks ago and I take this occasion to record the details while they are still fresh in my mind.

We have come here to Asheville, N. C., for two days of rest, being worn by the strain of the last four or five weeks. I have lost five pounds (it's an ill wind that blows nobody good) and Will has lost about four pounds. Let me say in the outset that Mr. Bryan has been absolutely loyal to his

WILLIAM JENNINGS BRYAN

chief and has never permitted a word of criticism. I know this so well because of the large mail which has come to me regarding post-office and appointments of various kinds. I have made it my work to bring these letters to Will's attention at spare moments (usually when he was shaving in the morning) and I have then called up the various departments and answered the inquiries. However great the President is, he does not understand the politics of the country and has appointed many reactionaries; this has caused fierce criticism in some of the letters above mentioned. In every instance Mr. Bryan has sharply rebuked the writer —even (as in more than one instance) when that writer has been a warm and personal friend. Will has been absolutely loyal—let that fact be firmly recorded.

The parting of the ways has come from a radical difference in foreign policy. In domestic policies the two have worked most harmoniously. Indeed, the tariff, and particularly the currency bill, have required the joint efforts of the two to secure their passage.

The first serious break was over the Fabula case, Mr. Bryan insisting that the American public should be warned off or out of the danger zone and that, while under international law they have a technical right to go where they please, there is a moral duty which they owe to their government to keep out of danger at such a critical time and thereby relieve their government from responsibility for their safety.

The President stood firmly on the ground of international law. Each instance widened the breach, Mr. Bryan standing for the principle of arbitration, the President regarding the time as inopportune.

Cabinet meeting day had become a hard day for Mr. Bryan. More than once he came home with bloodshot eyes and weary steps, and said words to this effect: "Mary, what does the President mean! *Why* can't he see that by keeping open the way for mediation and arbitration, he has

420

an opportunity to do the greatest work man can do! I cannot understand his attitude."

As the days wore on his sleep became broken. He would lie awake three and four hours at a time, tossing, jotting down memoranda for next day's work, etc. Upon such occasions I sometimes persuaded him to take a hot bath, to eat something light, to count monotonously—all the sleep-inducing remedies I knew, but without much result. He signed the first note to Germany, not because he fully agreed, but because it was the opening statement of our position and simply called for a similar statement on the part of Germany.

The evening we had word of the sinking of the *Lusitania* we were dining out. Coming home, Mr. Bryan said: "I wonder if that ship carried munitions of war? I will have Lansing investigate that! If she did carry them, it puts a different phase on the whole matter! England has been using our citizens to protect her ammunition!"

Lansing the next day had the clearance papers examined and reported ammunition on board. There is a ruling under international law, permitting ships to carry small ammunition, but, as Will said, cartridges, as well as bombs and shrapnel, were made to kill men. From that time Mr. Bryan took the position that, in order to maintain strict neutrality, we must send a note to England protesting against her interference with our shipping, as well as one to Germany for destroying the *Lusitania*.

One night he came home, his eyes shining and his face beaming. The President had consented to the principle of arbitration, or rather the principle of investigation by commission as provided in our thirty peace treaties. After the telegram had been drawn for communicating this statement to the German Government, the President directed that the telegram be not sent, because of information he had received, through a newspaper man, from the German Embassy. Another time a note was prepared for England reiterating our protest against interference with our trade with neutrals. The President ordered this stopped, because Mr. House, in London, thought it unwise.

So near did they come to an agreement!

When the second note was drawn the tension became more marked. Will said the note should be so modified as to give Germany a chance to express a willingness for mediation, or for investigation of facts, rather. That as phrased, and particularly with no protest sent to England, the note left Germany no chance to do anything but refuse to discontinue her submarine warfare. That could only be followed by a withdrawal of representatives, which was perilously near war. He said: "It will be Germany's turn to make the next move. If it were our turn, I could trust the President to find a way out. It is virtually placing the power to declare war in the hands of another nation."

The finished note was sent to the State Department Friday night and Will told me he could not sign it. He had told the President a few days before that he felt it would be unfair to all concerned for him to remain in the Cabinet. Mr. Bryan waited after the Cabinet meeting and called the President aside and told him his determination. The President was evidently surprised.

That Friday I went to luncheon with Mrs. Judge Howey. Mrs. Marye, the wife of the Ambassador to Russia, was guest of honor. Mrs. Marye had a great deal to say about war conditions—the ladies generally spoke very openly about many things pertaining to European affairs. Mrs. Daniels and I were the only officials (by marriage) there. We sat like statues, expressing no opinion upon anything excepting the weather. I had driven to the luncheon in my car, and as I was returning, while crossing Massachusetts Avenue I saw Will in the carriage on his way home. It was then about 3.30. I hailed him and he left the carriage and got in the car with me. He had just called on Secretary McAdoo to tell him he had decided to resign. Mr. Bryan had not consulted any of the Cabinet, as he did not wish to implicate anyone else. He told McAdoo because he was the son-in-law of the President.

On reaching the house, Mr. Bryan went to lie down and so remained during the afternoon. He passed an almost sleepless night. He told me what it would mean, how he would be abused, vilified, and misrepresented, but he said: "If I wait until this note goes and a curt rejoinder is returned, it will then be too late. The President evidently feels he is voicing the sentiment of the country. I feel sure there are comparatively few Americans who want our country to be involved in this cataclysm. If I resign now, I believe it will be possible to bring the real sentiments of the people to˜the surface. The President may then feel at liberty to take steps which he now feels are unwise to take."

Saturday morning Will went to his work as usual. I saw that something must be done. He must get out of town for Sunday. I decided to appeal to our old friend, Senator Blair Lee, whose beautiful old home, Silver Spring, was often our refuge from the frightful heat of last summer. (I shall never forget the great magnolia tree under which we spent several Sunday afternoons, eating a picnic supper, reading, and sleeping.)

I telephoned to Senator Lee, asking if we might go to Silver Spring Saturday night after dinner and stay until Sunday evening. His response was quick and cordial.

The following day Mr. Bryan came home from the Department rather early and when I told him my plan, he said he could not go, as the President might call for him and he would not be able to respond quickly if he were in the country. I felt very much discouraged, but fortunately Secretary McAdoo called up on the telephone. I happened to answer and consulted him. He assured me that the note would not be sent nor would the President call for Mr. Bryan. He strongly approved the plan of a rest in the country. Mr. Bryan then consented to go, and twilight found us listening to the good-night song of birds. We were beyond the reach of newspaper men.

We retired early—were in bed eleven hours, of which Mr. Bryan slept four. He was so restless I suggested that he read a little till he should become drowsy. He had in his handbag a copy of an old book printed in 1829 and called "A Wreath of Appreciation of Andrew Jackson." He found it very interesting and I was much impressed with his (Jackson's) early life. The experiences through which he passed tended to fit him for the work he had to do. Is not this a general truth—that our lives often bring with them certain experiences and opportunities which, if rightly improved, fit us for some definite and special work?

The next morning, Senator Lee took Mr. Bryan—more heavy-eyed than ever—out for a long walk. They were gone two and a half hours. I employed this time writing to the children. He then took a nap of about an hour, ate dinner, and took another long walk. We hoped by this exercise to get him so weary physically that he could sleep. He gave Senator Lee his view upon the note, but did not tell him he thought of resigning. As he went home, in desperation I went to Dr. Kelley, who gave me a harmless powder to induce sleep. This I gave Will and he slept at last.

Monday morning McAdoo came. He and Will discussed matters, without reaching any conclusion. Mr. Bryan then went to the White House. His interview with the President lasted about an hour and was conducted with calmness and earnestness. Mr. Wilson would not yield a point, nor would Mr. Bryan. That night the resignation was sent and accepted, but was not made public until the following evening.

We were dining that night with Mr. Roberts, the father of Mrs. Stotesbury of Philadelphia. This old gentleman is ninety years old and was a classmate of Mr. Bryan's father in college. We were just going in to dinner when an extra

424

was called by newsboys in the street. We sent out for papers and read "Bryan Resigned!" If all our friends receive the news in the same spirit as those about the table, it will not be a great trial.

June 30, 1915.

This date finds us near the end of a pleasant two days' visit in Lincoln. "Charlie," Mr. Bryan's brother, is now Mayor and "officially" received us. Will says he thinks it very fine of the Mayor to lay aside any partisan feelings he may have had and greet us so cordially. We were met at the station by a large committee of old friends, and conducted to "the home of the Mayor." We arrived at 10 A. M. and spent the day receiving callers. In the evening Mr. Bryan spoke from the south balcony of the Lindell Hotel. The street was full and also the grounds of the church opposite. Governor Morehead presided. The meeting was opened with prayer by Rev. Harmon of the Christian Church. Governor Morehead then introduced Mr. Bryan in a neat little speech. Mr. Bryan was greeted by prolonged applause. (Tom Allen, who is a conservative man, estimated the crowd at 6000.) Mr. Bryan first read the abstract which he had prepared for the press—a boring process for me. I *loathe* to have him read anything and I know the audiences are also relieved to have it over.

His subject was "The Farmer's Interest in Peace." He had some very appropriately applied statistics. He did not forget to pay his respects to the New York press. He congratulated the people upon living thirty-six hours from New York and said the Allegheny Mountains are the salvation of the rest of the country, as they serve as a dike to keep the prejudice, the venom, the insolence, and the ignorance of the New York press from inundating the Mississippi Valley. He spoke of the points of difference between the President and himself without any unfriendliness and explained his reasons for resigning.

The crowd cheered him lustily and were evidently in

hearty accord. After his speech a reception was organized and for more than an hour we shook hands. The Governor and his wife received with us. Then we went out to Fairview. It made me sick at heart. How soon a place shows it is without a tenant! My poor flower garden is pathetic; many things dead, others running riot. The trees have made remarkable growth and the view is as lovely as ever. But I must not dilate further upon Lincoln, as I have yet to speak of our last days in Washington.

As soon as the news became generally known, we were deluged with letters and telegrams. (We have with us a large valise filled with mail—letters, opened and tied in flat bundles which we have not yet read. I am spending my spare time sorting these.) I could not but feel sad and discouraged. There has come out of these days, however, one delightful fact. We were able to distinguish between our real friends and our official ones. The last social function for me was a luncheon given by Mrs. Cone Johnson, the invitations having been issued more than a week before the resignation.

I dreaded to go for fear it might be a sad occasion. The guests numbered fifty and were my nearest official and many of my personal friends. Our daughter Grace went with me. I wore my new white lace dress and white hat. Grace was also in white. We were a little late. Instead of being a gloomy affair, everyone took the position that we would soon meet again. I sat between Madame Riano, wife of the Spanish Ambassador, and Madame Cespedes, wife of the Minister from Cuba. I read in a Southern paper afterward that there had been much conjecture as to whether or not I would come, how I would look, what I would say, etc.

I was doubly glad that I was able to be perfectly calm.

In June, we attended a meeting in Carnegie Hall, New York. The meeting was given under the auspices of the something of Federated Labor. Mr. Bryan was urged to attend by Congressman Buchanan of Chicago, a labor member and a structural iron worker. Will has known him for a number of years. Most of the New York papers refused to mention the meeting—the Socialist paper being the only one that announced it—with the result that the audience was largely Socialistic. Carnegie Hall was full (and people standing on the first floor). I mention this because the New York papers said there were "1900 people." I sat on the stage by a minister—Episcopalian. He was, in some way, representing the labor unions "in the Bronx" (a mysterious region which I have never understood). His speech was short and clear and he himself was a gentle, sweet-natured, refined fellow. If more ministers were only willing to work among and with the common people! It seems to me the Church is making a grievous error in standing so aloof from the toiler. This was Will's first speech after his resignation. He wore his black alpaca coat and stepped out like a lion! How the people did cheer! It did my heart good to hear them! It was the genuine spontaneous applause —when the audience responds as one man—rather than the sort of applause which is artificially started and maintained by effort.

When Mr. Bryan explained his points of difference with the President which had preceded his resignation, the audience caught the point and gave assent. When he spoke of his wish to warn the people off the ships, the audience almost raised the roof. I met some prominent women suffragists on the platform and returned to the hotel with a feeling that in spite of the storm of criticism, there are still friendly people left.

Our visit to Asheville was shortened by the Peace meeting held in Madison Square Garden on June 19th. This was managed by the German-American societies with the *Staats Zeitung* in the lead. The Germans have been so bitter and vindictive toward Will, feeling that he was hostile toward Germany. Indeed, one editorial from a

427

German paper which came to our attention said that he could not be neutral; he could not help being pro-British, because he has a son-in-law in the British army. Will told me at the time that if he were only free to reply he would say: "Ties of relationship do not always bind. The Kaiser has a cousin on the throne of England and another on the throne of Russia, but it does not seem to bias him at all." Which I regarded as rather an able retort.

CHAPTER XVI

THE NEXT FIVE YEARS

From my Diary, July 15, 1915.

A GREAT event was the Independence Day celebration at the San Francisco Exposition on the morning of the 5th of July, 1915. A stand had been erected in a large space—I believe it was in front of the "Court of Honor." We arrived early, but even then many thousand people were already waiting. A guard told me many had been there two hours. A roadway was roped off for the passage of the parade. This consisted largely of troops and crews from two battleships. The parade was reviewed by Hon. C. M. Moore, the President of the Exposition, by Will and two or three other "distinguished visitors." There was a pause in the procession, the people broke through the ropes, and I understand a goodly part of the parade failed to arrive. They could not get through the crowd. Mrs. Moore (mother of the President of the Exposition) and I left the automobile and went to the platform, where we could both see and hear.

I never before saw such a throng and never expect to see such a one again. The gate boxes showed 120,000 people inside the grounds when Will began to speak, and it is estimated that 100,000 of them were gathered about the speaker's stand. On all sides they stood. It was one of those days which seem typical of San Francisco. The sun blazed out with great heat, as Will's poor head bore witness—his scalp was burned quite red—as he stood with bared head while he spoke. This bright sun gave place at frequent intervals to light showers, or as the San Franciscans call it, "a fog." They will not admit that it rains. I was reminded of the "Scotch mist" which makes one very wet and has clearly defined drops, but to a Scotchman is not a

429

rain. Occasionally an umbrella was raised, but most of the time people stood in the "fog" regardless of injury to their dresses and hats.

I was surprised to notice how far Mr. Bryan's voice carried. One can tell by the motion in the crowd just how far the voice is reaching. Many thousands heard, I am sure.

This gathering was unique in another respect, i. e., in the large number of women who fainted! Several succumbed quite near the platform. They were given water from the pitcher which supplied Mr. Bryan and once both glasses were gone giving "first aid" to the women and he had nothing out of which to drink himself. One young woman was dragged out of the throng and carried, very limp, to the platform. They laid her on the boards just behind our chairs. She was unconscious for several minutes and then lay with closed eyes till the speech was finished. The bunting hid her from the crowd and her husband sat on the floor beside her.

Will's speech was followed by two luncheons. The officers of the Exposition entertained Mr. Bryan, and the "Woman's Board" entertained for me. The gathering was a distinguished one. I sat on the right of the acting President of the Board and on my right was Madame Tingley, who is head of the theosophists and has a school at San Diego; Ida Husted Harper (author) was there; Mrs. May Wright Sewell, of suffragist fame; Miss Adelaide Johnston, sculptress from Rome; Mrs. Phoebe Hearst; several delegates from abroad to the convention of the Woman's Peace Party; a Miss Watson, suffragist, whom I liked very much, gentle and old, and an excellent speaker. There were over thirty women in attendance. We were officially dined, too. We had a ball in our honor, marched in at the head of the procession, preceded by soldiers in blue and white uniforms. Mr. Bryan spoke before the Convention of the International Press Association; quite an opportunity to reach the foreign press; also, before the

THE NEXT FIVE YEARS

Woman's Peace Congress; before the Spanish War Veterans; before the Woman's Democratic Club, and made after-luncheon and dinner speeches on several occasions; all of which interfered sadly with our seeing the fair.

We made a round of official visits to all the foreign buildings; heard some remarkable music at the Guatemala building—strange instruments resembling the xylophone.

We made our way north through Oregon and Washington. One of the pleasant experiences in Oregon was our trip to Crater Lake. The committee met us at the train with two automobiles and we drove one hundred and twenty miles to the Lake. It is more difficult of access and more rugged in surroundings than Lake Tahoe, but with the same wonderfully clear water, with its varied colors.

We found the people of Oregon and Washington fully as cordial as those of California. Tacoma and Spokane are particularly well provided with fine places for large meetings. I shall always remember the stadium at Tacoma. It is built in what was once a ravine running down to the Sound, a natural amphitheatre. It is said to seat 30,000. Our meeting there was held on Sunday at 6.30 P. M., just as twilight began to fall. We had come by motor from Seattle and were a little late; the audience was waiting. Tiers of seats rise sharply and every one of the audience can see the speaker's stand. The seats are concrete and the top rows lead out upon steep banks of grass and beds of flowers. Above all is the balustrade and electric light posts guarding the sidewalk of the street above. On the upper tier is a tall flagpole from which a large flag floated.

There were fully 15,000 people there. Our car was stopped at the speakers' stand so that we faced the audience. Some one had started "My Country, 'tis of Thee," and all sang. It was beautiful, the soft light, the clear sky, the great crowd so quiet and orderly, the flag, the flowers. Then, as darkness came, the lights were turned on, and Mr. Bryan began his speech.

WILLIAM JENNINGS BRYAN

At Spokane the meeting was in a park with a natural slope. This place had the best sounding board we have found anywhere—shell-shaped and a huge canvas projecting from above, which keeps the voice from going up too much and being lost in the trees. There were from 15,000 to 20,000 here according to different estimates. Everything was excellently managed. We got away without being caught in the crowd.

Mr. Bryan made several short speeches from the rear end of the train as people gathered at the stations through which we passed.

When we reached Nebraska about August 3, he began his lecture dates. I traveled with him for two very busy weeks. These days are full of trains and changing cars and small hotels and crowds and shouts and rain and wind and auto rides across country. He has been making two speeches daily. It is hard work. One night when he was very tired, he said: "Mama, maybe it is a good thing I make my living this way. I believe I do good and it needs the spur of necessity to keep me at it. I would not work like this if we had plenty without it."

I came home with regret, as I dreaded to leave him alone, but find plenty here to occupy me; I am reading at night; am almost through the second volume of Lamartine's "The Girondists." Have been tremendously interested, even if it does take me a year to read it, catching a moment now and then.

October 2.

Since my last entry, the time has been filled to overflowing, chiefly with herculean efforts to get our belongings packed and out of our Washington home. It is astounding how things accumulate!

I made an interesting trip with Will to Newark and Paterson, New Jersey, where he addressed large meetings on woman's suffrage. The people, however, voted down

432

the proposition. We were one day in New York and had rather an interesting luncheon with the Japanese Consul-General and wife as hosts. The Japanese Ambassador and Countess Chinda were there, the President of the Japanese Bank in New York, Marquis (somebody), who had recently arrived from London, where he had been attending Cambridge. I was interested to hear him speak with a strong English accent. The leading Japanese merchants were present, a company of twenty or twenty-five. We appreciated this courtesy very much, especially now that Will is no longer an official. The lunch was given at the Nippon Club and while we sat on chairs and ate at a long table, the food was Japanese and served in Japanese style. Everyone had chopsticks, excepting Will and myself. I must say I do not relish Japanese food, but, of course, ate, "asking no questions for conscience' sake."

At night we went to a suffrage meeting under German-American auspices. They made the mistake of playing "Wacht am Rhein" when Will got up to speak. The orchestra had no orders to play it, but did so of their own accord.

This last week has been an interesting one. Will has done his first real campaigning for prohibition. We entered Ohio at Steubenville and with a special train, upon which we lived, toured the state for a week. He made sixty speeches in forty counties to (it was estimated) between 200,000 and 250,000 people. It was in a sense a triumph for him. It demonstrated one thing clearly, i.e., that in spite of all the abuse from the press, he has lost none of his popularity. The audiences were so attentive and responsive, I do not see how he could have failed to convince many. I had some glimpses of what a national campaign on this subject would be—a veritable religious crusade.

I did not attend all the meetings; the most impressive one was that at Cincinnati. Their largest auditorium was packed, people standing all along the walls and the platform thronged. Mr. Bryan made a powerful appeal. He spoke

28

to the German-Americans, showing them that the brewers and distillers were connecting them with the liquor traffic to their detriment; that they gave millions to corrupt legislatures, but not one cent for the public good, etc. He was late about beginning his speech and when he closed it was nearly 11.00 P. M. We went out by the back way and around to the front of the auditorium, where a street full of people had been standing since eight o'clock, waiting for Will to come. Ex-Congressman John Lentz had been speaking to them. Will stood in the automobile and made them a good speech. They were mostly workingmen and seemed impressed by his arguments.

His prohibition speeches are full of wit and brightness, replete with stories and very apt illustrations. In all these meetings and among these thousands of people, there have been only two who mentioned the resignation. The effort of the press to brand him as a traitor has evidently failed. He seems not only to have kept his old friends, but to have added new ones.

Villa Serena, Jan. 6, 1916.

We have finally left Washington! Our Florida home is certainly a sweet little place. The bougainvillea vines now meet on the arch over the entrance and are blooming. I have never seen a prettier entrance anywhere! The little drive through the woods is perfect. The curves are graceful and the trees on either side par excellence! In the oval before the patio gates the palms have grown wonderfully. Our royal palm in the center is towering in a surprising way. The travelers' palm, date palm, screw palm, fish tail palm, etc., are all thriving. But the crowning glory is the poinsettias—a little over two years old and above the window sills of the second story! A wealth of bloom, we are so proud of them. Our scarlet bougainvillea is creeping along and will soon meet over the patio gates. This will also be wonderful. The blossoms are a lovely color. Our large tubs in the edge of the wood, filled with colia, are most effective. The nasturtiums, roses, sweet alyssum, geraniums, foxgloves, petunias, are growing well.

We lead a simple life. Will works three or three and a half hours each morning, felling trees (his greatest enjoyment), cutting off dead limbs, pruning, splitting wood, etc.

I have been reading to him as he works. We are going on with "The Life of John Bright," which we began at Asheville more than a year ago. In the morning, too, we have a little reading. Will can dress more quickly than I and so reads while I comb my hair. We are reading Ruskin's "Ethics of the Dust." After a few pages of that we read our Bible verses and say our prayers, little John joining. It is so sweet to be able to begin the day in this quiet way without any hurry. If it were not for the mail! This is the fly in the ointment! It takes a tremendous amount of patience to answer every sort of question. We have found quite an efficient young man who takes dictation. I open all the mail and sort it, answering some, entering requests for lectures in our book, etc. We have many telegrams too. This last month (December) was particularly bad on account of the effort to get Will to join the Ford Peace Party at The Hague. I paid the bill for telegrams, for the month, this week. It was $103.97. I regarded that a little excessive for people of moderate income.

July 16, 1916.

A recital of the winter would not be complete without a word about our days "at home." The public were like the poor—we always had them with us—and it did not take long to show us that we must have regulations or else have no time for ourselves. We decided to open the house formally on Fridays. We always had as many flowers as possible. Mrs. Brickell was very kind about giving me flowers from her garden and the house was really lovely. We always served tea and sandwiches with small cakes, or else had fruit punch in our big bowl that belonged to Thomas Jefferson. Our butler, Jefferson, who came with us from Washington, was very efficient. Four or five ladies assisted me, and the people came, numbering anywhere between two and five hundred, each Friday afternoon. They were from all parts of the United States. Will, in his famous alpaca coat, was usually on the front lawn. We were dead tired by night, but had time to ourselves on other days.

In Chicago Will spoke at a Peace Meeting under auspices of Woman's Peace Party, of which Jane Addams is the head. This meeting was held in the auditorium and it was packed, even to the top gallery and the stage. I wish to add that this is rather remarkable, as the newspapers refused to give any notice of the meeting and the paid advertisements were printed in out-of-the-way corners. The committee sent notices to the ministers of the city with request that they be read from the pulpits. But, in spite of opposition, it was a wonderful meeting. I was pleased with Judge Prentiss, an old friend, who was against Mr. Bryan in the last campaign. He came up after the meeting, his face aglow with enthusiasm, and said, "I am just as happy as can be. I am so glad to be with Mr. Bryan again! I am with him on peace so heartily. I came a hundred and thirty miles to attend this meeting."

August 20, 1917.

To resume after a long interruption. Will spoke in Brooklyn at a large gathering of Norwegians (their national holiday) and we also looked up some artists, with a view to having Will's portrait painted for the State Department.

We next visited Mohawk Lake, to attend the Peace Conference. Ex-President Taft was presiding. When we arrived, the Peace people were feeling a little blue. The people who propose to keep peace by preparing for war seemed to be in the ascendency. In the afternoon an Interstate Collegiate Oratorical Contest was held—orations on

30 November, 1916

THE WHITE HOUSE..
WASHINGTON.

My dear Mr. Bryan,

Now that the result of the election is nowhere questioned I want to express to you the feeling, not of triumph, but of profound encouragement and real elation that the Cause which we believe to have been the Cause of the people should have been so emphatically and unmistakably sustained and my gratitude to all who, like yourself, have assisted to make the verdict clear. I am sure that all Democrats admired your Course during the Campaign as I did

Cordially and Sincerely Yours,

Woodrow Wilson

Hon. William J. Bryan

Letter from Woodrow Wilson to Mr. Bryan expressing his indebtedness to him for his support during his second Presidential campaign.

peace—five young men representing different groups of states. The first prize was won by a fair-haired youth from the Black Hills; the second, by a young man from Cornell. Of course, I was delighted to see the West more than hold her own against the East and said so, which perhaps was not wise. Will spoke that night. He took up the League to Enforce Peace and discussed it point by point. He was clear, logical, and convincing. He spoke beyond his time and at last turned to Ex-President Taft (who was presiding and should have rung the bell) and said, "Isn't my time up?"

Mr. Taft started and said, "Yes, Mr. Bryan, but I have been following you and not the clock." Every one paid rapt attention and some who came to scoff remained to pray.

Returning to New York, we took a train for Atlantic City, where Mr. Bryan addressed the Presbyterian General Assembly. It is always interesting to see great masses of people animated by a common purpose and I thought the delegates most interesting. We found the newly elected Moderator, Rev. Marquis, of Des Moines, a strong Bryan man, had read the *Commoner* from its first issue and always voted for him. We went to hear the Moderator's sermon. All the high church officials were seated on the pulpit platform. The church was filled to overflowing. We were taken in through the pastor's study and I was very proud to have Will taken up to the platform and given place next the Moderator.

In the afternoon he spoke on prohibition in the large auditorium on the Steel Pier. All the Presbyterian preachers from Nebraska (about forty) came to the hotel in a body and acted as our escort. They marched two by two in front of us and made quite a procession going down the boardwalk. People in the crowd recognized Mr. Bryan and greeted him. The auditorium was packed. People had pulled the upper sashes of the window down and were standing on the window sills outside. There were throngs at the doors who could not get in.

June 28, 1916.

Dear Bro. Bryan:

Will you just let me take a second of
your time, just long enough to grasp your
hand and shake it. You don't know how much
good it does me to hear the enthusiastic
things that are said about you by those who
have returned from St. Louis.

Cordially yours,

Hon. William Jennings Bryan,
Lincoln, Nebraska.

Letter from Franklin K. Lane, Secretary of the Interior, after the St. Louis
Convention of 1916.

In Chicago, Mr. Bryan and I attended the Republican and the Progressive conventions. He was reporting them for a syndicate of newspapers. It was most interesting to attend them in alternation and note the difference in the two bodies. The Republican, cut and dried; no spontaneity; all stiffness and dignity. The Progressives, full of enthusiasm and affection for their leader.

The weather in Chicago was dreadful; rain, almost continuous. I sat in my window at the hotel and watched the women parading for suffrage. The wind blew so they could not hold their banners; it took three or four to control one. The rain came in gusty torrents, but still the women marched! It was much more impressive than if the day had been fine, though, of course, the numbers were greatly reduced. I felt mean, sitting up, literally "high and dry," while they were sacrificing for me as well as for themselves. I am going to make some real suffrage speeches this fall.

Sunday night we went to St. Louis to attend the Democratic Convention. The situation was a little trying. Will, having been defeated by the "wets," was not even a delegate. I had dreaded these days for him and am glad to record that they were easier than I had supposed possible.

In the first place, there was a very marked tendency among the delegates to approve the things for which he has stood. It was not my imagination, but was remarked upon by others. In our rooms he was busy all the time receiving callers; his brother Charlie and I assisting. The temporary chairman, Governor Martin Glynn, talked over his speech with Will, and a most satisfactory speech it was from our point of view; the permanent chairman, Hon. Ollie James, came to discuss matters; delegates to give assurances of loyalty, etc. It became apparent that while the delegates and galleries had made up their mind that Will should speak, those in control were not inclined to permit it. After the permanent organization had been effected, cries of "Bryan! Bryan!" rose from all parts of the hall (excepting here and there where there were groups of hostile people, such as the New York delegation). The chairman was not able to restore order, though he pounded vigorously. The band was then signaled to play, which it did. Order was restored, but the moment the band finished the cries began again. Mr. Bryan was in the press gallery when the commotion began, but went out to speak at a business men's luncheon. The chairman discovered he had gone, but could not get the crowd quiet enough to be able to tell them so. They called for fifteen minutes after Mr. Bryan had gone and then Chairman James by much shouting got them still and told them he was not there.

At the next session they began at once, "Bryan, Bryan!" It was music to my ears to hear them. The rules were suspended; a committee went into the press gallery and conducted Will to the platform. He made a fine speech, entirely loyal to the party and saying that he expected to support the candidate. The real enthusiasm of the convention was shown during this speech. Applause rang out in a way I know so well. It was not necessary to support it by signals from the platform, by the bass drum and by other artificial means, as I saw at some other stages of the proceedings.

The papers were more respectful the next day than they had been at any time since he resigned. Some of the reporters really admitted that it was a Bryan convention at heart. It was a convention which had met to re-nominate President Wilson, and yet a convention which refused to permit the adoption of a platform or the nomination of a candidate until their uncrowned leader had spoken to them.

For two and a half days the clamor continued.

I forgot to report one incident of the convention which is worthy of record. When the platform was up for adoption, the convention began to call again for Will. He saw he was about to become an obstruction to business, and still it was necessary for him to hear the proceedings. He slipped out and put a chair under the speakers' platform, from which point he could hear everything and still not be seen. He stayed under there the remainder of the session. Many men would have kept in view and received the tribute the people evidently wished to pay! Here is an illustration of his modesty and self-effacement. It was a tremendous relief to me to have the convention over without any humiliations to Will. Bless his poor heart. How much abuse he has had to bear.

After the convention we went to Salem, Illinois, Will's old home, for Sunday. They had expected us in the early evening and had almost the entire population and the band out to welcome us. We, however, did not arrive until 11.00 P. M., but even then the band and several hundred people were at the station. I thought it rather sweet of the band, as it was entirely a voluntary tribute. They played without pay and marched ahead of us through the sleeping little town, tooting lustily.

Next day we went to the church Will joined at the age of fourteen; went to the cemetery and scattered flowers over the graves of Will's father and mother, brothers and sisters. The cemetery is much prettier, the trees have grown so much. The rest of the day was spent in greeting friends.

Monday morning we visited the little library which Mr. Bennett and Mr. Bryan presented to the town. It is a neat little place and built on the site of the house in which Mr. Bryan was born. The house itself now stands on an adjoining lot. We spent the night there with Will's aunt. I tried to imagine that his first little baby wails had sounded through those rooms, but did not succeed.

The remainder of the summer has passed swiftly and pleasantly. I have been at Fairview, our Nebraska home, quite alone with faithful Martha. On the 25th of June I began my music lessons. I have always wanted to play the pipe organ, and this seemed an opportunity to begin.

THE NEXT FIVE YEARS

I drive five miles across country in my little car to University Place and practice in the Methodist Episcopal church. The mornings are so lovely. I rise at 6.00 A. M. and am on the way at 7.30.

I shall always remember the lovely drives I have had; the country so peaceful, the wide fields, the wider skies, the little birds at breakfast, the timid cotton-tails occasionally crossing the road, the growing corn, the yellow grain, the low hills, so covered with fertility and thrift. There is no finer land in the whole world than this same Nebraska! My teacher is excellent and she is teaching me exactly the things I need so much to know, and oh! the pleasure of it all! When I make even the briefest pipe organ melody, I am so delighted. I know I am learning rapidly in spite of my fifty-five years. But people can always learn the things they really wish to know. If we would only keep alive the ambitions of youth until the opportunity comes!

November 27, 1917.

I have been and am sick at heart during these months when our country has been on the verge of war and when she has finally gone into it.

We have had periods of great anxiety and great depression, but there is nothing now but to accept the inevitable. I have kept notes of events, so am able to fill in these months with tolerable accuracy. The autumn of 1916 was spent at Fairview. The morning rides to University Place were continued until the weather and packing household effects made them impossible. I shall never forget those days, quite as beautiful as the summer. The "fodder in the shock"; blue mist on the horizon; a reddish-gold globe of a sun pushing through the mist; frost on freshly ploughed fields; shivering weeds by the roadside; rabbits running to cover. I saw and loved them all.

Mr. Bryan had an exceedingly busy autumn. His regular Chautauqua dates closed September 1. He then

443

rested (?) three days in Lincoln, looking after his heavy mail and then went with his brother on a hunt near Alliance. I heard that this hunt was very successful—prairie chickens. He then went South to Prescott, Arizona, where our son was attending court; then on to Tucson, resting and visiting William. Mr. Bryan spoke to large audiences at Phœnix, Tucson, and Prescott. His work in the National Campaign began September 17 at Reno, Nevada, and from then until the night before election, he averaged four or five speeches daily, speaking in nineteen different states. While he spoke under the auspices of the National Committee, the states in which he spoke were largely his own selection.

He suggested to the committee that as he favored prohibition, he could help most in the states where prohibition has been adopted or where prohibition campaigns were on, and as he favors Woman's Suffrage, he could help counteract the work of the Woman's Congressional Union which had endorsed Hughes. He was anxious also to assist in the reëlection of Senators Myers of Montana, Pittman of Nevada, Ashurst of Arizona, Burke of North Dakota, Kendrick of Wyoming, King of Utah, and Jones of New Mexico. By speaking in these states, he could make the Presidential campaign aid in the senatorial election. He had record-breaking meetings in all these states. Salt Lake City was probably the most enthusiastic, though all were so large it would be difficult to select any as unusually good.

Mr. Bryan came through the campaign in good voice, though considerably worn. As usual, the last night was given to his Lincoln speech. There was a great crowd and much enthusiasm. Election day he voted at the schoolhouse in Normal, visited with his country neighbors and at night we had our last family dinner at Fairview. We were fourteen at table and had an excellent turkey dinner and a fruit cake sent for our wedding anniversary by Mr. Titus, the head of a Dining Car Service. While a trifling thing, it was so unique as to merit description. The cake was excel-

444

lent in quality, rich and toothsome. It was baked in the shape of a book, perhaps 14 inches long by 8 inches wide and 3 inches thick. The outside cover was made of glazed gingerbread, so skilfully done that it looked exactly like brown leather. The edges of the leaves were perfect in ivory colored frosting. On the back in beautiful white sugar letters were the words "Happy Days, Vol. 32." (we had been married thirty-two years) and on the front were the words (lettering everywhere was absolutely perfect):

"Presented to Hon. and Mrs. Wm. Jennings Bryan on their thirty-second wedding anniversary, with compliments and best wishes," etc., etc.

We have had many cakes sent us first and last, but this was the most perfect one.

After dinner we all awaited election returns in our sitting room, and by the time we disbanded at 10.30, everything pointed to the election of Hughes. Will, Tom, and Charlie were still trying to see hope in later returns, but every one was discouraged. The Republicans were confident. Then one after another the Western states swung into line. California turned the scales and Wilson was reëlected by the West, on the slogan, "He has kept us out of war." Naturally after such a campaign, the West was bitterly disappointed when war was so soon declared.

Our little Church at Normal gave us a farewell dinner. The farmers brought different (prescribed) food in their baskets and the result was a feast of well-prepared viands. Long tables were laid in the church basement. The women brought their prettiest dishes, their best linen, vases and table ornaments. The tables were very pretty. The young men and women of the Sunday school waited on the table. The food was hot and excellent. Dr. and Mrs. Bailey, our old friends, were invited over from the sanitarium. The tables were filled several times before all were fed, and then everyone gathered in the church proper. "America" was sung by all. The minister spoke of following Will twenty-five years in politics and of what our home at Fairview had meant to the neighborhood. Mr. Brown spoke in behalf of the Sunday school. Dr. Bailey spoke as one who had met us when we first came West, twenty-nine years before. He made a most beautiful speech. Then I was called upon and said a few words which seemed to please, though they amounted to little. Then Will spoke on Friendship and kindred themes. The meeting was a charming thing, beautiful in thought and in expression. They sang "Blest be the tie that binds" and "God be with you till we meet again." Mr. Bryan's brother-in-law, James W. Baird, led the singing. The whole gathering was so full of good will and friendliness it pleased us very much. We were touched by the evident affection of our country neighbors.

In the meantime it began to filter through the minds of men that Will had been a great factor in the election of Wilson. It was proposed to give him a banquet in Washington. Once started, the idea grew and by the appointed night every nook and corner of the La Fayette dining room was filled with tables and chairs (and people in the chairs, of course) and one hundred and fifty had asked for tickets who could not be supplied. It was a representative gathering. The Cabinet was represented by Secretaries of State and Navy, the Comptroller of the Currency, the Treasurer of the United States, many Senators and Members of Congress and Members of various Boards and Commissioners and personal friends. I went in to hear the speeches.

Will spoke last and at considerable length, outlining different policies he regarded as important and ripe for action. His portrait, painted for the State Department, had been sent down from New York and put at the end of the dining room and at the psychological moment was unveiled amidst great applause. A letter was read from the President. Tumulty was present. Altogether it was an enthusiastic tribute. We dined at the White House next day. Everyone was most cordial.

The winter in Miami was very broken. Appeals came from many quarters for Will to come North for this meeting and that, mostly peace and prohibition meetings. He made three trips during the brief winter in Florida. The first was made in order to attend the meeting of the National Intercollegiate Prohibition Association which met in Louisville, Ky., on December 28. He also met with the "dry" Democrats of Kentucky to start the state fight for the submission of a constitutional amendment for prohibition. This was the beginning of what promises to be a successful fight.

On the second trip he went to Columbus, Ohio, and spoke in favor of prohibition and woman suffrage. A federation of "dry" Democrats was organized and the fight for a state prohibition amendment was begun. He addressed the Legislature which afterward granted presidential suffrage to the women of Ohio. He spoke to the Legislature of Indiana and helped organize the "dry" Democrats. In this state statutory prohibition was adopted and presidential suffrage was granted to women. This was later nullified by the Supreme Court. He spoke at Madison, Wisconsin, and Springfield, Illinois, and both these capitals voted "dry" soon after. He spoke to the Legislatures at Jefferson City, Missouri, Nashville, Tennessee, and New Orleans. All winter the war clouds were gathering and at times Will was greatly depressed. He would look haggard and worn and I feared for his health if America should enter the war.

We met some interesting people in Miami. John Wanamaker came to see us, very much troubled about the war situation. John Sargent, the great portrait painter, was doing some interiors in James Deering's home and we were invited to luncheon to meet him. From his appearance he is the last man I would have guessed to be an artist. Tall, heavy, florid, sandy-grey hair with bushy whiskers to match, blue eyes and rather a gruff manner. He and Will had a congenial time. Mr. Sargent and Mr. Charles Deering called later, but unfortunately I was out. I had a caladium leaf I wanted to show him—a most wonderful bit to color. I am sure he would have liked it. We very much enjoyed the annual visit of our good friends for many years, Mr. and Mrs. Samuel Untermeyer.

March 17, 1920.

I may say that the National Prohibition Amendment was ratified in January while we were in Baltimore. Will went over and was "in at the death," so to speak. After the signing of the amendment, leaders of the various temperance organizations had a luncheon and Will was presented with a large silver loving cup. He came back to Washington "bearing his blushing honors thick upon him" and full of cheer. The winter was not particularly busy. Will made a number of short trips for lectures, but was not gone long at any one time. He seemed to want to stay with me.

Will has had a comparatively restful winter. He was gone a month, leaving about the 8th of January. It was at this time that he "came back," as the newspapers say. Ever since he resigned as Secretary of State there has been an organized effort to ignore him. His work and speeches have been unnoticed by the eastern press. He went to Washington to attend the banquet given by the National Committee. The report was circulated that the gathering was being "packed" against him by Secretary Tumulty. Tumulty wrote Mr. Bryan and denied the rumor. But that was enough. Mr. Bryan's friends bought tickets in such numbers that it was necessary to have the banquet in two hotels, the speakers speaking in both places. Most of the speakers were presidential candidates. The President, not long before, had advocated making the ratification of the Versailles treaty an issue in the next campaign. When Mr. Bryan's turn came, he took the opposite side (reading

448

his speech at the first banquet, so that he could not be mis-quoted, and speaking extempore at the second). He argued that ratification now is necessary to quiet the business unrest in the country and to permit us to take our place in the League of Nations.

The newspapers suddenly awoke. "Bryan splits with the President" was the usual headline. The Republican papers praised him, being in favor of anything which would foment dissension in the Democratic ranks. The business interests of the country for once approved his course of action.

At this writing (March 25) Mr. Bryan is again in the North. He celebrated his sixtieth birthday in New York; 800 guests were at the tables; a cake 2 feet by 3 feet in size and sixty red, white, and blue candles.

CHAPTER XVII

RELIGIOUS WORK

LIKE other deep convictions, Mr. Bryan's religion was with him from the beginning. The description which he has given of his parents and home shows how completely he was hedged about by Christian precepts, and how smoothly his life ran on within the prescribed limits.

As I reread the letters of our rather lengthy courtship (four years) I find his diversions to have been Sunday school, church, prayer meeting, an occasional church social, and at long intervals, a circus or an evening at the theater. I select a letter written on his twenty-first birthday, beginning—

"Have just signed a fictitious name, '*Lazarus*,' to my essay *Pauperism* and learned my Sunday-school lesson for tomorrow, and now, though it is nearly eleven P. M., am going to write to you. . . .

"The day (my twenty-first birthday) has been spent very quietly; took a glance over my boyhood, at its pleasures gone beyond recall, at its few successes, its few sorrows. Then full of gratitude for the blessings of the past, I turned, with some trembling, to contemplate the unknown future, its responsibilities, its possible successes, and its probable misfortunes. I would dread to be compelled to set forth upon this sea with nothing but the light of my reason to aid me. What a blessing it is that we have that guide, the Bible. The future looks bright. I have almost graduated and will be prepared for work. I have good health, good friends, and best of all, a loving, faithful sweetheart."

My first impressions of Mr. Bryan were of a tall, slender youth, wearing a black frock coat and leading his class of

450

boys into the Sunday-school room. My classmates in boarding school sometimes warned me that he was too good, but after considering the matter, I decided that I preferred marrying a man who was too good rather than one who was not quite good enough.

During his earlier years he took no conspicuous part in church work for reasons which he set forth in a statement which I quote below.

"After the election in 1900 there was no certainty of my being a candidate again and I felt that I was no longer justified in avoiding religious activity. I felt free to devote more time to religious addresses, and possibly, with advancing age, I felt an increasing desire to render such service as I could. I therefore began to accept the invitations as they came in to speak at Y. M. C. A. meetings and church gatherings. One of the reasons which led me to do so was that some young men seem to think it smart to be skeptical. They regard it as larger intelligence to scoff at creeds and to refuse to connect themselves with churches. I thought that possibly I might reach and influence some young men who avoided the churches. I had made a sufficient success in life to answer any objection that might be made to my mental ability and I felt that I might make a defense of the Christian religion and reach some who might not be so easily reached from the pulpit. It was with this object in view that I prepared my lecture known as 'The Prince of Peace,' (See page 509) which has been more widely published than any other of my lectures and which has, I am convinced, been of service to some young men. It was with this idea also that I inserted in my lecture on 'The Value of an Ideal,' a brief defense of Christianity. While the discussion of religious themes has brought down upon me the criticism of some agnostics and infidels, it has brought me into closer

451

contact with the churchgoing element, and I have been amply rewarded for the use of my Sundays by the consciousness of having been instrumental in clearing away the doubts in the minds of many. The speeches which are delivered on Sunday at the Y. M. C. A. and at churches are religious in their character—I have never discussed political questions on Sunday—and are made without a compensation; not even traveling expenses are accepted. When I have spoken on Sunday at Chautauquas, I have permitted admission to be charged, because admission could not be made free on Sunday without greatly interfering with the Chautauqua's work, and when I have lectured at Chautauquas I have received compensation as on other days, but otherwise my Sunday speeches are without compensation, and in almost every case they have been public meetings where no admission was charged. In very rare exceptions admission has been charged, but I have not shared in the proceeds on such occasions."

A pleasant development of his religious work was Mr. Bryan's great Bible class in Miami. Beginning in the First Presbyterian Church, his class crowded out the Sunday school and then moved to the park, where, from the bandstand, he has taught the Sunday-school lessons to thousands. There was a distinct charm about these meetings, beneath the open sky, under the shade of graceful palms, and on the shore of our beautiful Biscayne Bay. Mr. Bryan's assistant in this work, and his loving friend as well, Mr. W. S. Witham, of Atlanta and Miami, always took charge of the opening exercises of the Sunday-school class. His little grandson, aged four, seemed to me to voice the feeling of many people. One day he was attending Mr. Bryan's class with his grandmother, and said, "I am not going back to my own Sunday school any more; I am coming to Mr. Bryan's class." His grandmother said, "Why

452

EXPOUNDER OF THE WORD OF LIFE

Mr. Bryan and his Bible Class at Miami, Florida.

should you want to leave your own Sunday school?" The boy replied, "But, Grandma, God can see us here."

I recall an occasion when the throng had come to greet Mr. Bryan at the close of the meeting; and one man said to him:

"Mr. Bryan, this is a wonderful meeting."

Mr. Bryan told him he was hoping to reach people who never go to church. The man said: "I am sure you had some of them here this morning. I was standing in the aisle near the front and a man was interfering with my view. I asked him to stand over a little, and he rejoined, 'You go to hell. I will stand where I damn please.'" This man was evidently not a church member in good standing.

Upon another occasion two men were quarreling under their breath about standing room, and one was heard to say to the other: "I want to hear Bryan and won't stir from here while he is speaking. After he finishes, just come outside and I'll show you whether you can order me around."

I have seen shabby men standing behind bushes or trees, whose interest has grown under his words until they have boldly marched up the aisle and found seats. No one can estimate the good which was done by this class, numbering anywhere from two to five or six thousand each Sunday.

I recall last winter Mr. Bryan told me of four young men who had come to him and said the morning talk had so deeply impressed them that they wanted to begin a Christian life. Mr. Bryan took their addresses and offered to give one of his books to each. Two came for the books. He found the third man had left town. The fourth failed to appear. Mr. Bryan decided to carry the book to him. I went with him. When we reached the neighborhood we found the streets torn up by sewer trenches. It had rained and pools of water alternated with splashy mud. I said: "Don't try to go. Wait until the road is finished." He said, "It won't take long to walk over. The boy may need the book; we cannot tell." So he went, picking his way for between two and three blocks to give this book to an unknown boy. In his zeal for souls, he was like an evangelist. Because of his deep interest in young men, the Y. M. C. A. made a strong appeal to him. He had joined the organization in his youth and was always ready to aid wherever possible. His wife and children were not too enthusiastic about this branch of his work. The Y. M. C. A. men's meeting at four o'clock on Sunday afternoon was our deadly rival. Often Sunday was his only day at home. We wanted his company, but the men's meeting would break up the afternoon and take him from us. We laid this sacrifice on the altar, but with unwilling hands, and I doubt if the recording angel gave us any credit.

My wrath against this great organization was somewhat appeased when the International Y. M. C. A. asked Mr. Bryan to assist in establishing a line of Y. M. C. A.'s in Canada. The development of the wheat lands along the Western Canadian Pacific had caused a great influx of population. Many towns needed help in perfecting these organizations. We began at Victoria in British Columbia, thence to Vancouver, and on East. My memories of this journey are most pleasant. We traveled by day. Each night found us in a new town. The local people planned a meeting at which a new Y. M. C. A. was organized. A more delightful way of seeing the country could not be imagined —nor is there a more delightful country to be seen.

A little incident which amused us both may be worthy of record. Earl Grey was at that time Governor-General of Canada and had shortly before gone across the country on the Canadian Pacific Railway on a tour of inspection. We had been told much about "Sunny Alberta," but when we reached Alberta, we found cloudy weather. In his speech Mr. Bryan mentioned this fact and then rashly ventured upon a pun, saying, "The day is probably 'gray' out of compliment to the Governor-General." I thought this quite neat. Imagine our feelings when an English reporter quoted Mr. Bryan as saying, "The day was 'dull' out of compliment to the Governor-General."

In church government Mr. Bryan's work was recognized. He was long an elder and then a ruling elder in the Presbyterian Church. He was for several years a delegate to the General Assembly and the year before his death was Vice Moderator of that body.

At a public meeting, held in the Academy of Music, Philadelphia, in 1920, during a session of the Presbyterian General Assembly, Mr. Bryan was present on the platform but not scheduled to speak. At the close of the meeting calls came from the audience for "Bryan! Bryan! Bryan!" A spectator describes what followed.

"Stepping to the front of the platform Mr. Bryan began, 'Friends, you have heard tonight—' and then he took in turn each of the addresses of the evening, analyzing and summarizing each, so that one could carry home the addresses in concise and comprehensive form; and this with that eloquence for which he was so justly noted. It was an astonishing exhibition of memory and of the remarkable ability of Mr. Bryan to sum up in such a masterly manner the salient features of each address: an intellectual feat which few men would have attempted and none accomplished with the precision and effectiveness of William Jennings Bryan."

To the laying of corner stones, the dedication of churches, drives for raising funds, he gave his time and strength without regard for his own health. One can hardly feel surprised that he went when he did. The wonder is that he did not go sooner. Here is a report of one afternoon, taken from a letter Mr. Bryan wrote to me:

"Yesterday was the day I spoke at the Y. M. C. A. men's meeting at Indianapolis; 2801 present, all men, and I had to speak to 2000 more for a few minutes outside. They could not get in. It was as enthusiastic as any political meeting I ever had. I was afraid they would break the stage down when they came to congratulate me. Before the meeting I spoke for half an hour to the younger boys on 'My Yoke is Easy.' I learned later from the superintendent that seventeen boys came up after I left and announced their intention to begin a Christian life. I then went by automobile to Upland to speak at a Methodist college. When we arrived we found the crowd too large for the hall, so we first filled the hall with visitors and I spoke to them. When they went out, we filled the hall with students and I spoke to them. One of the teachers was a missionary in Tokio when we were there. She said she had had a class of thirteen Japanese boys; of them ten had been converted by my 'Prince of Peace.' "

Up and down the land he spoke for the Y. M. C. A., the Y. W. C. A., the Epworth League, the Christian Endeavor, to all Protestant denominations, to Catholics and to Jews. I once said to him, "It seems strange to me that all denominations seem so pleased to have you speak. I should think it would be easy to give offense." He replied, "The underlying truth of all religions is the same. One can discuss these great principles before any audience and in the presentation each one recognizes his own belief."

The only time I ever knew him defeated in religious work was one night when we went to a mission along the water front in New York City. Among the wretched group gathered in the hall, Mr. Bryan looked like a creature from another world—his skin so fair, his eyes so clear, his dress so tidy, and his speech so different. When asked to speak, he did not know what to say, and told me afterwards, "It takes a man who has been saved from the depths to reach men like these. I cannot do it. I lack the necessary past."

If anyone who reads these pages doubts the presence of God's power in the world, I commend him to investigate the city missions. There the power of God may be seen beyond a peradventure. Human help alone could not transform a hopeless drunkard, a gambler, a libertine, into a steady, clear-eyed, earnest man, free from bad habits. It is a fine thing to be perfectly sure that God's power is working even now in the world.

A source of tremendous strength to Mr. Bryan was his freedom from doubt. Others might waver, drift, and struggle—he went serenely on, undisturbed. This may be explained by his conviction that man was much too puny and finite to understand the ways of God. He said more than once: "What do these men know? Pitting their poor little knowledge against omniscience! The infinite power which rules and controls is far beyond our finite mind." He had a firm faith in the inspiration of the Bible in which he had been nurtured, a strong belief in a guiding and protecting power, and a comforting reliance on the efficacy of prayer.

Miracles, a troublesome question to many, did not perplex him. A brief summary of his views may be of interest:

"Miracles are performed today—miracles as marvelous as anything recorded in Holy Writ. There is such a thing as a new birth; the heart can be so transformed that it loves the things it formerly hated and hates the things it formerly loved. The feeding of five thousand with a few loaves and fishes is not nearly so great a mystery nor, measured by man's rules, so seemingly impossible as the cleansing of a heart and the changing of a life. The spiritual gravitation that draws a soul toward heaven is just as real as the physical gravitation that draws matter toward the earth's center. We judge the law of gravitation by the influence it exerts; the proof of the spiritual law is as abundant and as conclusive. If we imagine a line drawn from the lowest plane to which man can descend to the highest point that man can reach, we can assume that every human being is at some point on that line and going in one direction or the other. When we find some beginning under the most unfavorable circumstances and rising, we know that there is a power above that is drawing them: 'I, if I be lifted up from the earth, will draw all men unto me.' So when we see people beginning under the most favorable surroundings but falling lower and lower, we know that they have not taken advantage of that lifting power which is theirs for the asking.

"There are realities in the spiritual world which science cannot explain because spiritual things are spiritually discerned, but these things are no less demonstrable than the things with which science deals.

"We affirm, therefore: First, that God can perform any miracle He may see fit to perform, whether it be by laws unknown to man, or by the overcoming of natural forces by forces greater than nature; second, that it is not unreasonable to believe that an infinite God may have reasons for performing miracles that finite man does not now, and possibly never can, comprehend; third, that the evidence of the Bible, which is trustworthy, furnishes convincing proof that miracles have been performed by characters in the Old Testament and by Christ and His apostles, all drawing from the same source of infinite power. Belief in the power of God to perform miracles, in the willingness of God to perform miracles, and in the actual performance of miracles, is confirmed and corroborated by man's experience in his own heart and life, and by his observation of similar changes in the hearts and lives of others."

Mr. Bryan was a firm believer in the doctrine of complete separation of Church and State. He believed in absolute equality before the law of all religious denominations. He claimed nothing on the score of conscience that he was not willing to accord to others. He believed in his religion with all his might, and with all his soul, and with all his strength, but he thought that it was unworthy of the true religion to ask or accept any favors from the State. He believed that all sects should advance their religion by their own efforts and at their own expense, unaided by the State. But his soul arose in righteous indignation when he found from the many letters he received from parents all over the country that state schools were being used to undermine the religious faith of their children. He argued that if the power of the State could not be properly used to advance religion, it followed as a matter of course that the power of the State must not be used to attack religion. In his Preface to Volume VIII of "The Writings of Thomas Jefferson," Mr. Bryan said:

"He lacks reverence who believes that religion is unable to defend herself in contest with error. He places a low estimate upon the strength of religion, who thinks that the wisdom of God must be supplemented by the force of man's puny arm."

His position is also shown in the text of the resolution written by him and passed by the Legislature of Florida in 1924. One paragraph of the preamble of it reads as follows:

"Whereas, the public schools and colleges of this State, supported in whole or in part by public funds, should be kept free from any teachings designed to set up and promulgate sectarian views, and should also be equally free from teachings designed to attack the religious beliefs of the public. . . . Therefore, it is the sense of the Legislature of the State of Florida that it is improper and subversive to the best interest of the people of this State for any professor, teacher or instructor in the public schools and colleges of this State, supported in whole or in part by public taxation, to teach or permit to be taught atheism or agnosticism or to teach *as true* Darwinism or any other hypothesis that links man in blood relationship to any other form of life."

Why restrain the public-school teacher from teaching as true any hypothesis which links man in blood relationship to any other form of life? Because such teaching is an attack on the religious beliefs of millions of our citizens whose money supports the public schools.

To illustrate. The American doctrine of the separation of Church and State would prohibit a Catholic teacher from teaching Catholicism in the public schools. But who would argue that this is an interference with freedom of conscience or freedom of speech, or even with "academic" freedom? Suppose the Protestant public-school teacher should attack Catholicism in the public schools and the law should restrain him, who but a bigot would charge that we were interfering with that teacher's freedom of conscience or of speech? And yet this was the charge hurled at Mr. Bryan when he said that the government schools which cannot teach religion must not attack religion.

The following letter from the great Russian, Tolstoy, pleased Mr. Bryan and shows the religious grounds for the congeniality between the two men:

DEAR MR. BRYAN:

The receipt of your letter gave me great pleasure as well as reminiscence of your visit. If you wish to have Bandareff's book and my letter to politicians, please write to my friend Vladimir Thertkoff, Herts Christ Church, England. He will forward to you all that you wish to have.

RELIGIOUS WORK

I had, in the Russian papers, news about you. I wish with all my heart success in your endeavor to destroy the trusts and to help the working people to enjoy the whole fruits of their toil, but I think this is not the most important thing of your life. The most important thing is to know the will of God concerning one's life, i.e., to know what he wishes us to do and fulfill it. I think that you are doing it and that is the thing in which I wish you the greatest success.

Yours truly,

LEO TOLSTOY.

2 February, 1907.

CHAPTER XVIII

The Vindication of Mr. Bryan's Policies

HENRY WATTERSON once said that Mr. Bryan was a moral philosopher—not a statesman. "He is no statesman," said Mr. Watterson, "who has not learned to detach his policies from his visions. He is no statesman who has not emancipated himself from that which for the want of a better name dreamers call the ideal. He is no statesman who does not apply his means to his ends, going fast or slow, as occasion requires, but making no mistakes in reading the riddle of the time, in deciphering the mathematics of the moment, in translating the spirit of the people."

Mr. Bryan certainly refused to detach his policies from his ideals. In advocating a measure, he never asked, "Is it popular?" He spent his life advocating unpopular causes which he felt to be right. Phillips Brooks characterizes such a man when he says, "Great is the condition of a man who lets rewards come, if they will or fail to come, but goes on his way true to the truth simply because it is true, strongly loyal to the right, for its pure righteousness."

If a successful political career can be gauged by the public offices held, Mr. Bryan was only moderately successful, but Wayne C. Williams in his book "Bryan—A Study in Political Vindication," gives another standard of success. "No other man in American public life has ever lived to see so many of his ideas and reforms accepted by his political opponents and the people at large and established in the fundamental law and the institutions of the land."

As all of Mr. Bryan's life was so closely interwoven with constructive policies, it will be necessary to set down a

462

partial list of these measures in order to prove the justice of the claim.

Mr. Bryan advocated a federal income tax. It has been adopted.

Mr. Bryan advocated popular election of U. S. Senators. The people now choose their senators.

Mr. Bryan advocated publicity in campaign contributions. It has come.

Mr. Bryan advocated a declaration that the United States would not permanently hold the Philippines. The declaration has been made.

Mr. Bryan advocated Prohibition. It is now a part of the fundamental law of the land.

Mr. Bryan advocated Woman Suffrage. The women now vote.

Mr. Bryan advocated the impartial investigation of all international disputes before any hostilities could be begun. It is now embodied in treaties with thirty nations of the world.

Mr. Bryan advocated a representation of labor in the Cabinet. A man with a "Union card" now sits as an adviser to the President.

Mr. Bryan opposed government by injunction. It was abolished.

Mr. Bryan advocated rail-rate regulation. The rates are regulated.

Mr. Bryan advocated initiative and referendum. It now prevails in twenty states.

Mr. Bryan advocated currency reform. It has been reformed.

FEDERAL INCOME TAX

When Mr. Bryan was in Congress (1891–95) he served on the sub-committee which prepared the income-tax clause of the revenue bill. President Cleveland and Secretary Carlisle opposed the clause. Mr. Bryan circulated a petition calling for a Democratic caucus and secured the passage of a resolution making the income tax a part of the revenue bill and thus insured its passage. The President allowed the measure to become a law without his signature.

The law was declared unconstitutional by the Supreme Court of the United States by a vote of five to four, one justice having changed his mind between the two arguments of the case.

But Mr. Bryan did not give up the fight. The platforms of 1896, 1900, and 1908 on which he ran for the Presidency all contained an income-tax plank. In 1904 he tried to have the plank inserted in the Democratic platform but failed. President Taft, who had defeated Mr. Bryan in 1908, recommended an income-tax amendment to the Constitution, after having contended that Mr. Bryan's plan of amending the Constitution was unnecessary.

The amendment was submitted to the states and was ratified just before Mr. Bryan became Secretary of State, and the law in pursuance of the amendment was passed during a Democratic administration. Thus Mr. Bryan, after nearly twenty years, at first almost alone among the leaders of his own party—and often in direct conflict with them—and after having created a strong public sentiment in its favor, by his numerous speeches and writings, saw one of his cherished reforms accomplished, having in the meanwhile had the pleasure of seeing two Republican Presidents, Roosevelt and Taft, espouse the measure.

When Mr. Bryan first advocated the income tax thirty years ago, he was called "anarchist," "nihilist," "socialist," "enemy of wealth."

And yet the federal income tax is now an accomplished fact. No political party, no public man, would dare advocate its repeal. It is generally accepted throughout the world as an instrument through which the tax burden is more fairly distributed.

THE VINDICATION OF HIS POLICIES

POPULAR ELECTION OF SENATORS

When Mr. Bryan ran for Congress the first time in 1890, one of the planks in his platform was the election of U. S. Senators by the people. He voted in Congress for the submission of the necessary amendment embodied in a resolution which was the first passed on the subject by either house. Mr. Bryan had this reform embodied in the Democratic national platform of 1900, which was reaffirmed in the three succeeding national platforms. A proposition to put such a plank in the Republican platform in 1908 was defeated by a vote of 7 to 1. But the struggle continued, and in 1913 the Constitution was amended and another one of Mr. Bryan's measures found its way into fundamental law.

Popular election of Senators was advocated by Mr. Bryan in 1890, before either house of Congress had ever adopted it. He wrote it into the platforms of his party. He spoke for it for twenty years and from hundreds of platforms, and as Secretary of State he signed the proclamation declaring it a part of the Constitution.

INDEPENDENCE OF THE PHILIPPINES

At the close of the Spanish War when Colonel Bryan resigned from the army, he immediately declared against an American colonial policy. Here the expression "imperialism" had its birth. Mr. Bryan advocated the Bacon amendment to the treaty with Spain. This amendment declared that the United States had no intention of exercising permanent control over the Philippines. The amendment was defeated by the Vice President breaking the tie vote in the Senate.

In 1900 when Mr. Bryan again ran for President he declared this issue to be paramount, and for more than fifteen years his voice was heard against this departure from American principles. In 1916 he saw his ideal written in

the Jones bill and passed by both houses and signed by
President Wilson.

PROHIBITION

Mr. Bryan was a total abstainer throughout his entire
life. His influence was always cast against the use of intoxicating liquor. The liquor interests recognized in him a
powerful enemy. They set about to destroy his leadership
of the Democratic Party by attempting to eliminate him
as a factor in his own state, and they succeeded in defeating
him for delegate to the National Democratic Convention of
1916. In 1915 and 1916 he spoke in several states for
prohibition. Up to the first election of Wilson he had
opposed making it a national issue, on the theory that,
without being able to secure the necessary Constitutional
amendment, it would interfere with the adoption of the
economic reforms which had already become national issues.

But when these economic reforms had become certain
of adoption, he threw himself into the fight and supported
the amendment in many speeches throughout the country.
His own state, Nebraska, happened to be the thirty-sixth
and last state necessary to the adoption of the amendment.

As to his part in the great achievement, let the leaders
of the cause speak. The legislative committee of the Anti-
Saloon League, after the fight was won, addressed Mr.
Bryan a formal letter in which they said:

"As democracy's greatest prophet of reform you
have many times rendered conspicuous service for the
right; never more so than in the present case. During
all the recent months leading up to the final battle, your
voice has sounded the high note of idealism in this
fight for humanity, has inspired your friends to confidence and enthusiasm, and has sent the shock of alarm
throughout the ranks of the liquor forces. This period
of continued and distinguished service found fit comple-

466

THE VINDICATION OF HIS POLICIES

tion in your great address at the Metropolitan M. E. Church and the overflow meeting at the First Presbyterian Church before the annual convention of the Anti-Saloon League of America; in your return to the national Capital for the final struggle in the house, and in your history-making and memorable reply to Mr. Gompers which, added to your unquestioned influence with the members of the Congress, did so much to put the cause of temperance and prohibition 'over the top.' "

Woman Suffrage

When woman suffrage became a real issue before the American people, Mr. Bryan took his stand. He had already in 1914 canvassed Nebraska when it was a local issue in that state. When the national amendment was submitted he rendered great service in many speeches and through the columns of the *Commoner*. His famous "Mother Argument," first delivered in 1916, is given on page 506. Here, too, as in the cause of Prohibition, he was one of the foremost workers in securing the adoption of the necessary Constitutional amendment.

The Thirty Peace Treaties

On February 17, 1905, in an editorial in the *Commoner* appears Mr. Bryan's first recorded advocacy of the principle embodied in the "thirty treaties." The same year he addressed a letter to President Roosevelt on the subject. In 1906 he advocated it before the American Society at London and before the Interparliamentary Union in the same city.

When Mr. Taft was President Mr. Bryan also submitted the plan to him and secured his approval. Mr. Taft afterwards, in a London speech, gave Mr. Bryan credit for the plan. When President Wilson tendered Mr. Bryan the office of Secretary of State the President gave Mr. Bryan's plan his hearty approval.

The subject is treated elsewhere in this volume, and it is not necessary to say here more than that the principle of the Bryan treaties now forms the "heart" of the Covenant of the League of Nations.

A DEPARTMENT OF LABOR

The establishment of a separate Department of Labor, with a representative in the Cabinet, was one of the measures which Mr. Bryan was first among the political leaders to advocate. He had a plank on the subject inserted in the Democratic platform of 1900 upon which he ran for the Presidency. He continued to advocate the measure in his speeches and through the columns of the *Commoner*.

In his Labor Day speech delivered at Chicago Sept. 7, 1908, he said:

"I regard the inauguration of this reform as the opening of a new era in which those who toil will have a voice in the deliberations of the President's council chamber."

In 1913 the Department of Labor in the President's Cabinet was established.

GOVERNMENT BY INJUNCTION

No position taken by Mr. Bryan aroused more opposition on the part of the big corporations than his stand against government by injunction. Mr. Bryan not only looked upon government by injunction as an attempt on the part of judges to invade the field of legislation, but also as a suspension of the constitutional right of trial by jury.

In his platforms and in his speeches he spoke against this abuse during a period of twenty years. He was called an enemy of the courts, and of law and of order, by the reactionary forces in both parties, but he fought on and he lived to see the protection of the right of labor against the

"MARYMONT"
The Bryan Home at Coconut Grove.
STARTING FOR A RIDE
Mr. Bryan and "Don." From photo taken in front of "Marymont" in 1925.

unwarranted issuance of injunctions written into law and the guarantee of the right of trial by jury in cases of alleged contempt committed outside the presence of the court.

REGULATION OF RAILROADS

After ten years of constant effort by Mr. Bryan to secure more effective railroad regulation, based on the Democratic platforms of 1896, 1900, and 1904, President Roosevelt, to the consternation of his Republican associates, took up the cause and with the support of the Democrats in Congress, accomplished the reform.

While the Democrats under Mr. Bryan's leadership had been demanding this measure of relief, the Republicans had been fighting it, but they were at last compelled to surrender under the weight of public opinion.

INITIATIVE AND REFERENDUM

In 1902 when the movement for the initiative and referendum was young, Mr. Bryan, before any other national leader had declared for it, put his influence behind this movement to make representative government more representative.

This stand was declared by Mr. Bryan's opponents to be another evidence of extreme radicalism, but one by one the states began to adopt it until they reached twenty in number, including the old conservative Commonwealth of Massachusetts. Other political leaders were converted to it, among them Presidents Roosevelt and Wilson.

CURRENCY REFORM

The Federal Reserve Act has proven itself to be a great piece of monetary legislation. It was bitterly opposed by the banking interests of the country, but it was the salvation of the country in the World War and has since proven its merit on many occasions.

WILLIAM JENNINGS BRYAN

Mr. Bryan did not write the act, but those on the inside know how he so changed its provisions as to save it from defeat. The story is told by Mr. Tumulty in his book, "Woodrow Wilson As I Knew Him."

The bill as drawn contained the bank-note feature which was in opposition to a plank in the Democratic platform of 1896 which Mr. Bryan had written and which was bitterly assailed at the time. It was also in opposition to other Democratic platform declarations. Mr. Bryan informed President Wilson of his opposition to the feature and after considerable difficulty succeeded in convincing the President that he (Bryan) was right.

It was through Mr. Bryan's influence, therefore, that a serious defect was removed from the bill, and the way cleared for the passage of this most important economic measure.

Bimetallism

Mr. Bryan's political enemies look upon his stand on "free silver" as the rankest of heresy and they point to the defeat of this measure as a proof of its unsoundness.

In the first place, let it not be forgotten that the Republican, as well as the Democratic, platform of 1896 declared for the free coinage of silver, the only difference being that the Republican Party wanted it by agreement with other nations which it pledged itself to promote.

After the election, President McKinley's first act was to send a commission to Europe to bring about the free coinage of silver. But then the unexpected happened; there was an enormous increase in the world's production of gold and a great cheapening in the cost of extracting it. The increase in the supply of money came from a hitherto unseen and entirely unexpected source. The quantitative theory of money, advocated by Mr. Bryan, was vindicated by events, but the need for the free coinage of silver gradually eliminated by the increased money supply,

470

THE VINDICATION OF HIS POLICIES

This vindication, however, is none the less complete. To show that the result which his followers desired, and for which they labored with intelligence and earnestness, has come from causes which no one could have anticipated, Mr. Bryan used this illustration: "Suppose the citizens of a town were divided, nearly equally, on the question of water supply, one faction contending that the amount should be increased, and suggesting that the increase be piped from Silver Lake, the only available body of water, the other faction insisting that no more water was needed; suppose that at the election the opponents of an increase won (no matter by what means); and suppose, soon after the election, a spring which may be described as Gold Spring, broke forth in the very center of the city, with a flow of half as much water as the city had before used; and suppose the new supply was turned into the city reservoir to the joy and benefit of all the people of the town. Which faction would, in such a case, have been vindicated?

"Just such a result has followed a similar increase in the nation's supply of money to the joy of all—thus proving the contentions of bimetallists."

CHAPTER XIX

THE FINAL YEARS

CHRONOLOGICALLY considered, the Democratic National Convention of 1920 at San Francisco takes first place in a record of Mr. Bryan's last five years. I was glad Mr. Bryan made the campaign for delegate-at-large. It did him good to meet his old friends again. The result of this canvass made Mr. Bryan a delegate-at-large with ten of the sixteen delegates supporting him, a notable victory. Condensing the convention details, there was a strong movement in the Democratic party to stand for an increase in the alcoholic content of beer and wine, and many delegates had been chosen in harmony with that plan. The convention was "wet" and had no use for Mr. Bryan and his temperance policies. Mr. Bryan stood his ground, bringing in a minority report from the Committee on Resolutions, and explaining the proposition included in this report. I append a brief extract from his remarks:

"On the night of the sixteenth day of last January when, at the nation's Capital, we celebrated the Passover from the old era to the new, I was honored by the leaders of this great cause with the privilege of being the last speaker at the meeting. I watched the clock, and when it was within one minute of the time when this nation would become saloonless for evermore, I quoted a passage from the Bible—the language in which the angel assured Joseph and Mary that it was safe to take the young child Jesus back to the Holy Land—you recall the words: 'They are dead that sought the young child's life.' [Applause.] When you remember that King Alcohol has slain a million more children than Herod

472

ever did, what language can more appropriately express the joy in the hearts of parents today than those words: 'They are dead that sought the young child's life'?

"Are you afraid that we shall lose some votes? Oh, my countrymen, have more faith in the virtue of the people. If there be any here who would seek the support of those who desire to carry us back into bondage to alcohol, let them remember that it is better to have the gratitude of one soul saved from drink than the applause of a drunken world. [Great applause.] . . .

"Let me give you a bit of history; the District of Columbia went dry and the white flag of prohibition was raised over the nation's Capital, never to be hauled down. It was a Democratic Senate and a Democratic House that passed the bill and a Democratic President who signed it. Are you ashamed of what your party did? [Applause.] Are you ashamed that a Democratic Senate and House submitted prohibition, and that every Democratic state ratified? Are you ashamed that three fourths of the Democratic Congressmen and two thirds of the Democratic senators voted for the enforcement law?

"Be not frightened; time and again in history the timid have been afraid. But they have always found that they underestimated the number of those who had not bowed the knee to Baal. The Bible tells us of a time when the great Elisha was told by his servant that the enemy was too great for them, the prophet answered: 'Fear not, they that be with us are more than they that be against us.' And then he drew aside the veil and on the mountain top the young man could see horses and chariots that had been invisible before. In just a few days another state will ratify the Suffrage Amendment, and then on the mountain tops you will see the women and children, our allies in every righteous cause. We shall not fail. [Great and prolonged applause.]"

WILLIAM JENNINGS BRYAN

The convention nominated Honorable James M. Cox for President and Honorable Franklin D. Roosevelt for Vice President, both excellent men who were worthy of high honor, but who misjudged the sentiments of the country.

During these years Mr. Bryan delivered a series of James Sprunt lectures at the Union Theological Seminary at Richmond, Va. These lectures were nine in number and were published by the faculty under the title "In His Image." This week spent in the Theological Seminary was a very happy one. He spoke several times of the joy it gave him to speak connectedly upon such themes to a body of students, and expressed a hope that if he lived to be old, he might arrange lectures at a series of colleges, and "you can go with me and meet these pleasant friends," he said.

One can only condense the work of these busy years. He addressed the Legislatures of West Virginia, of Kentucky, and of Florida. He spoke to the students at the State University of Florida, at Brown University, at Dartmouth, at Phillips Brooks House in Harvard. He lectured at the Moody Bible Institute, at the Bible Institute of Los Angeles, California, at the Lane Theological Seminary in Cincinnati, at Winona Lake Bible Conference, at Carnegie Hall, at the Presbyterian General Assembly, at the Miami Bible Conference, at the National Christian Endeavor Convention. He made a campaign of Florida to raise an endowment fund for the State University at Gainesville, spent one summer on the Chautauqua platform, campaigned the State of Florida for election as delegate-at-large to the National Democratic Convention in New York, speaking in the county seat of each of Florida's sixty-six counties, making the journey by automobile, coming home tanned by the sun and bright-eyed, full of happiness because he was beginning to know people all over the state, and found them such "fine fellows." The result of this campaign was also most gratifying, as Mr. Bryan ran 45,000 votes ahead of the next man on the list of candidates for delegate.

During the winter of 1924–25 he spoke at noon each day to the tourists at Coral Gables. His subject was not real estate, but he spoke of Florida generally, of its advantages and pleasures. This was a sparkling little speech which Mr. Bryan enjoyed making, for he was full of enthusiasm for his state. He had transferred his citizenship from Nebraska to Florida in 1922.

On March 30, 1923, Mr. Bryan wrote to Hon. George Huddleston in reply to the latter's suggestion that he (Mr. Bryan) ought to be the nominee of the Democratic party in 1924:

"I have not felt that I should ever make a fight for a Presidential nomination. My past nominations have come to me without contest, and it would be mortifying to have to make a contest; and whenever a contest is necessary, there is a possibility of defeat, which would be still more mortifying. I do not want the office and would not consider a nomination unless it came to me as a call from my party, and under circumstances that made me seem to be able to do more for the party than anybody else could. Such a situation is, of course, highly improbable—a very remote contingency."

The Democratic Convention in June, 1924, was held in New York City, and the metropolis made elaborate preparations for the coming of the great throng of delegates. The personal popularity of Governor Al Smith packed the galleries of Madison Square Garden with thousands of enthusiastic New Yorkers, while the delegates filled the body of the auditorium. Mr. Bryan, as delegate-at-large from Florida, was seated with that delegation. When a minority report from the Committee on Platform added to the plank on religious liberty a clause specifically condemning the Ku Klux Klan by name, Mr. Bryan spoke in support of the majority report. Although at no time a member of the Klan or connected with it in any way, Mr. Bryan deplored the condemnatory resolution for two reasons; first, that singling out such an organization by a great political party in its platform served to give it undue prominence, and second, that the direct result of such a resolution would be to foment fierce intolerance and strife.

The friends of Governor Smith rallied to the defense of the measure and Mr. Bryan was repeatedly interrupted during his speech by the bitterest abuse. He was no longer a young man. Although a rugged vigor still upheld him and although his ardor burned as intensely as in the very beginning of his political life, the cares and toil of years had taken their toll. He was more weary and worn than his age alone would justify.

The issue of the Klan was debated at great length in committee. One memorable Friday night the discussion continued until the early hours of the morning before decisions were finally reached. Describing the scene that followed, one of the members of the committee, reporting the session before the convention, said:

"When we had completed our deliberations and had begun to feel once more welling up into our hearts the spirit of fraternity and were about to disperse, one of the members (Judge John H. McCann of Pennsylvania) arose and recited the Lord's Prayer; and then at the close Mr. Bryan lifted up his voice in an invocation for guidance and for Divine help in this hour of stress." He added: "I do not know that I ought to say these things, but they did occur, and so I have come to report to you exactly what happened in that committee."

A hush fell on the great assemblage, followed by tumultuous applause. Mr. Bryan's prayer, now known as the "Daybreak Prayer," follows:

476

ATTENDING THE DEMOCRATIC CONVENTION OF 1924

THE FINAL YEARS

"Our Heavenly Father, we come into Thy presence conscious that Thou art infinite in wisdom, love and power, while we are limited in knowledge and prone to err.

"Thou dost care for Thy children, and hast promised to reveal Thyself and Thy will to those whose hearts are open to Divine suggestion.

"We need Thy counsel, Lord. We are carrying great responsibilities and dealing with mighty problems that vex and trouble us. We are subject to prejudice and passion and unconscious bias.

"Cleanse our minds from all unworthy thoughts and purge our hearts of all evil desires. Show us Thy way, and help us to know what Thou wouldst have us say and do and be.

"We would consecrate ourselves wholly unto Thee and Thy service. 'Thy kingdom come, Thy will be done, on earth as it is in Heaven.'

"Help us to advance in our day and this day the brotherhood Thou didst establish. May it include all mankind.

"So guide and direct us in our work today that the people of our party and of our country and of the world may be better for our coming together in this convention and in this committee.

"Bless us, not for ourselves, but that we may be a blessing. We ask in Jesus' name. Amen."

When Mr. Bryan faced his last convention and tried to guide the party which had held his devotion unswervingly since the days when he had spoken in its defense as a schoolboy, he faced it as a veteran of many political battles. He was scarred and aged, but still faithful to his party and zealous for its good. His voice, without the silver ring of youth, was still a powerful, resounding organ as he pleaded in the convention. But the angry galleries and opposing delegates repeatedly drowned his voice with the clamor of jeers.

WILLIAM JENNINGS BRYAN

Perhaps realizing that his years were numbered, Mr. Bryan paused in his speech to say to them, "This is probably the last convention of my party to which I shall be a delegate." Some of the audience broke into applause, but Mr. Bryan, facing the hostility inside the ranks of his own party as resolutely as he had faced the enemies of the party in earlier years, countered, with good humor; "Don't applaud. I may change my mind."

I will not record in detail the slurs which were hurled at him. For the reputation of our party I am sorry that these indignities should find a place in the record of the National Convention. But if Mr. Bryan felt the wounds, he gave no sign. He met wave after wave of prejudice and animosity as an old weathered rock will stand against angry seas.

These demonstrations, however, did little toward affecting results. Mr. Bryan stood for McAdoo, who received the votes of very nearly half the delegates, while Smith received at no time more than one third.

The resolution which Mr. Bryan opposed failed of adoption and such a platform was written and such candidates were nominated as were in harmony with his views.

When the final choice of the party was made, Hon. John W. Davis of West Virginia became the Presidential candidate, and Ex-Governor Charles W. Bryan of Nebraska was the Vice Presidential nominee. Mr. Bryan gave the ticket his hearty support.

It was during the New York Convention that Mr. Bryan gave the reporters a piece of news which had filled him with delight. Gathering the newspaper men about him, he told them that he had a most important item for them. With a pencil he wrote on a piece of paper the following:

"A great-granddaughter was born today to Mr. Bryan. The parents are William P. Meeker and Kitty Owen Meeker, Mr. Bryan's oldest grandchild."

478

THE FINAL YEARS

During these years he felt more and more the importance of religious work and devoted an increasing amount of time to it.

Friends and enemies alike have been interested to know why Mr. Bryan took up the question of evolution. This is a matter I can easily explain. When delivering religious lectures he found his audiences were in some respects different from his political audiences. He learned to know many Sunday-school teachers, pastors, and members of their congregations. After the address when people came to shake his hand, he often heard such remarks as these:

Happy father: "Mr. Bryan, I just wanted to come and tell you that our daughter heard you speak in ——. She is a student in the University there and your lecture has steadied her."

Weeping mother: "How I wish our son could have heard you speak. He has lost his faith."

Tall youth: "Mr. Bryan, I have been slipping away from the Church, but you have brought me back."

In a Western town a Japanese man came to him bringing a square wooden box which contained a really lovely vase, which I still prize. In picturesque English, he told Mr. Bryan that his son had heard him speak in Seattle. "He is a much better boy, a much better boy. I bring you this little present to show my thanks."

These repeated indications of unbelief, especially among college students, puzzled him. Upon investigation he became convinced that the teaching of evolution as a fact instead of a theory caused the students to lose faith in the Bible, first, in the story of creation, and later in other doctrines which underlie the Christian religion. He then read numerous books, and as always when investigating a subject, he read widely on both sides of this question.

Just why the interest grew, just how he was able to put

fresh interest into a question which was popular twenty-five years ago, I do not know. An editorial of last year offers an explanation. The clever writer was showing "why Mr. Bryan, more than any other man of the generation, has kept on the front page all the time." I regret that I am unable to quote verbatim, but the central idea of the argument was that whenever Mr. Bryan took a stand upon any subject, the matter at once became an issue. People began to fall in line. Sides grew distinct. The public divided and stood ready to do battle. There is some truth in this statement. The vigor and force of the man seemed to compel attention.

In May, 1923, the Presbyterian General Assembly had issued a pronouncement on the subject. In November following the Bishops of the Protestant Episcopal Church reiterated their acceptance of the Apostles' Creed as the foundation of their Church's belief, especially emphasizing the Virgin Birth. The Northern Baptist, the Baptist Bible Union, the Methodist Church North and South, the Christian Church, the Foreign Missionary Society, colleges, church papers of all denominations took up the argument. Occasionally a teacher was dismissed from a public school, a professor was dropped from the staff of a college, or a pastor resigned from his pulpit as a result of these discussions. During the spring of 1925 the United States Supreme Court rendered a decision emphasizing the parents' interest in the child's religion and affirming the state's right to control the schools. Legislatures here and there began to take notice. The Legislature of Tennessee became interested early in 1925.

While it is not my purpose to enter upon a general defense of Mr. Bryan's position, some misrepresented points in this connection may well be cleared. The press asserted that Mr. Bryan had worked for the introduction of this bill. The following letter from Attorney W. B. Marr, of Nashville, is illuminating;

July 6, 1925.

Hon. W. J. Bryan,
c/o Hicks & Hicks,
Dayton, Tenn.

DEAR SIR:

. . . We appreciate your kindly words of appreciation for the interest we have taken in the case.

We feel that we are almost the proximate cause of this statute in that we heard you present your great lecture "Is the Bible True?" Later we had several thousand of them published and distributed generally. Later when the Legislature first convened we sent about 500 copies to the members. Evidently this caused Mr. Butler to read and think deeply on this subject and prompted him to introduce his bill. Later, after it was introduced we presented the issue by sending your pamphlets again to the Legislature and believe they, as champions, quietly accomplished sufficient to overcome the active efforts of the advocates of Evolution, who opposed the bill. . . .

If we can be of further assistance to you, command us.

Respectfully,

W. B. MARR.

The following letter shows that Mr. Bryan, far from wishing a more drastic measure, wrote, asking that the penalty clause be omitted:

February 9, 1925.

Hon. Jno. A. Shelton,
The Senate,
Nashville, Tenn.

MY DEAR MR. SHELTON:

I had just learned before receipt of your letter of the

action taken by the Legislature of Tennessee and had intended writing to the author of the bill. Your letter, therefore, is very welcome. . . .

The special thing that I want to suggest is that it is better not to have a penalty. I suggest this for two reasons; in the first place, our opponents, not being able to oppose the measure on its merits, are always trying to find something that will divert attention, and the penalty furnishes the excuse. That is the way they defeated the bill in Kentucky a few years ago.

The second reason is that we are dealing with an educated class that is supposed to respect the law. It will be easier to pass the bill without a penalty attached. If the declaration made by the Legislature in the form of a law without penalty is not obeyed, a penalty can be added by a subsequent Legislature. In Florida, it was put in the form of a joint resolution which read substantially as follows:

"Be it Resolved by the Senate and House of Representatives of the Legislature of Florida that it is detrimental to the welfare of the state for any teacher or school official in any educational institution supported in whole or in part by taxation to teach or permit to be taught as true either Darwinism or any other evolutionary hypothesis that links man in blood relationship to any lower form of life."

Wishing you success in the effort to protect students from the demoralizing influence of this materialistic view of man's ancestry, I am

Very truly yours,

W. J. BRYAN.

That Mr. Bryan was asked to assist in the Scopes case, and did not offer his services unsolicited, is shown by the following letter:

THE FINAL YEARS

HICKS & HICKS
Attorneys and Counsellors at Law
Dayton, Tenn.

May 14, 1925.

Hon. William J. Bryan
Miami, Florida

MY DEAR SIR:

We have been trying to get in touch with you by wire to ask you to become associated with us in the prosecution of the case of the State against J. T. Scopes, charged with violation of the anti-evolution law, but our wires did not reach you.

We will consider it a great honor to have you with us in this prosecution. We will have no difficulty in obtaining the consent of the attorney general and the circuit judge for you to appear in the case.

Scopes has been bound over to the Grand Jury which meets the first Monday in August. We anticipate no trouble in getting a true bill against him by the grand jury. This will make the case be set for trial in the Circuit Court here the latter part of the first week in August, or in the first part of the second week in August.

Please get in touch with us and we will send you a copy of the text book taught in the school and a copy of the statute under which we are prosecuting Scopes.

Yours very truly,

SUE K. HICKS.

This does not seem the place for a discussion of the arrest and prosecution of John T. Scopes of Dayton, Tennessee, for the violation of the statute passed by the Legislature. A recital of the principles involved is found in the Appendix ("Who Shall Control?") and also the full text of Mr. Bryan's last speech upon the subject, "The Tennessee Case."

The question involved was a purely legal one, namely, had Scopes violated the law, and the efforts of the opposition to make the case hinge on the truth or lack of truth in the theory of evolution were out of place. I attended every session of the trial and felt that, as the question in point was purely technical, it was irrelevant to the subject when men of far from unblemished reputation, exclaimed, "I am a Christian; just as good a Christian as Mr. Bryan." It was incongruous to see men, whose hopeless faces proclaimed them without faith of any sort, rise to defend what they called religious freedom.

Mr. Scopes' defense was defeated at every point and the decision of the court a triumph for the Tennessee statute. It was agreed that no closing speeches should be made, which led Mr. Bryan to commit to writing the speech which he would have delivered in court. This work occupied the days following the close of the trial.

Our last automobile trip together was on Saturday, July 25, from Chattanooga to Winchester, Tennessee, the home of Judge Ralston and State Attorney General Stewart. Mr. Bryan had spent the preceding day and night in Chattanooga correcting the proof of his speech, and we (our faithful chauffeur, William McCartney, and I) left Dayton at 6.30 A. M., drove thirty miles to Chattanooga, where, by previous arrangement, we met Mr. Bryan outside the city where the highway, an excellent one, turned into the Winchester Road. I can see him now, standing by the side of the road, so vigorous and smiling.

After we had enjoyed the beauties of the river gorge with its morning shade and coolness, we drove into wider valleys and to the town of Jasper, where he was to make a short speech. The meeting was held under fine trees where the speaker's stand had been erected and a huge flag floated. I wish to record one fact which impressed me. I did not go to the stand, but sat in the car on the outskirts of the crowd. The fringe of the gathering consisted of many standing farmers in their simple but tidy overalls and shirts. When Mr. Bryan asked one of the local clergy to lead in

484

DEFENDER OF THE FAITH
Mr. Bryan upon arrival at Dayton, Tenn., to assist in the prosecution of the Scopes case. *Photo. Underwood & Underwood*

MR. BRYAN WITH OTHER MEMBERS OF THE COUNSEL FOR THE STATE
H. K. Hicks, Gordon McKenzie, Wallace Haggard, William Jennings Bryan, and Sue Hicks. *Photo. Pacific & Atlantic Photos*

prayer, every hat in these ranks was removed and every head bowed in reverence. I know of no part of our country where the toilers would be found more thoroughly religious.

I had brought a heavy wrap which could be used as a pillow, and when we had left Jasper, Mr. Bryan lay down on the back seat and took a long nap. We crossed the mountain range and over roads none too smooth, but the swaying and jolting did not disturb him. He had a fine, deep sleep, and awoke thoroughly rested.

I had been waiting till the close of the trial to discuss with him the future of his work. The time seemed opportune and we had our last serious talk. Beginning with the assertion of Tolstoy that religion is the relation which man fixes between himself and his God, we spoke of the sacredness of that relation; that almost everyone has some little irregularities in his belief which he mentions to no one—a matter between himself and his God—but his religion is to him a satisfactory faith. Mr. Bryan and I spoke of his work thus far; his effort to prove the presence, both in the Church and school, of a theory which when taught as fact tended to destroy belief in the truth of the Bible; that having proved the existence of such a situation, he was trying to do three things; first, to establish the right of taxpayers to control what is taught in their schools; second, to draw a line between the teaching of evolution as a fact and teaching it as a theory; and third, to see that teachers proven guilty of this offense should be given an opportunity to resign.

We spoke of the narrow margin between this perfectly legitimate work as touching the public servant, and an encroachment on individual religious belief which is a sacred domain. We agreed that care must be taken at this point that no religious zeal should invade this sacred domain and become intolerance.

Mr. Bryan said, "Well, Mamma, I have not made that mistake yet, have I?" And I replied, "You are all right

so far, but will you be able to keep to this narrow path?"
With a happy smile, he said, "I think I can." "But,"
said I, "can you control your followers?" and more gravely
he said, "I think I can." And I knew' he was adding mentally, "by the help of God."

I hope I may be pardoned for relating so personal a
matter as our last conversation. I do it to show that Mr.
Bryan in his attitude toward the theory of evolution had
only the desire to protect Christian faith from influences
which tended to undermine it.

Winchester, with its natural beauty, with its college
atmosphere, its flavor of age and refinement, pleased us
very much. As we drove through the village, we passed
the building in which the gentlemen of Winchester and
three adjoining towns were to meet Mr. Bryan at luncheon.
They were gathered on the lawn, 132 in number—such a
splendid body of men! I had a delicious luncheon with
Mrs. Judge Ralston and other friends, and afterward upon
the veranda, which was a bower of flowers, we received the
ladies of the community. When the hour arrived for Mr.
Bryan's speech, I returned to Dayton, as it was a long and
difficult drive, leaving Mr. Bryan to return to Chattanooga
with friends, where he spent the evening giving final correction to the proof of his speech.

Next morning he came breezing into my room at 9 A. M.
telling me how pleased he was with the new speech, how
very accurate the linotype man had been, how fine the
general appearance of the speech would be, etc. In his
mail was a very gratifying letter from our oldest grandson.
He brought it and read it to me, so pleased with its loving
appreciation. A friend had sent a basket of honeydew
melons; how kind everyone was. He reviewed the fact
that our son had been with us during the trial; what a
fine logical mind he had shown; how proud he was of him.
He was pleased with everyone and his heart was full of
cheer.

486

THE FINAL YEARS

At 11 o'clock he went to church, where, I am told, he made a beautiful prayer, his last public utterance. The pastor of the little church told us later that Mr. Bryan had seemed to address his God, not as a being far away across worlds, but as a very near and loving Heavenly Father.

At the midday meal he told me of having had a physical examination the day before—"just to ease your mind." His blood pressure was exactly between the extremes prescribed for men of his age; his heart action normal; his other tests entirely satisfactory. "According to that, Mamma, I have several more years to live," he concluded. After the meal he made several long-distance telephone calls concerning arrangements for the coming week, which we were to spend in Smoky Mountains. I was sitting on the side porch studying a touring map when he finished with the telephoning. "Well, that is finished," he said. "I will take my nap and write to Perrine when I get up."

As the shadows began to lengthen, I said to McCartney: "Go in and waken Mr. Bryan. Such a long nap will break his rest tonight." McCartney went and returned, saying that Mr. Bryan was sleeping so peacefully that it seemed a pity to waken him. A sudden foreboding ran through me like a shock. I said, "Go back, raise the window curtains, and see if he is only sleeping." He went in and called back to me: "Something is wrong. I cannot waken him." Unable as I was to leave my wheel chair, I directed McCartney how to search for Mr. Bryan's pulse and for his heart beat, and was soon convinced that he was gone. Then followed frantic telephone calls for doctors, two of whom were soon there, but no human help could avail. As I look back upon that day, the phrase which recurs to my mind is, "He was not, for God took him." I believe God loved this servant of his and had watched his years of service. God took him and spared him the infirmities of age, the weakness and pain of prolonged illness; the dreary, slow approach to the grave. God took him when he was facing the sunset with radiant contentment, a happy close to a life of consecration.

Although during the next day I was alone except for my companion and chauffeur, distance preventing any of our children from reaching me at once, the warm neighborliness of the village people enveloped me. Though I was without members of my own family, I was not alone. All that loving friends could do in hours of sorrow was done for me in Dayton. By their unfailing kindness expressed in fruit from their orchards, blossoms from their gardens, dainties from their tables, these new-made friends helped me.

Mr. Bryan lay in the parlor of the little cottage guarded in death by the young attorneys who had learned to know and love him during the course of the trial. Early on Tuesday morning our elder daughter Ruth and her husband, Major Owen, reached Dayton, and they remained with me through the journey to Washington. During Monday and Tuesday afternoon there were hours when Mr. Bryan lay in state, and the lawn before the cottage was crowded with people from Dayton and the surrounding countryside. On Tuesday afternoon a brief service was held by the local clergy. The veranda served as a pulpit. The crowd filled the lawn facing the house and their prayers and songs rang through the quiet of the summer afternoon.

The following morning, when day had scarcely dawned, we began our journey to Washington. Mr. Bryan was carried to our railway coach, which was waiting. Dayton was already stirring and a crowd had gathered at the station. A quiet, sorrowing throng watched our train depart. The crowds which assembled at railway stations on that journey were in a way reminiscent of the many campaign trips which Mr. Bryan and I had made together. It seemed natural to see the throngs of people crowding the platforms and filling the crossroads from side to side. The long lines of parked cars and wagons at the outskirts of the crowds were all familiar. For thirty years these crowds had gathered in the little towns, eagerly pushing their way around the back platform of the observation coach, and always Mr. Bryan had gone to greet them. He loved the little towns as they loved him, and whether by day or night, when they gathered at the station, he was never too busy or too weary to speak to them.

This last journey was like the early campaigns, except that now there was sorrow on the faces that pressed around the windows. The great crowds of people were silent and no one came to the back platform to greet them.

Of the throngs who gathered at Chattanooga and Nashville, only a small fraction were able to file through the car where Mr. Bryan lay in state. When the train, even after delaying its departure, began to move, many thousands who had wished to enter were disappointed. In the smaller towns the train stopped so short a time that the waiting crowds could not be admitted to the car, but the rear door was left open so that the people could file by close enough to see the flag-covered casket and the mounds of flowers which grew greater at every stop the train made.

At Jefferson City, Tennessee, a quartet of young men were standing on a pile of railway ties, hymn books in hand, singing as our train drew in, "One Sweetly Solemn Thought." Near by an older man supported a large American flag, and all around them was a crowd which seemed too great to have been recruited in one town.

> "One sweetly solemn thought
> Comes to me o'er and o'er,
> I am nearer home today
> Than I have been before,"

sang the quartet. Then the train began to move away. As we passed on, another portion of the crowd had begun to sing, but this time the hymn rose in a great chorus. They had paid their tribute through the voice of song and had conveyed their message of sympathy and love to us within the train.

At another town so small that the train did not stop, there had been a church service arranged so that it should close as the funeral train passed by, and the congregation came in a body from the little chapel to the railway embankment, where they stood with bowed heads as our train passed. At one point where the train did not stop, the waiting crowd held up a banner on which was printed, "We are honoring the memory of William Jennings Bryan."

Little knots of people gathered at the crossroads; sometimes four or five cars would be parked, and a little group waited there in the dust for the train to whirl by. As night fell, the crowds at the stations were undiminished. I shall never forget the throng at Bristol, on the border line of Virginia and Tennessee. It stretched away at both sides of the train. Little children were lifted up so that they could catch a glimpse through the car windows, but saddest of all to me were the old men. It was not curiosity which had brought them to the station, or courtesy. They were mourning a friend. I could see these old men here and there in all the crowds. They were the friends of the early campaigns and they had lost their champion. I said to my daughter, "They have indeed lost a friend who never broke faith with them." If the sympathy of friends can sustain one in sorrow, then we were upborne on the very wings of love as we journeyed to Washington.

Knowing the strain of the days to follow, we tried to sleep that night, but heard the murmur of voices at every stop the train made, and were told the following morning how the crowds had gathered all through the night. At Washington our son, William, Jr., and our daughter, Grace B. Hargraves, Mr. Bryan's brother, Charles W. Bryan, and his two sisters, Mrs. James Baird and Mrs. T. S. Allen, joined us. We found that the funeral arrangements, which had been made by his old friend and former secretary, Ben

490

G. Davis, were of the simplicity which would have accorded completely with Mr. Bryan's own wishes. In connection with the funeral service, a curious coincidence may not be omitted. I had expressed a wish that the funeral services should be held in the New York Avenue Presbyterian Church where Mr. Bryan and I had worshiped. I was told that Dr. Radcliffe, the pastor, was absent in Europe, but that Dr. Joseph Sizoo, who was filling the pulpit, would conduct the service if I wished. I assented, although this clergyman was personally unknown to me. It came then as a complete surprise and as a coincidence of dramatic impressiveness to learn that Dr. Sizoo had been brought into the ministry through the influence of one of Mr. Bryan's speeches, and that fact added weight to his impressive and beautiful address.

While Mr. Bryan lay in state in the church, guarded by two Spanish-American war veterans, more than 20,000 people filed past. Our rooms at the Lafayette Hotel were the meeting place for relatives and friends who had gathered from every part of the country.

Mr. Bryan's eldest grandchild, Mrs. William P. Meeker, and his youngest grandchild, Evelyn Hargraves, and his only great-grandchild, baby Ruth Meeker, represented youth and hope in our broken family circle.

I had hoped that we would not have the gloom of rainy skies to bear on the day of his funeral. But when the day dawned, there were overcast skies, against which we saw the flags at half-mast on all the government buildings. Rain fell at intervals during the entire day. I noticed twice when the rain ceased; once, for a few minutes as Mr. Bryan's casket was carried down the steep steps from the church into the waiting car, and again at Arlington as the long file of khaki-clad soldiers met us at the gate and formed a military guard to his last resting place, the clouds lifted and there was a suggestion of sunlight in the sky.

In any funeral there is material for sorrow and grief,

491

and in the very words which can be pronounced by any clergyman at any service for the dead there is a solemnity which overshadows the trivial concerns of life. But there was something more in the service for Mr. Bryan which, for the comfort of his friends, I wish that I could set down in words. The church had an atmosphere of dignity and peace. The flowers which were massed across the entire end of the church had transformed it into a bower; with tall crosses of lilies and roses standing high against a wall of bloom. But I wish to record more than the dignity of the place and more than the beauty of the funeral sermon. We who are closest to Mr. Bryan had entered the church full of grief, wondering if we could bear the strain which the hymns and prayers would put on already full hearts. As the first hymn ended and Dr. Sizoo began to speak, we found that our attention had left the casket beneath the flag; that it had ceased to seem the repository of our loved one. A sense of peace and of Mr. Bryan's contentment, a sense of his presence and benediction came to us and remained with us; not to his family alone but, as we afterward found, to a number of his friends as well. When Dr. Sizoo closed his sermon with "Thank God for the memory and heritage of William Jennings Bryan," and the great cross of white lilies was carried down the aisle of the church before the casket, we followed, all sure in our hearts that we followed only the tired, worn-out body which was being carried to the National Cemetery, and that somewhere just beyond our mortal vision his firm, unfaltering faith had been justified to him, and that beyond the reach of sorrow or pain, our Christian soldier was marching on.

THE MEMORIAL AMPHITHEATER IN BEAUTIFUL ARLINGTON NATIONAL CEMETERY, NEAR WHICH MR. BRYAN LIES AT REST

Photo, Underwood & Underwood, Washington

CHAPTER XX

CONCLUSION

WHEN a biography is finished and the subject has been followed to his grave, in most cases the work is complete. This is particularly true of one whose life has been devoted to a single purpose. Narration of the life of one who gave his entire time to mechanical invention, to electricity, to chemistry, or similar interests carries its evident conclusions. One sees from afar the ruling purpose, the later course, and the place in history. But when a man has been identified with many differing lines of work, the task of estimating him is more complex, and it seems necessary to draw together the separate threads and weave them into one strand.

What is it that has caused this man to be so widely known, so greatly loved, and so ardently hated? What quality in the man caused his influence, unaided by any official position, to extend far beyond the confines of his own country and called forth at his death, expressions of sorrow from all parts of the world, even from such distant lands as Persia, South Africa, and India?

Wayne C. Williams has recently published an admirable epitome of Mr. Bryan's public services, and, in conclusion, he has ventured to designate the place which Mr. Bryan should hold in history. I quote this summary of his achievement, knowing well its accuracy, and I quote also the eulogy, hoping that a wife may endorse praise where she could not with propriety express it:

"What gave Mr. Bryan the title of the greatest liberal and progressive leader in America? What made him the unmatched popular orator, the refuge and champion of the oppressed? Great as was his elo-

493

quence—and it was unsurpassed in this or probably in
any generation—yet this did not account for the Bryan
who has just left us. It was his deep sincerity of conviction and his courageous, constructive advocacy of great
principles that made him the real leader of progressivism
in this generation.

"Look at the record: Began his fight for popular
election of Senators in 1890, when he stood almost
alone. Kept it up until he wrote it into all his party
platforms and saw two amendments to the Constitution of the United States ratified. The first leader of
national prominence to come out for national prohibition and stuck to it, even when it was unpopular, until
he saw the Eighteenth Amendment written into the
Constitution; fought for Woman's Suffrage until he
saw it, too, written into the Constitution. Here is
achievement enough for one life. But this is not the
whole record by any means. Bryan's thirty peace
treaties negotiated while he was Secretary of State are
a powerful factor in the peace of the world. His work
for peace has counted in every land on the globe. He
was a champion of democracy, of the plain people, of
their right to determine their own policies. He spoke
for democracy in Russia and India and under nearly
every flag. He took up the cause of the Filipinos when
the whole country was wild for annexation and imperialism. He lived to see his party endorse his principles
and his pledge of free government for the Islands translated into law.

"But the record is not yet complete. Bryan cham-
pioned the right of labor. He fought for the toiling
masses against every species of injustice and wrong.
He stood for shorter hours, the right of trial by jury in
contempt cases (indeed, he was the real author of that
reform); he was the sole author of the law compelling
publicity of campaign expenditures. To him alone

CONCLUSION

belongs the credit for that great reform. Without him the Federal Reserve Act could not have been passed in the Wilson Administration. He fought to lower the tariff, to make wealth pay its share of the burdens of government. He proclaimed the only constructive anti-trust law remedy every proposed—a remedy that is fast coming to receive universal approval in America.

"He alone made the first nomination of Woodrow Wilson possible. He stood like a rock for prohibition when the wet Democratic leaders at New York would have repudiated the Eighteenth Amendment.

"And even this is only a partial list of the Bryan achievements. It is wonderful to see how his views have been vindicated by the passing of time. Abused and reviled as no public man has been in our time, he smilingly waved it all aside and triumphed over every bitter foe. He kept sweet in spirit to the end. What more can be said of any public man?

"Bryan was the John Bright and the Gladstone of American politics."

While one reads here a condensed record of his work, the compelling power in his life is not revealed. Looking back over our record, is it not true that through his youth, through his middle life, and through his declining years, there ran a clearly defined force which has given him strength and patience to walk his way? A deep love for his fellow man; a sympathetic interest in his fortunes; an understanding of his needs; an anxious wish to foster and to serve—these explain his course.

Some have questioned his wisdom; some have ridiculed his methods, but the common human heart understood his efforts and gave response.

"He was my friend."

495

CHAPTER XXI

SOME SELECTIONS FROM HIS SPEECHES

NO review of Mr. Bryan's life would be complete without the addition of certain passages from his speeches which may convey an impression of the form in which he presented his ideas to his audiences.

I have made these selections because I believe they will convey, in so far as printed words can convey, the simplicity of his expression. The first quotation is from his valedictory oration at Illinois College, where as a youth of twenty-one he took leave of his alma mater—with this exception the speeches represent his maturer years.

"We launch our vessels upon the uncertain sea of life alone, yet not alone, for around us are friends who anxiously and prayerfully watch our course. They will rejoice if we arrive safely at our respective havens, or weep with bitter tears, if one by one, our weather-beaten barks are lost forever in the surges of the deep.

"We have esteemed each other, loved each other, and now must from each other part. God grant that we may all so live as to meet in the better world, where parting is unknown.

"Halls of learning, fond Alma Mater, farewell. We turn to take one 'last, long, lingering look' at thy receding walls. We leave thee now to be ushered out into the varied duties of active life.

"However high our names may be inscribed upon the gilded scroll of fame, to thee we all honor give, to thee all praises bring. And when, in after years, we're wearied by the bustle of a busy world, our hearts will often long to turn and seek repose beneath thy sheltering shade."

496

"When God made man He gave him a soul and warned him that in the next world he would be held accountable for the deeds done in the flesh; but when man created the corporation he could not endow that corporation with a soul, so that if it escapes punishment here it need not fear the hereafter. And this man-made giant has been put forth to compete with the God-made man. We must assume that man in creating the corporation had in view the welfare of society, and the people who create must retain the power to restrict and to control. We can never become so enthusiastic over the corporation, over its usefulness, over its possibilities, as to forget the God-made man who was here first and who still remains a factor to be considered."

During Mr. Bryan's candidacy for President in 1900 the paramount political issue was "Imperialism." Against the attempt to add colonial dependencies to our republic Mr. Bryan threw himself with all the vehement force of his eloquence; and his definition of the ideal republic, delivered at that time, became one of the best known of his utterances.

"I can conceive of a national destiny surpassing the glories of the present and the past—a destiny which meets the responsibilities of today and measures up to the possibilities of the future.

"Behold a republic, resting securely upon the foundation stones quarried by revolutionary patriots from the mountain of eternal truth—a republic applying in practice and proclaiming to the world the self-evident propositions that all men are created equal; that they are endowed by their Creator with inalienable rights; that governments are instituted among men to secure these rights and that governments derive their just powers from the consent of the governed.

"Behold a republic in which civil and religious

help us, we reply that, instead of having a gold standard because England has, we will restore bimetallism, and then let England have bimetallism because the United States has it. If they dare to come out into the open field and defend the gold standard as a good thing, we will fight them to the uttermost. Having behind us the producing masses of this nation and the world, supported by the commercial interests, the laboring interests, and the toilers everywhere, we will answer their demand for a gold standard by saying to them: 'You shall not press down upon the brow of labor this crown of thorns, you shall not crucify mankind upon a cross of gold.' "

The great corporations of the country looked upon Mr. Bryan as a "dangerous man," but he was never an enemy to wealth honestly acquired. He insisted, however, on exalting the man above the dollar.

Following is a quotation from his speech before the Chicago Association of Commerce:

"There are many differences between the natural man and the corporate man. There is a difference in the purpose of creation. God made man and placed him upon His footstool to carry out a divine decree; man created the corporation as a money-making machine. When God made man He did not make the tallest man much taller than the shortest; and He did not make the strongest man much stronger than the weakest; but when the law creates the corporate person that person may be an hundred, a thousand, ten thousand, a million times stronger than the God-made man. When God made man He set a limit to his existence, so that if he was a bad man he could not be bad long; but when the corporation was created the limit on age was raised, and it sometimes projects itself through generation after generation.

In connection with the phrases quoted above there occurred an incident which, though it must have been embarrassing to the young Congressman, was a source of amused reminiscence to Mr. Bryan in after years. It was during this speech that Mr. Bryan made one of his very few lapses linguæ.

I have recorded the passage as Mr. Bryan intended to deliver it. He actually made, in ringing tones, the assertion that "he put *ears* in the wax of his sailors!" This error did not, however, mar the total effect of his first important speech in Congress.

In Chapter VI, Part One, Mr. Bryan quotes his definition of a "business man" as given in the famous speech which brought him his first nomination for the Presidency in 1896.

But the part of this speech which attracted wider attention and which was more frequently quoted was his closing paragraph:

"My friends, we declare that this nation is able to legislate for its own people on every question, without awaiting for the aid or consent of any other nation on earth; and upon that issue we expect to carry every state in the Union. I shall not slander the inhabitants of the fair state of Massachusetts nor the inhabitants of the state of New York by saying that, when they are confronted with the proposition, they will declare that this nation is not able to attend to its own business. It is the issue of 1776 over again. Our ancestors, when but three millions in number, had the courage to declare their political independence of every other nation; shall we, their descendants, when we have grown to seventy millions, declare that we are less independent than our forefathers? No, my friends, that will never be the verdict of our people. Therefore, we care not upon what lines the battle is fought. If they say bimetallism is good, but that we can not have it until other nations

SELECTIONS FROM HIS SPEECHES

Mr. Bryan first attracted attention in Congress when, in 1892, he delivered a speech on the tariff. The Republicans had impressed on the country the importance of protecting "home industries," meaning the manufactories, but Mr. Bryan insisted that there was a yet more important "home industry" which had a prior right to protection.

"When some young man selects a young woman who is willing to trust her future to his strong right arm; when they start to build a little home, that home which is the unit of society and upon which our government and our prosperity must rest; when they start to build this home, and the man who sells the lumber reaches out his hand to collect a tariff upon it; the men who furnish the carpets, table-cloths, knives, forks, dishes, furniture, spoons, everything that enters into the construction and operation of that home—when all these stretch out their hands, I say, from every direction to lay their blighting weight upon that cottage, the Democratic party says, 'Hands off, and let that home industry live.' It is protecting the grandest home industry that this or any other nation ever had."

.   .   .   .

"It is said that when Ulysses was approaching the island of the Sirens, warned beforehand of their seductive notes, he put wax in the ears of his sailors and then strapped himself to the mast of the ship, so that, hearing, he could not heed. So our friends upon the other side (the Republicans) tell us that there is depression in agriculture, and a cry has come up from the people; but the leaders of your party have, as it were, filled with wax the ears of their associates, and then have so tied themselves to the protected interests, by promises made before election, that, hearing, they can not heed."

JUSTICE SHOULD BE DONE   JUSTICE MUST BE DONE   JUSTICE SHALL BE DONE

Mr. Bryan in action.

SELECTIONS FROM HIS SPEECHES

liberty stimulate all to earnest endeavor and in which the law restrains every hand uplifted for a neighbor's injury—a republic in which every citizen is a sovereign, but in which no one cares or dares to wear a crown.

"Behold a republic standing erect while empires all around are bowed beneath the weight of their own armaments—a republic whose flag is loved while other flags are only feared.

"Behold a republic increasing in population, in wealth, in strength and in influence, solving the problems of civilization and hastening the coming of an universal brotherhood—a republic which shakes thrones and dissolves aristocracies by its silent example and gives light and inspiration to those that sit in darkness.

"Behold a republic gradually but surely becoming the supreme moral factor in the world's progress and the accepted arbiter of the world's disputes—a republic whose history, like the path of the just, 'is as the shining light that shineth more and more unto the perfect day.'"

In another speech of that period he cites the teachings of Christ as an argument against "Imperialism":

"If true Christianity consists in carrying out in our daily lives the teachings of Christ, who will say that we are commanded to civilize with dynamite and proselyte with the sword? He who would declare the divine will must prove his authority either by Holy Writ or by evidence of a special dispensation.

"Imperialism finds no warrant in the Bible. The command, 'Go ye into all the world and preach the gospel to every creature,' has no gatling gun attachment. When Jesus visited a village of Samaria and the people refused to receive him, some of the disciples suggested that fire should be called down from Heaven to avenge the insult; but the Master rebuked them and said: 'Ye

501

know not what manner of spirit ye are of; for the Son of man is not come to destroy men's lives, but to save them.' Suppose he had said: 'We will thrash them until they understand who we are,' how different would have been the history of Christianity! Compare, if you will, the swaggering, bullying, brutal doctrine of imperialism with the Golden Rule and the commandment, 'Thou shalt love thy neighbor as thyself.'

"Love, not force, was the weapon of the Nazarene; sacrifice for others, not the exploitation of them, was His method of reaching the human heart. A missionary recently told me that the Stars and Stripes once saved his life because his assailant recognized our flag as a flag that had no blood upon it."

When the advocates of Imperialism had failed in every other argument they fell back on "destiny" as the justification for denying the right of self-government to the Philippines. To this argument Mr. Bryan replied:

"History is replete with predictions which once wore the hue of destiny, but which failed of fulfilment because those who uttered them saw too small an arc of the circle of events. When Pharaoh pursued the fleeing Israelites to the edge of the Red Sea he was confident that their bondage would be renewed and that they would again make bricks without straw, but destiny was not revealed until Moses and his followers reached the farther shore dry shod and the waves rolled over the horses and chariots of the Egyptians.

"When Belshazzar, on the last night of his reign, led his thousand lords into the Babylonian banquet hall and sat down to a table glittering with vessels of silver and gold, he felt sure of his kingdom for many years to come, but destiny was not revealed until the hand wrote upon the wall those awe-inspiring words, 'Mene, Mene, Tekel, Upharsin.'

SELECTIONS FROM HIS SPEECHES

"When Abderrahman swept northward with his conquering hosts his imagination saw the Crescent triumphant throughout the world, but destiny was not revealed until Charles Martel raised the cross above the battlefield of Tours and saved Europe from the sword of Mohammedanism.

"When Napoleon emerged victorious from Marengo, from Ulm and from Austerlitz, he thought himself the child of destiny, but destiny was not revealed until Blücher's forces joined the army of Wellington and the vanquished Corsican began his melancholy march toward St. Helena.

"When the redcoats of George the Third routed the New Englanders at Lexington and Bunker Hill there arose before the British sovereign visions of colonies taxed without representation and drained of their wealth by foreign made laws, but destiny was not revealed until the surrender of Cornwallis completed the work begun at Independence Hall, and ushered into existence a government deriving its just powers from the consent of the governed."

His apostrophe to Moses occurred in the course of a speech on Imperialism:

"Shame upon a logic which locks up the petty offender and enthrones grand larceny. Have the people returned to the worship of the Golden Calf? Have they made unto themselves a new commandment consistent with the spirit of conquest and lust for empire? Is 'thou shalt not steal upon a small scale' to be substituted for the law of Moses?

"Awake, O ancient law giver, awake! Break forth from thine unmarked sepulchre and speed thee back to cloud-crowned Sinai; commune once more with the God of our fathers and proclaim again the words engraven upon the tables of stone—the law that was, the law that is today—the law that neither individual nor nation can violate with impunity!"

In his speech at the inauguration of the first President of Cuba in 1902 Mr. Bryan said:

"Let me borrow a story which has been used to illustrate the position of the United States: A man wended his way through the streets of a great city. Unmindful of the merchandise exposed on every hand he sought out a store where birds were kept for sale. Purchasing bird after bird he opened the cages and allowed the feathered songsters to fly away. When asked why he thus squandered his money, he replied: 'I was once a captive myself, and I find pleasure in setting even a bird at liberty.'

"The United States once went through the struggle from which you have just emerged; the American people once by the aid of a friendly power won a victory similar to that which you are now celebrating, and our people find gratification in helping to open the door that barred your way to the exercise of your political rights.

"I have come to witness the lowering of our flag and the raising of the flag of the Cuban republic; but the event will bring no humiliation to the people of my country, for it is better that the Stars and Stripes should be indelibly impressed upon your hearts than that they should float above your heads."

The following passage is taken from Mr. Bryan's speech at the Democratic National Convention in St. Louis in 1904:

"Eight years ago a Democratic national convention placed in my hand the standard of the party and commissioned me as its candidate. Four years later that commission was renewed. I come tonight to this demo-

"How like a human life! Man, flung into existence without his volition, bearing the race-mark of his parents, carrying the impress of their lives to the day of his death, hedged about by an environment that shapes and molds him before he is old enough to plan or choose, how these constrain and hem him in! And yet he, too, leaves his mark upon all that he touches as he travels, in obedience to his sense of duty, the path that leads from the cradle to the grave. But here the likeness ends. The Colorado, pure and clear in the mountains, becomes a dark and muddy flood before it reaches the ocean, so contaminated is it by soil through which it passes; but man, if controlled by a noble purpose and inspired by high ideals, may purify, rather than be polluted by, his surroundings, and by resistance to temptation make the latter end of his life more beautiful even than the beginning.

"The river also teaches a sublime lesson of patience. It has taken ages for it to do its work, and in that work every drop of water has played its part. It takes time for individuals or groups of individuals to accomplish a great work and because time is required those who labor in behalf of their fellows sometimes become discouraged. Nature teaches us to labor and to wait. Viewed from day to day the progress of the race is imperceptible; viewed from year to year, it can scarcely be noted, but viewed by decades or centuries the upward trend is apparent, and every good work and word and thought contributes toward the final result. As nothing is lost in the economy of nature, so nothing is lost in the social and moral world. As the stream is composed of an innumerable number of rivulets, each making its little offering and each necessary to make up the whole, so the innumerable number of men and women who recognize their duty to society and their obligations to their fellows are contributing according to their strength

SELECTIONS FROM HIS SPEECHES

Always a lover of Nature, Mr. Bryan drew inspiration from the vast handiwork of God. The following thoughts were evoked by a sunrise seen from Darjeeling, India:

"How puny seem the works of man when brought into comparison with majestic nature! His groves, what pigmies when measured against the virgin forest! His noblest temples, how insignificant when contrasted with the masonry of the hills! What canvas can imitate the dawn and sunset! What inlaid work can match the mosaics of the mountains!

"Is it blind chance that gives these glimpses of the sublime? And was it blind chance that clustered vast reservoirs about inaccessible summits and stored water to refresh the thirsty plains through hidden veins and surface streams?

"No wonder man from the beginning of history has turned to the heights for inspiration, for here is the spirit awed by the infinite and here one sees both the mystery of creation and the manifestations of the Father's loving-kindness. Here man finds a witness, unimpeachable though silent, to the omnipotence, the omniscience and the goodness of God."

Referring to the Grand Canyon of the Colorado, Mr. Bryan said:

"There are 'sermons in stones,' and the stones of this canyon preach many impressive ones. They not only testify to the omnipotence of the Creator but they record the story of a stream which both molds and is molded by, its environment. It can not escape from the walls of its prison and yet it has made its impress upon the granite as, in obedience to the law of gravitation, it has gone dashing and foaming on its path to the sea.

"The strongest argument in favor of woman suffrage is the mother argument. I love my children—as much, I think, as a father can; but I am not in the same class with my wife. I do not put any father in the same class with the mother in love for the child. If you would know why the mother's love for a child is the sweetest, tenderest, most lasting thing in the world, you will find the explanation in the Bible: 'Where your treasure is, there will your heart be also.'

"The child is the treasure of the mother; she invests her life in her child. When the mother of the Gracchi was asked: 'Where are your jewels?' she pointed to her sons. The mother's life trembles in the balance at the child's birth, and for years it is the object of constant care. She expends upon it her nervous force and energy; she endows it with the wealth of her love. She dreams of what it is to do and be—and, O, if a mother's dreams only came true, what a different world this would be! The most pathetic struggle that this earth knows is not the struggle between armed men upon the battlefield; it is the struggle of a mother to save her child when wicked men set traps for it and lay snares for it. And as long as the ballot is given to those who conspire to rob the home of a child it is not fair—no one can believe it fair—to tie a mother's hands while she is trying to protect her home and save her child. If there is such a thing as justice, surely a mother has a just claim to a voice in shaping the environment that may determine whether her child will realize her hopes or bring her gray hairs in sorrow to the grave.

"Because God has planted in every human heart a sense of justice, and because the mother argument makes an irresistible appeal to this universal sense, it will finally batter down all opposition and open woman's pathway to the polls."

cratic national convention to return the commission. You may dispute whether I have fought a good fight, you may dispute whether I have finished my course, but you cannot deny that I have kept the faith."

In this selection from his lecture on "America's Mission" Mr. Bryan gives again his ideal of American civilization:

"Standing upon the vantage ground already gained, the American people can aspire to a grander destiny than has opened before any other race.

"Anglo-Saxon civilization has taught the individual to protect his own rights; American civilization will teach him to respect the rights of others.

"Anglo-Saxon civilization has taught the individual to take care of himself; American civilization, proclaiming the equality of all before the law, will teach him that his own highest good requires the observance of the commandment: 'Thou shalt love thy neighbor as thyself.'

"Anglo-Saxon civilization has, by force of arms, applied the art of government to other races for the benefit of Anglo-Saxons; American civilization will, by the influence of example, excite in other races a desire for self-government and a determination to secure it.

"Anglo-Saxon civilization has carried its flag to every clime and defended it with forts and garrisons; American civilization will imprint its flag upon the hearts of all who long for freedom.

" 'To American civilization, all hail!
Time's noblest offspring is the last.' "

Mr. Bryan rendered yeomen service to the cause of woman suffrage, and the following argument is quoted from his speech at the Washington banquet in 1916:

505

LAST PHOTOGRAPH OF WILLIAM JENNINGS BRYAN TAKEN ON
THE MORNING OF HIS DEATH

to the sum total of the forces that make for righteousness and progress."

While reference to Nature's great wonders found place in his public utterances, Mr. Bryan also drew upon the humble vegetable to carry his messages to an audience. In his lecture, "The Value of an Ideal," he discusses the radish as follows:

"Did you ever raise a radish? You put a small black seed into the black soil and in a little while you return to the garden and find the full-grown radish. The top is green, the body white and almost transparent, and the skin a delicate red or pink. What mysterious power reaches out and gathers from the ground the particles which give it form and size and flavor? Whose is the invisible brush that transfers to the root, growing in darkness, the hues of the summer sunset? If we were to refuse to eat anything until we could understand the mystery of its creation we would die of starvation—but mystery, it seems, never bothers us in the dining room; it is only in the Church that it causes us to hesitate."

In his lecture, "The Prince of Peace," he made use of the melon for his illustration:

"I was eating a piece of watermelon some months ago and was struck with its beauty. I took some of the seeds and dried them and weighed them and found that it would require some five thousand seeds to weigh a pound; and then I applied mathematics to that forty-pound melon. One of these seeds, put into the ground, when warmed by the sun and moistened by the rain, takes off its coat and goes to work; it gathers from somewhere two hundred thousand times its own weight, and, forcing this raw material through a tiny stem, constructs a watermelon. It ornaments the outside with a covering of green; inside the green it puts a layer of white, and within the white a core of red, and all through the red it scatters seeds, each one capable of continuing the work of reproduction. What architect drew the plan? Where does the little seed get its tremendous power? Where does it find its coloring matter? How does it collect its flavoring extract? How does it build a watermelon? Until you can explain a watermelon, do not be too sure that you can set limits to the power of the Almighty or say just what He can do or how He would do it. I cannot explain the watermelon, but I eat it and enjoy it."

The following passages from the same speech, touching the subjects of Immortality and the Resurrection are perhaps most widely quoted and loved:

IMMORTALITY

"If the Father deigns to touch with divine power the cold and pulseless heart of the buried acorn and to make it burst forth from its prison walls, will He leave neglected in the earth the soul of man, made in the image of his Creator? If He stoops to give to the rose bush, whose withered blossoms float upon the autumn breeze, the sweet assurance of another springtime, will He refuse the words of hope to the sons of men when the frosts of winter come? If matter, mute and inanimate, though changed by the forces of nature into a multitude of forms, can never die, will the imperial spirit of man suffer annihilation when it has paid a brief visit like a royal guest to this tenement of clay? No, I am sure that He who, notwithstanding His apparent prodigality, created nothing without a purpose, and wasted not a single atom in all His creation, has made provision for a future life in which man's universal longing for immortality will find its realization. I am as sure that we live again as I am sure that we live today."

THE RESURRECTION

"In Cairo I secured a few grains of wheat that had slumbered for more than thirty centuries in an Egyptian tomb. As I looked at them this thought came into my mind: If one of those grains had been planted on the banks of the Nile the year after it grew, and all its lineal descendants had been planted and replanted from that time until now, its progeny would today be sufficiently numerous to feed the teeming millions of the world. An unbroken chain of life connects the earliest grains of wheat with the grains that we sow and reap. There is in the grain of wheat an invisible something which has the power to discard the body that we see, and from earth and air fashion a new body so much like the old one that we can not tell the one from the other. If this invisible germ of life in the grain of wheat can thus pass unimpaired through three thousand resurrections, I shall not doubt that my soul has power to clothe itself with a body suited to its new existence when this earthly frame has crumbled into dust."

In 1912 Mr. Bryan delivered at the Baltimore Convention the following tribute to Democracy in his speech on the chairmanship:

"The Democratic party has led this fight until it has stimulated a host of republicans to action. I will not say they have acted as they have because we acted first; I will say that at a later hour than we, they caught the spirit of the times and are now willing to trust the people with the control of their own government.

"We have been traveling in the wilderness; we now

come in sight of the promised land. During all the weary hours of darkness progressive democracy has been the people's pillar of fire by night; I pray you, delegates, now that the dawn has come, do not rob it of its well-earned right to be the people's pillar of cloud by day."

In his Thanksgiving address in London Mr. Bryan spoke on the international ideal as follows:

"The world is coming to understand that armies and navies, however numerous and strong, are impotent to stop thought. Thought inspired by love will yet rule the world. I am glad that there is a national product more valuable than gold or silver, more valuable than cotton or wheat or corn or iron—an ideal. That is merchandise—if I may call it such—that moves freely from country to country. You can not vex it with an export tax or hinder it with an import tariff. It is greater than legislators, and rises triumphant over the machinery of government. In the rivalry to present the best ideal to the world, love, not hatred, will control; and I am glad that on this Thanksgiving Day I can meet my countrymen and their friends here assembled, return thanks for what my country has received, thanks for the progress that the world has made, and contemplate with joy the coming of that day when the rivalry between nations will be, not to see which can injure the other most, but to show which can hold highest the light that guides the footsteps of the human race to higher ground.

This passage on "The Bible" is quoted from Mr. Bryan's lecture, "The Making of a Man."

"To the young man who is building character I present the Bible as a book that is useful always and

everywhere.   It guides the footsteps of the young; it
throws a light upon the pathway during the mature
years, and it is the only book that one cares to have
beside him when the darkness gathers and he knows that
the end is near.   Then he finds consolation in the promises of the Book of Books and his lips repeat, even when
his words are inaudible, 'Yea, though I walk through
the valley of the shadow of death, I shall fear no evil;
for thou art with me; thy rod and thy staff they comfort me,' or 'I go to prepare a place for you,' 'that where
I am, there ye may be also.' "

The following passage is taken from the lecture which
Mr. Bryan called "The Fruits of the Tree."

"Example is the means of propagating truth.
"What bloodshed might have been avoided; what
slaughter might have been prevented, if all who bore
the name of Christian had been willing to trust to the
life for the evangelization of the world, instead of resort-
ing to the sword!
"It is a slow process, this winning of converts by
example, but it is the sure way—it is Christ's way.   A
speech may be disputed; even a sermon may not convince, but no one has yet lived who could answer a
Christian life; it is the unanswerable argument in support
of the Christian religion."

This quotation from his speech on Sam Houston expressed the underlying principle of Mr. Bryan's own political
philosophy.

"With the orator and the statesman, however,
breadth of sympathy is indispensable.   We labor for
those whom we love; no other motive is sufficient to
direct a large life and nothing begets love but love itself.

WILLIAM JENNINGS BRYAN

'They love him because he first loved them' can be said of all who have been loved by the people. Only when orators and statesmen devote themselves unselfishly to the welfare of the whole people do they link themselves to those eternal forces which give assurance of permanent progress. They enter into partnership with nature, as it were, and grow with the cause which they aid."

APPENDIX

THE DENVER CONVENTION

[Telegrams sent by Mr. Bryan to his brother, Charles W. Bryan, during the Denver Convention, 1908.]

Gentlemen of the Convention:

More than two-thirds of the members of this convention have been either instructed to vote for my nomination or have been openly pledged to my nomination before being selected as delegates. On the fifth of March last, the Nebraska state convention adopted a platform which contained the plank which the minority proposes as a substitute. This platform was printed throughout the United States and it was generally understood, being so represented by Republican and Democratic papers, that it represented my views on the subjects covered. Only three conventions, if I am correctly informed, were held before the fifth of March, the conventions of Wisconsin, Oklahoma and Kansas. I had been advocating for more than twelve years the remedies outlined in the substitute. The idea was presented in the platform of 1900, which was endorsed by more than six millions of Democrats. And I have a right to assume that the Democratic voters who sent you as delegates to this convention, were fully informed as to my position on the trust question. The committee has given the convention a splendid platform on other questions, but I regard the plank on this question as not sufficiently strong, and as not a full response to public sentiment. Believing that it will mean a loss of hundreds of thousands of votes to the ticket if the convention shows any timidity in dealing with this question, I am constrained to make this appeal to the convention for an anti-trust plank upon which I can make an honest fight in behalf of the whole people. If the convention votes down this substitute, I shall at least have placed myself upon record and given to the public assurance that I have not faltered and shall not falter in my effort to rid this country of the evils that have grown up under industrial monopolies. Having made this appeal, I await the judgment of the convention.

WILLIAM JENNINGS BRYAN.

———

To C. W. Bryan: I appreciate very much the opinion of Haskell, Williams and the other friends, but I think a failure to put in a

515

strong trust plank will lose me a million votes. I will ask, therefore, that they allow the platform to be adopted with the exception of the trust plank, and that those who are willing to do so will join in a minority report substituting the Nebraska anti-trust plank for the one proposed by the committee. I will submit a brief statement of my reasons for asking that it be substituted for the committee plank and then leave the convention to vote on a roll call. If they vote me down it will at least protect me, and those who vote it down can take the responsibility when they go home. I do not intend to be a party to the surrender which is proposed.

W. J.

To C. W. Bryan: No. That plank is not sufficient. I want a trust plank that we can make a fight on and shall insist upon a provision which will make it impossible for one corporation to control more than a certain per cent of the total product. I prefer to state it at fifty per cent but will not object at sixty-five, but there must be some per cent and I think there ought to be a lower proportion, say twenty-five to forty per cent, when they come under federal supervision; the word "wholesome" before the word "competition" is objectionable. It contains the same idea that Taft expressed when he suggested that only unreasonable restraint of trade should be condemned. Our friends are at liberty to say that I object to this plank as not strong enough and that I am not willing to have the party put in the position of being frightened by these monopolies. They have scared the Republican Party. They ought not be permitted to scare ours. If necessary make the fight in the convention.

W. J.

MR. BRYAN OPPOSES PARKER FOR TEMPORARY CHAIRMAN AT BALTIMORE CONVENTION

(From the Official Proceedings of the Democratic National Convention, 1912, page 3)

Mr. William Jennings Bryan, of Nebraska: Mr. Chairman and gentlemen of the Convention, I rise to place in nomination for the office of temporary chairman of this convention the name of Hon. John W. Kern, of Indiana. [Applause.] And in thus dissenting from the judgment of our National Committee as expressed in its recommendation, I recognize that the burden of

APPENDIX

proof is upon me to overthrow the assumption that the committee can claim that it is representing the wishes of this Convention and of the party in the nation. [Applause.] I call your attention to the fact that our rules provide that the recommendation of the committee is not final. I remind you that the very fact that this Convention has the right to accept or reject that recommendation is conclusive proof that the presumption in favor of this convention is a higher presumption than that in favor of the wisdom of the committee. [Applause.]

If any of you ask me for my credentials, if any of you inquire why I, a mere delegate to this Convention from one of the smaller states, should presume to present a name and ask you to accept it in place of the name they presented, I beg to tell you, if it needs to be told, that in three campaigns I have been the champion of the Democratic party's principles, and that in three campaigns I have received the vote of six millions and a half of Democrats. [Applause.] If that is not proof that I have the confidence of the party of this nation, I shall not attempt to furnish proof. I remind you that confidence reposed in a human being carries with it certain responsibilities, and I would not be worthy of the confidence and the affection that have been showered upon me by the Democrats of this nation if I were not willing to risk humiliation in their defense.

I recognize that a man can not carry on a political warfare in defense of the mass of the people for sixteen years without making enemies, and I recognize that there has been no day since the day I was nominated in Chicago when these enemies have not been industrious in their efforts to attack me from every standpoint. The fact that I have lived is proof that I have not deserted the people. If for a moment I had forgotten them, they would not have remembered me.

I take for my text this morning the text that the committee has been kind enough to place upon the wall for my use. He "never sold the truth to serve the hour." That is the language of the hero of Monticello, and I would not be worthy of the support I have received if I were willing to sell the truth to serve the present hour.

We are told by those who support the Committee's recommendation that it is disturbing harmony to oppose their conclusions. Let me free myself from any criticism that any one may have made heretofore or may attempt hereafter. Is there any other delegate in this body of more than ten hundred who tried earlier than I to secure harmony in this Convention? I began several weeks ago. I announced to the sub-committee that I would not be a candidate for Temporary Chairman. I might have asked without presumption that at the end of sixteen years of battle, when I find the things I have fought for not only triumphant in my own party but even in the Republican party, the modest honor of standing before this Convention and voicing the rejoicing of my party. [Applause.] But I was more interested in harmony than I was in the chance to speak to this Convention. Not only that, but I advised this Committee to consult the two leading candidates, the men who together have nearly two-thirds of this Convention instructed for them, and get their approval of some man's nomination, that there might be no contest in this Convention. [Applause.] My friends, what suggestion could I have then made more in the interest of harmony than to ask this Committee to allow two-thirds of this Convention a voice in the selection of its temporary chairman?

In the discussion before the sub-committee the friends of Mr. Clark and the friends of Mr. Wilson were not able to agree; one supported Mr. James and the other supported Mr. Henry; but in the full committee last night the friends of Mr. Wilson joined the friends of Mr. Clark in the support of Mr. James, Mr. Clark's choice, and yet the Committee turned down the joint request thus made.

I submit to you that the plan that I followed was the plan for the securing of harmony; and that the plan which the Committee followed was not designed to secure harmony. [Applause.]

Let me for a moment present the qualifications of one fitted for this position. This is no ordinary occasion. This is an epoch-making Convention. We have had such a struggle as was never seen in politics before. I have been in the center of this fight, and I know something of the courage that it has brought forth, and something of the sacrifice that has been required. I know that men working upon the railroad for small wages, with but little laid up for their retiring years, have defied the railroad managers and helped us in this progressive fight at the risk of having their bread and butter taken from them. I have known men engaged in business and carrying loans at banks who have been threatened with bankruptcy if they did not sell their citizenship, and yet I have seen them, defying these men, walk up and vote on the side of the struggling masses against predatory wealth. [Applause.] I have seen lawyers risking their future,

518

APPENDIX

alienating men of large business, in order to be the champions of the poor. I have seen this struggle go on. I have seen men who had never made a speech before go out and devote weeks of time to public speaking, because their hearts were stirred. It seems to me that now, when the hour of triumph comes, the song of victory should be sung by one whose heart has been in the fight.

John W. Kern has been faithful every day in those sixteen years. It has cost him time, it has cost him money, and it has cost him the wear of his body and his mind. He has been free always with all that he had; and four years ago, when the foundation was laid for the present victory, it was John W. Kern who stood by my side when we took the last stronghold of the enemy. It was John W. Kern who stood with me and helped to bring into the campaign the idea of publicity before the election, that has now swept the country, until even the Republican party was compelled by public opinion to give it unanimous endorsement only a few weeks ago. [Applause.] It was John W. Kern who stood with me on the Denver platform that demanded the election of Senators by direct vote of the people, when a Republican National Convention had turned it down by a vote of seven to one; and now he is in the United States Senate, where he can make a Senator look as big as a Senator ought to look to the American people. [Applause.] He helped in the fight for the Amendment authorizing an income tax, and he has lived to see a President who was opposed to us take that plank out of our platform and put it through Senate and House, and thirty-four States of the Union have ratified it; and now he is leading the fight in the United States Senate to purge that body of Senator Lorimer, who typifies the supremacy of corruption in politics. [Applause.]

What better man could we have to open a convention? I repeat, what better man could we find to represent the militant spirit of democracy? [Applause.] My friends, when I come to contrast him with the candidate presented by the Committee, I can do it without impeaching his character or his good intent.

But, my friends, not every man of high character or good intent is a fit man to sound the keynote of a progressive campaign. There are seven million Republicans in this country, or were at the time of the last election, and I have never doubted that the vast majority of them were men of high character and good intent, but we would not invite one of them to be Temporary Chairman of our Convention. We have a great many Democrats who vote

519

the ticket who are not in full sympathy with the purposes of the party. I not only voted the ticket, but I made speeches for the candidate when I was not at all satisfied with either the candidate or the influences that nominated him and directed the campaign of 1904. [Applause.] And I assume that no friend of Judge Parker will contend that he was entirely satisfied in 1908 with either the candidate or all of the plans and purposes of our party.

I remind you that this is not a question where personal ambitions or personal compliments or the pleasant things are uppermost. We are writing history today, and this Convention is to announce to the country whether it will take up the challenge thrown down at Chicago by a Convention controlled by predatory wealth, or answer it by putting ourselves under the same control and giving the people no party to represent them. [Applause.]

We need not deceive ourselves that that which is done in a National Convention is done in secret. If every member of this Convention entered into an agreement of secrecy we would still act under the eyes of the representatives of the press, who know not only what we do, but why we do it, and who told us to do it. [Applause.] And the delegates of this Convention must not presume upon the ignorance of those people who did not come, either because they had not influence enough to be elected delegates or money enough to pay the expenses of the trip, but who have as much interest in the party's welfare as we who speak for them today. [Applause.] Those people will know that the influences which dominated the Convention at Chicago and made its conclusion a farce before the country are here and are more brazenly at work than they were at Chicago. [Applause.]

I appeal to you: Let the commencement of this Convention be such a commencement that the Democrats of this country may raise their heads among their fellows and say, "The Democratic party is true to the people. You can not frighten it with your Ryans nor buy it with your Belmonts." [Applause.]

My friends, if the candidate selected by the Committee were an unknown man we would judge him by the forces that are back of him, and not by you gentlemen who may try to convince yourselves that you owe it to the Committee to sustain its action even though you believe it a mistake.

That, my friends, is not the question. We know who the candidate is as well as the men behind him. We know that he is the man chosen eight years ago when the Democratic party, beaten in two campaigns, decided it was worth while to try to

APPENDIX

win a campaign under the leadership of those who had defeated us in the campaigns before. The country has not forgotten that that Convention was influenced to its act by the promise of large campaign funds from Wall Street, and it has not forgotten the fact that after the corporation management of that campaign had alienated the rank and file of the party, Wall Street threw the party down and elected the other man. [Applause.] It has not forgotten that when the votes were counted we had a million and a quarter less votes than we had in the two campaigns before, and a million and a quarter less than we had in the election four years afterward. It has not forgotten that it is the same man backed by the same influence that is to be forced on this Convention to open a progressive campaign with a paralyzing speech that will dishearten every man in it. [Applause.]

You ask me how I know without reading it that that speech would not be satisfactory. Let me tell you; a speech is not so many words; it is the man and not the words that makes the speech.

We have been passing through a great educational age, and the democratic movement has been sweeping all obstacles before it around the world. In Russia emancipated serfs have secured the right to a voice in their government. In Persia the people have secured a constitution. In Turkey the man who every hour was in danger of being cast into prison without an indictment, or beheaded without a charge against him, now has some influence in the molding of the laws. And China, the sleeping giant of the Orient, has risen from a slumber of two thousand years and today is a republic waiting for recognition. And while the outside world has been marching at double quick in the direction of more complete freedom, our nation has kept step, and on no other part of God's footstool has popular government grown more rapidly than here. In every State the fight has been waged.

The man whom I present has been the leader of the progressive cause in his State, and once joint leader in the nation.

I challenge you to find in sixteen years an occasion where the candidate presented by the Committee has, before an election, gone out and rendered any effective service in behalf of any man who was fighting the people's cause against plutocracy.

Now this is the situation which we have to meet. The Democratic party has led this fight until its action has stimulated a host of Republicans to imitation. I will not say these Republicans have acted as they have because we acted first; I would rather

APPENDIX

say that they at a later hour than we have caught the spirit of the time and are now willing to trust the people with the control of their own government. [Applause.]

We have been traveling in the wilderness. We have now come in sight of the promised land. During all the weary hours of darkness progressive democracy has been the people's pillar of fire by night. I pray you, delegates, now the dawn has come, do not rob our party of the right so well earned to be the people's pillar of cloud by day. [Applause.]

WHY BRYAN CHANGED FROM CLARK TO WILSON

(From the Official Proceedings of the Democratic National Convention, 1912, page 233)

Mr. Bryan, of Nebraska: Nebraska is a progressive State. Only twice has she given her vote to a Democratic candidate for President, in 1898 and in 1908, and on both occasions her vote was cast for a progressive ticket, running upon a progressive platform. Between these two elections, in the election of 1904, she gave a Republican plurality of 85,000 against a Democratic reactionary. In the recent primaries the total vote cast for Clark and Wilson was over 34,000, and the vote cast for Harmon something over 12,000, showing that the party is now more than three-fourths progressive. The Republican party of Nebraska is progressive in about the same proportion. The situation in Nebraska is not materially different from the situation throughout the country west of the Alleghenies. In the recent Republican primaries, fully two-thirds of the Republican vote was cast for candidates representing progressive policies.

In this convention the progressive sentiment is overwhelming. Every candidate has proclaimed himself a progressive. No candidate would have any considerable following in this convention if he admitted himself out of harmony with progressive ideas.

By your resolution, adopted night before last, you, by a vote of more than four to one, pledged the country that you would nominate for the Presidency no man who represented or was obligated to Morgan, Ryan, Belmont, or any other member of the privilege-seeking, favor-hunting class. This pledge, if kept, will have more influence on the result of the election than the platform or the name of the candidate. How can that pledge be made effective? There is but one way; namely, to nominate a candidate who is under no obligation to those whom these influ-

522

ences directly or indirectly control. The vote of the State of New York in this convention, as cast under the unit rule, does not represent the intelligence, the virtue, the Democracy or the patriotism of the ninety men who are here. It represents the will of one man—Charles F. Murphy—and he represents the influences that dominated the Republican convention at Chicago and are trying to dominate this convention. [Applause.] If we nominate a candidate under conditions that enable these influences to say to our candidate, "Remember now thy creator," we cannot hope to appeal to the confidence of the progressive Democrats and Republicans of the nation. Nebraska, or that portion of the delegation for which I am authorized to speak, is not willing to participate in the nomination of any man who is willing to violate the resolution adopted by this Convention, and to accept the high honor of the Presidential nomination at the hands of Mr. Murphy. [Applause.]

When we were instructed for Mr. Clark, the Democratic voters who instructed us did so with the distinct understanding that Mr. Clark stood for progressive Democracy. [Applause.] Mr. Clark's representatives appealed for support on no other ground. They contended that Mr. Clark was more progressive than Mr. Wilson, and indignantly denied that there was any coöperation between Mr. Clark and the reactionary element of the party. Upon no other condition could Mr. Clark have received a plurality of the Democratic vote of Nebraska. The thirteen delegates for whom I speak stand ready to carry out the instructions given in the spirit in which they were given, and upon the conditions under which they were given [applause]; but some of these delegates—I can not say for how many I can speak, because we have not had a chance to take a poll—will not participate in the nomination of any man whose nomination depends upon the vote of the New York delegation. [Applause.]

Speaking for myself and for any of the delegation who may decide to join me, I shall withhold my vote from Mr. Clark as long as New York's vote is recorded for him. [Applause.] And the position that I take in regard to Mr. Clark, I will take in regard to any other candidate whose name is now or may be before the convention. I shall not be a party to the nomination of any man, no matter who he may be, or from what section of the country he comes, who will not, when elected, be absolutely free to carry out the anti-Morgan-Ryan-Belmont resolution and make his administration reflect the wishes and the hopes of those who believe in a government of the people, by the people and for the people. [Applause.]

If we nominate a candidate who is under no obligation to these interests which speak through Mr. Murphy, I shall offer a resolution authorizing and directing the presidential candidate to select a campaign committee to manage the campaign, in order that he may not be compelled to suffer the humiliation and act under the embarrassment that I have, in having men participate in the management of his campaign who have no sympathy with the party's aims, and in whose Democracy the general public has no confidence.

Having explained the position taken by myself and those in the delegation who view the subjects from the same standpoint, I will now announce my vote——

[Mr. Bryan was here interrupted. Continuing, he said:]

Now I am prepared to announce my vote, unless again interrupted. With the understanding that I shall stand ready to withdraw my vote from the one for whom I am going to cast it whenever New York casts her vote for him, I cast my vote for Nebraska's second choice, Governor Wilson. [Applause.]

[NOTE.—The Nebraska State Democratic Convention held soon after the Baltimore Convention endorsed Mr. Bryan's action. If Mr. Bryan's constituents approved his course, who else has the right to complain?]

MR. BRYAN DECLINES TO BECOME A CANDIDATE FOR VICE-PRESIDENT IN 1912

(From the Official Proceedings of Democratic National Convention, 1912, page 382)

Mr. William J. Bryan, of Nebraska: Mr. Chairman and members of the Convention, you have been so generous to me in the allowance of time that I had not expected to trespass upon your patience again; but the compliment that has been paid me by the gentleman from the District of Columbia justifies, I hope, a word in the form of a valedictory. [Applause.]

For sixteen years I have been a fighting man. Performing what I regarded as a public duty I have not hesitated to speak out on every public question which was before the people of the nation for settlement; and I have not hesitated to arouse the hostility and the enmity of individuals where in behalf of my country I felt it my duty to do so. [Applause.] I have never advocated any man except with gladness, and I have never opposed any man except in sadness. [Applause.] If I have any enemies in this country, those who are my enemies have a monopoly of hatred. There is not one human being for whom I feel a hatred. [Applause.] Nor is there one American citizen, in my own party or any other, whom I would oppose for anything, unless I believed that in not opposing him I was surrendering the interests of my country, which I hold above any person. [Applause.]

I recognize that a man who fights must carry scars, and long before this campaign commenced I decided that I had been in so many battles and had alienated so many, that my party ought to have the leadership of some one who had not thus offended, and who thus might lead with greater hope of victory. [Applause.]

Tonight I come with joy to surrender into the hands of the one chosen by this Convention a standard which I have carried in three campaigns, and I challenge my enemies to declare that it has ever been lowered in the face of the enemy. [Applause.]

The same belief that led me to prefer another for the Presidency, rather than to be the candidate myself, leads me to prefer another rather than myself to be a candidate for Vice-President. It is not because the Vice-Presidency is lower in importance than the Presidency that I decline it. There is no office in this nation so low that I would not take it if I could serve my country by so doing. [Applause.]

I believe that I can render more service to my country when I have not the embarrassment of a nomination and have not the suspicion of a selfish interest than I could as a candidate; and your candidates will not be more active in this campaign than I shall be. [Applause.] My services are at the command of the party, and I feel a relief now that the burden of leadership is transferred to other shoulders. Having, in this Convention, given us a platform, the most progressive that any party of any size has ever adopted, and having given us a candidate who I believe will appeal not only to Democratic votes, but to some three or four million Republicans who have been alienated by the policies of their party, there is but one thing left to do, and that is to give us a candidate for Vice-President in harmony with our candidate for President, so there may be no joint debate between our candidates. [Applause.]

APPENDIX

WHO SHALL CONTROL?

[NOTE.—This statement on the Tennessee case was prepared by Mr. Bryan at Coconut Grove, Florida, in June, 1925.]

The first question to be decided is: Who shall control our public schools? We have something like twenty-six millions of children in the public schools and spend over one billion and seven hundred thousand dollars a year upon these schools. As the training of children is the chief work of each generation, the parents are interested in the things to be taught the children.

Four sources of control have been suggested. The first is the people, speaking through their legislatures. That would seem to be the natural sources of control. The people are sovereigns and governments derive their just powers from the consent of the governed. Some seem to think that schools are excepted from the control of the people. Legislatures enact all state laws, and in most states the decision is made without the possibility of a referendum. Legislatures fix the death penalty for crime and the form and extent of other punishments. Legislatures regulate marriage and divorce, property rights, descent of property, care of children, and all other matters between citizens. Why are our legislatures not competent to decide what kind of schools are needed, the requirements of teachers, and the kind of instruction that shall be given?

If not the legislatures, then who shall control? Boards of Education? It is the legislature that authorizes the election of boards and defines their duties, and boards are elected by the people or appointed by officials elected by the people. All authority goes back at last to the people; they are the final source of authority.

Some have suggested that the scientists should decide what shall be taught. How many scientists are there? And how shall their decrees be proclaimed? Professor Steinmetz put the number of scientists at about five thousand; Professor Leuba, in one of his books, puts the number at about fifty-five hundred. The American Society for the Advancement of Science has about eleven thousand members, but that includes Canadians as well as citizens of the United States. If the number is put at eleven thousand, it makes about one scientist for every ten thousand people—a pretty little oligarchy to put in control of the education of all the children, especially when Professor Leuba declares that

526

APPENDIX

over half of the scientists agree with him in the belief that there is no personal God and no personal immortality.

The fourth source suggested is the teacher. Some say, let the teacher be supreme and teach anything that seems best to him. The proposition needs only to be stated to be rejected as absurd. The teacher is an employee and receives a salary; employees take directions from their employers, and the teacher is no exception to the rule. No teacher would be permitted to teach students in the United States that a monarchy is the only good government and kings the only chief executives. No teacher would be permitted to slander presidents and libel our form of government. No teacher would be permitted to go from the South and teach in a northern school that the northern statesmen and soldiers of the Civil War were traitors; neither would a northern teacher be permitted to go from the North and teach in a southern school that the southern soldiers and statesmen were traitors. These three illustrations are sufficient to show that a teacher must respect the wishes of his employers on all subjects upon which the employers have a deep-seated conviction. The same logic would suggest that a teacher receiving pay in dollars on which is stamped, "In God We Trust," should not be permitted to teach the children that there is no God. Neither should he be allowed to accept employment in a Christian community and teach that the Bible is untrue.

That is the Tennessee case. Evolution disputes the Bible record of man's creation, and the logic of the evolution eliminates as false the miracles of the Bible, including the virgin birth and the bodily resurrection of Christ. Christians are compelled to build their own colleges in which to teach Christianity; why not require agnostics and atheists to build their own colleges if they want to teach agnosticism or atheism?

The Tennessee case is represented by some as an attempt to stifle freedom of conscience and freedom of speech, but the charge is seen to be absurd when the case is analyzed. Professor Scopes, the defendent in the Tennessee case, has a right to think as he pleases—the law does not attempt to regulate his thinking. Professor Scopes can also say anything he pleases—the law does not interfere with his freedom of speech. As an individual, Professor Scopes is perfectly free to think and speak as he likes and the Christians of Tennessee will protect him in the enjoyment of these inalienable rights. But that is not the Tennessee case and has nothing to do with it.

APPENDIX

Professor Scopes was not arrested for doing anything as an individual. He was arrested for violating a law as a *representative* of the *state* and as an employee in a school. As a representative, he has no right to misrepresent; as an employee, he is compelled to act under the direction of his employers and has no right to defy instructions and still claim his salary. The right of free speech cannot be stretched as far as Professor Scopes is trying to stretch it. A man cannot demand a salary for saying what his employers do not want said, and he cannot require his employers to furnish him an audience to talk to, especially an audience of children or young people, when he wants to say what the parents do not want said. The duty of a parent to protect his children is more sacred than the right of teachers to teach what parents do not want taught, especially when the speaker demands pay for his teaching and insists on being furnished an audience to talk to. Professor Scopes can think whatever he wants about evolution, but he has no right to force his opinion upon students against the wishes of the tax payers and the parents.

And, I may add, Professor Scopes is doing more harm to teachers than to anyone else. If he establishes the doctrine that a teacher can say anything he likes to the students, regardless of the wishes of his employers, who are the parents and tax payers, it will become necessary to enquire what teachers think before they are employed. At present, teachers are not examined as to their thoughts on religion; if, however, a teacher when once employed is at liberty to rob Christian children of their religious beliefs, then atheists, agnostics, infidels, and all others who seek to undermine the Christian religion will find it difficult to secure employment as teachers in Christian communities, and the school boards will become much more important official bodies than they are now. If religion has to be protected in the election of school boards, then school board elections may become the most important elections held, for parents are much more interested in their children and in their children's religion than they are in any political policies or in the election of any particular candidates— even more interested in their children than in who shall be governor or president. Professor Scopes has raised a question of the very first magnitude and the ones most likely to suffer by the raising of the issue are those who think they can ignore the right of the people to have what they want in government, including the kind of education they want.

528

APPENDIX

MR. BRYAN'S LAST SPEECH

[NOTE.—This address was to have been delivered by Mr. Bryan as the closing argument for the State in the case of The State of Tennessee vs. John Thomas Scopes, at Dayton. The decision to submit the case to the jury without argument prevented Mr. Bryan from delivering the speech. The jury returned a unanimous verdict in favor of the State, which Mr. Bryan represented, but he arranged to have his speech printed, to be given out for publication. Just after he had finished the revised proof, came his unexpected death.]

May It Please the Court,
 and Gentlemen of the Jury:
 Demosthenes, the greatest of ancient orators, in his "Oration on The Crown," the most famous of his speeches, began by supplicating the favor of all the gods and goddesses of Greece. If, in a case which involved only his own fame and fate, he felt justified in petitioning the heathen gods of his country, surely we, who deal with the momentous issues involved in this case, may well pray to the Ruler of the Universe for wisdom to guide us in the performance of our several parts in this historic trial.

Let me, in the first place, congratulate our cause that circumstances have committed the trial to a community like this and entrusted the decision to a jury made up largely of the yeomanry of the State. The book in issue in this trial contains on its first page two pictures contrasting the disturbing noises of a great city with the calm serenity of the country. It is a tribute that rural life has fully earned.

I appreciate the sturdy honesty and independence of those who come into daily contact with the earth, who, living near to nature, worship nature's God, and who, dealing with the myriad mysteries of earth and air, seek to learn from revelation about the Bible's wonder-working God. I admire the stern virtues, the vigilance and the patriotism of the class from which the jury is drawn, and am reminded of the lines of Scotland's immortal bard, which, when changed but slightly, describe your country's confidence in you:

"O Scotia, my dear, my native soil!
 For whom my warmest wish to Heaven is sent,
Long may thy hardy sons of rustic toil
 Be blest with health, and peace, and sweet content!

APPENDIX

"And, oh, may Heav'n their simple lives prevent
From luxury's contagion, weak and vile!
Then, howe'er crowns and coronets be rent,
A virtuous populace may rise the while,
And stand, a wall of fire, around their much-loved isle."

Let us now separate the issues from the misrepresentations, intentional or unintentional, that have obscured both the letter and the purpose of the law. This is not an interference with freedom of conscience. A teacher can think as he pleases and worship God as he likes, or refuse to worship God at all. He can believe in the Bible or discard it; he can accept Christ or reject Him. This law places no obligations or restraints upon him. And so with freedom of speech; he can, so long as he acts as an individual, say anything he likes on any subject. This law does not violate any rights guaranteed by any constitution to any individual. It deals with the defendant, not as an individual, but as an employee, an official or public servant, paid by the State, and therefore under instructions from the State.

The right of the State to control the public schools is affirmed in the recent decision in the Oregon case, which declares that the State can direct what shall be taught and also forbid the teaching of anything "manifestly inimical to the public welfare." The above decision goes even farther and declares that the parent not only has the right to guard the religious welfare of the child, but is in duty bound to guard it. That decision fits this case exactly. The State had a right to pass this law, and the law represents the determination of the parents to guard the religious welfare of their children.

It need hardly be added that this law did not have its origin in bigotry. It is not trying to force any form of religion on anybody. The majority is not trying to establish a religion or to teach it—it is trying to protect itself from the effort of an insolent minority to force irreligion upon the children under the guise of teaching science. What right has a little irresponsible oligarchy of self-styled "intellectuals" to demand control of the schools of the United States, in which twenty-five millions of children are being educated at an annual expense of nearly two billions of dollars?

Christians must, in every State of the Union, build their own colleges in which to teach Christianity; it is only simple justice that atheists, agnostics and unbelievers should build their own colleges if they want to teach their own religious views or attack the religious views of others.

530

APPENDIX

The statute is brief and free from ambiguity. It prohibits the teaching, in the public schools, of "any theory that denies the story of Divine creation as taught in the Bible," and teaches, "instead, that man descended from a lower order of animals." The first sentence sets forth the purpose of those who passed the law. They forbid the teaching of any evolutionary theory that disputes the Bible record of man's creation and, to make sure that there shall be no misunderstanding, they place their own interpretation on their language and specifically forbid the teaching of any theory that makes man a descendant of any lower form of life.

The evidence shows that defendant taught, in his own language as well as from a book outlining the theory, that man descended from lower forms of life. Howard Morgan's testimony gives us a definition of evolution that will become known throughout the world as this case is discussed. Howard, a fourteen-year-old boy, has translated the words of the teacher and the text-book into language that even a child can understand. As he recollects it, the defendant said, "A little germ of one cell organism was formed in the sea; this kept evolving until it got to be a pretty good-sized animal, then came on to be a land animal, and it kept evolving, and from this was man." There is no room for difference of opinion here, and there is no need of expert testimony. Here are the facts, corroborated by another student, Harry Shelton, and admitted to be true by counsel for defense. Mr. White, Superintendent of Schools, testified to the use of Hunter's Civic Biology, and to the fact that the defendant not only admitted teaching evolution, but declared that he could not teach it without violating the law. Mr. Robinson, the chairman of the School Board, corroborated the testimony of Superintendent White in regard to the defendant's admissions and declaration. These are the facts; they are sufficient and undisputed. A verdict of guilty must follow.

But the importance of this case requires more. The facts and arguments presented to you must not only convince you of the justice of conviction in this case but, while not necessary to a verdict of guilty, they should convince you of the righteousness of the purpose of the people of the State in the enactment of this law. The State must speak through you to the outside world and repel the aspersions cast by the counsel for the defense upon the intelligence and the enlightenment of the citizens of Tennessee. The people of this State have a high appreciation of the value of

531

APPENDIX

education. The State Constitution testifies to that in its demand that education shall be fostered and that science and literature shall be cherished. The continuing and increasing appropriations for public instruction furnish abundant proof that Tennessee places a just estimate upon the learning that is secured in its schools.

Religion is not hostile to learning; Christianity has been the greatest patron learning has ever had. But Christians know that "the fear of the Lord is the beginning of wisdom" now just as it has been in the past, and they therefore oppose the teaching of guesses that encourage godlessness among the students.

Neither does Tennessee undervalue the service rendered by science. The Christian men and women of Tennessee know how deeply mankind is indebted to science for benefits conferred by the discovery of the laws of nature and by the designing of machinery for the utilization of these laws. Give science a fact and it is not only invincible, but it is of incalculable service to man. If one is entitled to draw from society in proportion to the service that he renders to society, who is able to estimate the reward earned by those who have given to us the use of steam, the use of electricity, and enabled us to utilize the weight of water that flows down the mountainside? Who will estimate the value of the service rendered by those who invented the phonograph, the telephone, and the radio? Or, to come more closely to our home life, how shall we recompense those who gave us the sewing machine, the harvester, the threshing machine, the tractor, the automobile, and the method now employed in making artificial ice? The department for medicine also opens an unlimited field for invaluable service. Typhoid and yellow fever are not feared as they once were. Diphtheria and pneumonia have been robbed of some of their terrors, and a high place on the scroll of fame still awaits the discoverer of remedies for arthritis, cancer, tuberculosis and other dread diseases to which mankind is heir.

Christianity welcomes truth from whatever source it comes, and is not afraid that any real truth from any source can interfere with the divine truth that comes by inspiration from God Himself. It is not scientific truth to which Christians object, for true science is classified knowledge, and nothing therefore can be scientific unless it is true.

Evolution is not truth; it is merely an hypothesis—it is millions of guesses strung together. It had not been proven in the days of Darwin; he expressed astonishment that with two or

532

three million species it had been impossible to trace any species to any other species. It had not been proven in the days of Huxley, and it has not been proven up to today. It is less than four years ago that Prof. Bateson came all the way from London to Canada to tell the American scientists that every effort to trace one species to another had failed—every one. He said he still had faith in evolution but had doubts about the origin of species. But of what value is evolution if it cannot explain the origin of species? While many scientists accept evolution as if it were a fact, they all admit, when questioned, that no explanation has been found as to how one species developed into another.

Darwin suggested two laws, sexual selection and natural selection. Sexual selection has been laughed out of the class room, and natural selection is being abandoned, and no new explanation is satisfactory even to scientists. Some of the more rash advocates of evolution are wont to say that evolution is as firmly established as the law of gravitation or the Copernican theory. The absurdity of such a claim is apparent when we remember that anyone can prove the law of gravitation by throwing a weight into the air, and that anyone can prove the roundness of the earth by going around it, while no one can prove evolution to be true in any way whatever.

Chemistry is an insurmountable obstacle in the path of evolution. It is one of the greatest of the sciences; it separates the atoms—isolates them and walks about them, so to speak. If there were in nature a progressive force, an eternal urge, Chemistry would find it. But it is not there. All of the ninety-two original elements are separate and distinct; they combine in fixed and permanent proportions. Water is H_2O, as it has been from the beginning. It was here before life appeared and has never changed; neither can it be shown that any thing else has materially changed.

There is no more reason to believe that man descended from some inferior animal than there is to believe that a stately mansion has descended from a small cottage. Resemblances are not proof—they simply put us on inquiry. As one fact, such as the absence of the accused from the scene of the murder, outweighs all the resemblances that a thousand witnesses could swear to, so the inability of science to trace any one of the millions of species to another species, outweighs all the resemblances upon which evolutionists rely to establish man's blood relationship with the brutes.

But while the wisest scientists cannot prove a pushing power,

533

APPENDIX

such as evolution is supposed to be, there is a *lifting* power that any child can understand. The plant lifts the mineral up into a higher world, and the animal lifts the plant up into a world still higher. So, it has been reasoned by analogy, man rises, not by a power within him, but only when drawn upward by a higher power. There is a spiritual gravitation that draws all souls toward heaven, just as surely as there is a physical force that draws all matter on the surface of the earth towards the earth's center. Christ is our drawing power; He said, "I, if I be lifted up from the earth, will draw all men unto me," and His promise is being fulfilled daily all over the world.

It must be remembered that the law under consideration in this case does not prohibit the teaching of evolution up to the line that separates man from the lower forms of animal life. The law might well have gone farther than it does and prohibit the teaching of evolution in lower forms of life; the law is a very conservative statement of the people's opposition to an anti-Biblical hypothesis. The defendant was not content to teach what the law permitted; he, for reasons of his own, persisted in teaching that which was forbidden for reasons entirely satisfactory to the law-makers.

Most of the people who believe in evolution do not know what evolution means. One of the science books taught in the Dayton High School has a chapter on "The Evolution of Machinery." This is a very common misuse of the term. People speak of the evolution of the telephone, the automobile, and the musical instrument. But these are merely illustrations of man's power to deal intelligently with inanimate matter; there is no growth from within in the development of machinery.

Equally improper is the use of the word "evolution" to describe the growth of a plant from a seed, the growth of a chicken from an egg, or the development of any form of animal life from a single cell. All these give us a circle, not a change from one species to another.

Evolution—the evolution involved in this case, and the only evolution that is a matter of controversy anywhere—is the evolution taught by defendant, set forth in the books now prohibited by the new State law, and illustrated in the diagram printed on page 194 of Hunter's Civic Biology. The author estimates the number of species in the animal kingdom at five hundred and eighteen thousand, nine hundred. These are divided into eighteen classes, and each class is indicated on the diagram by a circle,

534

proportionate in size to the number of species in each class and attached by a stem to the trunk of the tree. It begins with protozoa and ends with the mammals. Passing over the classes with which the average man is unfamiliar, let me call your attention to a few of the larger and better known groups. The insects are numbered at three hundred and sixty thousand, over two-thirds of the total number of species in the animal world. The fishes are numbered at thirteen thousand, the amphibians at fourteen hundred, the reptiles at thirty-five hundred, and the birds are thirteen thousand, while thirty-five hundred mammals are crowded together in a little circle that is barely higher than the bird circle. *No circle is reserved for man alone.* He is, according to the diagram, shut up in the little circle entitled "Mammals," with thirty-four hundred and ninety-nine other species of mammals. Does it not seem a little unfair not to distinguish between man and lower forms of life? What shall we say of the intelligence, not to say religion, of those who are so particular to distinguish between fishes and reptiles and birds, but put a man with an immortal soul in the same circle with the wolf, the hyena and the skunk? What must be the impression made upon children by such a degradation of man?

In the preface of this book, the author explains that it is for children, and adds that "the boy or girl of average ability upon admission to the secondary school is not a thinking individual." Whatever may be said in favor of teaching evolution to adults, it surely is not proper to teach it to children who are not yet able to think.

The evolutionist does not undertake to tell us how protozoa, moved by interior and resident forces, sent life up through all the various species, and cannot prove that there was actually any such compelling power at all. And yet, the school children are asked to accept their guesses and build a philosophy of life upon them. If it were not so serious a matter, one might be tempted to speculate upon the various degrees of relationship that, according to evolutionists, exist between man and other forms of life. It might require some very nice calculation to determine at what degree of relationship the killing of a relative ceases to be murder and the eating of one's kin ceases to be cannibalism.

But it is not a laughing matter when one considers that evolution not only offers no suggestions as to a Creator but tends to put the creative act so far away as to cast doubt upon creation itself. And, while it is shaking faith in God as a beginning, it is also creating doubt as to a heaven at the end of life. Evolutionists do not feel that it is incumbent upon them to show how life began or at what point in their long-drawn-out scheme of changing species man became endowed with hope and promise of immortal life. God may be a matter of indifference to the evolutionists, and a life beyond may have no charm for them, but the mass of mankind will continue to worship their Creator and continue to find comfort in the promise of their Saviour that He has gone to prepare a place for them. Christ has made of death a narrow, star-lit strip between the companionship of yesterday and the reunion of tomorrow; evolution strikes out the stars and deepens the gloom that enshrouds the tomb.

If the results of evolution were unimportant, one might require less proof in support of the hypothesis, but before accepting a new philosophy of life, built upon a materialistic foundation, we have reason to demand something more than guesses; "we may well suppose" is not a sufficient substitute for "Thus saith the Lord."

If you, your honor, and you, gentlemen of the jury, would have an understanding of the sentiment that lies back of the statute against the teaching of evolution, please consider the facts that I shall now present to you. First, as to the animals to which evolutionists would have us trace our ancestry. The following is Darwin's family tree, as you will find it set forth on pages 180–181 of his "Descent of Man":

"The most ancient progenitors in the kingdom of Vertrebrata, at which we are able to obtain an obscure glance, apparently consisted of a group of marine animals, resembling the larvae of existing ascidians. These animals probably gave rise to a group of fishes, as lowly organized as the lancelot; and from these the Ganoids, and other fishes like the Lepidosiren, must have been developed. From such fish a very small advance would carry us on to the amphibians. We have seen that birds and reptiles were once intimately connected together; and the Monotremata now connect mammals with reptiles in a slight degree. But no one can at present say by what line of descent the three higher and related classes, namely, mammals, birds, and reptiles, were derived from the two lower vertebrate classes, namely, amphibians and fishes. In the classes of mammals the steps are not difficult to conceive which led from the ancient Monotremata to the ancient Marsupials; and from these to the early progenitors of the placental mammals. We may thus ascend to the Lemuridæ; and the interval is not very wide from these to the Simiadæ.

536

APPENDIX

The Simiadæ then branched off into two great stems, the New World and Old World monkeys; and from the latter, at a remote period, Man, the wonder and glory of the Universe, proceeded. Thus we have given to man a pedigree of prodigious length, but not, it may be said, of noble quality." (Ed. 1874, Hurst.)

Note the words implying uncertainty; "obscure glance," "apparently," "resembling," "must have been," "slight degree," and "conceive."

Darwin, on page 171 of the same book, tries to locate his first man—that is, the first man to come down out of the trees—in Africa. After leaving man in company with gorillas and chimpanzees, he says, "But it is useless to speculate on this subject." If he had only thought of this earlier, the world might have been spared much of the speculation that his brute hypothesis has excited.

On page 79 Darwin gives some fanciful reasons for believing that man is more likely to have descended from the chimpanzee than from the gorilla. His speculations are an excellent illustration of the effect that the evolutionary hypothesis has in cultivating the imagination. Professor J. Arthur Thomson says that the "idea of evolution is the most potent thought economizing formula the world has yet known." It is more than that; it dispenses with thinking entirely and relies on the imagination.

On page 141 Darwin attempts to trace the mind of man back to the mind of lower animals. On pages 113 and 114 he endeavors to trace man's moral nature back to the animals. It is all animal, animal, animal, with never a thought of God or of religion.

Our first indictment against evolution is that it disputes the truth of the Bible account of man's creation and shakes faith in the Bible as the Word of God. This indictment we prove by comparing the processes described as evolutionary with the text of Genesis. It not only contradicts the Mosaic record as to the beginning of human life, but it disputes the Bible doctrine of reproduction according to kind—the greatest scientific principle known.

Our second indictment is that the evolutionary hypothesis, carried to its logical conclusion, disputes every vital truth of the Bible. Its tendency, natural, if not inevitable, is to lead those who really accept it, first to agnosticism and then to atheism. Evolutionists attack the truth of the Bible, not openly at first, but by using weazel-words like "poetical," "symbolical" and "allegorical" to suck the meaning out the inspired record of man's creation.

APPENDIX

We call as our first witness Charles Darwin. He began life a Christian. On page 39, Vol. I of the Life and Letters of Charles Darwin, by his son, Francis Darwin, he says, speaking of the period from 1828 to 1831, "I did not then in the least doubt the strict and literal truth of every word in the Bible." On page 412 of Vol. II of the same publication, he says, "When I was collecting facts for 'The Origin' my belief in what is called a personal God was as firm as that of Dr. Pusey himself." It may be a surprise to your honor and to you, gentlemen of the jury, as it was to me, to learn that Darwin spent three years at Cambridge *studying for the ministry.*

This was Darwin as a young man, before he came under the influence of the doctrine that man came from a lower order of animals. The change wrought in his religious views will be found in a letter written to a German youth in 1879, and printed on page 277 of Vol I of the Life and Letters above referred to. The letter begins: "I am much engaged, an old man, and out of health, and I cannot spare time to answer your questions fully,—nor indeed can they be answered. Science has nothing to do with Christ, except in so far as the habit of scientific research makes a man cautious in admitting evidence. For myself, I do not believe that there ever has been any revelation. As for a future life, every man must judge for himself between conflicting vague probabilities."

Note that "science has nothing to do with Christ, except in so far as the habit of scientific research makes a man cautious in admitting evidence." Stated plainly, that simply means that "the habit of scientific research" makes one cautious in accepting the only evidence that we have of Christ's existence, mission, teachings, crucifixion, and resurrection, namely the evidence found in the Bible. To make this interpretation of his words the only possible one, he adds, "For myself, I do not believe that there ever has been any revelation." In rejecting the Bible as a revelation from God, he rejects the Bible's conception of God and he rejects also the supernatural Christ of whom the Bible, and the Bible alone, tells. And, it will be observed, he refuses to express any opinion as to a future life.

Now let us follow with his son's exposition of his father's views as they are given in extracts from a biography written in 1876. Here is Darwin's language as quoted by his son:

"During these two years (October, 1838, to January, 1839) I was led to think much about religion. Whilst on board the

538

APPENDIX

Beagle I was quite orthodox and I remember being heartily laughed at by several of the officers (though themselves orthodox) for quoting the Bible as an unanswerable authority on some point of morality. When thus reflecting, I felt compelled to look for a First Cause, having an intelligent mind in some degree analogous to man; and I deserved to be called an atheist. This conclusion was strong in my mind about the time, as far as I can remember, when I wrote the 'Origin of Species'; it is since that time that it has very gradually, with many fluctuations, become weaker. But then arises the doubt, can the mind of man, which has, as I fully believe, been developed from a mind as low as that possessed by the lowest animals, be trusted when it draws such grand conclusions?

"I cannot pretend to throw the least light on such abstruse problems. The mystery of the beginning of all things is insoluble by us; and I for one must be content to remain an Agnostic."

When Darwin entered upon his scientific career he was "quite orthodox and quoted the Bible as an unanswerable authority on some point of morality." Even when he wrote "The Origin of Species," the thought of "a First Cause, having an intelligent mind in some degree analogous to man" was strong in his mind. It was *after* that time that "very gradually, with many fluctuations," his belief in God became weaker. He traces this decline for us and concludes by telling us that he cannot pretend to throw the least light on such abstruse problems—the religious problems above referred to. Then comes the flat statement that he "must be content to remain an Agnostic"; and to make clear what he means by the word, agnostic, he says that "the mystery of the beginning of all things is insoluble by us"—not by him alone, but by everybody. Here we have the effect of evolution upon its most distinguished exponent; it led from an orthodox Christian, believing every word of the Bible and in a personal God, down and down and down to helpless and hopeless agnosticism.

But there is one sentence upon which I reserved comment—it throws light upon his downward pathway. "Then arises the doubt, can the mind of man which has, as I fully believe, been developed from a mind as low as that possessed by the lowest animals, be trusted when it draws such grand conclusions?"

Here is the explanation; he drags man down to the brute level, and then, judging man by brute standards, he questions whether man's mind can be trusted to deal with God and immortality!

How can any teacher tell his students that evolution *does not*

539

tend to destroy his religious faith? How can an honest teacher *conceal* from his students the effect of evolution upon Darwin himself? And is it not stranger still that preachers who advocate evolution never speak of Darwin's loss of faith, due to his belief in evolution? The parents of Tennessee have reason enough to fear the effect of evolution on the minds of their children. Belief in evolution cannot bring to those who hold such a belief any compensation for the loss of faith in God, trust in the Bible, and belief in the supernatural character of Christ. It is belief in evolution that has caused so many scientists and so many Christians to reject the miracles of the Bible, and then give up, one after another, every vital truth of Christianity. They finally cease to pray and sunder the tie that binds them to their Heavenly Father.

The miracle should not be a stumbling block to any one. It raises but three questions: 1st. *Could* God perform a miracle? Yes, the God who created the universe can do anything He wants to with it. He can temporarily suspend any law that He has made or He may employ higher laws that we do not understand. 2nd. *Would* God perform a miracle? To answer that question in the negative one would have to know more about God's plans and purposes than a finite mind can know, and yet some are so wedded to evolution that they deny that God *would* perform a miracle merely because a miracle is inconsistent with evolution.

If we believe that God *can* perform a miracle and *might* desire to do so, we are prepared to consider with open mind the third question, namely, *Did* God perform the miracles recorded in the Bible? The same evidence that establishes the authority of the Bible establishes the truth of the record of miracles performed.

Now let me read to the honorable court and to you, gentlemen of the jury, one of the most pathetic confessions that has come to my notice. George John Romanes, a distinguished biologist, sometimes called the successor of Darwin, was prominent enough to be given extended space in both the Encyclopedia Britannica and Encyclopedia Americana. Like Darwin, he was reared in the orthodox faith, and like Darwin, was led away from it by evolution (see "Thoughts on Religion," page 180). For twenty-five years he could not pray. Soon after he became an agnostic, he wrote a book entitled, "A Candid Examination of Theism," publishing it under the assumed name, "Physicus." In this book (see page 29, "Thoughts on Religion"), he says:

"And forasmuch as I am far from being able to agree with

540

those who affirm that the twilight doctrine of the 'New Faith' is a desirable substitute for the waning splendor of 'the old,' I am not ashamed to confess that with this virtual negation of God the universe to me has lost its soul of loveliness; and although from henceforth the precept to 'work while it is day' will doubtless but gain an intensified force from the terribly intensified meaning of the words that 'the night cometh when no man can work,' yet when at times I think, as think at times I must, of the appalling contrast between the hallowed glory of that creed which once was mine, and the lonely mystery of existence as now I find it,—at such times I shall ever feel it impossible to avoid the sharpest pang of which my nature is susceptible."

Do these evolutionists stop to think of the crime they commit when they take faith out of the hearts of men and women and lead them out into a starless night? What pleasure can they find in robbing a human being of "the hallowed glory of that creed" that Romanes once cherished, and in substituting "the lonely mystery of existence" as he found it? Can the fathers and mothers of Tennessee be blamed for trying to protect their children from such a tragedy?

If anyone has been led to complain of the severity of the punishment that hangs over the defendant, let him compare this crime and its mild punishment with the crimes for which a greater punishment is prescribed. What is the taking of a few dollars from one in day or night in comparison with the crime of leading one away from God and away from Christ?

Shakespeare regards the robbing one of his good name as much more grave than the stealing of his purse. But we have a higher authority than Shakespeare to invoke in this connection. He who spake as never man spake, thus describes the crimes that are committed against the young. "It is impossible but that offences will come: but woe unto him through whom they come. It were better for him that a millstone were hanged about his neck, and he cast into the sea, than that he should offend one of these little ones."

Christ did not overdraw the picture. Who is able to set a price upon the life of a child—a child into whom a mother has poured her life and for whom a father has labored? What may a noble life mean to the child itself, to the parents, and to the world?

And, it must be remembered, that we can measure the effect on only that part of life which is spent on earth; we have no way of calculating the effect on that infinite circle of life of which existence here is but a small arc. The soul is immortal and religion deals with the soul; the logical effect of the evolutionary hypothesis is to undermine religion and thus affect the soul. I recently received a list of questions that were to be discussed in a prominent Eastern school for women. The second question in the list read, "Is religion an obsolescent function that should be allowed to atrophy quietly, without arousing the passionate prejudice of outworn superstition?" The *real* attack of evolution, it will be seen, is not upon *orthodox* Christianity, or even upon *Christianity*, but upon *religion*—the most basic fact in man's existence and the most practical thing in life.

But I have some more evidence of the effect of evolution upon the life of those who accept it and try to harmonize their thought with it.

James H. Leuba, a Professor of Psychology at Bryn Mawr College, Pennsylvania, published a few years ago, a book entitled "Belief in God and Immortality." In this book he relates how he secured the opinions of scientists as to the existence of a personal God and a personal immortality. He used a volume entitled "American Men of Science," which, he says, included the names of "practically every American who may properly be called a scientist." There were fifty-five hundred names in the book. He selected one thousand names as representative of the fifty-five hundred, and addressed them personally. Most of them, he said, were teachers in schools of higher learning. The names were kept confidential. Upon the answers received, he asserts that over *half* of them *doubt* or *deny* the existence of a personal God and a personal immortality, and he asserts that *unbelief increases* in proportion to prominence, the percentage of unbelief being greatest among the most prominent. Among biologists, believers in a personal God numbered less than thirty-one per cent, while believers in a personal immortality numbered only thirty-seven per cent.

He also questioned the students in nine colleges of high rank and from one thousand answers received, ninety-seven per cent of which were from students between eighteen and twenty, he found that unbelief increased from fifteen per cent in the Freshman class up to forty to forty-five per cent among the men who graduated. On page 280 of this book, we read, "The students' statistics show that young people enter college, possessed of the beliefs still accepted, more or less perfunctorily, in the average

542

home of the land, and gradually abandon the cardinal Christian beliefs." This change from belief to unbelief he attributes to the influence of the persons "of high culture under whom they studied."

The people of Tennessee have been patient enough; they acted none too soon. How can they expect to protect society, and even the church, from the deadening influence of agnosticism and atheism if they permit the teachers employed by taxation to poison the minds of the youth with this destructive doctrine? And remember, that the law has not heretofore required the writing of the word "poison" on poisonous doctrines. The bodies of our people are so valuable that druggists and physicians must be careful to properly label all poisons; why not be as careful to protect the spiritual life of our people from the poisons that kill the soul?

There is a test that is sometimes used to ascertain whether one suspected of mental infirmity is really insane. He is put into a tank of water and told to dip the tank dry while a stream of water flows into the tank. If he has not sense enough to turn off the stream, he is adjudged insane. Can parents justify themselves if, knowing the effect of belief in evolution, they permit irreligious teachers to inject skepticism and infidelity into the minds of their children?

Do bad doctrines corrupt the morals of students? We have a case in point. Mr. Darrow, one of the most distinguished criminal lawyers in our land, was engaged about a year ago in defending two rich men's sons who were on trial for as dastardly a murder as was ever committed. The older one, "Babe" Leopold, was a brilliant student, nineteen years old. He was an evolutionist and an atheist. He was also a follower of Nietzsche, whose books he had devoured and whose philosophy he had adopted. Mr. Darrow made a plea for him, based upon the influence that Nietzsche's philosophy had exerted upon the boy's mind. Here are extracts from his speech:

"Babe took philosophy. . . . He grew up in this way; he became enamoured of the philosophy of Nietzsche. Your honor, I have read almost everything that Nietzsche ever wrote. A man of wonderful intellect; the most original philosopher of the last century. A man who made a deeper imprint on philosophy than any other man within a hundred years, whether right or wrong. More books have been written about him than probably all the rest of the philosophers in a hundred years. More college professors have talked about him. In a way, he has reached more people, and still he has been a philosopher of what we might call the intellectual cult.

"He wrote one book called 'Beyond the Good and Evil,' which was a criticism of all moral precepts, as we understand them, and a treatise that the intelligent man was beyond good and evil, that the laws for good and the laws for evil did not apply to anybody who approached the superman. He wrote on the will to power.

"I have just made a few short extracts from Nietzsche that show the things that he (Leopold) has read, and these are short and almost taken at random. It is not how this would affect you. It is not how it would affect me. The question is, how it would affect the impressionable, visionary, dreamy mind of a boy—a boy who should never have seen it—too early for him."

Quotation from Nietzsche: "Why so soft, oh, my brethren? Why so soft, so unresisting and yielding? Why is there so much disavowal and abnegation in your heart? Why is there so little fate in your looks? For all creators are hard and it must seem blessedness unto you to press your hand upon' millenniums and upon wax. This new table, oh, my brethren, I put over you: Become hard. To be obsessed by moral consideration presupposes a very low grade of intellect. We should substitute for morality the will to our own end, and consequently to the means to accomplish that. A great man, a man whom nature has built up and invented in a grand style, is colder, harder, less cautious and more free from the fear of public opinion. He does not possess the virtues which are compatible with respectability, with being respected, nor any of those things which are counted among the virtues of the herd."

Mr. Darrow says: that the superman, a creation of Nietzsche, has permeated every college and university in the civilized world.

"There is not any university in the world where the professor is not familiar with Nietzsche, not one. . . . Some believe it and some do not believe it. Some read it as I do and take it as a theory, a dream, a vision, mixed with good and bad, but not in any way related to human life. Some take it seriously. . . . There is not a university in the world of any high standing where the professors do not tell you about Nietzsche and discuss him, or where the books are not there.

"If this boy is to blame for this, where did he get it? Is there any blame attached because somebody took Nietzsche's philosophy seriously and fashioned his life up on it? And there is no question in this case but what that is true. Then who is to blame? The *university* would be more to blame than he is; *the scholars* of the world would be more to blame than he is. *The publishers* of the world . . . are more to blame than he is. Your honor, it is hardly fair to hang a nineteen-year-old boy for the philosophy that was taught him at the university. It does not meet my ideas of justice and fairness to visit upon his head the philosophy that has been taught by university men for twenty-five years."

In fairness to Mr. Darrow, I think I ought to quote two more paragraphs. After this bold attempt to excuse the student on the ground that he was transformed from a well-meaning youth into a murderer by the philosophy of an atheist, and on the further ground that this philosophy was in the libraries of all the colleges and discussed by the professors—some adopting the philosophy and some rejecting it—on these two grounds, he denies that the boy should be held responsible for the taking of human life. He charges that the scholars in the universities were more responsible than the boy, and that the universities were more responsible than the boy, because they furnished such books to the students, and then he proceeds to exonerate the universities and the scholars, *leaving nobody responsible*. Here is Mr. Darrow's language:

"Now, I do not want to be misunderstood about this. Even for the sake of saving the lives of my clients, I do not want to be dishonest and tell the court something that I do not honestly think in this case. I do not think that the universities are to blame. I do not think they should be held responsible. I do think, however, that they are too large, and that they should keep a closer watch, if possible, upon the individual.

"But you cannot destroy thought because, forsooth, some brain may be deranged by thought. It is the duty of the university, as I conceive it, to be the great storehouse of the wisdom of the ages, and to have its students come there and learn and choose. I have no doubt but what it has meant the death of many; but that we cannot help."

This is a damnable philosophy, and yet it is the flower that blooms on the stalk of evolution. Mr. Darrow thinks the universities are in duty bound to feed out this poisonous stuff to their students, and when the students become stupefied by it and commit murder, neither they nor the universities are to blame. I am sure, your honor and gentlemen of the jury, that you agree with me when I protest against the adoption of any such a philosophy in the state of Tennessee. A criminal is not relieved from responsibility merely because he found Nietzsche's philosophy in a library which ought not to contain it. Neither is the university guiltless if it permits such corrupting nourishment to be fed to the souls that are entrusted to its care. But, go a step farther, would the state be blameless if it permitted the universities under its control to be turned into training schools for murderers? When you get back to the root of this question, you will find that the legislature not only had a *right* to protect the students from the evolutionary hypothesis but *was in duty bound to do so.*

While on this subject, let me call your attention to another proposition embodied in Mr. Darrow's speech. He said that Dicky Loeb, the younger boy, had read trashy novels, of the blood and thunder sort. He even went so far as to commend an Illinois statute which forbids minors reading stories of crime. Here is what Mr. Darrow said: "We have a statute in this state, passed only last year, if I recall it, which forbids minors reading stories of crime. Why? There is only one reason; because the legislature in its wisdom thought it would have a tendency to produce these thoughts and this life in the boys who read them."

If Illinois can protect her boys, why cannot this state protect the boys of Tennessee? Are the boys of Illinois any more precious than yours?

But to return to the philosophy of an evolutionist. Mr. Darrow said: "I say to you seriously that the parents of Dicky Loeb are more responsible than he, and yet few boys had better parents. . . ." Again, he says, "I know that one of two things happened to this boy; that this terrible crime was inherent in his organism, and came from some ancestor, or that it came through his education and his training after he was born." He thinks the boy was not responsible for anything; his guilt was due, according to this philosophy, either to heredity or to environment.

But let me complete Mr. Darrow's philosophy based on evolution. He says: "I do not know what remote ancestor may have sent down the seed that corrupted him, and I do not know through how many ancestors it may have passed until it reached Dicky Loeb. All I know is, it is true, and there is not a biologist in the world who will not say I am right."

Psychologists who build upon the evolutionary hypothesis teach that man is nothing but a bundle of characteristics inherited from brute ancestors. That is the philosophy which Mr. Darrow applied in this celebrated criminal case. "Some remote ancestor"

546

APPENDIX

—he does not know how remote—"sent down the seed that corrupted him." You cannot punish the ancestor—he is not only dead but, according to the evolutionists, he was a brute and may have lived a million years ago. And he says that all the biologists agree with him—no wonder so small a per cent of the biologists, according to Leuba, believe in a personal God.

This is the quintessence of evolution, distilled for us by one who follows that doctrine to its logical conclusion. Analyze this dogma of darkness and death. Evolutionists say that back in the twilight of life a beast, name and nature unknown, planted a murderous seed and that the impulse that originated in that seed throbs forever in the blood of the brute's descendants, inspiring killings innumerable, for which the murderers are not responsible because coerced by a fate fixed by the laws of heredity! It is an insult to reason and shocks the heart. That doctrine is as deadly as leprosy; it may aid a lawyer in a criminal case, but it would, if generally adopted, destroy all sense of responsibility and menace the morals of the world. A brute, they say, can predestine a man to crime, and yet they deny that God incarnate in the flesh can release a human being from this bondage or save him from ancestral sins. No more repulsive doctrine was ever proclaimed by man; if all the biologists of the world teach this doctrine—as Mr. Darrow says they do—then may heaven defend the youth of our land from their impious babblings.

Our third indictment against evolution is that it diverts attention from pressing problems of great importance to trifling speculation. While one evolutionist is trying to imagine what happened in the dim past, another is trying to pry open the door of the distant future. One recently grew eloquent over ancient worms, and another predicted that seventy-five thousand years hence everyone will be bald and toothless. Both those who endeavor to clothe our remote ancestors with hair and those who endeavor to remove the hair from the heads of our remote descendants ignore the present with its imperative demands. The science of "How to Live" is the most important of all the sciences. It is *desirable* to know the physical sciences, but it is *necessary* to know how to live. Christians desire that their children shall be taught all the sciences, but they do not want them to lose sight of the Rock of Ages while they study the age of the rocks; neither do they desire them to become so absorbed in measuring the distance between the stars that they will forget Him who holds the stars in His hand.

547

APPENDIX

While not more than two per cent of our population are college graduates, these, because of enlarged powers, need a "Heavenly Vision" even more than those less learned, both for their own restraint and to assure society that their enlarged powers will be used for the benefit of society and not against the public welfare.

Evolution is deadening the spiritual life of a multitude of students. Christians do not desire less education, but they desire that religion shall be entwined with learning so that our boys and girls will return from college with their hearts aflame with love of God and love of fellow-men, and prepared to lead in the altruistic work that the world so sorely needs. The cry in the business world, in the industrial world, in the professional world, in the political world—even in the religious world—is for consecrated talents—for ability plus a passion for service.

Our fourth indictment against the evolutionary hypothesis is that, by paralyzing the hope of reform, it discourages those who labor for the improvement of man's condition. Every upward-looking man or woman seeks to lift the level upon which mankind stands, and they trust that they will see beneficient changes during the brief span of their own lives. Evolution chills their enthusiasm by substituting aeons for years. It obscures all beginnings in the mists of endless ages. It is represented as a cold and heartless process, beginning with time and ending in eternity, and acting so slowly that even the rocks cannot preserve a record of the imaginary changes through which it is credited with having carried an original germ of life that appeared sometime from somewhere. Its only program for man is scientific breeding, a system under which a few supposedly superior intellects, self-appointed, would direct the mating and the movements of the mass of mankind—an impossible system! Evolution, disputing the miracle, and ignoring the spiritual in life, has no place for the regeneration of the individual. It recognizes no cry of repentance and scoffs at the doctrine that one can be born again.

It is thus the intolerant and unrelenting enemy of the only process that can redeem society through the redemption of the individual. An evolutionist would never write such a story as The Prodigal Son; it contradicts the whole theory of evolution. The two sons inherited from the same parents and, through their parents, from the same ancestors, proximate and remote. And these sons were reared at the same fireside and were surrounded by the same environment during all the days of their youth; and

548

APPENDIX

yet they were different. If Mr. Darrow is correct in the theory applied to Loeb, namely, that his crime was due either to inheritance or to environment, how will he explain the difference between the elder brother and the wayward son? The evolutionist may understand from observation, if not by experience, even though he cannot explain, why one of these boys was guilty of every immorality, squandered the money that the father had laboriously earned, and brought disgrace upon the family name; but his theory does not explain why a wicked young man underwent a change of heart, confessed his sin, and begged for forgiveness. And because the evolutionists cannot understand this fact, one of the most important in the human life, he cannot understand the infinite love of the Heavenly Father who stands ready to welcome home any repentant sinner, no matter how far he has wandered, how often he has fallen, or how deep he has sunk in sin.

Your honor has quoted from a wonderful poem written by a great Tennessee poet, Walter Malone. I venture to quote another stanza which puts into exquisite language the new opportunity which a merciful God gives to every one who will turn from sin to righteousness.

"Though deep in mire, wring not your hands and weep;
   I lend my arm to all who say, 'I can.'
No shame-faced outcast ever sank so deep
   But he might rise and be again a man."

There are no lines like these in all that evolutionists have ever written. Darwin says that science has nothing to do with the Christ who taught the spirit embodied in the words of Walter Malone, and yet this spirit is the only hope of human progress. A heart can be changed in the twinkling of an eye and a change in the life follows a change in the heart. If one heart can be changed, it is possible that many hearts can be changed, and if many hearts can be changed it is possible that all hearts can be changed—that a world can be born in a day. It is this fact that inspires all who labor for man's betterment. It is because Christians believe in individual regeneration and in the regeneration of society through the regeneration of individuals that they pray, "Thy kingdom come, Thy will be done in earth as it is in heaven." Evolution makes a mockery of the Lord's Prayer!

To interpret the words to mean that the improvement desired must come slowly through unfolding ages,—a process with which each generation could have little to do—is to defer hope, and hope deferred maketh the heart sick.

Our fifth indictment of the evolutionary hypothesis is that, if taken seriously and made the basis of a philosophy of life, it would eliminate love and carry man back to a struggle of tooth and claw. The Christians who have allowed themselves to be deceived into believing that evolution is a beneficent, or even a rational process, have been associating with those who either do not understand its implications or dare not avow their knowledge of these implications. Let me give you some authority on this subject. I will begin with Darwin, the high priest of evolution, to whom all evolutionists bow.

On pages 149 and 150, in "The Descent of Man," already referred to, he says:

"With savages, the weak in body or mind are soon eliminated; and those that survive commonly exhibit a vigorous state of health. We civilized men, on the other hand, do our utmost to check the process of elimination; we build asylums for the imbecile, the maimed, and the sick; we institute poor laws; and our medical men exert their utmost skill to save the life of everyone to the last moment. There is reason to believe that vaccination has preserved thousands who from a weak constitution would formerly have succumbed to smallpox. Thus the weak members of civilized society propagate their kind. No one who has attended to the breeding of domestic animals will doubt that this must be highly injurious to the race of man. It is surprising how soon a want of care, or care wrongly directed, leads to the degeneration of a domestic race; but, excepting in the case of man himself, hardly anyone is so ignorant as to allow his worst animals to breed.

"The aid which we feel impelled to give to the helpless is mainly an incidental result of the instinct of sympathy, which was originally acquired as part of the social instincts, but subsequently rendered, in the manner previously indicated, more tender and more widely diffused. How could we check our sympathy, even at the urging of hard reason, without deterioration in the noblest part of our nature. . . . We must therefore bear the undoubtedly bad effects of the weak surviving and propagating their kind."

Darwin reveals the barbarous sentiment that runs through evolution and dwarfs the moral nature of those who become obsessed with it. Let us analyze the quotation just given. Dar-

550

APPENDIX

win speaks with approval of the savage custom of eliminating the weak so that only the strong will survive and complains that "we civilized men do our utmost to check the process of elimination." How inhuman such a doctrine as this! He thinks it injurious to "build asylums for the imbecile, the maimed, and the sick," or to care for the poor. Even the medical men come in for criticism because they "exert their utmost skill to save the life of everyone to the last moment." And then note his hostility to *vaccination* because it has "preserved thousands who, from a weak constitution would, but for vaccination, have succumbed to smallpox"! All of the sympathetic activities of civilized society are condemned because they enable "the weak members to propagate their kind." Then he drags mankind down to the level of the brute and compares the freedom given to man unfavorably with the restraint that we put on barnyard beasts.

The second paragraph of the above quotation shows that his kindly heart rebelled against the cruelty of his own doctrine. He says that we "feel *impelled* to give to the helpless," although he traces it to a sympathy which he thinks is developed by evolution; he even admits that we could not check this sympathy "even at the urging of hard reason, without deterioration of the noblest part of our nature." "*We must therefore bear*" what he regards as "the undoubtedly *bad effects* of the weak surviving and propagating their kind." Could any doctrine be more destructive of civilization? And what a commentary on evolution! He wants us to believe that evolution develops a human sympathy that finally becomes so tender that it repudiates the law that created it and thus invites a return to a level where the extinguishing of pity and sympathy will permit the brutal instincts to again do their progressive (?) work.

Let no one think that this acceptance of barbarism as the basic principle of evolution died with Darwin. Within three years a book has appeared whose author is even more frankly brutal than Darwin. The book is entitled "The New Decalogue of Science" and has attracted wide attention. One of our most reputable magazines has recently printed an article by him defining the religion of a scientist. In his preface he acknowledges indebtedness to twenty-one prominent scientists and educators, nearly all of them "doctors" and "professors." One of them, who has recently been elevated to the head of a great state university, read the manuscript over *twice* "and made many invaluable suggestions." The author describes Neitzsche who, according to

551

APPENDIX

Mr. Darrow, made a murderer out of Babe Leopold, as "the bravest soul since Jesus." He admits that Nietzsche was "gloriously wrong," not certainly, but "perhaps," "in many details of technical knowledge," but he affirms that Nietzsche was "gloriously right in his fearless questioning of the universe and of his own soul."

In another place, the author says, "Most of our morals today are jungle products," and then he affirms that "it would be safer, biologically, if they were more so now." After these two samples of his views, you will not be surprised when I read you the following:

"Evolution is a bloody business, but civilization tries to make it a pink tea. Barbarism is the only process by which man has ever organically progressed, and civilization is the only process by which he has ever organically declined. Civilization is the most dangerous enterprise upon which man ever set out. For when you take man out of the bloody, brutal, but beneficent, hand of natural selection you place him at once in the soft, perfumed, daintily gloved, but far more dangerous, hand of artificial selection. And, unless you call science to your aid and make this artificial selection as efficient as the rude methods of nature, you bungle the whole task."

This aspect of evolution may amaze some of the ministers who have not been admitted to the inner circle of the iconoclasts whose theories menace all the ideals of civilized society. Do these ministers know that "evolution is a bloody business"? Do they know that "barbarism is the only process by which man has ever organically progressed"? And that "civilization is the only process by which he has ever organically declined"? Do they know that "the bloody, brutal hand of natural selection" is "beneficent"? And that the "artificial selection" found in civilization is "dangerous"? What shall we think of the distinguished educators and scientists who read the manuscript before publication and did not protest against this pagan doctrine?

To show that this is a world-wide matter, I now quote from a book issued from the press in 1918, seven years ago. The title of the book is "The Science of Power," and its author, Benjamin Kidd, being an Englishman, could not have any national prejudice against Darwin. On pages 46 and 47, we find Kidd's interpretation of evolution:

"Darwin's presentation of the evolution of the world as the product of natural selection in never-ceasing war—as a product,

552

APPENDIX

that is to say, of a struggle in which the individual efficient in the fight for his own interests was always the winning type—touched the profoundest depths of the psychology of the West. The idea seemed to present the whole order of progress in the world as the result of a purely mechanical and materialistic process resting on force. In so doing it was a conception which reached the springs of that heredity born of the unmeasured ages of conquest out of which the Western mind has come. Within half a century the Origin of Species had become the bible of the doctrine of the omnipotence of force."

Kidd goes so far as to charge that "Nietzsche's teaching represented the interpretation of the popular Darwinism delivered with the fury and intensity of genius." And Nietzsche, be it remembered, denounced Christianity as the "doctrine of the degenerate," and democracy as "the refuge of weaklings."

Kidd says that Nietzsche gave Germany the doctrine of Darwin's efficient animal in the voice of his superman, and that Bernhardi and the military textbooks in due time gave Germany the doctrine of the superman translated into the national policy of the super-state aiming at world power. (Page 67.)

And what else but the spirit of evolution can account for the popularity of the selfish doctrine, "Each one for himself, and the devil take the hindmost," that threatens the very existence of the doctrine of brotherhood.

In 1900—twenty-five years ago—while an International Peace Congress was in session in Paris, the following editorial appeared in *L'Univers*:

"The spirit of peace has fled the earth because evolution has taken possession of it. The plea for peace in past years has been inspired by faith in the divine nature and the divine origin of man; men were then looked upon as children of one Father, and war, therefore, was fratricide. But now that men are looked upon as children of apes, what matters it whether they are slaughtered or not?"

When there is poison in the blood, no one knows on what part of the body it will break out, but we can be sure that it will continue to break out until the blood is purified. One of the leading universities of the South (I love the State too well to mention its name) publishes a monthly magazine entitled "Journal of Social Forces." In the January issue of this year, a contributor has a lengthy article on "Sociology and Ethics," in the course of which he says:

APPENDIX

"No attempt will be made to take up the matter of the good or evil of sexual intercourse among humans aside from the matter of conscious procreation, but as an historian, it might be worth while to ask the exponents of the impurity complex to explain the fact that, without exception, the great periods of cultural afflorescence have been those characterized by a large amount of freedom in sex-relations, and that those of the greatest cultural degradation and decline have been accompanied with greater sex repression and purity."

No one charges or suspects that all or any large percentage of the advocates of evolution sympathize with this loathsome application of evolution to social life, but it is worth while to inquire why those in charge of a great institution of learning allow such filth to be poured out for the stirring of the passions of its students.

Just one more quotation: The Southeastern Christian Advocate of June 25, 1925, quotes five eminent college men of Great Britain as joining in an answer to the question, "Will civilization survive?" Their reply is that:

"The greatest danger menacing our civilization is the abuse of the achievements of science. Mastery over the forces of nature has endowed the twentieth century man with a power which he is not fit to exercise. Unless the development of morality catches up with the development of technique, humanity is bound to destroy itself."

Can any Christian remain indifferent? Science needs religion to direct its energies and to inspire with lofty purpose those who employ the forces that are unloosed by science. Evolution is at war with religion because religion is supernatural; it is, therefore, the relentless foe of Christianity, which is a revealed religion.

Let us, then, hear the conclusion of the whole matter. Science is a magnificent material force, but it is not a teacher of morals. It can perfect machinery, but it adds no moral restraints to protect society from the misuse of the machine. It can also build gigantic intellectual ships, but it constructs no moral rudders for the control of storm-tossed human vessels. It not only fails to supply the spiritual element needed but some of its unproven hypotheses rob the ship of its *compass* and thus endanger its cargo.

In war, science has proven itself an evil genius; it has made war more terrible than it ever was before. Man used to be content to slaughter his fellowmen on a single plain—the earth's surface. Science has taught him to go down into the water and shoot up from below, and to go up into the clouds and shoot down

APPENDIX

from above, thus making the battlefield three times as bloody as it was before; but science does *not* teach brotherly love. Science has made war so hellish that civilization was about to commit suicide; and now we are told that newly discovered instruments of destruction will make the cruelties of the late war seem trivial in comparison with the cruelties of wars that may come in the future. If civilization is to be saved from the wreckage threatened by intelligence not consecrated by love, it must be saved by the moral code of the meek and lowly Nazarene. His teachings, and His teachings alone, can solve the problems that vex the heart and perplex the world.

The world needs a Saviour more than it ever did before, and there is only one "Name under heaven given among men whereby we must be saved." It is this Name that evolution degrades, for, carried to its logical conclusion, it robs Christ of the glory of a virgin birth, of the majesty of His deity and mission, and of the triumph of His resurrection. It also disputes the doctrine of the atonement.

It is for the jury to determine whether this attack upon the Christian religion shall be permitted in the public schools of Tennessee by teachers employed by the State and paid out of the public treasury. This case is no longer local; the defendant ceases to play an important part. The case has assumed the proportions of a battle-royal between unbelief that attempts to speak through so-called science and the defenders of the Christian faith, speaking through the Legislators of Tennessee. It is again a choice between God and Baal; it is also a renewal of the issue in Pilate's court. In that historic trial—the greatest in history—force, impersonated by Pilate, occupied the throne. Behind it was the Roman government, mistress of the world, and behind the Roman Government were the legions of Rome. Before Pilate, stood Christ, the Apostle of Love. Force triumphed; they nailed Him to the tree and those who stood around mocked and jeered and said, "He is dead." But from that day the power of Caesar waned and the power of Christ increased. In a few centuries the Roman government was gone and its legions forgotten; while the crucified and risen Lord has become the greatest fact in history and the growing figure of all time.

Again force and love meet face to face, and the question, "What shall I do with Jesus?" must be answered. A bloody, brutal doctrine—Evolution—demands, as the rabble did nineteen hundred years ago, that He be crucified. That cannot be the

555

APPENDIX

answer of this jury representing a Christian State and sworn to uphold the laws of Tennessee. Your answer will be heard throughout the world; it is eagerly awaited by a praying multitude. If the law is nullified, there will be rejoicing wherever God is repudiated, the Saviour scoffed at and the Bible ridiculed. Every unbeliever of every kind and degree will be happy. If, on the other hand, the law is upheld and the religion of the school children protected, millions of Christians will call you blessed and, with hearts full of gratitude to God, will sing again that grand old song of triumph:

> "Faith of our fathers, living still,
> In spite of dungeon, fire and sword;
> O how our hearts beat high with joy
> Whene'er we hear that glorious word—
> Faith of our fathers—holy faith;
> We will be true to thee till death!"

Published Works of William Jennings Bryan

Seven Questions in Dispute
In His Image
Heart to Heart Appeals
Orthodox Christianity vs. Modernism

The Prince of Peace
The Royal Art
Famous Figures of the Old Testament

Selected Speeches of William Jennings Bryan

The People's Law
The Price of a Soul
The Value of an Ideal

Man
The Signs of the Times; To which is added Faith

The above books may be obtained through any bookseller.

The phonograph records of Mr. Bryan's speeches are made by
The Starr Piano Co., Richmond, Ind.

556

INDEX

INDEX

INDEX

INDEX